Developments in the
Roman Catholic Church
in Scotland
1789-1829

Developments in the Roman Catholic Church in Scotland
1789-1829

CHRISTINE JOHNSON

JOHN DONALD PUBLISHERS LTD
EDINBURGH

ISBN 0 85976 092 8

Exclusive distribution in the United States
of America and Canada by Humanities
Press Inc., Atlantic Highlands,
NJ 07716, U.S.A.

Phototypesetting by R D Composition Ltd., Glasgow
Printed in Great Britain by Bell & Bain Ltd., Glasgow

Contents

Introduction

THE Roman Catholic seminary of Aquhorties, opened in 1799 for the education of Scots boys intended for the priesthood, stands at the watershed between the older Catholic Mission in Scotland of the 17th and 18th centuries, with its roots in the pre-Reformation era; and the new Catholic Mission of the 19th and 20th centuries.

The college itself, endowed as it was with a government grant, illustrates a radical change in the official policy of the British government. Fifty years previously Scottish priests had been hunted down, imprisoned and banished as Jacobite agents who constituted a threat to the rule of the House of Hanover. Now, in 1799, the government was actively supporting the training of priests for the Scottish Mission, while the priests themselves were praying, in their chapels, for 'our Sovereign King George'.[1]

Symptomatic, too, of the changing climate of opinion was the formation in 1794 of the Glengarry Fencibles. Although this was by no means the first British regiment to recruit Catholics, it was the first regiment in post-Reformation Scotland to have a Catholic priest as its official chaplain. The formation of a predominantly Catholic regiment to defend Britain against France was also symptomatic of international political change. France, which had been the traditional refuge for Catholics, had, with the outbreak of the French Revolution, become an enemy to the Roman Catholic religion, and instead of Scottish priests fleeing to France, French priests were escaping in large numbers to Britain.

Not only did the seminary of Aquhorties witness profound political changes in Europe, it also witnessed a no less profound change in the pattern of Catholicism in Scotland. In the 18th century there were only two major strongholds of Catholicism in Scotland: Banffshire in the north-east, and the Morar area, including some of the Hebridean Islands, in the west. These areas apart, there were only small pockets of Catholicism in Galloway, Perthshire, Angus, Peeblesshire and Edinburgh, mainly centred on the houses of Catholic nobles and lairds. In the Glasgow area, and around the estuary of the Clyde, Catholics were almost non-existent. Webster[2] lists two Catholics in Renfrewshire, and none at all in Ayrshire.

By the time that the seminary of Aquhorties had been transferred to Blairs in 1829, this pattern had radically altered. In 1764 Bishop Hugh MacDonald estimated that there were 13,166 Catholics in the Highland Vicariate.[3] Arisaig and South Morar were entirely Catholic; Canna, Eigg, South Uist and Benbecula, and Barra, were Catholic except for a few Protestants on Canna and Eigg, and several Protestant gentry on Barra.[4] Between 1770 and 1829 thousands of

Highland Catholics left Scotland for Canada. Mr Austin MacDonald, writing in 1791, estimated that about 4,000 Catholics had emigrated since 1772.[5] By 1829, although it is difficult to arrive at any exact figure, this number must have more than doubled.

Not only did Highland Catholics emigrate to Canada; from 1790 many, driven from their homes by starvation and by the rack-renting of the landowners, moved south to find employment in the cotton mills of Glasgow and Paisley. For these incomers a Catholic mission was established in Glasgow, in 1790, under the care of a Gaelic-speaking priest. Thirty years later this was to be the largest mission in Scotland.

Although Highlanders formed the initial Catholic population in Glasgow, their numbers were soon swamped by the ever-growing tide of Irish immigrants. In 1786 there had only been about seventy Catholics in Glasgow.[6] In 1792 the congregation at the chapel averaged 200.[7] In 1812 the thousand-odd communicants received at Easter by Mr Scott fell far short of the total number of Catholics in Glasgow.[8] In 1828 Mr Scott, now Bishop, estimated that between Morar in the north and Galloway in the south, in the new Western Vicariate, there were 70,000 Catholics, of whom only 4,000 spoke only Gaelic.[9] As the Catholics who lived in the Highlands still, in most cases, in 1828, spoke only Gaelic, Bishop Scott's figures show clearly the dramatic alteration that had taken place in the structure of the Catholic population of Scotland between 1790 and 1830.

The transfer of Aquhorties to Blairs in 1829 was one result of this population change. In 1827 the division of Scotland into two Vicariates, Highland and Lowland, was replaced by a new division into three Vicariates: Eastern, Northern and Western.[10] The Northern Vicariate, consisting of Banffshire, Aberdeenshire, and eastern Inverness-shire, centred on the traditional Catholic strongholds of the old Lowland Vicariate. The Eastern Vicariate, encompassing the Lothians, Peeblesshire, the Borders as far west as Kirkcudbrightshire, Perthshire, Fife and Angus, acknowledged the new urban populations, largely Irish, which had by now rendered insignificant the old enclaves round Catholic houses like Traquair and Munshes. Most striking, however, was the Western Vicariate, which included not only the traditionally Catholic, Gaelic-speaking West Highlands and Islands, but the newly Catholic, Irish-dominated areas of the south-west, which stretched from the Clyde to Wigtownshire. Indeed, it was the Irish Catholic south-west which dominated this Vicariate. The Highlands, which had been the most important Catholic stronghold, in terms of numbers, throughout most of the 18th century, had by this time been greatly changed by emigrations and clearances.[11]

Aquhorties was the last seminary to serve the old Lowland Vicariate. On the 4th of September 1828,[12] the pupils from the Highland seminary at Lismore were transferred to Aquhorties, and in the following summer all the boys, Highland and Lowland, moved to the new foundation at Blairs, which was to be the college for all three new Vicariates, and which continues to this day to train boys intended for the priesthood in Scotland.

On a purely domestic level the running of Aquhorties, with its farm and policies, reflects the enthusiasm for both agricultural improvement and for raising the general standard of living which was current in Scotland in the late 18th and early 19th centuries.

This book was originally intended as a study of the history of the college at Aquhorties. I discovered, however, that there is no adequate history of the Scottish Mission between 1789 and 1829 against which such a study could be placed. I therefore extended the scope of the book to include all the major developments which took place in the Scottish Mission between these years. This is a large topic to cover adequately, but two factors have placed limits on it. Firstly, the paucity of Highland source material has forced me to concentrate primarily on developments in the Lowland Vicariate. Secondly, certain topics, such as Catholic emancipation and Irish Catholic politics, have already been more than adequately covered in other works, and these topics I have only discussed as and when they affected the internal affairs of the Scottish Mission, its priests and its bishops.

The different developments which took place within the Roman Catholic Church in Scotland between 1789 and 1829 were interdependent and must be considered in that light. Where only one development is considered in isolation, it is easy to misconstrue its significance. An example of such a misconstruction is the undue emphasis which has been placed in the past on the religion of the goldsmith, David Downie, a Catholic who was charged with high treason in 1794. In attempting to trace all the major developments which took place in the Scottish Mission during forty of the most crucial years of its existence, I have been forced to treat some individual topics in less depth than would have been possible had I taken a narrower subject. I have tried, however, to place these developments within the context of Scottish history as a whole, to show that the Roman Catholic Church in post-Reformation Scotland, although proscribed for over two centuries, nevertheless continued to be involved in developments which took place in Scotland as a whole.

NOTES

1 Bishop Hay to Bishop Geddes, 5th January 1795, Blairs Letters, Columba House. [B.L.]

2 'Webster's Analysis of Population, 1755', in *Scottish Population Statistics*, edited by J. G. Kidd, Scottish History Society (1975 reprint), pp. 31, 28 respectively.

3 'Bishop Hugh MacDonald's report on the Highland Vicariate, 1764', edited by the Rev. Roderick MacDonald, *Innes Review*, 1964, p.150.

4 *Ibid.*, pp. 147-148.

5 Mr Austin MacDonald to Bishop Hay, 11th July 1791, B.L.

6 Stothert 'Life of Bishop Hay', in J. F. S. Gordon *Journal and Appendix to Scotichronicon and Monasticon*, Vol. I, p. 265 (1874).

7 Bishop Geddes to Bishop Hay, 25th October 1792, B.L.

8 Mr Andrew Scott to Bishop Cameron, 6th April 1812, B.L.

9 Bishop Scott to Bishop Paterson, 22nd January 1828, B.L.

10 *Catholic Directory*, 1831, pp. 63, 66, 71.

11 Although the population of the West Highlands shows an overall increase in the early 19th century, evidence from priests' letters suggests that there was a significant decrease in the number of Catholics in these areas during that period.

12 Rev. W. J. Anderson, 'The College for the Lowland District of Scotland at Scalan and Aquhorties, Registers and Documents', *Innes Review*, no. XIV, 1963, pp. 181-182.

1

Historical Background

THE Beggars' Summons of 1559 marked the beginning of the Reformation in Scotland.[1] In August 1560 the Scottish Parliament accepted the Reformed Confession of Faith, which abrogated papal authority and forbade the celebration of Mass. Three bishops remained in Scotland within the reformed church, as did those priests who, by subscribing to the Confession of Faith and taking the Oath of Supremacy, retained their benefices after 1573. Throughout the last thirty years of the 16th century Parliament regularly passed acts against Roman Catholicism: Jesuits and priests were ordered to leave the country; 'unlawful hearers of mass' were to be executed and their goods escheat to the king; pilgrimages to chapels and wells were forbidden, as were 'card-singers, bonfires and other superstitious and papistical rites'.[2]

On the 29th of January, 1611, George Home, earl of Dunbar, died. He had been High Commissioner of the General Assembly at Glasgow, and had used his influence to enforce the Acts of Parliament against Roman Catholics. After his death the Catholics found that the persecution against them was relaxed, and the superior of the Scottish Jesuit Mission took the opportunity to send more priests into Scotland.[3] The respite, however, was short-lived. In 1628 Charles I issued a proclamation to the effect that, twice each year, the bishops and ministers of the Church of Scotland should send to the Privy Council a list of all the Catholics who refused to attend services in their churches. The denounced Catholics were to be taken prisoner, treated as rebels, and their property confiscated to the Crown.[4]

In 1685 Charles II died, and was succeeded by his Catholic brother, James VII. At last there seemed to be some hope that Catholics would be allowed to worship freely. James told the Privy Council that Catholics should be given freedom of worship. He attempted to bribe the Scottish Parliament to pass an Act of Toleration by holding out the promise of free trade with England, but he was unsuccessful. In spite of this, in 1687 he ordered all Scottish priests on the continent to return to Scotland.[5] In 1689, Parliament declared that James VII had forfeited the throne. Protestant William and Mary were declared his successors, and the Catholics were once again faced with persecution.[6]

The Scottish Reformation had political as well as religious implications. It led to a closer connection with Protestant England, a connection which was confirmed by the Union of the Crowns in 1603. The Reformation also spelt the end of Scotland's 'Auld Alliance' with France. Although trade between the two countries continued, France could no longer expect Scotland to invade England on her behalf.

As far as the Scottish Catholics were concerned, however, the ties with France remained strong. France provided a refuge for exiled priests and laymen, and the Scots Colleges at Douay and at Paris provided an education, not only for intending priests, but for the sons of those Catholics who could afford to send them there. French nunneries provided a similar education for Catholic girls.

After James VII was exiled in 1689, the link between Scottish Catholics and France assumed a new political significance. The Scots College at Paris housed the official archives of the exiled Stuart cause,[7] and became a centre for Jacobite activity.

It must always be borne in mind that the Catholics were not the only people in Scotland to support the Jacobite cause. Numerically the greatest support for the exiled Stuarts came from the Episcopalians. However, this survey does not pretend to be an analysis of Jacobitism, but merely of Catholic involvement in it, in order to show how that religion came to be identified with Jacobite politics for most of the 18th century.

In 1689 Viscount Dundee raised the first Jacobite army, drawing most of his support from the Highland clans, as the gentry of the north-east, although in sympathy with his cause, did not come out in active support of him. Some of the Highland support derived from a personal desire to plunder, or from hatred of the Earl of Argyll, as much as from loyalty to James VII, but this made it no less dangerous in the eyes of government. Although Dundee achieved a victory at Killiecrankie, his followers were repulsed at Dunkeld, and routed at Cromdale, where they refused to submit but took to the safety of the mountainous West Highlands. By itself, Dundee's rising might perhaps have been dismissed as relatively unimportant, but it coincided with a rising in Ireland led by James VII, and with France's declaration of war on Britain. The government was therefore afraid that the rebels might be reinforced from Ireland or France. The pacification of the Highlands became a matter of importance. In 1691 a settlement was agreed upon, whereby the chiefs agreed to take the oath of allegiance, but the massacre of the allegedly Catholic MacDonalds of Glencoe, in February 1692, undid the good effects of the settlement, and did more than any other single event to promote the Jacobite cause in the Highlands.

Among the chiefs who had taken part in Dundee's rising were Clanranald and Glengarry, both of whom, along with their followers, were Catholic.

The Jacobite cause was further strengthened among the Scottish Catholics by an Act of Parliament passed in 1700. This Act placed a price on the heads of priests; anyone seizing a priest who had once been banished, and delivering him up as prisoner, would receive 500 merks. The Act also aimed at preventing children from being brought up as Catholics:

> . . . for preventing all seduction by papists no person professed or suspected to be papists shall be capable to be imployed in the education of youth or the trust or management of their affairs: And especially that none such shall be capable to be Governours, Chaplains, Pedagogues or Schoolmasters, Tutors or Curators, Chamberlains and Factors, and that none presume to imploy papists or such as are suspect of popery in any of the said trusts until first they purge

themselves of popery and sign the formula aftermentioned under the pain of ane years valued rent or one thousand merks . . . [8]

Furthermore, the Protestant relatives of children of Catholic parents were empowered to take legal action to ensure that these children were brought up as Protestants.

Not only were Catholics deprived of any legal authority over their children; they were also denied any legal right of inheritance or disposal of

. . . any lands houses tenaments anualrents or other real rights or tacks of lands or teinds.

All such rights were to devolve on the nearest Protestant heirs, who

. . . would succeed [as] if they [the Catholic landholders] and all intervening popish heirs were naturally dead.

In other words the laws of inheritance and of conveying simply ignored the existence of Catholics, and allowed the nearest Protestant heirs to claim, as of right, any lands or other property in Catholic hands.

In 1708 further penal laws were passed which declared Catholics incapable of acquiring moveables or recovering just debts.[9]

Faced with laws which attacked their two most vulnerable points — their children and their property — it is little wonder that those Catholics who refused to renege on their religion should have supported the Stuart cause. As Bishop John Geddes put it:

The Scottish Catholics were generally desirous of the restoration of the family of Stuart to the throne of Britain; nor is this to be wondered at. They inherited those principles from their fathers. There were princes of that house claiming the right of their ancestors, which they had a prospect of recovering, from the great number of their friends. Besides, the Scottish Catholics were discouraged and much exposed to oppression; it was therefore natural for them to wish for an event that was likely to release them and put them again in possession of the privileges of free-born citizens.[10]

In 1700, Anne's last surviving child died, and in 1702 she succeeded William. In 1701 the English Act of Settlement provided for a Protestant succession in the event of Anne's dying without issue. It named Sophia, Dowager Electress of Hanover, as Anne's heir to the English throne. Scotland passed no corresponding Act and Jacobite hopes were raised. In 1707, however, with the Union of Parliaments, Scotland concurred in the Hanoverian succession, and it became clear that only through war could the Stuarts regain the throne. In 1701 England had become involved in the War of the Spanish Succession, and in March 1702 Scotland also declared war on France. It was in France's interest, at this time, therefore, to support a Jacobite rebellion in Scotland. 5,000 French troops were supplied for the proposed landing on the shores of the Firth of Forth in 1708, but the plans miscarried and no landing took place. The government, however, was sufficiently alarmed to take the precaution of sending soldiers into the Highlands.

It was in the Highlands in particular that the real threat to the House of Hanover was to be found. English Jacobites may have toasted the 'king over the water', but it was in the Highlands that words were backed by weapons. There were several reasons for this. In the first place Highland society was kin-based and steeped in genealogy; in the eyes of such a society the Stuart right to the kingship would be seen as unquestionable, the Hanoverian right at best tenuous. Secondly there was a Gaelic tradition, referred to in the 'Song of the Clans', that a battle on the Clyde would restore the Gaels to their former supremacy.[11] Thirdly the MacDonald kindred resented the territorial expansion of the Campbells at their expense and saw war as an opportunity to regain their lands. Finally, those clans which were still Catholic at the beginning of the 18th century saw in the Stuarts their only hope for the restoration of their freedom of worship and their legal identity.

The north-east of Scotland, too, being a stronghold both of Catholicism and of Episcopalianism, espoused the Jacobite cause. In 1707 Colonel Nathaniel Hooke, the so-called Jacobite agent for Louis XIV, visited Scotland, where he stayed on more than one occasion in Banffshire with the Catholic Bishop Nicolson.[12] In 1715 the standard of King James was raised at Braemar, and the Earl of Mar, self-appointed leader of the rebellion, was joined by men from the north-east, and by west Highland clans: Camerons, MacIntoshes, MacDonalds and others, including a substantial number of Catholics.

In the Rebellion of 1745, 70% of Prince Charles's army was Episcopalian and 30% was Catholic. But although Catholics formed only a minority of the army, their support for the Jacobite cause is well attested, for priests as well as laymen followed the Prince.

The Highland Vicar Apostolic, Bishop Hugh MacDonald, son of MacDonald of Morar, who was later to tell Bishop Geddes that he had advised the Prince to return to France rather than endanger the lives of himself and his friends, nevertheless felt himself obliged by honour to support the rising. On the 19th of August he blessed Prince Charles's standard at Glenfinnan. There, Catholics from Moidart, Arisaig, Knoydart, Morar, Glengarry and Lochaber took up arms under their respective chiefs, and formed a considerable part of the army which the Prince led to Edinburgh. Priests from the Highlands also joined the Jacobite army. Mr Allan MacDonald was made confessor to the Prince as well as chaplain to Clanranald's men. Mr MacGillis joined as chaplain to Glengarry's men. Both these priests wore Highland dress with sword and pistol and were given the rank of Captain. They both escaped alive from Culloden in 1746; another priest, Mr Colin Campbell, lost his life in that battle.

In the north-east, too, priests supported Prince Charles. Mr John Tyrie joined up as chaplain to the Catholic followers of Gordon of Glenbucket. Mr Gordon, priest at Rathven in the Enzie, preached the Jacobite cause in his chapel, and succeeded in enrolling about a dozen men. This small band was the beginning of a company of about fifty formed under the captaincy of Charles Gordon. Mr John Gordon, the priest, accompanied them to Edinburgh, leaving them when they were incorporated in the Duke of Perth's regiment, and returning to Rathven.[13]

At least four priests — Mr Alan MacDonald, Mr James Tyrie, Mr Angus MacGillis and Mr Robert Leith (afterwards Abbot of Ratisbon) — accompanied the Jacobite army into England.

Inevitably Catholic participation in the Jacobite rebellions brought government retribution. The Catholic position was worsened in 1717 when James VIII, the old Pretender, having been forced to leave France, took up residence in Rome, where the Pope bestowed on him the honour of a Papal Guard.[14] When the Pope so favoured the exiled Stuarts it is little wonder that, to the British government, Catholicism and Jacobitism seemed to be two sides of the same coin.

In 1715 the situation of Scottish Catholics and their priests was, in the opinion of John Thomson, agent at Rome 1782-1792, and author of a *History of the Scottish Mission*, precarious because the ministry was

> ... doubly animated against them both on account of their religion and loyalty to King James. Hence the Catholics behaved as quietly and cautiously as possible.[15]

By 1716 the failure of the Jacobite rising had made life even more difficult for Catholics. Even the little seminary on Eilean Ban, in Loch Morar, was forced to close because of the activity of government soldiers in the area.

After the '45 Rebellion the whole Highlands were 'pacified' by Cumberland's soldiers. The clans were disarmed, estates of Jacobites were forfeited to the Crown, and Highland dress, and the playing of the bagpipe, were forbidden. Catholics suffered with the rest. Catholic landowners like the Duke of Perth lost their estates; Catholic homes, like Balquhain Castle, were burned. Burned, too, were many Catholic chapels as well as the little seminary at Scalan. Priests were imprisoned.

It was the Highlands which suffered most in the aftermath of Culloden. When Bishop Hugh MacDonald returned from France in 1749, he found Banffshire a safer retreat than Morar. He did, however, return to the Highlands, eluding the searches made for him by government troops, until 1752. But, in 1752, Presbyterian ministers persuaded the government that Bishop Hugh was recruiting soldiers for the French army. Searches were intensified and the Bishop was forced to retire to the Lowlands under an assumed name.[16] He was finally arrested in 1755, and in 1756 he was brought to trial before the Justiciary Court at Edinburgh on an indictment of being 'by habit and repute a Popish priest'. In March the Court pronounced sentence of banishment on him, but the Bishop, under the names of 'MacKenzie' and 'Scott', went, not abroad, but to Shenval in the Cabrach district of Banffshire,[17] where he remained with John Geddes (later to become Bishop) until 1762, when he was finally able to return to his Highland Vicariate. He died there in March 1773.

Although Bishop Hugh was forced to remain in exile from his Vicariate for a good many years, his experience was not typical. Generally speaking, Catholic priests, after the '45 Rebellion, were treated comparatively leniently.[18] Mr Allan MacDonald, Mr Alexander Forrester, and Fathers John and Charles Farquharson, S.J., after a lengthy imprisonment on board a ship, were banished. Father Alexander Gordon, S.J., died in irons in Inverness prison. Father Alexander Cameron, S.J., of the family of Locheil, died a prisoner at sea. On no priest was the death penalty inflicted; indeed many priests suffered only a short imprisonment. Priests who died in prison died of illness caused by the unhealthy conditions in which they were forced to live, and not at the hands of executioners. Father Peter Gordon, S.J., of Braemar, was imprisoned in Aberdeen, but was at once released on bail following the intervention of Menzies of Pitfoddels, and returned to Braemar. Mr James Grant, priest on Barra, was brought in irons to Inverness

Castle, but was released the following year, thanks to the intervention of his brother, John Grant of Wester Boggs in Banffshire, and 'the gentlemen of the clan'.[19] His bail was granted on condition that he present himself when called for — he never was.

The history of four of the priests mentioned above, Allan MacDonald, Alexander Forrester, and John and Charles Farquharson, illustrates how quickly government panic abated after the suppression of the '45 Rebellion. The four priests were taken to London, where they were eventually brought before the Secretary of State, the Duke of Newcastle:

> His Grace told them that they were banished upon the condition of their finding bail to the amount of £1000 each that they would never return to Britain. Upon their representing that it would be impossible for them to find such high bail, the Duke smiled, and said, that as he knew they were honest men, he would accept of the one's bail for the other. On the same occasion one of the gentlemen present took notice, in good humour, that to go to Scotland by Holland was not very far out of the way.[20]

Although the government must have been aware of the presence in Scotland of banished men — like the above Mr Forrester in 1747 — it is not surprising that it took no action against them unless forced to do so by the protests of Presbyterian ministers. The Jacobite threat was evaporating. In 1750, Prince Charles paid a visit to London, where he went sightseeing, accompanied by one Colonel Brett.[21] Before he left England, the Prince became a Protestant in the hope of gaining Protestant support for the Jacobite cause. The Prince's visit was no secret to the British government, which, however, saw no necessity to take action. Nor can his visit have helped the Stuart cause. His conversion to Protestantism was a gesture aimed at Scottish Presbyterians and at members of the Church of England, but neither of these two bodies had any sympathy for the exiled Stuarts. At the same time, his conversion made it clear to Catholics that religion was, for him, merely a political tool. Furthermore, by this time areas of active Jacobitism had become very restricted. The clan chiefs who had come to the Prince's army in 1745 had done so reluctantly and with little hope of success. The 'pacification' of 1746 can only have served to crush the last forlorn hope of a Stuart restoration. Even the Pope withdrew his support from the Jacobite cause. In 1766, following the death of his father, Prince Charles visited the English, Scots and Irish Colleges in Rome. The Pope, afraid that the Catholics in Britain would be made to suffer as a result of such an imprudent visit, showed his disapproval by dismissing the superiors of these colleges and ordering them to leave Rome.[22]

In 1778 the English Catholic Relief Bill was passed, and it was hoped that the Bill would be extended to Scotland. The Scottish Bill, like its English counterpart, would have required Catholics to take an oath of allegiance to the Hanoverian King George III. This nearly all the Scottish Catholics were prepared to do. For this they were condemned by Dr Abernethy Drummond, a non-juring clergyman in Edinburgh. Stothert, in his 'Life of Bishop Hay', gives Drummond's reasons for so doing:

> The party which he [Drummond] represented was, at this time, especially exasperated against the Catholic Body for having, as it was alleged, deserted its Political principles of adherence to the almost extinct Jacobite Cause, and by this sacrifice outbid the Non-jurors in the favour and

protection of Government.[23]

But, by 1788, leading Catholics had recognised that the Jacobite cause was lost. Only Henry, Cardinal Duke of York, and brother of Prince Charles, still clung to his family's dynastic pretensions. In 1788, when Prince Charles died, the Cardinal published a protest, in which he declared that neither his profession, nor the character he bore, should prejudice his title to the crown of Great Britain.[24] In 1789, following the death of Prince Charles's widow, he had a medal struck in which he had himself designated 'Henricus IX', with the motto, 'non desideriis hominum sed Dei voluntate', on the reverse side.[25] This medal the Cardinal was still presenting to British visitors to Rome in 1803,[26] but by this time the gesture had no political undertones. By 1794, the Cardinal Duke of York, the last of the Stuart line, was prepared to be friends with the House of Hanover, and in particular with Prince Augustus, the son of George III, who was, that year, visiting Rome. Abbé MacPherson, who was by this time the Scots Agent at Rome, sent Bishop Geddes this charming account:

> The Cardinal Duke and Prince Augustus are on the most friendly terms with each other. The Prince has passed this summer at Grotta Feretta. He had often occasion of meeting the Cardinal; never met him but he caused his Phaeton to stop, and stood up with his hat in hand till the Cardinal was passed. This continued attention produced the effect which the Prince desired. Lately the Cardinal ordered his carriage to stop too, and kindly inquired after the Prince's health, expressing at the same time his affection towards him and his friends, and how much he wished to be on the most intimate footing with His Royal Highness, his dear Cousin; that he hoped Political disputes between their families in past times, could now no longer give umbrage. The Prince was so much struck with this friendly and unexpected behaviour of the Cardinal, that he could not find words to express his feelings, only repeated three times: I thank you Royal Highness. The following day he made amends for this; walked with the Cardinal for more than two hours; has dined with him, and frequents his Conversation every evening. The Cardinal is delighted with his amiable qualifications. It is hoped he will come to inherit some of the rich jewels which the Cardinal possesses.[27]

In 1798 the French army of Napoleon entered Rome. The Cardinal Duke of York was forced to flee the city, a penniless refugee. In 1799 the British government granted him £2,000 for his immediate assistance, together with a pension of £4,000 per annum for the rest of his life.[28]

By 1799 the Jacobite rebellions had become a matter of history; a bygone era which furnished Bishop Hay with stories to tell the students at his new seminary of Aquhorties, when they gathered round the fire on winter evenings.[29]

NOTES

1 See Gordon Donaldson, *The Scottish Reformation* (1960) for a detailed account.

2 *General Index to the Acts of the Parliaments of Scotland*, pp. 924-925.

3 J. F. S. Gordon, *Journal and Appendix to Scotichronicon and Monasticon*, Vol. I, p. 582.

4 *Ibid.*, p. 573.

5 *Ibid.*, p. 567.

6. For a general account of the 1689 Revolution settlement, and of the 18th century Jacobite rebellions, see Dr William Ferguson, *Scotland, 1689 to the Present* (1968).

7 David MacRoberts, 'The Scottish Catholic Archives, 1560-1978', *Innes Review* XXVIII, 1977, p. 74.

8 *Acts of the Parliaments of Scotland (A.P.S.)*, vol. X, pp. 215-218.

9 Forbes Leith, *Memoirs of Scottish Catholics during the XVIIth and XVIIIth Centuries*, vol. II, 1647-1793 (1909), p. 239.

10 Bishop John Geddes, 'Some Account of the State of the Catholic Religion in Scotland during the years 1745-6-7', copied by Abbé MacPherson into his continuation of John Thomson's 'History of the Scottish Mission' (Mss Vols, Columba House). (Also printed in Forbes Leith, *Memoirs of Scottish Catholics*, vol. II, p. 332 *et seq.*)

11 For this information I am indebted to Mr MacInnes of the School of Scottish Studies, Edinburgh University (Scottish Literature I lecture).

12 Peter Anson, *Underground Catholicism in Scotland* (1970), p. 109.

13 Bishop Geddes, 'Account of the Catholic Religion . . . 1745-6-7', Forbes Leith, Vol. II, pp. 334-335.

14 Peter Anson, *Underground Catholicism in Scotland*, p. 115.

15 John Thomson, 'History of the Scottish Mission' (Mss Vols, Columba House), vol. II, p. 45.

16 Paul MacPherson's continuation of Thomson's 'History' (Mss Vols, Columba House), vol. II, p. 237.

17 *Ibid.*, p. 260.

18 Bishop Geddes, 'Account of the Catholic Religion . . . 1745-6-7', Forbes Leith, vol. II, pp. 340-343.

19 Bishop Geddes, 'Account of the Catholic Religion . . . 1745-6-7', in Forbes Leith, vol. II, pp. 342-3.

20 *Ibid.*, p. 341.

21 Margaret Forster, *The Rash Adventurer* (B.C.A. edition 1974), pp. 256-257.

22 J. F. S. Gordon, *Scotichronicon and Monasticon*, p. 51.

23 *Ibid.*, p. 151.

24 J. F. S. Gordon, *Scotichronicon and Monasticon*, p. 273.

25 *Ibid.*, p. 294.

26 Ian Docherty, 'Cardinal Erskine and the Cardinal Duke of York', *Innes Review* XVI, 1965, pp. 217-218.

27 Abbé MacPherson, Rome, to Bishop Geddes, 5th September 1794, B.L.

28 J. F. S. Gordon, *Scotichronicon and Monasticon*, p. 422.

29 *Ibid.*, p. 420.

2

Persecution and Toleration, 1700-1778

IN 1700 the Scottish Parliament passed the very harsh 'Act for preventing the grouth of Popery' which, had it been rigorously enforced, would have deprived all Catholics of their lands and property, and would have seen all children of Catholic parents educated as Protestants. It would have closed all chapels and banished all priests from Scotland. In fact, for the most part, the penal laws were not rigidly enforced, except when a threat of Jacobite rebellion made Catholics, along with non-juring Espiscopalians, a political threat. This is why Catholic sources mention 'persecutions' in years like 1702, 1708, 1716 and 1746.

It should also be remembered that from 1707 Scotland was governed from Westminster. Members of Parliament living in London were used to the presence of Catholic foreign ambassadors, with their chapels and chaplains, in which Mass was openly celebrated. A London-based politician was bound to see Catholicism from a different viewpoint to that of a Presbyterian minister in, say, Glasgow.

The Scottish Catholics were well aware of this situation. Their bishops might request the help of the exiled King James in obtaining money for the Mission; or in obtaining Propaganda's consent to their proposals; but they also requested the help of the British government when their people were faced with persecution. The bishops could not petition government directly, but they could, and did, obtain the assistance of foreign ambassadors. In 1724, for instance, the new oath of allegiance, prescribed the previous year, had its penal clauses much reduced following such intervention.[1]

In England, many powerful noble families remained Catholic, and in Scotland in the opening years of the 18th century there were also a number of Catholic nobles. These men helped to protect their co-religionists from the worst of the penalties that could be enforced. In 1710 they tried to convince the Lords of Justiciary that Catholics were being unjustly treated. When this failed, the nobles took their case to London. Catholic nuncios, particularly those whose courts were in alliance with Britain, were asked to intervene. As a result an order was sent out in the Queen's name to the Lords of Justiciary, ordering them not to persecute the Catholics in any manner on account of their religion, provided they lived peacefully and created no disturbance.[2] In 1751, when vigorous action was again being taken against Scottish Catholics, the Pope requested the Catholic powers to order their ambassadors to Britain to protest. In this instance, the Imperial, Bavarian and Sardinian ministers were of great help, and the Dukes of Newcastle and Argyll promised that the persecutions would stop.[3]

The most consistent enemies of the Roman Catholics in Scotland were the Presbyterian ministers. For much of the 17th century there had been a conflict over whether the Church of Scotland would be Presbyterian or Episcopalian. Alongside the religious struggle was a political struggle which swept both Scotland and England into Civil War, and gave the Presbyterians the ascendancy. With the restoration of Charles II in 1660 the Scottish Church became Episcopalian again. In 1689, the Revolution, which put William and Mary on the throne, finally restored the Established Church to Presbyterianism.

By 1689 the ranks of the Presbyterian ministers had thinned, and it took some time for them to regain their full strength. But, according to one source, it was not so much lack of Presbyterian strength as lack of Episcopalian effort that had allowed Catholicism to regain its hold on the north-east of Scotland. In 1718, the Presbytery of Kincardine O'Neil complained bitterly:

> ... about fifty years ago there was hardly a papist to be found in all this countrey. But after the Restoration while the projects and power of the Courts were employed against another sett of people, when protestants were persecuted in the South, popery was Connived at in the north and there unwearied Emissaries Laboured to Spread their poison as far as they could with Immunity ... [4]

The General Assembly survey of 1714 noted an increase of Catholicism, mainly in Banffshire, Lochaber, Glengarry and Aberdeenshire, but with a few converts in Perthshire and Galloway. Such reports might be dismissed as exaggeration on the part of the Presbyterian ministers, were their claims not corroborated by Catholic sources. The report of the Scottish mission of the Society of Jesus of 1702 lists many converts, as does Thomson's 'History of the Scottish Mission' for the first decades of the 18th century.[5] A specific example of the concurrence of Catholic and Presbyterian sources concerns Perthshire. In 1714 the General Assembly was told of the conversions made by a Perthshire priest, and of how:

> ... the late Lord Drummond had a son within these —— years baptized publickly by a popish priest and a popish Bishop was sent for to be Godfather, and many gentlemen in the Countrey about were invited to be there, and came accordingly, most of whom were said to be present at the baptism.[6]

Under the year 1708, John Thomson, the Catholic historian, recorded:

> About twenty years before there was scarcely a Catholic in Perthshire, and all the conversions since that time were owing, under God, to the singular zeal of the Duke of Perth, who, when he was Chancellor, settled two missioners on his estate; and their number was still increasing under the protection of that noble family [i.e. the Drummonds].[7]

It must, of course, be borne in mind that, when Catholic sources refer to 'conversions', they are often referring to people who would have considered themselves to have been always Catholic, but who had hitherto been prevented, by the scarcity of priests, from receiving religious instruction, or being confirmed, or perhaps even baptised.

The Presbyterians blamed the increase in the number of Catholics on a variety of causes. One obvious difficulty encountered by the Church of Scotland occurred when a Catholic was the sole heritor for a parish, as was MacDonald of Glengarry for parishes in Knoydart and Morar. On the heritors devolved the responsibility for the maintenance of minister and schoolmaster, and the upkeep of manse, church and school. A Catholic heritor could make life very difficult for a Presbyterian minister who preached anti-popery.

More generally, Presbyterian ministers blamed the increase on mixed marriages. They also attempted to have enforced the clause of the 1700 Penal Act which forbade ' . . . any papist to be entertained as a domestick servant by any protestant'.[8] Both these situations, it was feared, might result in conversions to Catholicism.

One complaint made against priests by the ministers is an inadvertent condemnation of the harsh treatment meted out by the established church to the parents of illegitimate children:

> [The Priest] Baptizes Children begotten in fornication and takes the parents obliged to be of the Communion of the Church of Rome, and such delinquents resort to him to evade discipline, which weakens the hands of the Protestant ministers . . . [9]

In 1794 the Protestant parents of illegitimate children were still asking Catholic priests to perform the baptisms,[10] preferring a Catholic rite to the harsh discipline of the stool of repentance.

Another complaint made to the General Assembly in the early 18th century was that ministers had to cope with very large parishes, while often being paid only very small salaries, many livings being worth less than 600 merks (£400 Scots). Ministers were therefore forced to spend much time and effort in farming their glebes to provide for their families, instead of devoting their energies to their congregations. Furthermore, when ministers became old and infirm, they had to continue, unaided, in parishes with which they could no longer cope. All these problems the Presbyterian ministers wanted to see remedied, and a start was made in 1725, when the General Assembly set up a committee, financed by a grant of £600 per annum from the king. This committee's function was to determine which areas of the Highlands and the north-east were most in need of help in the form of more ministers and catechists, and to supply that need. Over the next few years, the committee was inundated with appeals for help from many different presbyteries which had to cope with over-large parishes and scattered congregations.[11]

The king had provided the General Assembly with a grant because that body had informed him that ' . . . Popery and Ignorance did increase and prevail in several places in the Highlands and Islands'.[11] In the eyes of Mr Thomson the Committee had been appointed:

> . . . under the specious pretext of converting infidels, but the real design of it was to pervert the Catholics, especially in the Highlands.[12]

The Catholics generally blamed the Presbyterian ministers for persecutions against them, with some justice. In 1709 some Catholic nobles and gentlemen, who lived in areas with large Catholic populations, were charged with high treason for hearing mass, and for harbouring priests.[13] In the same year, an attempt was made to persuade landowners to evict their Catholic tenants unless the latter bound themselves to attend the Established Church.[14] In 1754, soldiers were brought to Uist to apprehend the priest there; the priest had to take temporary refuge in Ireland.[15] In each case Catholic sources blame the action taken against Catholics on the Presbyterian ministers.

Presbyterian sources confirm Catholic sources in attesting to the activity of ministers. Indeed one of the problems faced by Presbyterians in attempting to have the Penal laws enforced was, according to the five Highland parishes round Braemar, that:

> ... Ministers and they only are the informers, and thereby made odious to the papists, and therefore are the less fit to deall with them, and convince them, and tempts the priest to think and speak evill of them, and the cause they maintain.[16]

In other words the ministers admitted that it was they alone who brought prosecutions against Catholics, and that by doing so they spoiled any chance they might otherwise have had of converting Catholics to Protestantism.

The strongest argument that the ministers could use to try to obtain the enforcement of the penal laws against Catholics was to equate Catholicism with Jacobitism, especially at times when Jacobite rebellions had just occurred. Thus, in 1718, the synod of Moray, enlarging on the iniquities of Catholic priests, bishops and Jesuits, pointed out that:

> One great branch of their work and design is to sow the seeds of disaffection to our Protestant king and government, and their success in this is so considerable that the most part of the Nominal protestants in those countreys are bloody and avowed Jacobites.[17]

Even when the ministers did succeed in bringing prosecutions to the courts, their aim was often thwarted by local magistrates. The parishes round Braemar listed:

> The disappointments we meet with in persecutions against them [i.e. Catholics]: (1) when we give in presentments against them to be put in the portois Rolls, by some underclerks or others that have the management of that affair, there are such alterations made that the Inditement comes to nothing when brought to be tryed before the Honourable Judges. (2) In case the Delinquents or their friends are slow in gaining upon those Clerks or are not successfull, but the Lybell is bound Relevant, then the witnesses are prevailed upon to absent, and no fines enacted of them for their Contumacy. (3) When all is rightly managed, witnesses compear, the party found guilty, which seldom happens, he is either absent and declared fugitive, or is present and banished according to Law, but in both cases they are free and safe as ever being never more minded, but live peaceablie at home and enjoy the privileges of the best Subjects.[18]

From a Catholic standpoint, much the same picture emerges:

> ... this very year [1724] they [the ministers] obtained an order from Court to all Sheriffs to make strict search for priests and to cast them into prison ... But the missioners were not much alarmed by this order which was given merely to please the ministers but not designed to be put into execution.[19]

In 1764 the government actively intervened to prevent the persecution of Catholics. After the '45 rebellion, the estates of Jacobites had been forfeited, and a Commission set up to manage them. On one such Highland estate the factor, at the instigation of some of the more extremist ministers, gave notice to all the tenants that, if they did not at once begin to attend the Presbyterian Church, they would have to leave their farms at the next term. The tenants, even though they had had little opportunity for instruction in the Catholic religion, due to the scarcity of priests, refused to abandon their faith, and faced eviction. Government, however, being apprised of their plight, intervened to prevent the factor's threat from being implemented.[20]

In the second half of the 18th century, after all threat of Jacobite rebellions had receded, and the promise of a new prosperity had reconciled most of Scotland to a parliamentary union under the House of Hanover, the government began to realise that in the Highland clans it had a rich source of manpower to feed the British army. Many of the West Highland clans were still predominantly Catholic, and so Highland Catholics began to be drafted for foreign service, even though this meant that they had to take an anti-Catholic oath. The Bishops' report to Propaganda of 1763-64 estimated that, since the outbreak of war with France in 1756, not less than 6,000 Scottish Catholics had been drafted for foreign service, mainly in the East and West Indies.[21] It was because of their potential value as soldiers that Catholics first saw some hope of having the Penal Acts against them repealed.

On December 11th, 1770[22] a motion was put forward in the House of Commons by General Burgoyne, and seconded by General Conway, with a view to recruiting Catholics into the British army. It proposed the relaxation of the oath laid down by the Act of 1700 whereby Catholics joining the army were forced to swear:

> I, ———, Do sincerely from my heart Profess and Declare before God who searcheth the heart that I do deny disown and abhore these tenets and doctrines of the Papal Romish Church viz the Supremacy of the Pope and Bishop of Rome over all Pastores . . . His power of dispenseing and pardoning. The doctrine of Transubstantiation and the corporal presence with the Communion without the Cup in the Sacraments of the Lords Supper. The adoration and sacrifice professed and practised by the Popish Church in the Mass . . . [23]

General Burgoyne told of how he had commanded five hundred Catholics in the last war. These men had pretended they were Protestants, but had attended Catholic chapels when they could, an action which the General had not opposed, as they went there out of uniform. He pointed out to the House that these men were as brave as any soldiers in the army; and mentioned that foreign nations were astonished that so many good soldiers should be forced into the service of foreign powers because of oaths imposed in Britain. The General's motion was prompted by the need for more soldiers to serve in America. Nothing came of it, but his idea was revived eight years later.

Sir John Dalrymple, who had been the author of a plan to raise Catholic regiments in Ireland, saw a possibility of the same being done in Scotland. He therefore asked Bishop Hay what was the attitude of Scottish Catholics towards the American rebellion; whether they would be willing to engage in Government service if so required; and what terms they would expect for so doing.[24] Bishop Hay replied that the Scottish Catholics were loyal to the government, and that, though the law prevented them from serving in the army, they tried to be good citizens in so far as the law permitted. In the bishop's estimation most Scottish Catholics disapproved of the conduct of the Americans; and, as he pointed out, the Highland emigrants now living in Canada were fighting on the side of the British. Even in Britain, and in spite of the Penal Laws, many Catholics were enlisting in the army. To encourage more Catholics to enlist, Bishop Hay suggested that the Penal Laws be repealed, at least in so far as they forbade the saying or hearing of mass, and the purchase or inheritance of property. He also insisted that the oath be amended so as to omit all religious references and retain only the clause referring to loyalty to the King and 'Obedience to the Laws of War'.[25]

At about the same time that Sir John Dalrymple approached Bishop Hay, one of the Judges of the Court of Session approached Mr Alexander Gordon, principal of the Scots College, Paris, who was temporarily in Scotland, and asked him whether the Scottish Catholics might be prepared to raise a body of men for the service of the government, and on what terms. According to Mr Lewis, a government official:

> In order to procure certain information on that head, Principal Gordon set out in the middle of winter for the Highlands of Scotland, where the Catholicks are most numerous, and where he had to travel over hills covered with ice and snow, sometimes at the peril of his life. He either found the Catholicks well inclined to the measure or he contrived to make them so; and if the penal statutes disabling them from serving in the army had been repealed, he saw reason to believe that from two to three thousand men might have been got willing to serve in any part of G. Britain or America, without asking bounty money, rank, or half pay if disabled after the war.
>
> The Judge went to London to see what could be done in the business of the wished for repeal of the statutes disqualifying Catholics from serving in the army. By Pl. Gordon's advice, and with the assistance of letters which were procured the Judge brought the English Catholics to unite with the Scots; thus it became a common measure of the R. Catholics of G. Britain. Accordingly in a joint address presented to the King on the 2nd of May 1778 'they made an humble tender of their service to be employed as he in his wisedom and the sense of the nation might direct'.[26]

It was the Scottish insistence that English Catholics should be included in the petition for relief that was to lead to the failure to procure a Scottish Relief Bill in 1778. After a co-operative start the Committee of English Catholic nobles and gentry decided to act independently of its Scottish counterpart. It decided to ask for the repeal of an English Act passed during the reign of King William, which chiefly affected rights over property. As the Scottish Penal Act of 1700 was very similar, the Scottish Catholics hoped for a Repeal Bill which would cover both Acts. The English Committee, however, refused to allow a joint bill to be presented;[27] and on the 3rd of June 1778, it was only the English Penal Act which was repealed.

The Scottish Catholics hoped that their Relief Bill would automatically follow, if not in this, then at least in the next session of Parliament. On August 14th, 1778 the Irish Relief Bill received the Royal Assent in the National Parliament at Dublin. On September 12th the principal Scottish Catholics held a meeting at Edinburgh together with the Scottish bishops. At Bishop Hay's instigation, the meeting passed several resolutions. Firstly it was agreed that Lord Linton, Mr Maxwell of Munshes and Mr Glendonwyn should wait on the Lord Advocate. They were to thank him for his help in the past and to inform him that the meeting was considering the heads of a proposed Relief Bill. Secondly, a draft of the proposed Bill was to be sent to Mr Crosbie, the advocate, for his approval, after which it would be shown to Lord North before the next session of Parliament. Thirdly, the meeting resolved, albeit reluctantly on the part of the Lowland gentry, to offer to raise a Catholic regiment of a thousand men for the public service.[28] No doubt Bishop Hay remembered that the first hope of relief had coincided with the government's desire to recruit Catholic soldiers.

By this time, however, the passage of the English and Irish Relief Bills had fanned into flames the ever-smouldering Scottish Presbyterian hatred of 'popery'. The Scottish nobles had generally been in favour of the Relief Bill, as had some of the moderate Presbyterian ministers, including Dr William Robertson, Principal of Edinburgh University. Many, many ministers, however, were violently opposed to any measure of Catholic relief. Some idea of the extent of this anti-Catholic feeling can be gained from reading the book, *Scotland's Opposition to the Popish Bill*,[29] published in Edinburgh in 1780, which contains all the resolutions against a Scottish Relief Bill passed by synods such as those of Glasgow, Perth and Dundee. Parliament was petitioned; ministers preached anti-popery from their pulpits; associations and committees were formed to oppose the Bill. On Saturday, 30th January 1779, an Edinburgh mob gathered outside the newly built chapel and priest's house in Chalmers Close, broke windows, and shouted insults. On Tuesday they gathered again, throwing so many stones that the two priests who lived there, Mr Cameron and Mr Mathison, fled to Edinburgh's other chapel, in Blackfriars Wynd, taking with them what few valuables they could carry. As soon as they had left, the mob broke into the house, wrecked the interior, and then set fire to the building. Bishop Hay returned from London to Edinburgh just in time to see his house in flames. The following day the mob looted the house and chapel in Blackfriars Wynd; they only refrained from setting it on fire too because of the dangerous proximity of other houses. The mob also damaged the houses both of Catholic laymen and of people known to favour Catholic relief.[30] Bishop Hay and Principal Robertson were forced to take refuge for a few days in Edinburgh Castle. Further riots occurred in Glasgow, Dundee, Peebles and at Stobhall.[31]

The anti-Catholic hysteria caused so much anxiety that Bishop Hay and the government concurred in deciding to discard the proposed Scottish Relief Bill, at least for the moment. It was not until 1793, by which time the political climate had radically changed, that a Scottish Relief Act was finally passed.

NOTES

1 Thomson, 'History of the Scottish Mission', vol. II, p. 103.

2 Thomson, 'History of the Scottish Mission', quoted in Forbes Leith, vol. II, pp. 266-273.

3 MacPherson's Continuation of Thomson's History, vol. II. p. 232.

4 N. M. Wilby 'The *Encreasce of Popery* in the Highlands, 1714-1747'; transcript of Document NLS MS 976 ff. 147-149; *Innes Review* XVII 1966, p. 97.

5 'Encreasce of Popery', Document NLS MS 976, ff. 143; *Innes Review* 1966, pp. 92-96.

6 *Ibid.*, p. 94.

7 Thomson's 'History of the Scottish Mission', quoted in Forbes Leith, vol. II, p. 242.

8 *A.P.S.*, vol. X, p. 218.

9 'Encreasce of Popery', Document NLS MS 976 p. 143; *Innes Review* 1966, p. 93.

10 'Queries Relating to the Roman Catholics in Scotland' January 1794, B.L.

11 'Register of the Acts and Proceedings of the Committee of the General Assembly of the Church of Scotland for the Reformation of the Highlands and Islands of Scotland and for Management of the Kings Bounty for that End', Ms Vol, Register House CHI/5/51.

12 Thomson, 'History of the Scottish Mission', vol. II, p. 110.

13 Thomson's 'History', quoted in Forbes Leith, vol. II, p. 246.

14 *Ibid.*, p. 248.

15 MacPherson's Continuation of Thomson's 'History', vol II, p. 252.

16 'Encreasce of Popery', Document NLS MS 976 ff 147-9; *Innes Review* 1966, p. 99.

17 'Encreasce of Popery', Document NLS MS 976 f.151; *Innes Review*, 1966, p. 103.

18 'Encreasce of Popery', Document NLS MS 976, ff. 147-9; *Innes Review*, 1966, p. 99.

19 Thomson, 'History of the Scottish Mission', vol. II, pp. 103-4.

20 *Scotichronicon*, p. 50.

21 *Ibid.*, p. 46.

22 *Ibid.*, p. 143.

23 *A.P.S.* vol. X, p. 218.

24 *Scotichronicon*, p. 144; also Bishop Hay to Abbé Grant, 22nd April 1778, printed in Forbes Leith, Vol. II, pp. 368-380.

25 *Scotichronicon*, p. 145 quotes the letter of Bishop Hay to Sir John Dalrymple, 16th February, 1778.

26 'Statement of facts in consideration of which fifty pounds yearly was granted by Government in 1778 to Alexander Gordon then Principal of the Scots College in Paris' — contained in a letter written by Mr M. Lewis, 11th November 1808, B.L.

27 Bishop Hay to Bishop Grant, 22nd April 1778, quoted in Forbes Leith, Vol. II, pp. 368-372.

28 *Scotichronicon*, p. 153.

29 *Scotland's Opposition to the Popish Bill*, printed by Paterson, Edinburgh, 1780.

30 *Scotichronicon*, pp. 158-160.

31 *Ibid.*, pp. 162-163.

3

Growth of Toleration, 1778-1793

THE British government had demonstrated its sympathy towards Catholics when, in 1778, it had passed the English Catholic Relief Act. This official attitude of toleration had perhaps received some impetus in 1763 at the conclusion of the Seven Years War. Under the terms of the Peace of Paris, Britain had acquired extensive new territories, in Canada and in various West Indian islands. In these new colonies most of the people were Catholic, and their religious liberties had been specially secured under the terms of the treaty. When the British Colonies were granted toleration, it must have seemed to many quite incongruous that Catholics in Britain should be denied freedom of worship.

Although the Scottish Relief Bill was not passed in 1779, Scottish Catholics were aware that they were viewed in a favourable light by the government. The Dundas regime which, in Henry Cockburn's eyes, was synonymous with restrictive practices, and with fear of reform,[1] was, nevertheless, a champion of the Catholic cause. Bishop Cameron regarded Lord Melville as ' . . . our first and greatest Protector, . . . our chief Patron'.[2] This toleration was repeated in other branches of officialdom.

In 1778, encouraged by the more tolerant attitude then prevalent in the British Army, Bishop Hay instructed all Catholics who wished to enlist to state openly that, as Catholics, they must refuse to take the oath as it stood. Those who followed their bishop's instructions were applauded for their honesty, and were allowed to omit the anti-Catholic clauses of the oath, swearing only to be obedient and faithful.[3] This was an important concession, won without noise or fuss by taking advantage of the political situation.

In the same year, some Catholic soldiers were forbidden by their Major to attend chapel. Bishop Hay wrote to the Commander-in-Chief, General Sir Adolphus Oughton, at Caroline Park, and the General granted permission for the soldiers to attend chapel, so long as they went a few at a time to avoid attracting attention.[4] With the passage of the Relief Bill in 1793, the army dispensed with this restriction. In 1795 the Catholics in the Fencible Regiment stationed at Dundee were ordered to march to chapel ' . . . in rank and file, with a drummer and piper at the head'.[5] In 1798, on the first of December, the Adjutant General's office published a General Order to the effect that non-commissioned officers and men were to be allowed to attend the chapels, churches and meeting-houses of their respective religious denominations, whenever the opportunity for so doing arose.[6]

The magistrates of Edinburgh demonstrated their religious tolerance in rather a macabre fashion. In 1776 they allowed Bishop Hay every facility for attending two Irishmen who were lying under sentence of death for a street robbery.[7] In 1790 they invited Bishop Geddes to attend another Irishman on the scaffold itself — and to have dinner with them afterwards. Bishop Geddes prudently declined both invitations, preferring to administer absolution, as on previous occasions, from a nearby window.[8] Edinburgh extended its religious toleration to the poor as well as to the condemned. The Catholic inmates of the city's Poor House were allowed to go to chapel when they pleased, and a priest was allowed to visit any who were ill.[9]

It would have benefited the Edinburgh magistrates had they been able to protect the welfare of the city's chapels as well as they did that of the condemned Irishmen. After the riots of 1779, Bishop Hay petitioned Parliament for compensation: £1,306 for the house in Chalmers Close, £400 for that in Blackfriars Wynd; together with £300 for the furniture and £1,000 for the books that had been destroyed. Tradesmen and tenants in the Bishop's house petitioned for a further £572.10.0. Parliament ruled that it was on Edinburgh's magistrates that the onus of providing compensation must fall.[10]

Other cities also demonstrated their sympathy towards Catholics, sympathy which prompted Bishop Hay to write to Bishop Geddes in December 1792:

> The Magistrates of Dundee some time ago offered to Mr Pepper [the priest there] to apply to higher powers to extend the English Bill in favour of the Catholics there to Scotland; now in the present disposition of Glasgow, could not some means be fallen upon to get the four leading towns of Edinburgh, Glasgow, Aberdeen and Dundee to lay their heads together for that purpose? If they did I dare say it would succeed . . . who knows but Providence intends that those very places which lately were most against us should be the means of befriending us.[11]

Although Bishop Hay's plan was not implemented, his letter demonstrates how far the main Scottish cities had demonstrated their sympathy towards Catholics by 1792.

Another body which extended its goodwill to the Scottish Catholics was the Commission for Forfeited Estates. In 1777 the titular Duchess of Perth, a Catholic, died, leaving the priest for the Perth area, who had lived at Stobhall as her chaplain, without a home. Bishop Hay, who was acquainted with one of the Commissioners, Lord Kames, applied to him for the lease of the farm of Park on the Stobhall estate. Lord Kames, aided by Mr Colquhoun Grant, persuaded another of the Commissioners, Lord Gardenstone, to agree to this request, and Bishop Hay was granted the lease of Park in the name of its former Catholic tenant, in spite of opposition from the factor, who had, in the interim, granted that lease to someone else.[12]

The army had adopted a more lenient attitude towards the taking of the oath by Catholics, because it needed recruits. Other bodies saw toleration as a necessary step towards stemming the flow of emigrants, many of whom were Catholic, from the West Highlands and Islands. In 1770, Glenaladale had bought land on St John's Island [Prince Edward Island] from Henry Dundas, and in 1771 the first large Catholic emigration had taken place when many of Boisdale's tenants left South Uist to settle there.[13] The tide of emigration was stemmed by the American War of Independence, but had resumed by 1790, and in 1791 one of the Highland priests estimated that, to date, about four thousand Catholics had emigrated from the West Highlands and Islands to Canada and Nova Scotia.[14] The Scottish bishops, in their letter to Propaganda in 1791, expressed grave concern at the numbers of Catholics who were emigrating:[15] Catholicism in America might benefit, especially as many priests were emigrating with their congregations; but the Scottish Mission could ill afford such a drain on its members.

A desire to stem the tide of emigration gave the Scottish bishops new and unexpected allies, in the traditionally Covenanting city of Glasgow. The reason was economic. In 1755, when Webster had conducted his census, he had found no Catholics in Glasgow. By 1786 Bishop Geddes was paying fairly regular visits to Glasgow to say Mass for the Catholics there. He described his congregation in his 'Autobiographical Notes':

> The Catholics who are known are few; the two Miss Fletchers, Mr and Mrs Bonet who teach dancing; Henry and Anthony Straubach, Anthony's wife and two or (three?) children; they are German glass-cutters; John Mungall, Mrs Hair and her two children, George Hossac and some other poor persons.[16]

By 1791 Bishop Geddes estimated that Glasgow had about twenty-nine communicants. This means that by then there must have been about sixty Catholics living in the city.[17] In 1789 the Bishop leased an apartment in Montrose's lodging for use as a chapel. In the following year he had the partitions removed from this apartment to make a chapel big enough to seat a hundred.[18] By now he was considering the possibility of stationing a priest permanently in the city, instead of making frequent journeys there himself from Edinburgh. In 1791, Bishop Geddes sent a hopeful account to Bishop Hay:

> Some Protestants of note, among the rest the procurator Fiscal, expressed a wish to be at our meeting: I thought it most prudent to beg they would not come, because it might occasion too much Observation; and I suspected their Motive was Curiosity only. I was not ill-pleased however to have with us five or six Soldiers in their Regimentals. I was assured that three rich Merchants had said in a private Company that they would readily contribute something to the maintenance of a Catholic priest in their town, to let the World see that they are not there so bigotted as is commonly imagined. Mr Wilson, your old friend, now Town's Clerk, and our landlord . . . told me that prejudices against us are much more subsided within these three or four years than he could have expected.[19]

By this time the Catholic congregation in Glasgow was being augmented by Gaelic-speaking Highlanders who relied for Confession and so on on the occasional visits of Mr MacDonald, the Highland priest at Crieff.

In the beginning of 1792, Mr Kemp, of the Society for Preventing Emigration, seems to have approached Bishop Hay about the possibility of persuading Highlanders to come to the factories of Glasgow rather than to emigrate to Canada. In February, Bishop Hay informed Bishop Geddes that:

> . . . after consulting with several of our friends, I wrote a letter to Mr Kemp, telling him how happy we should be to keep the poor people of the Highlands at home, and willing to concur in his plan, but that the only objection was their not having any exercise of their Religion etc. To this I got no answer. But Mr Alexander [MacDonell, priest in] Badenoch informed me that all who were able to pay their freight would not be kept from America, especially after the good accounts sent from those who went last year . . . ; but the poor people, who could not pay the freight, nor go to America, were greatly pitied, and something must be done for them.

Accordingly he went to see our friends at Glasgow and get what accounts he could of the people thereabouts . . . Then he went to Mr Dale, and told who he was, and wished to concur with his wishes, if the point of Religion could be accomodated. Then he went to Professor Anderson, who was keen on the matter, and by his means got acquaint with others, as much in want of hands as Mr Dale. The Consequence of all which was that they had laid their heads together . . .[20]

By May 1792, the manufacturers, who had previously expressed their willingness to subscribe towards a chapel, were beginning to doubt the wisdom of so doing while the penal laws were in force, in case they should be acting unlawfully.[21] Bishop Hay asked Bishop Geddes, who was then in London, to discuss the whole question with Mr Dundas. The discussion had a favourable outcome, and by August of the same year, the bishops could report to Mr Thomson, Scots Agent at Rome:

At Glasgow . . . there is a very large Hall taken from the Duke of Hamilton and the Provost for the publickly avowed purpose of being a Catholic Chapel. The principal Manufacturers are actually placing 300 seats in this Hall, and are the Cautioners for the Rent which is no less than £40 . . . The Town's Clerk, is, I think, a sincere friend; we are recommended by the Board of Trade and Society for Preventing Emigration supports us; the Manufacturers know it is their Interest to have many industrious sober men; and above all we have God to trust in.[22]

A comment made by Mr Thomson earlier that year sums up these developments:

Who would have thought that those who a dozen of years ago burnt our houses and Chappels would in so short a time think of building Chappels for us themselves.

Mr Thomson did not live to see an even greater change take place in Glasgow as Irish immigration transformed its Catholic mission from a small outpost to one of the major centres of the Catholic Church in Scotland.

By 1794, Mr MacDonell estimated that there were about five hundred and sixty Highlanders in Glasgow, attracted by the prospect of employment in the cotton industry.[23] In 1803, when he returned to Glasgow after eight years spent as chaplain to the Glengarry Fencibles, Mr MacDonell found only about twenty Highlanders attending the chapel.[24] He was, however, informed that, in Greenock, there were about two hundred Highland Catholics, even though only a handful went to the chapel, so there may have been a considerable number in Glasgow too, who did not attend the chapel, perhaps because Mr MacDonell's successor spoke hardly any Gaelic. There was still a sufficient number of Highland Catholics in Glasgow in 1808 to warrant Mr MacLachlan's being sent to the Highlands to learn Gaelic before being stationed there as priest.[25] By 1811, however, Mr Scott found that there were few Catholics in Glasgow who did not speak English.[26]

Already in November 1793 Mr MacDonell was finding among his congregation Irish immigrants, many of whom were ' . . . pining away on the bed of sorrow in this town and miserable objects . . . '[27] In 1801 Mr MacDonell's successor, Mr Farquharson, described the Glasgow chapel as ' . . . wholly on the Irish establishment'.[28] Four years later he wrote to Mr Mathison, priest at Auchinhalrig:

Many thousands of Irish Catholics are actually at Glasgow, could they be brought round [to attend chapel]; and could another Labr, active, equally zealous and versed in the Gaelic, be spared for between Glasgow and Paisley, several hundreds of poor Highlanders who understand not a word of English could be soon collected.[29]

In 1826 a Highland priest was still visiting Glasgow very occasionally to give Confession etc. to the few Gaelic-speaking Highlanders there, but by this time the enormous problem of coping with the Irish Catholics had driven the problems of the relatively insignificant number of Highlanders into the background. In 1830 Mr Scott, now bishop, estimated that in the preceding year he had baptised over a thousand children.[30] This figure would make the total Catholic population of the Glasgow mission somewhere in the region of 36,000. Almost all of them were of Irish extraction. There were by this time priests at Ayr, serving about 6,000 people; in Wigtownshire 3,000; in Dumfries 3,000; in Greenock 4-5,000; and in Paisley 5,000. These congregations, too, were almost entirely of Irish extraction.[31] Throughout the years between 1792 and 1830 the wealthy Protestants of Glasgow continued to help the struggling Catholic mission. The merchants gave up their commitment to the chapel in 1795 after subscribing towards a new building. They and others continued to donate money at intervals, and, in 1817, when Catholic schools were established in Glasgow, it was the generosity of Protestants which kept them open.[32]

It was not only in government circles and among officials that Catholics were being viewed with increasing sympathy and toleration as the eighteenth century drew to a close. As early as 1787 Bishop Geddes remarked that evidence for this could be seen by the fact that the new chapels being built at that time at Huntly, Glenlivet and Strathavon all had slated roofs.[33]

In 1790 the Scots College at Douay was threatened with closure as the French wanted to take it over. Some Protestant lairds in Scotland agreed to sign a protest against this takeover so long as lawyers would confirm that they could do so legally.[34]

In the same year an Episcopalian minister showed his friendship for Catholics, as Bishop Geddes informed Bishop Hay:

> Dr Webster is building a fine Chapel beyond the Infirmary [in Edinburgh] . . . and he has very seriously offered to me the second story, immediately above him, for a chapel to us . . . You may therefore let me know what you think of this curious proposal. I believe you will not much like it, but it shows the Temper of the Times.[35]

Although the Catholic bishops refused this generous offer, one of the Edinburgh priests was present at the laying of the foundation stone.[36] Other Protestants in Edinburgh were also showing a friendly interest towards Catholics in 1790, even attending Mass at the chapels in Blackfriars Wynd[37] — probably to satisfy their curiosity.

The Catholic bishops were, by this time, accepted into Edinburgh's fashionable social circles. In 1786, for instance, Bishop Geddes wrote to Mr Thomson:

> There is an excellent poet started up in Ayrshire, where he has been a ploughman; he has made many excellent poems in old Scotch, which are now in the press for the third time. I shall send them to you. His name is Burns. He is only twenty eight years old; he is in town just now, and I supped with him once at Lord Monboddo's, where I conversed a good deal with him, and think him a man of uncommon genius; and he has yet time, if he lives, to cultivate it.[38]

Bishop Geddes was a man of singular charm who did a great deal towards promoting goodwill towards Catholics. He made many influential friends who, in time, were to help in the obtaining of the Scottish Relief Bill. In 1789 alone the

Bishop numbered among his correspondents Principal Robertson, General Hutton, Dr John Gregory, Sir William Forbes, Sir Alexander Livingstone, and the Earl of Buchan, all of whom expressed their regard for him.[39] In 1790 Bishop Geddes had, on one occasion

... within these eight days dined or supped with four of our Lords of Session, and all of them seem to be very favourable.[40]

Even his much less gregarious colleague, Bishop Hay, enjoyed Lord Monboddo's hospitality.[41]

The Scottish bishops and priests, in the last decades of the eighteenth century, were also very much part of the contemporary literary scene. From London George Chalmers kept up a vigorous correspondence with Bishops Hay and Geddes about new books that were being published.[42] He borrowed from them some of their valuable manuscripts, including the 'Life of James II', now in The Scottish Catholic Archives.[43] He requested of them information for inclusion in the topography, *Caledonia,* which he was compiling.[44]

In 1782 the Society of Antiquaries of Scotland was founded. Bishop Geddes, who had taken an active interest in its establishment, presented to its library a copy of Leslie's *History of Scotland,* and was asked by Lord Buchan to write a biography of the 'good Bishop of Ross'.[45] In 1790 Bishop Geddes was made an honorary member of the Society.[46]

The combined literary output of Bishops Hay and Geddes was considerable. Bishop Hay's numerous publications were limited to the field of Catholic theology, but he also wrote out mathematical texts to be used by scholars at his seminary at Scalan. Bishop Geddes wrote on more general topics. Many of his most interesting pieces of work were not published until the twentieth century. These include his history of the Scottish Mission's involvement in the '45 rebellion; his autobiographical notes; and his account of his journey to Orkney in 1790; all of which are of historical value.[47] Popular works published during his lifetime include a pamphlet on duelling published in 1791,[48] a *Life of St Margaret* published in 1794; and articles on the Pope and on Boscovich which were included in Dr Gleig's edition of the *Encyclopaedia Britannica.*[49]

Scottish Catholics had been pioneers in the use of original records in the field of historical research. The *Critical Essay on the Ancient Inhabitants of the Northern Parts of Britain or Scotland,* written by the Scottish priest, Thomas Innes, paved the way to a new understanding of Dark Age history. Mr Innes also rescued from oblivion the valuable archives of the Scots College at Paris, which included the Stuart Papers, the Memoirs of James VII and II, and four volumes pertaining to the pre-Reformation Archbishopric of Glasgow.[50] (Sadly many of the College's papers were lost at the time of the French Revolution.)

The Scots College at Rome also had its historians. The successive Scots Agents at Rome, who lived in the College, were in a unique position to obtain source material, because all the business conducted between the Scottish Mission and the Sacred College of Propaganda was conducted through them. The archives at Rome housed, therefore, a rich treasure of official documents relating to the Scottish Mission, as well as the many personal letters by which friends at home kept the agents up to date with domestic affairs and with gossip. It was largely from these sources that John Thomson started to compile, in 1789, his 'History of the Scottish Mission'.[51] In 1792 Mr Thomson died, and in 1795 his successor, Abbé Paul MacPherson, picked up the 'History' from 1731, where Mr Thomson had stopped, and continued it up to 1759. Although he collected further notes and memoirs for the period up to 1780 he did not manage to incorporate them into the 'History'. Both Mr Thomson and Abbé MacPherson expressed, in the 'History of the Scottish Mission', some very prejudiced opinions of events. Nevertheless, the work is scholarly, and shows a keen appreciation of the importance of original sources.[52]

The Highland Vicariate, too, had its scholars; priests who were, not surprisingly, particularly interested in the poems of Ossian. In the 1760s James MacPherson had caused a great stir when he had published several books of what he claimed were translations of the Gaelic poetry of Ossian. The authenticity of his translations was challenged by, among others, Dr Samuel Johnson. A committee, appointed after MacPherson's death in 1796, reported that he ' . . . liberally edited traditional Gaelic poems and inserted passages of his own'.[53] A series of letters written in 1806 between Sir John Sinclair and Bishop Cameron, suggests, however, that this judgement may have been too severe. A scroll letter written by Bishop Cameron about the Jesuit priest, John Farquharson (1699-1782), contains the following information:

> I knew the Rev. John Farquharson personally. He had resided in Strathglass, as Roman Catholic Clergyman, for some years, before the middle of last century. It was there he became acquainted with Gaelic poetry. The winter evenings, even at a later period, were generally spent in hearing those compositions sung or recited and Mr Farquharson frequently copied them . . . Mr MacPherson's Translation was sent to Mr Farquharson by Mr Glendonwyne of Parton, about the year 1766, and the attention of everyone was then drawn to [Mr Farquharson's] Ms. Mr MacGillivray was a classical scholar and great admirer of the poems. He assures me he has, a hundred times, seen Mr Farquharson turning up his folio to compare the translation with the Gaelic. His general complaint was that MacPherson fell short of the beauty and energy of the original, which he used to repeat and translate literally. Mr MacGillivray is, and was at the time, convinced that the Ms contained the original of all the poems translated by MacPherson for he never saw Mr Farquharson at a loss in his collations, and he heard him frequently regret that the other poems in his Ms nowise inferior in merit to those published had not been laid before the public.[54]

Unfortunately Father Farquharson's manuscripts were thrown out, or used to light fires, by people who were unaware of their value. Father Farquharson was quite unaware of the importance of his manuscripts, not realising that the sweeping changes which were taking place in the Highlands by the second half of the eighteenth century were threatening the survival of Gaelic oral tradition.

Father Farquharson's collections of poetry from Gaelic oral tradition are comparable to the collection of old Scots and English songs published by Allan Ramsay, in 1724-1727, under the title of the *Tea Table Miscellany*.

Generally speaking, the Scottish Catholic priests and bishops were regarded, in government circles and among men of letters, as peaceable, scholarly men who ministered quietly to their small congregations. Among the less well-informed, Catholicism was still, in 1779, regarded in the same light that had led Church of

Scotland ministers half a century before to equate it with ignorance and superstition. Many people seem to have been hardly aware of the existence of priests in the Highlands at all, so unobtrusively did they go about their duties. In 1773 there were fourteen priests, as well as a bishop, working in the Highlands. In that year Dr Johnson made his famous tour through the Highlands and Islands. To his regret his tour did not take him through any Catholic areas. As he remarked:

> Popery is favourable to ceremony; and among ignorant nations, ceremony is the only preservation of tradition. Since Protestantism was extended to the savage parts of Scotland, it has perhaps been one of the chief labours of the ministers to abolish stated observances, because they continued the remembrance of the former religion. We therefore who came to hear old traditions, and see antiquated manners should probably have found them amongst the Papists.[55]

Had Dr Johnson ventured among the Catholics of Morar or of South Uist or Barra he might have met with some of the fourteen Highland priests. As it was he could only comment:

> If any missionaries [i.e. Catholic priests] are busy in the Highlands, their zeal entitles them to respect, even from those who cannot think favourably of their doctrine.[56]

By 1790 the Catholic priests had indeed won the respect of a large section of the population of Scotland. It was inevitable, however, that some of the 'anti-popery' fanaticism which had led to such ugly scenes in 1779 should survive into the nineteenth century. Bishop Hay, for one, never relaxed in his efforts to keep the Catholic Church in Scotland out of the limelight, and to this end he was always extremely reluctant to permit any innovations in the form of worship used in the chapels of his vicariate, even after the penal law of 1700 had been repealed.

NOTES

1 Henry Cockburn, *Memorials of his Time* (Edinburgh and London, 1910), p. 103.

2 Bishop Cameron to Robert Dundas, Lord Chief Baron, Scroll letter, 9th September 1803, B.L.

3 *Scotichronicon*, p. 144.

4 *Ibid.*, p. 154.

5 John Pepper to Abbé MacPherson, 19th November, 1795, B.L.

6 *Scotichronicon*, p. 409.

7 *Ibid.*, p. 133.

8 Bishop Geddes to Bishop Hay, 18th February 1790, B.L.

9 Bishop Hay to John Gordon, Aberdeen; 3rd November 1791, B.L.

10 *Scotichronicon*, pp. 168 and 172.

11 Bishop Hay to Bishop Geddes, 17th December 1792, B.L.

12 *Scotichronicon*, p. 135.

13 *Ibid.*, pp. 80-82.

14 Austin MacDonald, Knoydart to Bishop Hay, 11th July 1791, B.L.

15 *Scotichronicon*, p. 316.

16 'The Autobiographical Notes of Bishop John Geddes', edited by W. J. Anderson, *Innes Review*, 1967, p. 57.

17 Bishop Geddes to Bishop Hay, 10th February 1791, B.L.

18 Bishop Geddes to George Mathison, Auchinhalrig, 28th January, 1790, B.L.

19 Bishop Geddes to Bishop Hay, 10th February, 1791, B.L.

C

20 Bishop Hay to Bishop Geddes, 21st February 1792, B.L. Note: the 'Mr Dale' mentioned by Bishop Hay is David Dale, famous for the founding, in 1786, along with Arkwright, of the cotton mills at New Lanark. This was the first really large-scale cotton-spinning enterprise to be undertaken in Scotland.

21 Bishop Hay to Bishop Geddes, 28th May 1792, B.L.

22 Bishops Hay and Geddes to Mr Thomson, Rome, 28th August 1792, B.L.

23 Mr Thomson, Rome to Bishop Hay, 24th March 1792, B.L.

24 Alexander MacDonell to Bishop Cameron, 24th October 1803, B.L.

25 Andrew Scott to Bishop Cameron, 7th July 1808, B.L.

26 Andrew Scott to Bishop Cameron, 13th May 1811, B.L.

27 Alexander MacDonell, Glasgow, to Bishop Hay, 26th November 1793, B.L.

28 John Farquharson to Abbé MacPherson, 7th May 1801, B.L.

29 John Farquharson to George Mathison (enclosed in a letter from Bishop Cameron), 7 Nov. 1805, B.L.

30 *Catholic Directory*, 1831, p. 67.

31 These figures are obtained from various reports printed in the *Catholic Directories* of 1831-1835.

32 Andrew Scott to Bishop Cameron, 21st April 1818, Preshome Letters, Columba House.

33 *Scotichronicon*, p. 270.

34 Bishop Geddes to Bishop Hay, 19th August 1790, B.L.

35 Bishop Geddes to Bishop Hay, 20th September 1790, B.L.

36 James Robertson to Bishop Geddes, 5th July 1790, B.L.

37 Bishop Geddes to Mr Thomson, 12th April 1790, B.L.

38 Bishop Geddes to Mr Thomson, 1786, quoted in *Scotichronicon*, p. 264.

39 *Scotichronicon*, p. 288.

40 Bishop Geddes to Mr Thomson, 12th April, 1790, B.L.

41 Bishop Hay to Bishop Geddes, 21st February 1792, B.L.

42 E.g. George Chalmers to Bishop Geddes, 2nd May 1795 B.L.

43 Mr Farquharson to Abbé MacPherson, 19th September 1800, B.L.

44 George Chalmers to Bishop Geddes, 2nd May 1795; 5th August 1794. B.L.

45 *Scotichronicon*, pp. 225-6.

46 James Cummyng to Bishop Geddes, 26th February 1790, B.L.

47 Manuscripts are in Columba House.

48 Mr Thomson to Bishop Geddes, 27th December 1791, B.L.

49 Bishop Geddes to Abbé MacPherson, 13th March 1794, B.L.

50 David MacRoberts, 'The Scottish Catholic Archives 1560-1978', *Innes Review*, 1977, pp. 69-74.

51 John Thomson to Bishop Geddes, 15th July 1789, B.L.

52 Mss volumes together with notes and memoirs are preserved in Columba House.

53 Sir Paul Harvey, *Oxford Companion to English Literature*, 4th edition (1973), p. 503.

54 Bishop Cameron to Sir John Sinclair, Scroll letter, 1806, B.L.

55 Dr Johnson, *A Journey to the Western Islands of Scotland*, (London 1970), pp. 115-116.

56 *Ibid.*, p. 96.

4

The Relief Bill, 1793

THE Penal Act of 1700 had, it seemed, left Scottish Catholics with no legal rights whatsoever, so long as they adhered to their religion. Specific court cases, however, established that they did have a few legal rights.

The first case occurred in 1744. In 1743, after numerous scandals, Mr Francis MacDonald, a Highland priest, left the Catholic Church and became a licensed catechist and preacher under the Royal Bounty Committee at Strontian. In the following year he was brought before the Presbytery of Mull, accused of gross immorality. Bishop MacDonald came forward to give evidence against him. The right of a Catholic bishop to give evidence in a Presbyterian church court was challenged, but the church procurator, the future Lord Prestongrange, admitted his evidence.[1] It was quite a step forward for a presbytery to recognise as a witness a Roman Catholic bishop.

In 1783 a much more important case arose. In this year, Miss Gordon of Auchanacy, a Catholic, succeeded to an unexpired lease. Her right to do so was challenged by the nearest Protestant heir. The dispute was taken to the Court of Session. Lord Eskgrove referred it to the Inner House, where ten judges, including the Lord Justice Clerk and Lords Hailes, Monboddo, Gardenstone and Eskgrove, unanimously agreed that a Catholic had the same rights as a Protestant to succeed to and enjoy a lease of land in Scotland.[2] This was the first official recognition that Catholics had any legal rights with regard to land.

In 1789, when Scottish Catholics were still waiting to be given their first Relief Bill, the English Catholic Committee began to press hard for a second Relief Bill for English Catholics. This might have proved an opportunity for Scottish Catholics to act in conjunction with the English Committee to press home their own claims, had not the actions of the English Committee been condemned by the Scottish priests as at best misguided. Bishop Geddes voiced his fears in a letter to Mr Thomson:

> We must be very cautious in joining the English Catholics; for I am sorry to see little Prudence among them; yesterday I received a printed copy of a new oath proposed to be taken by them transmitted to our consideration by Bp. Gibson, but it is in such terms that I for one shall never take it.

Bishop Geddes further objected to the Committee's styling its members 'Protestant Catholic Dissenters' in an attempt to align themselves with other English dissenters.[3] Mr Farquharson, never one to mince words, expressed his opinion that the whole English Catholic Committee should be sent to Botany Bay.[4]

Scottish fears were increased in May 1790 when Bishop Gibson died, depriving the Committee of its most able and reliable adviser; but in 1791, when the Bill was passing through the House of Lords, the unexceptionable Irish oath was substituted for the one of which Bishop Geddes had disapproved. The second English Relief Bill, which became law in June 1791, proved, after all, to be perfectly acceptable to all Catholics, and Mr Alexander Geddes wrote from London to his cousin, Bishop Geddes, expressing astonishment that the Scottish Catholics had not asked for the Bill to be extended to them.[5]

In December 1792 Bishop Hay broached the matter of a Scottish Relief Bill, suggesting that Scotland's four major cities be asked to bring the Bill before Parliament. His coadjutor, however, did not think that such a scheme was practical. But by this time something had occurred which was to bring to a head the whole matter of Scottish Catholic Relief.

Towards the end of 1792 the elderly and childless Maxwell of Munshes was confronted, by his nearest Protestant heir, with an ultimatum: either Maxwell was to give this gentleman legal security that he would inherit the estate to the exclusion of Maxwell's sister and other Catholic relatives, or the said gentleman would take immediate steps to have Munshes disinherited under the Penal Act of 1700. Munshes at once posted to Edinburgh, where he and Bishop Geddes consulted with a number of lawyers, including the Lord Advocate.[6] The general consensus of opinion was that, while legal proceedings might delay the outcome for some time, Maxwell would ultimately lose his estate to the Protestant claimant. They advised an immediate application to Parliament for the repeal of the penal laws regarding ownership of property. An Irish Relief Bill was already being discussed in Parliament and was almost certain to be passed, so the moment was propitious for application for a Scottish Relief Bill.[7] The penal laws were, by this time, as Bishop Hay pointed out, singularly unfair, in that only Scotland was still burdened with them:

> I am longing to hear what way this attack against Munshes will be received by the Judges: it will make a curious appearance in the eyes of the world, if whilst Catholicks are getting every indulgence they can reasonably desire throughout the whole British Dominions, he should be deprived of such an estate merely because he is a Catholick.[8]

Bishop Geddes, remembering the outburst of anti-Catholic feeling triggered off by the proposal of a Scottish Relief Bill in 1779, thought that, in the present instance, the Scottish Catholic landowners should merely petition for a repeal of the penal laws which referred to property, and that as few people as possible should be told of the petition.[9] Bishop Hay, however, insisted that his coadjutor use all his influence to further a much wider Bill than Maxwell had intended to bring forward, giving his reasons for so doing:

> The general run of the Country is in our favour, and I do not think that your using your endeavours with your great friends could do any harm; if they do not incline to it you have done at least your part. If matters were carried through at once, there would not be the least danger, but if property alone be sought and obtained this might raise a sputter (if any were inclined to make one) to prevent our getting more, of which property would be considered as a prelude. This was the rock our friends split upon, when the first application was made; had Scotland been included in the first bill, there probably would have been no disturbance. And from the

experience of what happened then, I am fully persuaded that it would be much easier to get the whole at once just now, than to get a part now, and the rest hereafter. Might you not at least suggest these reflections to Mr Constable [Maxwell of Munshes] as well as to your other friends?[10]

Munshes and the other Catholic landowners were afraid that if they asked for too sweeping a reform they might fail even to obtain rights over property. Moreover, Henry Dundas, the Home Secretary, felt that the Bill should cover only property. But Bishop Geddes, encouraged by Bishop Hay, appealed to the many friends he had made over the years. He spoke to the nobility and to the Protestant ministers in Edinburgh; he wrote to powerful friends in other cities; he then wrote assuring Mr Dundas that he had the full support of everyone he had consulted regarding the Relief Bill. The government, on the Bishop's advice, then consulted the magistrates and principal clergymen of every city in Scotland. So favourable were the replies that the government decided to accept a Bill which, if passed, would repeal the penal laws regarding Catholic worship as well as property. The Lord Advocate was asked to present the Bill, which was read in the House of Commons on April 25th and on May 1st. By June 5th it had passed the House of Lords.[11] Bishop Geddes was delighted to observe that:

... there has scarcely been a murmur that I have heard, which, I believe, is owing greatly to the quiet manner with which the affair has been gone about and to the very obliging disposition of the Publishers of our Newspapers who unanimously agreed to reject every inflammatory composition that was offered them for publication. There was no mention made of us in the General Assembly. Its Moderator, Dr Hardie, had seen the Bill at London, and had said that it was not favourable enough to us. The Lord Advocate has behaved extremely well, and, last week, when I thanked him he seemed happy with what he had done; and assured me that the few exceptions had been left merely for peace's sake but that they will never be minded.[12]

Under the 1793 Relief Act,[13] Scottish Catholics were allowed freedom of worship; they were specifically authorised to inherit and to purchase lands and property as freely as any other people in Scotland; and their priests were at last able to say Mass with impunity. The 'few exceptions' mentioned in Bishop Geddes's letter were the clauses which excluded Catholics from teaching, or acting as tutors or curators to, Protestant children. These clauses, however, as the Lord Advocate had mentioned, were never invoked, and Catholics became teachers in many schools throughout Scotland, chiefly in the burghs. It was inevitable that Catholics would still be barred from holding certain offices, as indeed they continued to be even after the passing of the 1829 Emancipation Bill. The 1793 Relief Act, however, removed the main legal disabilities under which Catholics had laboured for so long, on the sole condition that they took a totally acceptable oath of loyalty to the king, and to the Hanoverian succession.

In practical terms, the Relief Bill, although it removed, at last, fears of persecution and of disinheritance, provoked surprisingly little immediate change in the Scottish Mission itself. For many years before it had been passed, Scottish Catholics had been worshipping openly in their chapels, and their priests had been going unmolested throughout the country. After the Bill was passed, no innovations were immediately introduced into the form of worship, and no imposing chapels sprang up. These developments were still at least ten years away.

Of a far more immediate practical impact on the Scottish Mission were the French Revolution and the Napoleonic Wars.

NOTES

1 'Clergy Lists of the Highland District 1732-1828', F. Forbes and W. J. Anderson, *Innes Review*, 1966, p. 137.

2 *Scotichronicon*, pp. 227-228.

3 Bishop Geddes to Mr Thomson, 30th August 1789, B.L.

4 Mr Farquharson to Mr Thomson, 9th February 1790, B.L.

5 Dr Alexander Geddes, London, to Bishop Geddes, 5th July 1791, B.L.

6 Bishop Geddes to Bishop Hay, 7th February 1793, B.L.

7 Bishop Geddes to Bishop Hay, 7th February 1793, B.L.

8 Bishop Hay to Bishop Geddes, 1st February 1793, B.L.

9 Bishop Geddes to Bishop Hay, 25th March 1793, B.L.

10 Bishop Hay to Bishop Geddes, 18th March 1793, B.L.

11 Abbé Paul MacPherson, 'Relation of the Means by which the repeal of the Penal Laws against the Catholics of Scotland was obtained on the 3rd June 1793'. Printed in Forbes Leith, vol. II, pp. 388-391. (This account was drawn up and presented to Propaganda in March 1794).

12 Bishop Geddes to Bishop Hay, 5th June 1793, B.L.

13 *Statutes at Large*, Vol. 16, 33 George III, c.44, pp. 336-337.

5

The Scottish Mission, 1560-1793

THE Scottish Reformation of 1560 swept away within a few years the ordered hierarchy of the Catholic Church. Although many people in Scotland remained Catholic, there were no bishops left to co-ordinate and supervise the work of any remaining priests, and to ensure a continuing flow of new priests to the Scottish Mission. Furthermore, all the endowments and property of the Catholic Church in Scotland were ultimately lost to it, with the exception, for all practical purposes, of chapels in the remote and generally poorer areas, which remained in Catholic hands. Any priests venturing into Post-Reformation Scotland not only ministered under constant threat of imprisonment, banishment, or even death, but, unless they were supported by a religious order, had to endure grinding poverty, dependent for their sustenance on the charity of their congregations. It is not surprising, therefore, that it was regular rather than secular priests who dominated the Scottish Mission throughout the seventeenth century.[1] In 1668, for instance, there were, in Scotland, eleven Jesuits, three Dominicans and two Franciscans.[2] The Jesuits generally established their members as chaplains in the houses of nobles or lairds, while the Irish Franciscans, from their base in Ulster, maintained a supply of Gaelic-speaking priests to the Highlands.

The regular clergy who worked in Scotland were under the supervision of the superiors of their respective orders; their secular counterparts, for over sixty years after 1560, were under no such supervision. Moreover, there was no overall co-ordination to ensure that secular and regular priests worked together for the maximum benefit to Catholics in Scotland. What was needed was the appointment of someone to be in authority over all priests in Scotland.

The first step towards providing a regular supply of secular priests for Scotland was taken in June 1622. Pope Gregory XIII had set up a Commission of Cardinals to 'promote the reconciliation of the schismatic oriental churches'.[3] In 1622 Pope Gregory XV promoted the Commission into a Congregation, the Congregation 'de Propaganda Fide', usually referred to as 'Propaganda'. This Congregation was made responsible for the supervision of missionary activity throughout the world. In 1623 it appointed Mr William Bishop as the first Vicar Apostolic for England and Scotland.

In Protestant countries like England and Scotland Roman canon law was no longer recognised. In Scotland the judicial powers of the Catholic bishops with regard to marriages and testaments had been taken over by the secular courts: by local commissary courts for testaments of small value, by the Commissary Court at

Edinburgh, established in 1564, for testaments of higher value, and by the Court of Session for divorce cases. A Vicar Apostolic could exercise only the spiritual powers vested in him by Papal authority. He had no territorial diocesan jurisdiction, but he did have the power to ordain priests, to consecrate chapels and to give confirmation. He also had the power to co-ordinate and control the activities of the priests on his Mission.

The appointment of an Englishman as Vicar Apostolic over a united Anglo-Scottish Mission inevitably aroused antagonism among Scottish priests reared in the tradition of Scottish ecclesiastical independence which had been established in 1192 by the Papal Bull, 'Filia Specialis'. A more practical complaint against Bishop was that his jurisdiction in Scotland was little more than nominal and did little to promote the Catholic faith there. In 1649, when Mr William Leslie took up the post at Rome of Agent for the Scottish secular clergy, one of his main objects was to obtain a separate Vicar Apostolic for Scotland. He saw his object accomplished at last when, in 1694, Mr Thomas Nicolson was consecrated bishop, and was appointed as the first Vicar Apostolic over the again separate Scottish Mission.[4]

With Bishop Nicolson's appointment it became possible to organise more efficiently the supply of secular priests for Scotland. Priests who found promising boys could refer them to the Bishop who could then have them properly educated for the priesthood. Both students and secular priests could be supported by Mission funds derived partly from an annual payment by Propaganda, and partly from gifts of money made to the Mission and invested on the Continent. Although this income was less than adequate, it did much to ensure that secular clergy could be sent in larger numbers to Scotland. This had been one of Agent Leslie's main reasons for fighting to obtain the appointment of a Scottish Vicar Apostolic. Agent Leslie, like many other secular priests, was violently anti-Jesuit,[5] and hoped that Bishop Nicolson would replace the Jesuits on the Scottish Mission with secular priests.

The main complaints made by Leslie against the Jesuits were: firstly, that they endeavoured to syphon off for their own Order the most promising Scots boys, leaving only the less able to become secular priests;[6] secondly, that a Jesuit priest could easily leave Scotland in times of hardship or danger, and retire to the comfortable safety of a Jesuit house on the Continent;[7] and, thirdly, that the Jesuits made a point of concentrating their efforts on nobles and lairds, to the neglect of the ordinary people.[8]

As regards the first complaint, it was inevitable, since three of the four Scots Colleges on the Continent were run by Jesuits, that a proportion of the students studying in them would be attracted into the Society of Jesus. This in itself might not have affected the Scottish Mission had not many of these Scots Jesuits been sent to serve in Germany, France and eastern Europe rather than in Scotland. Not all of the Scots Jesuits, however, were lost to the Scottish Mission. In 1703 there were serving in Scotland nine Jesuits, as well as four Benedictines, five Irish Franciscans, and seventeen secular clergy;[9] in other words, a quarter of the priests were Jesuits. In 1763, of the seventeen priests stationed in the Lowland District, five — almost a third — were Jesuits.[10] The contribution made by the Society of Jesus to the preservation of Catholicism in Scotland, although it could have been much greater, was nevertheless of no small importance to a Mission chronically short of priests.

It would be a laborious task to search out figures which would either concur with or refute the claim that Jesuits deserted the Mission in time of trouble. In the seventeenth century, many Jesuits spent only a short time in Scotland before returning to the Continent, but many of them had been imprisoned and subsequently banished by the Scottish courts.[11] By the second half of the eighteenth century Scotland was safer, and Jesuits were spending all their working lives in the Scottish Mission. When the Society of Jesus was disbanded in 1773, four of its members were serving in the Highlands. All four continued in their stations as secular priests: Father Kenneth MacKenzie, who had come to Strathglass in 1756 remained there until shortly before his death, in Aberdeen, in 1775. Father Norman MacLeod served Strathglass from 1753 until his death in 1777; Father John Farquharson, who had been in Scotland since 1729, died at Balmoral in 1782, aged 83; and Father Charles Farquharson served Braemar from 1745 until his death in 1799.[12] There can be no criticism of the dedication with which these four Jesuits served in Scotland.

The Society of Jesus undeniably directed its mission activities towards the ruling classes, whether in its far-flung outposts in China and Japan, or in its more modest missions in the Protestant nations of Europe. In the latter, of course, the Jesuits could not hope to gain entry into court circles, and so had to concentrate their attention on any favourably disposed nobles. In Scotland, an example of the close connection established between lairds and Jesuits is to be found in the Maxwell families of Kirkconnel and Terregles. The boys of these families were almost all educated at the Jesuit-run Scots College at Douay; many of them became Jesuits themselves, often returning to Scotland as chaplains to their families.[13] Jesuit belief was that if a noble was a Catholic, then all his dependents, whether family members or tenants on his estates, would also become, or remain, Catholics. This belief was borne out in several instances. The Dukes of Gordon, for example, remained Catholic until 1728, and so did their tenants in the Enzie, Glenlivet, Strathavon, Badenoch and Lochaber. In Galloway, too, the tenants on the estates of the Maxwells and Glendonwyns remained Catholic in an area which had, in the seventeenth century, produced the most extreme of the Covenanters. Only at Traquair, in spite of the Earl's adherence to Catholicism, do the tenants appear to have diverged from their landlord and embraced the Protestant faith.[14] Perhaps this can be attributed to the situation of Traquair House in Peeblesshire, within easy reach of Edinburgh and the influence of the Reformed Kirk, and, before 1707, of Parliament. Galloway, Banffshire and Lochaber, by contrast, were remote, far less accessible areas.

The post of chaplain to a landowning family was by no means exclusive to the Society of Jesus. In 1703 there were Jesuit chaplains with the Earl of Nithsdale, the Countess of Seaforth, Leslie of Balquhain, and the lairds of Garlieston, Niddrie and Auchinhove; but there were also secular priests serving as chaplains at

Gordon Castle, Drummond Castle and Traquair House, as well as a Benedictine at Carnfield. Mr James Gordon, in his report to Propaganda, was at pains to point out that the secular priests

> ... depended on the Nobility only in this, that they made use of their protection to live with more safety and to exercise their functions with greater freedom, and ... served the neighbouring Catholics with no less attention than if they had not been attached to those Noblemen.[15]

The implication of this statement was that the Jesuits, unlike the secular priests, stayed comfortably in the lairds' houses and did not minister to the Catholics of the surrounding area. This, an accusation frequently made against the Jesuits, would seem to be refuted by the report made in 1702 by Father Hugh Strachan, S.J. to his superior. Father Strachan, who was chaplain to the laird of Auchinhove, as well as listing the converts he had made among the people living in his area, sent the following description of his life:

> The region I dwell in is steep and sterile, mountainous and rugged, and much hardship and inconvenience has to be put up with. The people are so poor that they keep their cattle in their own dwellings. We live as we can on butter, cheese and milk, rarely get flesh, fish hardly ever. We usually drink water, sometimes beer; wine we never taste but at the altar. We lie on the ground, or on a little straw or heather. These and other inconveniences perhaps still worse are telling upon my strength and my health is more often bad than good.[16]

In his report, Mr Gordon criticised the Jesuits for not confining themselves to fixed stations, but wandering about where they pleased, and not applying themselves properly to instruction and to preaching. The Jesuit report of 1702 suggests that this criticism, if not altogether unmerited, was at least greatly exaggerated. Father Innes, it is true, described how

> For nearly fifteen years I have been wandering over different parts of this, my native country.[17]

But the other Jesuits seem to have confined their activities each to a definite district. As to their wandering about, this is hardly surprising, considering the extensive and difficult terrains they had to cover. Father Alexander Macra's district was

> ... a tract of country twelve miles in length, broken up by many gulfs or firths both to the north and south, and containing a considerable number of villages ... [18]

Father Robert Seton had charge of a district in Braemar some sixty miles long. Nor could these areas have been decreased, since there were always too few priests available to cover the country adequately.

The chief criticism that can be made of the Society of Jesus is that it removed from Scotland men who, had they been secular priests and not Jesuits, would have served there rather than on the Continent. This the Society accomplished in the Scots colleges which it ran in Rome, in Madrid and in Douay, by recruiting to itself boys sent to the Colleges to be educated specifically for the Scottish Mission. On the other hand, the priests whom the Society sent to Scotland seem to have been just as hard-working and conscientious as their secular counterparts. There was, however, inevitably some friction between Jesuits and secular clergy.

In 1750 the Jesuits objected to the choice of the Paris-educated Mr Alexander Gordon as coadjutor to Bishop Smith. This was not the first time that the Society had run counter to Bishop Smith, and the Bishop took this occasion to obtain from

Propaganda a decree that

> These Religious [were submitted] so far to the bishop's jurisdiction that they were obliged to receive powers from him to preach and administer the sacraments; as likewise in case of improper behaviour he could remove them from their stations but not oblige them to serve any particular mission without the consent of their superior.[19]

Friction such as this, however, was not frequent. In 1709 Bishop James Gordon wrote to the General of the Jesuits, praising the Jesuit priests in Scotland, and saying that he did all he could to help them and to promote peace between Jesuits and secular clergy.[20] The fact that no Jesuit priest left Scotland when the Society was disbanded in 1773 is a good indication of the success with which the Jesuits had been integrated into the Scottish Mission since the beginning of the eighteenth century.

Not surprisingly, it was the question of money which caused the most bitter acrimony between Jesuits and secular clergy in the impoverished Scottish Mission.

If a priest served as a chaplain he was maintained by the household with which he stayed. In cases where a chaplain had to serve a large and numerous mission, a Jesuit chaplain benefited the Scottish Mission, which was thus freed from the necessity of maintaining that station, a blessing when both finances and manpower were in short supply. On the other hand, houses like Traquair and Terregles had relatively small missions attached to them. These were ideal stations for old secular priests who could no longer cope with the stringencies of a large country station. If such chaplaincies were filled by Jesuits, then the old priests had to be maintained by Mission funds along with younger priests who had to take over most of their duties.

It was, however, after the disbandment of the Jesuits in 1773 that the bitterest anti-Jesuit feelings were aroused. The Jesuits had been rich and well-endowed. In 1773 Mr Johnson, who had been the Jesuit provincial, took over the administration of the funds that had belonged to the Scottish Jesuits. In 1780 he died, leaving Mr George Maxwell, another ex-Jesuit, as his executor. In 1781 Bishop Hay persuaded Mr Maxwell to make over these funds to the Scottish Mission, on condition of their being refunded, without interest, should the Society of Jesus ever be re-established. In 1802 Mr Maxwell died, leaving the funds to the Scottish Mission on the same terms as had been agreed upon by Bishop Hay.[21]

By 1802, however, the re-establishment of the Jesuits was no longer just the pious hope that it must have seemed, in 1781, to Bishop Hay. They had already been restored in Russia, and pressure was being applied in Rome to have them universally re-established.[22] The possibility of such a re-establishment aroused the most violent feelings in the Lowland Vicariate of Scotland. There were, serving in the Lowland District, at that time, three ex-Jesuits: Mr Charles Maxwell, Mr MacGillivray and Mr John Pepper. Mr MacGillivray was living in semi-retirement at Traquair House, passing his spare time in binding books and in carving egg-cups and tobacco boxes for, among others, Bishop Cameron.[23] Mr Maxwell had been in charge of the Mission funds since 1798, an onerous appointment which he had discharged faithfully through some of the most difficult times the Mission had known in recent years. Mr Maxwell and Mr MacGillivray were in their fifties; Mr John Pepper, the chaplain at Terregles, was in his seventies. As soon as there seemed any likelihood of the Jesuits being restored, Bishop Cameron conceived an obsessive distrust of these men who had served the Mission as secular priests for thirty years. He determined to remove Mr Maxwell from the procuratorship, and Mr MacGillivray from the office of administrator in the Lowland Vicariate. He wrote to Mr MacPherson:

> Begging your pardon, I think you erred in promoting Mr Maxwell to be Procurator, and even in getting him and Mr MacGillivray made Administrators; you must have known that they never could give us their full confidence. No secular clergyman was ever admitted into the secrets of Jesuits; their finances, their political government, everything which could be kept from us was . . . scrupulously concealed. We now see that they had appointed laymen, to watch over their interests and be a check upon the Bishops and their clergy . . .[24]

Bishop Cameron was afraid that the Jesuits would soon be in a position to reclaim their funds from the Scottish Mission. He was afraid that, since the College of Stonyhurst in England, run as it was by ex-Jesuits, was to all intents and purposes a Jesuit college, the ex-Jesuits in Scotland would want Scottish Jesuit funds to be applied to it, rather than to the maintenance of secular clergy in Scotland.[25] He also seems to have been afraid that Mr Maxwell and Mr MacGillivray might abuse their positions of office to benefit Jesuits at the expense of the Scottish Mission.

In 1810 Mr Pepper died; in 1811 Mr Maxwell and Mr MacGillivray also died. Mr Davidson, priest at Greenock, echoed his bishop's sentiments when he wrote to Bishop Cameron, 'The Lowland Mission is now . . . happily cleared of Jesuits'.[26] It is a sad reflection on the Scottish Mission that money matters could engender such hostility towards priests who had served it so faithfully and for so long.

The appointment of Bishop Nicolson as Vicar Apostolic over a separate Scottish Mission was a step in the right direction. This appointment, by itself, however, was to prove inadequate in face of the linguistic division of Scotland into Gaelic-speaking Highlands and Scots-speaking Lowlands. A boy from Aberdeen or Edinburgh who trained for the priesthood could be of little benefit to Catholics in, say, Barra, who spoke only Gaelic. It was essential that as many Gaelic-speaking as Scots-speaking priests should be trained, a fact that was recognised by Agent Leslie in the late seventeenth century. Leslie, with this in mind, made the following proposal to Propaganda:

> . . . that for the future an equal number of Highlanders and Lowlanders should be kept in the college [at Rome]. Ever since its foundation one, or two at the most, had been received from the Highlands. These rude countries remained therefore all this time deprived of pastors to instruct, administer the sacraments or afford spiritual help of any kind. Those of the Lowlands, for want of the Erse language, could be of little service, and having too much ado in their own country scarcely ever thought on the Highlands. On some rare occasions, it is true, a few Irish priests visited them, but remained very little time among them; one or two of their own country who had studied at Rome laboured as much as they could till they were apprehended by the ministers and imprisoned. But though they continued at liberty what could two men only do in a country so wide, so rough and so stormy?[27]

In 1703, when James Gordon sent his report to Propaganda,[28] there were eight priests stationed in the Highlands and one in the Gaelic-speaking Deeside. Of these nine priests, five were Irish Franciscans, two were Jesuits, one was a Benedictine monk and only one was a secular clergyman. The Jesuits who were serving on the

Scottish Mission were not all Gaelic speakers, as their reports of 1702 show, but they were stationed in Braemar, Deeside and Strathglass, as well as in the Scots-speaking missions in Galloway, Fife and Midlothian. The Jesuit reports of 1702 illustrate the problems faced by non-Gaelic-speaking priests in the Highlands, and the difference in attitude between Highlander and Lowlander.

Father Alexander Macra, who, from his name, was probably a native Gaelic speaker, was obviously deeply attached to his mission station, an area 'broken up by many gulfs or firths' — probably Morar. He described the hardships and poverty of his congregation with sympathy, expressing admiration for their industry and their patience. He praised their piety and their inclination 'to good', giving many illustrations of this.[29]

Father Hugh Strachan, who was stationed with the Laird of Auchinhove at Deeside, found language a problem to begin with:

> [I] was at that time [1701] entirely ignorant of my native language, which, however difficult it is to learn, our Lord has enabled me to acquire so completely that I am now able to read, write, preach and catechise in the Vernacular. I have composed a catechism of controversy in this Highland tongue . . .[30]

Father Strachan, like Father Macra, sympathised with the hardships with which his people had to contend; he himself found the life hard and a toll on his health, but his report suggests that he adapted himself well both to the life and to his Gaelic-speaking congregation.

By contrast, the report of Father John Innes illustrates the problems that could occur if a priest was sent to a congregation with whose language and customs he was unfamiliar:

> For nearly fifteen years I have been wandering over different parts of this, my native country, with what difficulties, hardship and peril He only knows, who knows all things. I have had to accomodate myself to the manners and customs of the rudest and most uncouth country people . . . It cost me immense toil and much time to learn to speak the extremely difficult language of this country . . .[31]

Father Innes's report shows how much more satisfactory it would have been to have native Highlanders as priests, rather than incomers who had to adapt themselves to an alien way of life.

The West Highlands of Scotland had close links with Ireland, links forged by generations of migration, from the settlement of Argyll by the Scots in the sixth century to the settlement in Ireland in the seventeenth century of MacDonalds dispossessed by the Campbells. Linguistically and culturally the West Highlands and Catholic Ireland were so similar that Irish Franciscans were able to fit easily into West Highland society, and it was on these men that the Scottish Catholics chiefly relied, throughout the seventeenth century, to provide a Gaelic-speaking priesthood. Mr Thomson describes how, for instance, in 1704, Bishop Nicolson

> . . . used all his interest both in Ireland and on the Continent to procure a supply. He had, some years before, sent many Highland youths to the college at Paris, and some to that of Rome, to afford a constant supply to the country, but unfortunately most of them after all his trouble and expense misgave, which gave him great concern and increased his difficulties.[32]

In 1729 Bishop Gordon, again short of priests for the Highlands, wrote urgently to France, and managed to obtain one or two more Irish priests for the Mission.[33] As late as 1756 Irish priests were still needed:

> The Highlands were in a deplorable state for want of missioners. Bishop MacDonald earnestly entreated the Roman agent to prevail on some worthy Irish friars to take pity on the poor Catholics there, and go and succour them . . . Mr Grant, after using all his interest, could get none of these Fathers to accept of the offer.[34]

The Irish Franciscans could not be depended on for a continuing and steady supply of priests. If a friar retired, or was forced by ill-health to leave his station, no reliance could be placed on the Franciscans sending a replacement. In 1739 two Irish friars who absented themselves from Scotland on private business, promising to return in a short time, were detained in Ireland by their superiors.[35]

It was clear that only native Highlanders could be relied upon to spend their lives as priests among the Gaelic-speaking Catholics of Scotland; and that they should be secular priests, not attached to a religious order which might recall them at any time.

Bishop James Gordon concerned himself particularly with the Highlands. He went there several times on short visits, and then spent the whole winter of 1711-1712 there, returning to the Lowlands in June. The purpose of this long stay was to acquaint himself with the 'Nature and Genius' of the people, and to learn some Gaelic:[36]

> Bishop Gordon from that time saw the impossibility of one Vicar Apostolic being able to take proper care of the Catholics and promote the interests of religion in such a wide and extensive country as Scotland is, and especially in the Highlands so far separated from the low country and of so difficult access, and the necessity of having a proper Vicar Apostolic constantly on the spot in the Highlands and one who should know the language of the country to watch over the interests of religion.

On his return to the Lowlands, Bishop Gordon wrote to Mr Stuart, the Agent at Rome, asking him to propose to Cardinal Sacripanti that Bishop Nicolson be given another coadjutor for the Lowlands, leaving himself as Bishop in the Highlands. This scheme, however, was opposed by some of the Scottish priests, who wrote to Mr Stuart, telling him on no account to put Bishop Gordon's proposal to the Cardinal. The proposal was shelved, but Bishop Gordon did not reliquish his objective.[37]

In 1725 Bishop Gordon's arguments in favour of the appointment of a Highland Vicar Apostolic were reinforced. In that year a General Assembly Committee was set up to provide more ministers, catechists and schoolmasters for the Highlands in order to stamp out the 'Encrease of Popery'.[38] In the face of this increased Presbyterian activity, and of the long, difficult journeys that a Lowland-based Bishop had to make in order to confirm people in the Highlands, it became more vital than ever that there should be a resident Highland bishop to oppose Presbyterian encroachment on the Catholics there. Once again, Bishop Gordon petitioned Rome for a Highland Vicar Apostolic, this time with the support of the Scottish priests.[39]

In 1727 the Pope granted Bishop Gordon's request. The Bishop's choice for Highland Vicar Apostolic fell on the young, Gaelic-speaking priest, John Grant. Grant, at his own request, was sent to Rome to procure the approval of Propaganda. Having been given that approval, Mr Grant set out on a lengthy tour of Italy, during the course of which he became ill, and his money ran out. He became profoundly depressed, to the point of insanity, saw everyone as his enemy, and refused the appointment as Bishop. He then disappeared and never rejoined the Scottish Mission.[40]

Bishop Gordon was understandably alarmed at John Grant's behaviour, fearing that he had perhaps jeopardised the chance of obtaining a Highland Vicar Apostolic. He wrote again, however, to Propaganda, in 1730, stressing the need for such an appointment especially as the number of Catholics was increasing in the Highlands. This time he recommended Mr Hugh MacDonald, of the MacDonalds of Morar, who carried great weight in that part of the country, who had received all his education in Scotland, and who was acceptable to all the priests and laymen whom the Bishop had consulted.[41] This time there was no hitch. Hugh MacDonald, son of MacDonald of Morar, was consecrated at Edinburgh on 13th October, 1731. The Bishops then divided Scotland into two districts, Highland and Lowland, taking language as the criterion for the division. The only exceptions to this rule were Glenlivet and Strathavon, which, though Gaelic-speaking, were kept in the Lowland Vicariate, because Bishop Gordon's seminary of Scalan was situated in Glenlivet.[42]

The creation of a Highland Vicariate was followed almost immediately by the founding of a Highland seminary. From 1732 until 1746, and again, from 1768 until 1829, Highland priests were able to obtain at least the rudiments of their education in the Highlands, only going abroad to the Scots Colleges when they were older. The impact of this was quite remarkable. Of the priests who were serving in the Highlands when the Highland Vicariate was created, or who were to serve in it within the next ten years and were then at College, six, apart from the Bishop, were Highland. Of the other eight, one was from Edinburgh, one from Cromarty, two were from Aberdeenshire, three were from Banffshire and one was from Elgin. One of the Highlanders had been converted to Catholicism while studying at Aberdeen University.[43] The dominant influence of the North-East is clear.

Of the sixty-one priests who served the Highland Vicariate, and who began their training after the first Highland seminary was opened, only two — both Irish — are known to have been other than native Highlanders. The vast majority came from the West Highlands and Islands, a few from Perthshire; and the rest, whose origins are unclear, had, with two exceptions, Highland names. By 1745 priests who had begun their training at the Highland seminary were beginning to arrive home, ordained, from the Colleges abroad. By 1781 the Highland priests consisted of one MacGillis, one Chisholm, and thirteen MacDonalds.[43]

Undoubtedly the various Highland seminaries contributed a great deal towards the establishment of a native priesthood, but there is also another factor which may have played a part, a factor which stems from the nature of Highland society.

As the eighteenth century wore on, many Highland chiefs abandoned their old standards, based on the clan system, a chief's importance being measured in terms of the manpower he could command. They turned instead to the Lowland standards whereby a man's status was measured in terms of money, not men. In short, they became landlords exploiting their lands for financial gain. Their tenants, however, still clung to the values of the kin-based society which can be traced back to the seventh and eighth-century Irish law tracts. In that society a bishop was accorded the rank of 'ri tuaithe' or clan chief.[44] It is surely no accident that the first five Highland bishops were all near relatives of clan chiefs. Bishop Hugh was the son of MacDonald of Morar; his successor, Bishop John, was a grandson of MacDonald of Morar; Bishop Alexander MacDonald was the son of MacDonald of Bornish; and Bishops John and Angus Chisholm were brothers, cousins to Chisholm of Strathglass.

Turning to the priests themselves, a definite pattern seems to emerge. Under the first three Highland bishops, all MacDonalds, forty-four priests began their training. Of these no fewer than thirty were MacDonalds. Of the remaining fourteen, three were MacEachans. In the fifteenth century, the MacEachans had been the most important local kindred in Kintyre, their chiefs holding the office of maer of the MacDonald Lords of the Isles. They retained this office, holding it of the Crown, after the forfeiture of Kintyre in 1745. Donald Munro, writing about 1550, describes MacEachan of Kilellan as a 'freeholder', the fourth grade of cenn cinnidh or head of kindred under the overlordship of the Lord of the Isles.[45] It would seem, therefore, in view of the very conservative society of the West Highlands, that there might be some justification for placing the eighteenth-century MacEachan priests under the umbrella grouping of 'MacDonald'. Such a presumption is less tendentious than might at first appear: Evan MacEachan appears in the register of the Scots College at Valladolid, as 'Evanus MacDonald'.[46] If, therefore, we can group MacEachans with MacDonalds, this would mean that thirty-three of the priests to start their training under the MacDonald bishops were themselves MacDonalds — just over 75%.

In 1792 the third MacDonald bishop died. He was succeeded in turn by John and Angus Chisholm from Strathglass. The two Chisholms seem to have been the only Strathglass students to have trained for the priesthood during the MacDonald espiscopacies. Of the first eight priests to start their training under the Chisholm bishops, five, including the only MacDonald, were from Strathglass. By 1803 much of Strathglass had been cleared of its people to make way for sheep, as had many areas in the West Highlands and Islands. Of the priests who started their training after about 1807, only three were MacDonalds, two of whom were from Lochaber. Of the other five who were ordained by 1828, one came from Glen Shee, and one, Ronald Rankine, came from Fort William. Of the other three, Terence MacGuire was from Ireland, Alexander MacSwein was of Irish extraction, and William Byrne knew no Gaelic.

None of the above statistics can be related in any way to the positioning of the different Highland seminaries. The figures do not take account of boys who started to train for the priesthood and fell by the wayside, but even so they must be taken as representative of the initial intake of boys. These statistics would suggest that each Highland bishop in turn claimed some sort of clan loyalty which influenced the candidature for the Highland priesthood. This loyalty seems to have broken down in the second decade of the nineteenth century, by which time emigration and clearances had taken their toll. The Highland priesthood, therefore, owed much to the survival of the kin-based society in the Western Highlands and Islands. In the light of this, the Highland Vicariate is seen to have been a vital factor in the continuation of Catholicism in these areas.

NOTES

1 *Scotichronicon* — Clergy lists — pp. 627-636, also biographical notes on priests, pp. 514-626.

2 *Ibid.*, p. 627.

3 Anson, *Underground Catholicism in Scotland*, p. 8.

4 Thomson, 'History of the Scottish Mission', Vol. I, pp. 16 *et seq.* gives general account.

5 Abbé Paul MacPherson, 'History of the Scots College, Rome', edited by W. J. Anderson, *Innes Review* 1961, pp. 33-34.

6 Abbé MacPherson, 'History of the Scots College, Rome', *Innes Review* 1961, p. 29.

7 Abbé MacPherson, 'History of the Scots College, Rome', *Innes Review* 1961, p. 29.

8 Thomson, 'History of the Scottish Mission', vol. I, pp. 548-549.

9 *Ibid.*, pp. 547-548.

10 Bishop Smith's report to Propaganda 1763; in Rev. R. MacDonald, 'The Highland District in 1764', *Innes Review* 1964, pp. 141-142.

11 *Scotichronicon*, biographical notes of Scottish priests, pp. 514-626.

12 F. Forbes and W. J. Anderson, 'Clergy lists of the Highland District', *Innes Review* 1966, p. 152.

13 *Scotichronicon* — biographical notes, pp. 580-582; also the Douay Register printed in *Registers of the Scots Colleges* — New Spalding Club, 1906.

14 Thomson, 'History of the Scottish Mission', Vol. I, pp. 547-48; Webster, *Scottish Population Statistics*, pp. 18, 21-24.

15 Thomson, Vol. I, pp. 548-49.

16 'Report of the Scottish Mission of the Society of Jesus for the year 1702', printed in Forbes Leith, Vol. II, p. 204.

17 *Ibid.*, p. 195.

18 'Report of the Scottish Mission of the Society of Jesus, 1702', Forbes Leith, Vol. II, p. 193.

19 Abbé MacPherson's continuation of Thomson's 'History', Vol. II, pp. 229-230.

20 Letter of Bishop Gordon, printed in Forbes Leith, Vol. II, p. 252.

21 George Maxwell to Bishop John Chisholm, 26th August 1796. Oban Letters, Columba House.

22 Bishop John Chisholm to Charles Maxwell, 30th April 1800, B.L.

23 Eg. Mr MacGillivray to Bishop Cameron, 8th November 1802, B.L.

24 Bishop Cameron to Abbé MacPherson, 3rd June 1807, B.L.

25 Thomas Bagnall to Bishop Cameron, 5th May 1811, B.L.

26 John Davidson to Bishop Cameron, 1811, B.L.

27 MacPherson, 'History of the Scots College, Rome', *Innes Review* 1961, pp. 65-66.

28 Thomson, 'History of the Scottish Mission', Vol. I, p. 547.

29 'Report of the Scottish Mission of the Society of Jesus, 1702', Forbes Leith, Vol. II, p. 193.

30 'Report of the Scottish Mission of the Society of Jesus, 1702', Forbes Leith, Vol. II, p. 204.

31 *Ibid.*, p. 195.

32 Thomson, 'History of the Scottish Mission', quoted in Forbes Leith, Vol. II, p. 219.

33 Thomson, 'History of the Scottish Mission', Vol. II, p. 169.

34 MacPherson's continuation of Thomson, Vol. II, p. 261.

35 *Ibid.*, p. 141.

36 Thomson, Vol. II, p. 6.

37 Thomson, Vol. II, p. 8.

38 'Register of the Acts and Proceedings of the Committee of the General Assembly of the Church

of Scotland for Reformation of the Highlands and Islands of Scotland and for management of the King's Bounty for that End.' CHI/5/51, Register House.

39 Thomson, Vol. II, pp. 114-115.

40 Thomson, Vol. II, pp. 136, 143.

41 Thomson, Vol. II, p. 183.

42 Abbé MacPherson's continuation of Thomson, Vol. II, p. 2.

43 F. Forbes and W. J. Anderson, 'Clergy Lists of the Highland District, 1732-1828', *Innes Review* 1966, pp. 129-184, supply the details from which these figures are obtained.

44 Kathleen Hughes, *The Church in Early Irish Society* (1966), p. 135.

45 Munro's *Western Isles of Scotland and Genealogies of the Clans* (1961), p. 103.

46 *Records of the Scots Colleges*, New Spalding Club, 1906, p. 210.

6

Catholic Landowners

IN 1703, after the formation of a separate Scottish Mission, James Gordon sent to Propaganda a report on the numbers of Catholics in Scotland. In about 1790 Mr Thomson, writing about this report in his 'History of the Scottish Mission', added his own comments on the numbers of Catholics in Scotland a century later:

> [Gordon] then gives a general account of the Catholics and of the places where they were most numerous. These were the same in which they are most numerous at this day, only he says that in Tweedale and Clydesdale there were considerable numbers where there are very few at present. He says that the Catholics lived with greatest peace and security in the Western Isles and that they did not live so peaceably in any part either in the Highlands or Lowlands as in the Duke of Gordon's estate. The Enzie at that time was the principal mission of the whole kingdom. The Bishop resided there for the most part and the procurator of the mission always; the meetings of the clergy were all held there. The Catholics were so numerous and their meetings so public that the Protestants called the Enzie the Papistical Country. They enjoyed the same freedom in Glenlivet and Strathboggy. Though the privy council and persons in power knew this yet they connived at it out of regard for the Duke of Gordon —— He adds —— that there were still among the Catholics a considerable number of persons conspicuous for their Birth and fortune such as the Dukes of Gordon and Perth, the Earls of Huntly Traquair Nithsdale Seaforth Aboyne and Melfort, the Lords Drummond, Semple, Oliphant and Banff, Count Leslie with many lairds both in Highlands and Lowlands besides the Earl of Middleton who had been received into the Church at St. Germans. From this numeration it appears that though the Catholics in Scotland are certainly increased in number since that time, yet many of the Nobility and Gentry have apostatized.[1]

Time, by 1790, had taken its toll of the Catholic nobles, partly through the enactment of the penal laws, partly due to Jacobitism, but also through the natural course of events. The widowed Countess of Seaforth, in 1702, foiled an attempt made under the penal Act to have her son educated as a Protestant when she stole him away and sent him to the Continent.[2] It was not the penal Act which resulted in the third Duke of Gordon's being brought up a Protestant, but a mixed marriage. When his Catholic father died, his mother, who was an Episcopalian, had him brought up in her faith. Indeed the penal laws regarding education occasionally backfired, as when John Thomson, who had been brought up a Protestant, was converted to Roman Catholicism while acting as preceptor to the Catholic family of Innes of Balnacraig.[3]

In 1822 Mr James Kyle (later bishop) reported to Propaganda that, of the nobles, only the Earl of Traquair was still Catholic. There were also still a few Catholic lairds, but most of the old Catholic landowners had long since apostatised. According to Bishop Kyle, this was no loss because, in former times, the Catholic nobles had 'contributed extremely little to the spread or defence of the faith'.[4]

Such an indictment of the Catholic landowners cannot be justified. Had it not been for the Maxwells and Glendonwyns in Galloway, the Catholic religion would surely have been completely wiped out there. Had it not been for the protection of the Dukes of Gordon, who remained Catholic until 1728, Catholicism could not have survived in such strength in the North-East. In 1718, for instance, the presbytery of Kincardine O'Neil attributed the growth of popery in that area, among other things, to

> Great men of the popish Religion such as the D[uke] of G[ordon] having Superiorities and Regalities and keeping Courts in them by their Corrupt Deputies ——[5]

A memorial drafted in 1720 accused Catholics on the Duke of Gordon's estates of persecuting with impunity the Protestants who lived there.[6] The second Duke of Gordon's death in 1728 was precipitated by his journey to London in the previous year to try to obtain protection for the Catholics on his estates who were being harried by the Presbyterians.[7]

Throughout the seventeenth and early eighteenth centuries, before the Scottish Mission was well established under the care of a properly organised priesthood headed by a Vicar Apostolic, the presence of Catholic landowners was a decisive factor in many parts of Scotland in the continuing of the Catholic religion. Only in the Western Highlands and Islands did the problems of distance and of finding Gaelic-speaking ministers prevent the Catholics from being much disturbed by Protestants in the seventeenth century. In the late eighteenth century Catholic landowners, who had commanded the loyalty of their tenants during the Jacobite rebellions, began to turn their backs on the people who had formerly looked to them for protection. In 1770, for instance, MacDonald of Boisdale, an ex-Catholic, opened a Protestant school in South Uist. When Catholic parents complained that their children were being given anti-Catholic teaching, Boisdale ordered them to abandon their religion or leave his lands. To a man the Catholics chose to leave their homes rather than turn their backs on their religion. Boisdale was taken completely by surprise. Afraid of losing his tenants and hence his rents, he withdrew his demands, and renewed all his leases for another year. But he demanded so much money from his tenants that Catholics throughout Britain were moved to subscribe to a fund to pay for these people to emigrate to St. John's Island in Canada:

> Boisdale, finding that the Catholics in Uist were so liberally assisted, and so strongly protected, finding also that numbers of them were leaving his lands, and dreading that others would follow their example, began to relent, and even to favour them in a particular manner. He entreated and begged of such as remained not to abandon the country, and gave them every assurance of not being molested in their religion for the future, and that they should have their possessions much below what they had hitherto paid for them.[8]

The refusal of Boisdale's tenants to abandon their religion in the face of the threat of eviction is a tribute to the strength of the Scottish Mission.

In the seventeenth century nobles and lairds had provided refuges for priests and protection for Catholic tenants. In the late eighteenth century Catholic landowners like Chisholm and Glengarry as well as the apostate Boisdale withdrew this protection. But by this time the Scottish Mission was in a strong enough position to help ordinary Catholics and to keep them loyal to their religion.

NOTES

1 Thomson, 'History of the Scottish Mission', Vol. I, pp. 546-547.

2 Thomson, Vol. II, p. 189.

3 Abbé MacPherson, 'Account of the Mission in Scotland 1792-1793', Ms. Scottish Catholic Archives.

4 James Kyle's Report to Propaganda, quoted in James Robertson, 'The Life and Times of James Kyle D.D., Vicar Apostolic in the Northern District', typescript, Scottish Catholic Archives.

5 'Encrease of Popery', document NLS MS 976 ff. 147-149; *Innes Review* 1966, p. 97.

6 *Ibid.*, Document NLS MS 68 ff. 31-32, p. 107.

7 Thomson, Vol. II, p. 127.

8 Forbes Leith, Vol. II, pp. 363-365.

7

The Scots Colleges Abroad:
Historical Background

THE continuation of the Roman Catholic faith in Scotland after 1560 depended on an adequate supply of priests, to prevent the Protestant church from winning converts in the still Catholic enclaves, to administer the sacraments of baptism, marriage and confession, and to instruct the people in the Catholic religion.

Until 1714 Scottish priests had to receive all their training abroad, at the Scots Colleges of France, Spain or Italy, or at the Scottish Benedictine monasteries of Ratisbon, or Wurzburg. Ideally it was hoped that boys would come to the Colleges when they were about seventeen years of age, leaving as ordained priests at the age of twenty-five. It was also hoped that boys coming to the Colleges would have a good knowledge of Latin, perhaps a little knowledge of Greek, and would be ready to start studying Philosophy.[1] In fact many boys were only about fourteen years old when they arrived, while some were as young as ten. Furthermore few of the younger boys can have had very much knowledge of Latin, because of the problems of educating Catholic children, partly due to the penal laws, but even more so to the inadequacy of the parish schools in the more remote areas of Scotland.

The first post-Reformation Scots College to be founded abroad was that of Douay.[2] In 1575 the combined English and Scottish college of Tournay broke up. Early in the following year Dr James Cheyne of Arnage, a Scottish secular priest, and principal and professor in the university of Douay, out of the revenues of his canonry at Tournay, founded a seminary for Scottish secular clergy. To begin with the seminary was situated at Tournay, but, sometime before 1581, it was transferred to Pont-a-Mousson. In 1593 it was moved again to a healthier and safer situation at Douay. In 1595 it was again transferred, this time to Louvain, and it was not until 1612 that it was finally settled at Douay, where it remained until it was closed by the French Revolution in 1793. The seminary was elevated to college status in 1632.

The College of Douay numbered among its benefactors Mary, Queen of Scots, who, in 1582, settled on it an annual pension of 1200 francs, subsequently augmenting the sum to four hundred gold crowns. This pension ceased with the death of Mary in 1587.

Although he had founded the seminary specifically to train boys for the secular priesthood, Dr Cheyne, in 1580, found it necessary to entrust its government to a Scottish Jesuit, Father Edmund Hay of Megginch. From that time, apart from short intervals when the Walloon Jesuits had charge of it, the Scots College of

Douay was in the hands of the Scots Jesuits until the Jesuits were expelled from France in 1765. When this happened the Scottish property at Douay was confiscated to the Crown as being Jesuit property. Mr Gordon, principal of the Scots College, Paris, on the instruction of the Scottish bishops, entered into negotiations with the French government, which admitted the claim of the Scottish Mission to the Douay property. Aided by the precedent of the English College at St Omers,[3] Principal Gordon secured Douay College for the Mission on these terms: the management of the Scottish property at Douay was given to a Bureau of French civilians, which permitted a given number of Scots students to be maintained and educated in the College under the supervision of a Scots Rector named by themselves on the recommendation of the Scottish bishops. The first secular priest to become Rector of the College was Mr Robert Grant, brother of the Scots Agent at Rome. When he arrived at Douay, he discovered that the Jesuits had taken with them all the best furniture and chapel ornaments, bequeathing only their debts to their successor.

In the years before 1765 Douay had produced many Jesuit priests, not all of whom returned to service in Scotland. Between 1765 and 1793 it supplied the Scottish Mission with five Highland priests and six Lowland priests, while of the boys who were students there in 1793 a further six were ordained, two of them — Andrew Scott and Andrew Carruthers — going on to become bishops. In 1793 the French Revolution closed the College of Douay, and its students were dispersed to complete their studies, some to Scotland and others to Valladolid.[4]

After the Reformation of 1560 Bishop Chisholm of Dunblane and Bishop John Leslie of Ross went to Rome seeking to establish a Scots College there. According to Abbé MacPherson:

> They represented to Clement VIII —— the woeful state of religion in Scotland, and the evident danger of its utter ruin unless speedy and efficatious means were adopted to prevent it: and that the most effectual would be to erect a seminary in Rome for the education of Scots youth, who would perpetuate a succession of Catholic clergy and labour in support of the Catholic faith. They added that the establishment of that nature already made fell very short of being proportionable to the crying necessity.[5]

On 9th December, 1600 the Scots College, Rome received its Bull of Foundation together with a grant of revenues from a house, an abbey and a small vineyard for its maintenance. Subsequent grants augmented this income. In 1602 the College received its first eleven pupils, but it found problems in obtaining a suitable rector:

> It would appear it was, even then, equally difficult to find proper subjects for the charge as it has been at a recent period. This is easily accounted for. In Rome numberless are the lucrative and honourable employments for the clergy —— The Rectorship of the poor Scots College never was either lucrative or of any distinguishing honour. It was only an object for such as had nothing [which] could recommend them to better places, while at the same time the duties annexed to the office required no mean qualifications.[6]

In 1616 the Pope consigned the administration of the College to the Italian Jesuits. Both Agent Leslie in the seventeenth century and Mr Thomson in the eighteenth complained bitterly of the mismanagement of the College by its Jesuit superiors. There may have been a certain amount of justification for these complaints. Some of the boys who were sent to the College to train for the secular priesthood joined the Society of Jesus, and many of these Jesuits were lost to the Scottish Mission. On the other hand, between 1712 and 1765 twenty-two out of twenty-nine Highland priests were educated at the Scots College, Rome.[7] In 1764 the Scottish bishops sent a report to Propaganda in which they mentioned that, of the secular priests then serving in the Lowlands, seven out of the twelve had been educated at Rome, as had all the Highland secular priests. The coadjutor bishop of the Lowland Vicariate, and the Vicar Apostolic and his coadjutor of the Highland Vicariate had also been educated at Rome.[8] All these priests had been at the College before the Jesuits in Rome were disbanded in 1773. Abuses there may have been, but the Jesuits at Rome supplied the vast majority of the secular priests who served the Scottish Mission. This the Mission itself was to acknowledge when, in 1773, the Jesuits were disbanded.

When, in 1773, the government of the Scots College, Rome was taken out of the hands of the Jesuits, the Scottish bishops were asked if they could supply a Scottish priest to take over as rector of the College. But, Scotland being short of priests, the bishops, with a surprising lack of foresight, replied that they could not see why the College should not be as well run by Italian secular priests as it had been by Italian Jesuits.[9] This was a strong vindication of the Jesuits, and contrasts sharply with the long catalogue of criticisms to be found in Mr Thomson's 'History of the Scottish Mission'.

The decision to allow Italian secular priests to take over the running of the Scots College at Rome was soon to be regretted. Due to mismanagement, many of the students sent out to Rome at the expense of the Scottish Mission became disillusioned and gave up their vocations. After the Jesuits left, the students in the College were sent to the schools of Propaganda, where arrangements both of classes and of term dates were different, making the changeover difficult and unsatisfactory. Friction was caused, too, when the anti-Jesuit Cardinal Caraffa (Protector 1774-1780) forbade the students to frequent the churches of ex-Jesuit priests.[10] Amid such confusion it is not surprising that many of the students renounced their vocations.

Cardinal Caraffa had been in favour of appointing a Scots priest as rector, but he had assumed that the Scottish bishops would themselves see the wisdom of such a move, and so had done nothing to prompt them to that course of action. By the time the bishops had realised their mistake in allowing an Italian rector to be appointed, Cardinal Caraffa had been succeeded as Protector by the less sympathetic Cardinal Albani. In 1781 Bishop Hay was sent to Rome as a result of complaints made by the students about their Italian rector. He petitioned Albani to allow a Scots priest to take over the rectorship of the College. Cardinal Albani and the Prefect of Propaganda, Cardinal Antonelli, agreed to Hay's request, and, in 1782, Mr John Thomson was sent to Rome as assistant Agent to Mr Peter Grant, on the understanding that he would, as promised, be appointed rector of the Scots College there.

Mr Thomson was, in the words of his successor, Abbé MacPherson:

> —— an honest upright man, had talents and was addicted to study. He had however some natural foibles that made him appear rather in an unfavourable light to such as were not well

acquainted with him. His manners were unpolished, his address was awkward, and his utterance embarrassed. He likewise was thought by some hasty in his resolutions and a little too quick in his resentment. These failings rendered him rather unacceptable to his fellow missionaries, and to the generality of Catholics.[11]

Thomson's fellow priests felt so strongly about him that some of them took the very rash step of sending an anonymous letter to Cardinal Albani, criticising both the appointment and Bishop Hay for making it. This letter proved a valuable weapon for the Italian superiors of the English and Irish Colleges in Rome, who saw that, if their counterpart at the Scots College were replaced, they too might soon lose their comfortable positions. They had protested about the proposed Scots rector to Cardinal Albani, and the Cardinal used the letter as an excuse for giving in to them. Mr Thomson therefore arrived in Rome only to find that Albani had resolved not even to allow him to lodge at the College, far less to take up the post of rector there.[12] Papal intervention secured bed and board for Mr Thomson at the College. In 1784 he succeeded Abbé Grant as Scots Agent at Rome, but he never succeeded in obtaining the rectorship. Indeed, even his lodging at the College was resented by the Italian rector, Marchioni. Abbé MacPherson describes the effect on the College of the ill-feeling between Thomson and Marchioni:

> Their brawls were extremely prejudicial to the discipline of the house by dividing the students into parties. Encouraged by Marchioni many of them behaved with much impropriety to Mr Thomson; the college, in fine, was now in as bad a condition as it had been in the worst of times.[13]

By 1788 the state of the College was so bad that Bishop Hay wrote to Bishop Geddes:

> Who knows but Scalan may yet turn to be of good service, in place of the Scots shop [college] in Rome.[14]

That Bishop Hay could even begin to compare the small, impoverished seminary of Scalan, lost in the wilds of Glenlivet, with the splendid College situated in the capital of the Catholic world shows just how bad he considered the situation in the College to be. Indeed it was so bad that in July 1789 Bishop Hay wrote to Mr Thomson that, until some security was given that the College would be reformed, he would send no more boys there.[15]

Not only was Mr Thomson at odds with his fellow priests, with Mr Marchioni, and with some of the College students, but also he succeeded in making a powerful enemy of Cardinal Albani, whom he had affronted by some incautious remarks, so that for several years before his death he was unable to obtain admittance to the Cardinal's presence.[16] It was a grave situation indeed when the Cardinal Protector refused to see the Scottish Agent.

In 1792 Mr Thomson died at Naples, where he had gone in the hope of recovering his health. His death was perhaps a blessing for the Scottish Mission in general, and for the Scots College at Rome in particular, both of which had suffered from his inability to get on with people. It is for his historical research rather than for his diplomacy that Mr Thomson has earned a place of honour in the annals of the Scottish Mission. His history of that Mission, and its continuation by his successor, Abbé MacPherson, have yet to be superseded.

Mr Thomson's successor, Abbé Paul MacPherson, who came to Rome in 1793, was an able diplomat. He soon established cordial relations with Cardinal Albani:

> If I can keep on such good terms with [Albani] as I am just now it will be in my power to be of
> very material service to our young Gentlemen [the students]. The Rector will willingly leave the
> inspection of the discipline of the house to me. It is only the name and emoluments he grasps at,
> he does not appear desirous of the charge.[17]

With Abbé MacPherson in charge of the discipline of the students, Bishop Hay no longer saw any reason to refuse to send boys to the College.[18] Neither he nor Abbé MacPherson, however, lost sight of their goal, the obtaining of Scottish instead of Italian priests as rectors. Abbé MacPherson did all that he could to further this end, but he had still not met with success when, in 1798, the College was closed by the Napoleonic Wars.

The Royal Scots College in Spain was founded at Madrid, in 1672, by William Semple of Lochwinnoch, who bequeathed it to Scotland as a seminary for the education of secular priests under Jesuit superiors. In 1767 the Jesuits were suppressed in Spain, and the College, assumed to be Jesuit property, was confiscated to the Spanish crown.[19]

During the first one hundred and forty years of its existence the College seems to have been of little use to the Scottish Mission. Between 1704 and 1771 not a single Highland priest received his education there.[20] In 1703 Mr James Gordon reported to Propaganda that the College, since its foundation, and although it had been endowed with more than 3,000 crowns per annum, had supplied only two secular priests for the Scottish Mission, and that it had been shut since about 1680.[21] In 1715 the Scots Jesuits managed to recover the College property from the hands of the Spanish Jesuits, and three students were sent at once from Douay to Madrid to reopen the College as a viable educational establishment. But more problems followed. According to Mr Thomson:

> The Scots Jesuits instead of peopling the College with Scots youths and educating them for the
> service of the Mission opened with great Eclat a magnificent seminary for the education of the
> sons of the nobility in Spain by whom they were greatly favoured, and there were no Scots
> students in the house but two or three novices of their own.[22]

Although Mr Thomson was violently anti-Jesuit, it would seem that his criticism of the Madrid College was justified. None of the priests who served in the Scottish Mission between 1730 and 1770 had received any part of his education in Spain.

The situation was to change dramatically in 1771 when Mr John Geddes was sent by the Scottish Mission to Spain. He succeeded in reclaiming the College for the Mission, and in having it transferred to the former Jesuit college of San Ambrosia in Valladolid. The College reopened with Mr Geddes as rector in charge of two professors and fifteen students. Under its charter of Royal Patronage the College was recognised as a continuation of the original Semple foundation. It was to be managed by the Scottish secular clergy, the Scottish bishops having the right to nominate the rector and the Spanish king officially appointing him. Valladolid was different from the other Scots Colleges in that it was the only one to teach the students on the College premises instead of sending them to the public University schools.

Mr Geddes's popularity with the court of Madrid earned him a pension of £120 per annum, when, in 1780, he returned to Scotland as coadjutor to Bishop Hay. His episcopal consecration was carried out in Spain by the archbishop of Toledo, primate of all Spain,[23] a singular honour and a mark of the esteem in which Mr Geddes was held in Spain.

Bishop Geddes was succeeded as rector by Mr Alexander Cameron, who bought vineyards for the College, added another wing to it, and built a country house at Boecillo where students and masters could spend the summer vacation.[24] On the death of Bishop Geddes in 1798 Mr Cameron succeeded him as coadjutor to Bishop Hay, and Mr John Gordon took over the rectorship of the College. Between 1771 and 1809 almost half of the priests who came to the Scottish Mission had attended the Scots College at Valladolid. Between 1798 and 1809 Valladolid was the only Scots College on the Continent that was still open. The Peninsular War finally closed it in 1809.

The only pre-Reformation Scots College was that of Paris.[25] In 1325 David, Bishop of Moray, endowed four bursaries in the University of Paris, for four boys from the diocese of Moray, to educate them for the principal ecclesiastical offices of the diocese. Bishop David provided for the maintenance of the students by the gift of a farm at Grisey, in Normandy, about thirty miles from Paris. In 1571, after the Scottish Universities became Protestant, Mary Queen of Scots added several bursaries to the Paris College. In 1603, under the terms of Archbishop Beaton's will, the College acquired the Archbishop's residual property, together with a house in the Rue des Amendiers for the accommodation of the students. Archbishop Beaton's request was made on condition that

> . . . besides Ecclesiastics some of the Children of the Catholic nobility and gentry should receive their education there without any obligation of taking to the Church, being deprived of the means of receiving a suitable education in their own Country by the change of Religion which had then taken place . . .[26]

In 1688 Louis XIV granted a new confirmation of all the previous gifts to the College by means of Letters Patent which defined the object of the College to be the education both of boys intended for the priesthood in Scotland, and of Scots boys who did not intend to take Holy Orders. The College was to be united to the University of Paris and was to enjoy all the rights and privileges accorded to other Colleges of the University. The sole superior was to be the prior of the Carthusians. Under him the superintendence of the students, all of whom were to be Scots by birth, was to devolve on two Scottish secular priests, viz. a principal and a procurator.[27]

The Scots College at Paris differed from the three other Scots Colleges abroad in several ways. Firstly, it was the only College never to have been in the hands of Jesuits, and to have been always staffed by Scottish secular priests. Secondly, although all the colleges accepted lay boarders from time to time, the Paris College was the only one obliged to do so under its constitution. Thirdly, because of its situation and its obligations to educate lay students, the Paris College alone became involved in Jacobite politics. Fourthly, and most important in the long term, the 1688 constitution of the Paris College was laid down before there were any Vicars Apostolic in Scotland. Overall control was therefore assigned to the prior of the Carthusians in Paris. This constitution was not altered after Scotland was granted a Vicar Apostolic, and so the Scottish bishops were in the invidious position of having no authority over the College other than that which the principal, out of courtesy, was pleased to permit.

In the mid-eighteenth century the reputation of the Paris College received a severe setback when it was accused of Jansenism.[28] The Thomson-MacPherson 'History of the Scottish Mission' suggests that the rumours were largely the work of two bodies of people, the Jesuits and the 'Pilgrims'. The Jesuits, it is suggested, tried to blacken the name of the College in the hope that it might then be handed over to them. The 'Pilgrims' had a more obscure motive.

The 'Pilgrims' were two Highland priests, Mr Colin Campbell and Mr James Tyrie, who came to Rome in 1735 where they laid charges

... against Lowland clergy, Paris, Scalan and Bishop Gordon himself as Jansenising if not actually Jansenist.[29]

Inter-clan hostility had prevented Campbell from realising his ambition to become Vicar Apostolic of the Highland District, and thwarted ambition may have prompted his wild accusations, accusations which did the Scottish Mission much harm:

... misled by the artifices of the Pilgrims, though otherwise a good, pious man [Cardinal Riviera] had conceived unreasonable prejudices against the College at Paris and the most respectable characters on the Mission.[30]

So upset was Cardinal Riviera by the alleged corruption of the Scots College at Paris that he ordered two students who were being sent to Scotland in 1750 to avoid Paris, even though this meant a longer, more expensive journey.

One of the most famous priests to emerge from the Paris College was Mr Thomas Innes, author of the *Critical Essay on the Ancient Inhabitants of Scotland,* a pioneering work in the field of Dark Age studies. Mr Innes, of the Drumgask family, a family which produced many priests, attended the College from 1681 to 1691, when he was ordained priest. From 1698 to 1701 he was stationed in Strathdon. From 1701 till 1727 he was prefect of studies in the Paris College, being succeeded in that office by his nephew, Mr George Innes. After a second period of two years in Britain, Thomas Innes returned to Paris for good. Under him and his brother Lewis Innes before him, the Paris College and its archives experienced what has been described as their 'golden age'.[31]

While the Paris College was in the hands of men of this calibre, there were no problems in the relationship of the College to the Scottish Mission. Indeed the precise nature of this relationship was not questioned until 1780.[32] In that year a problem arose as to whether College or Mission was responsible for the maintenance of a priest who had become insane. Were priests who had studied at the Paris College full members of the Scottish Mission with the mutual rights and obligations implied by such a membership, or were they, in some sense at least, independent of the Mission? Under the tactful management of Bishop Geddes, the Scottish bishops and the principal of the College — Principal Gordon — agreed that students of the College were bound to serve in the Scottish Mission when desired to do so by the principal. In return, the funds of the Mission, together with a subsidiary fund, called 'Hacket's money', should provide two-thirds of Mr Gordon's board, the remaining third being provided in equal shares by the Principal, and by Bishop Hay and his coadjutor out of their private income.[33]

Even after this problem had been settled, Bishop Hay still had cause for complaint. In 1781 he complained that the College was not supplying the priests that it should for the Mission. Propaganda granted the College a subsidy in the hope that that would improve matters. By 1784 it was becoming clear that, whatever agreement had been made in 1780, Principal Gordon regarded the College as his personal sinecure. In spite of the fact that the College was a traditional staging-post for masters and students travelling between Rome and Scotland, Principal Gordon, in 1784, refused to allow Abbé Grant any access at all to the College when the latter was on his way to Rome.[34]

The Paris College was the least valuable of all the Colleges in the eighteenth century as a source of priests. Of fifty-six Highland priests who were ordained between 1704 and 1790, only six had been educated at Paris. The College was, however, valuable in the education of Scottish Catholic laymen and so in helping to perpetuate the Catholic religion in Scotland. It also played an important role in preserving archives relating to the pre-Reformation Church in Scotland, and to the affairs of the exiled Stuarts, although many of these records were lost at the time of the French Revolution.

Although the Scots College at Paris was the oldest of the four Colleges on the Continent, it was the first one to be closed in the aftermath of the French Revolution. The last priest it had sent home was Mr James Cattanach, who was ordained in 1788. No further priests received any part of their education in Paris from that date until Principal Gordon abandoned it in 1792. Its closure was no great loss to the Scottish Mission.

The four Scots Colleges of Douay, Rome, Valladolid and Paris provided most of the education for the majority of the Scottish priests who were educated before the French Revolution. A few priests received all their education in Scotland, but they were the exceptions. There was, however, another source of education for future priests for Scotland. In 1703 Mr James Gordon listed, among the priests serving in Scotland, four Benedictine monks, two of whom were supported out of Mission funds.[35] These four monks had been educated at the Scots Benedictine monasteries of Ratisbon and Wurzburg.

The monastery at Ratisbon was founded in 1075 by an Irish monk from Donegal named Muiredach Mac Robartaig, usually known as Marianus Scotus. It is not clear which Rule this monastery followed, whether that of St Benedict or that of the Irish Church — the Rule of Columbanus — or perhaps a mixture of the two. The monastery flourished, and, in about 1110, a larger monastery, St James's, was built in Ratisbon. This new foundation was a Benedictine abbey. During the twelfth century it established seven daughter houses in Germany alone. The original foundation of Weih-Sankt-Peter survived as a priory dependent on the new abbey of St James.

Wurzburg had a continuous Irish tradition from as early as 689 when St Kilian was martyred there. Also associated with the city were Marianus Scotus the chronicler (not the Marianus Scotus of Ratisbon), and the ninth-century scholar, Clemens Scotus. In 1085 an Irish bishop, who seems to have been the head of a small community of monks, died there. Wurzburg was therefore an obvious place for the site of a daughter house of Ratisbon. There are two different accounts of the founding of Wurzburg. Both accounts agree that there were Irish monks there in 1142, but they disagree as to whether Wurzburg was founded from Ratisbon. By 1185, however, Wurzburg was definitely established as a daughter house of Ratisbon.

In 1497 the abbot of Wurzburg died, leaving no monk behind him, and German monks were introduced. In 1597 the monastery was handed over to the Scots Benedictines.

By the end of the fifteenth century there were very few Irish monks left in Germany. Ratisbon was one of the few foundations which still continued as an Irish community. The monks still called themselves 'Scoti' after the Irish monks who had been their predecessors. By now, however, the Irish 'Scoti' who had emigrated to Dalriada in the sixth century had given their name to what was by now called 'Scotland', and 'Scot' had come to mean an inhabitant of Scotland. In 1514 the abbot of Ratisbon was involved in a dispute with his bishop, and the matter was referred to the pope. In 1515 the pope issued a bull deposing the Irish abbot on the grounds that he was not a Scot, believing 'Scoti' to refer to Scottish and not Irish nationality. A Scottish secular priest was appointed in place of the Irish abbot. The same bull paved the way for the acquisition of Wurzburg by the Scottish Benedictines eighty-two years later.[36]

In 1680 Abbot Fleming of Ratisbon conceived the idea of founding a seminary for the education of priests for Scotland. The seminary was opened about five years later, but the boys were housed in the monastery, there being insufficient funds to build a separate foundation for these students.[37]

In 1711 there were several students at the Ratisbon seminary, some of them well advanced in their studies, and Abbot Fleming sent one of his monks to Scotland to recruit more boys. This the monk accomplished easily by promising parents that their sons would be educated free of charge. The Abbot proposed to ordain some of his students and send them to Scotland as secular priests, but the Scottish bishops were afraid that the best students at Ratisbon would be claimed for the Benedictine order, leaving only less able men to become secular priests. They therefore refused to accept any but monks for the Scottish Mission.[38]

In 1714 John Anthony, Bishop of Aichstätt, endowed the monks of Ratisbon with money to build a seminary at Aichstätt. The seminary, which was to be run by the monks, was to be for the education of twelve Scots boys who intended to become priests. It was to be financed by an income of 1000 florins per annum during the Bishop's life, and a bequest of 20,000 florins when he died. The boys were to be educated at Ratisbon until the seminary at Aichstätt was built. The monks, not thinking Aichstätt to be very convenient, put off building the seminary until the Bishop died, when they built it at Ratisbon.[39]

In 1716 Abbot Fleming, seeing that the Scottish Mission was desperately short of priests, persuaded the Pope to recommend the Ratisbon seminary to the Elector of Bavaria.[40] The resulting endowment allowed the Abbot to build a magnificent seminary, which was completed by 1718. According to Mr Thomson, the Scottish bishops felt that the Abbot had used the poverty of the Scottish Mission as a fund-raising plea, merely to convert the seminary into 'a nursery for the monastery'.[41]

Perhaps Ratisbon sent fewer monks to the Scottish Mission than had been hoped for, but in a Mission which was always chronically short of priests, the few who did come were of great help, not only for their pastoral work, but also because they were usually maintained by the monastery and so did not add to the burden on overstretched Mission funds.

Wurzburg, too, although it only possessed a small seminary, established to train its own recruits, nevertheless also sent monks as priests to Scotland. Father William Pepper, for instance, was the first priest in the new station of Dundee opened in 1787.

At about the beginning of the eighteenth century there was some talk of the Scottish Mission's establishing a seminary on the coast of Normandy.[42] Such a seminary would have saved the Mission much in the way of travelling expenses, being far closer to Scotland than Madrid, Rome, or even Paris. However, the scheme came to nothing. Instead a seminary was opened at Loch Morar in Scotland.

All the above foundations, although situated on the Continent, were owned either by Scots monks or by the Scottish Mission. There were, however, in addition, two places set aside for the education of Scots boys in one foreign establishment, The College of Propaganda in Rome. This college had granted two of its places to the Scottish Mission, one for a Lowland boy and one for a Highland. Although these places were generally filled, they produced very few priests. One reason for this was given by Mr Thomson in 1789:

> As to Propaganda little good is to be expected from it, for it is scarcely probable that anyone will keep his health.[43]

In that year the Highland boy at Propaganda College had been sent home to die while the Lowland boy, James MacDonald, was in poor health.

In 1794 Abbé MacPherson, Mr Thomson's successor, further condemned the practice of sending boys to Propaganda College, in a letter to Bishop Hay:

> Our establishment in Propaganda deserves a serious consultation at your meeting . . . From the experience of many years it is evident that we have greatly lost by it; of all the promising young men sent there since the first of it, Mr Norman only returned. Nor am I surprised at it. Neither will anyone who is acquainted with the discipline observed there, and which is necessary because of the heterogeneous humours and inclinations of so many tribes and languages. Our youth, subjected to rules so contrary to their nature, either conceive disgust at the Ecclesiastical State and leave the College, or else by observing them ruin their healths and soon finish their days.[44]

Abbé MacPherson suggested that Propaganda should be asked, instead of supporting two Scots boys at its own college, to provide bursaries whereby the boys could be educated elsewhere, preferably in Scotland. In this sentiment Bishop Geddes heartily concurred,[45] but nothing had been accomplished when, in

February 1798, the arrival of French troops in Rome closed Propaganda and its college.

From 1560 until 1714 almost all the Scottish priests were educated at the four Scots Colleges at Paris, Douay, Rome and Madrid. After 1714, although some of their early education could be given in Scotland, almost all the priests still received more advanced branches of their education on the Continent. A few priests were sent from the Scots monasteries in Germany to help the secular and Jesuit clergy in Scotland. Between them they kept the Catholic religion alive in Scotland.

NOTES

1 Father Patrick Anderson's rules for the Scots College, Rome; contained in Abbé Paul MacPherson, 'History of the Scots College, Rome', edited by W. J. Anderson, *Innes Review* 1961, p. 19.

2 *Scotichronicon*, pp. 90-94; MacPherson, 'History of the Scots College, Rome'', p. 12.

3 MacPherson's continuation of Thomson, printed in Forbes Leith, Vol. II, p. 361.

4 *Scotichronicon*, p. 94.

5 MacPherson, 'History of the Scots College, Rome', p. 13.

6 *Ibid.*, p. 15.

7 F. Forbes and W.J. Anderson, 'Clergy Lists of the Highland District', *Innes Review* 1966, pp. 133-184.

8 *Scotichronicon*, p. 46.

9 MacPherson, 'History of the Scots College, Rome', pp. 131-132.

10 *Ibid.*, p. 135.

11 *Ibid.*, p. 139.

12 *Ibid.*, p. 140.

13 *Ibid.*, p. 142.

14 Bishop Hay to Bishop Geddes, 6th November 1788, quoted in *Scotichronicon*, p. 281.

15 Bishop Hay to Mr Thomson, 28th July 1789, see *Scotichronicon*, p. 290.

16 Mr Smelt to Bishop Geddes, 30th March 1793, B.L.

17 Abbé MacPherson to Bishop Hay, 16th November 1793, B.L.

18 Bishop Hay to Abbé MacPherson, 17th December 1793, B.L.

19 'A letter from Valladolid from Mr John Geddes, in which he gives an Account of the Scots College venducated out of the hands of the Irish 1771, to Father Robert Leith, abbot of the monastery of Ratisbon.' Oban Letters I, envelope 1, S.C.A.

20 'Clergy Lists of the Highland District', *Innes Review* 1966.

21 Thomson, 'History of the Scottish Mission', Vol. I, pp. 533-534.

22 *Ibid.*, Vol. II, p. 117.

23 John Ritchie, *Reflection on Scottish Church History*, (Edinburgh, 1927) p. 303.

24 Alexander Cameron, Valladolid to Bishop Geddes, 27th July 1790, B.L; also John Gordon, Valladolid to Abbé MacPherson, 1st August 1796, B.L.

25 *Scotichronicon*, pp. 247-248.

26 Henry Innes to Bishop Hay, 27th October 1801, B.L.

27 *Scotichronicon*, pp. 247-248.

28 Jansenism was a puritan approach to Catholic worship etc condemned as heretical.

29 'Clergy Lists of the Highland District', *Innes Review* 1966, p. 134.

30 Abbé MacPherson's continuation of Thomson, Vol. II, p. 236.

31 David MacRoberts, 'The Scottish Catholic Archives', *Innes Review* 1977, pp. 69-71.

32 *Scotichronicon*, p. 185.

33 *Scotichronicon*, p. 185.

34 *Ibid.*, pp. 213, 240.
35 Thomson, Vol. I, pp. 547, 549.
36 Mark Dilworth, *The Scots in Franconia* (Edinburgh, 1974) pp. 11-21 gives a detailed history of Ratisbon and Wurzburg, from which this short account is taken.
37 Thomson, Vol. II, p. 42.
38 *Ibid.*, p. 25.
39 *Ibid.*, p. 43.
40 *Ibid.*, p. 51.
41 *Ibid.*, p. 56.
42 *Ibid.*, Vol. I, p. 532.
43 John Thomson to Bishop Hay, 4th July 1789, B.L.
44 Abbé MacPherson to Bishop Hay, 11th June 1794, B.L.
45 Bishop Geddes to Bishop Hay, 22nd October 1794, B.L.

E

8

The Seminary at Scalan, 1716-1799

ALTHOUGH the Scottish Mission, like those of England and Ireland, had colleges on the Continent to train its young men for the priesthood, these colleges were not entirely satisfactory for a number of reasons. There was, for instance, an understandable tendency for students at the three Jesuit-run colleges to be attracted into the Society of Jesus.

The original Bull of Foundation of the Scots College at Rome laid no obligation on students to become clerics, much less to return as missionaries to Scotland. In 1606 the situation was slightly improved when Monseigneur Paulini insisted that the purpose of the college must be to educate youths for the priesthood, and that the priests ordained there should be encouraged to return to work in Scotland. He also succeeded in obtaining, from the Pope's exchequer, the sum of seventy-two crowns to defray the journey of each priest to Scotland.[1]

Father Patrick Anderson, the first Jesuit superior of the College, ruled that each student, six months after entrance, might be required by the rector to take an oath that he would, if so required, take Holy Orders and return to Scotland.[2] The oath was modified by Pope Urban VIII, because it was pointed out to him that students could easily get dispensation from the part of the oath compelling them to return home once they were priests. A new clause bound the students of all Pontifical colleges to work as priests for three years in their native countries before they could join any religious order[3] — the problem of new priests refusing to work in their homelands having been common to all the colleges, and not just the Scots College.

This oath was a step in the right direction, but it still meant that, when times were difficult or dangerous for priests in Scotland, they were at liberty, after three years, to abandon their congregations and find safety and security in a religious house on the Continent, either as a Jesuit, or in one of the Scots Benedictine Monasteries.

This problem, best documented for the Scots College, Rome, must have been equally true of Douay. (Madrid College, before 1771, can virtually be discounted as it sent only two or three secular priests to Scotland in its first hundred and forty years of existence).

Another problem that arose when boys were sent to the Scots Colleges abroad was their high failure rate, which meant that the impoverished Scottish Mission was losing money on boys who would never serve it as priests, and also that fewer potential priests were filling the few available places at the colleges. Mr James

Gordon discussed the problem of boys' travelling expenses or 'viatics' in his 1703 report to Propaganda, where he pointed out that

> ... the Clergy and the Youths' Parents are in general so poor that they can scarce furnish them with genteel Cloaths much less give them what is necessary for so long a journey and that unless the Colleges allow them viatics the benefits of them to the mission will be in a great measure lost, as either the number of Alumni will not be complete which was often the case then, or such vagabonds will be admitted as are unfit for being Missioners on whom money, time and pains will be spent in vain who will either be sent away re infecta or if they are promoted will be a burden and a disgrace to the Mission.[4]

Mr Gordon proposed that the colleges should pay the viatics of students coming to them, financing this by accepting one or two fewer students and thus freeing money formerly used on maintaining these students.

Apart from the financial difficulty of sending boys abroad, there were, in the eighteenth century, political problems. In 1708, for instance, boys could not be sent directly to France, but had to be sent by the dangerous and expensive route through Norway and Denmark.[5] The reason for this was that the War of the Spanish Succession had involved Scotland and England in the war against France. In 1710 Bishop Gordon found the situation in Scotland itself was making it difficult to send off some boys to Rome:

> ... on account of the terror parents were in of the circuit courts where among other crimes they were challenged and impeached for sending their children to be educated abroad ... [also] the captains of vessels were so terrified by the threats and clamours of the ministers, that they absolutely refused to give a passage to any youths they suspected were going to foreign colleges.[6]

Educationally, too, there were problems in sending Scots boys to the colleges abroad. Not only did poor educational facilities for Catholics in Scotland mean that boys were often sent abroad when too young and insufficiently advanced in their studies, but also the instruction which they received at the colleges was often ill-suited to their subsequent missionary duties in Scotland. About the end of the seventeenth century Agent Leslie made some recommendations which illustrate this problem. In Mr Thomson's words:

> He [Leslie] earnestly recommends the students, as hitherto, not to be obliged to throw away so much of their time either in philosophy or divinity, or useless speculative questions under the delusive pretence that, being masters of these, they can by themselves and without the help of any one learn every other thing necessary in these sciences. It is to be observed that the Scots students, the moment they arrive on the mission must directly enter on the exercise of every pastoral duty, and that too in a country overspread with heresy and infidelity; that their necessary occupations as missionaries scarcely will leave them one day in the course of a whole year to be employed in study, and though they had time seldom are they provided with books necessary for those who have to begin the study of moral or dogmatic theory. The most our missionaries can do is not to forget what they learned in the schools; hence the necessity of applying there to useful and practical doctrine that on entering the mission they may be capable to catechise, preach, administer the sacraments, know the rites of the church and their signification, answer the objections of heretics, solve the doubts of Catholics and direct souls in the road of Christian perfection ... This knowledge must not be merely theoretical; a great part of it must be practical ... The Greek and Hebrew tongues should not be neglected, being very serviceable to answer the objections of our heretics, who greatly cultivate these languages.[7]

Briefly, Agent Leslie wanted the colleges to train priests to be able to cope with the particular circumstances which they would meet with in Scotland, rather than to follow the same methods that were used in the training of priests destined for officially Catholic countries.

In 1703 Mr James Gordon followed Leslie in criticising Rome for giving Scots students seven years' instruction in

> ... Philosophical Theological Speculations and Subtlties which were of no manner of use in the Mission as scarce once in twenty or thirty years did an occasion occur to use them ... it was highly absurd to spend so much time in laborious trifles and neglect those studies that were necessary and useful for instructing Catholics and confuting heretics. ... Mr David Burnet ... on his arrival in the mission from Rome, finding he knew so little of what was necessary for a Missioner was so discouraged that he was tempted to leave the mission ...[8]

It was Mr James Gordon in 1703 who first suggested that a way of overcoming all the problems surrounding the training abroad of priests would be to open a seminary in Scotland. He envisaged the seminary as an extension of, or development from, the Catholic schools already in being in the Highlands of Scotland. He believed that, if boys could receive all their training, and be ordained, in Scotland, this would be the most effectual means of promoting Catholicism there:

> ... as those who had studied and had been ordained at home would be exempt from many dangers to which young men going abroad or Missioners returning home were exposed, and they would never think of abandoning the country in time of persecution. Moreover they would be less obnoxious to the Protestants as seminary priests from foreign countries were principally aimed at by the penal laws.[9]

In support of his idea Mr Gordon mentioned that Bishop Nicolson was about to ordain one Peter Frazer, born in the Highlands, who, after some years in Paris, had completed his studies under one of the Missioners in Scotland.[10]

It was not, however, until nine years later, that the subject of a Scottish seminary was again seriously raised. In 1706 Mr Gordon had been consecrated as Bishop Nicolson's coadjutor, and in 1712 he wrote a letter to Mr Lewis Innes at the Scots College, Paris, in which he referred to his plans for a seminary.[11] In the following year he wrote to Propaganda, pointing out how beneficial such a seminary would be for the Scottish Mission, and begging for financial assistance towards establishing it.[12] In 1714 he wrote to Mr Thomas Innes that the seminary had opened.[13] To begin with there were seven boys at the seminary, but more arrived later. Their superior was Mr George Innes, nephew of Lewis and Thomas Innes. This, the first seminary for the training of boys for the priesthood to be opened in Britain since the Reformation, was situated on Eilean Ban in Loch Morar, in the 'Garbh Chriochan' or 'Rough Bounds'. It is possible that Bishop Gordon had chosen this site when he spent a night there, on 23rd June 1707, on his first visit to the Highlands.[14] The site was certainly chosen with an eye to security, for it was remote, inaccessible, and in the heart of Catholic Clanranald country.

In 1715 two boys, Allan MacDonald and John MacLachlan, were sent to Rome; they were both already well advanced in their studies when they arrived at the College, so it is likely that they had previously studied at the Loch Morar seminary.[15] Another pupil who began his ecclesiastical education at Loch Morar was Hugh MacDonald, who was to become the first Vicar Apostolic of the Highland District. The year after his consecration, Bishop Hugh MacDonald was to re-establish, on Eilean Ban, the first Highland seminary to be opened to train Gaelic-speaking priests for his Vicariate.

Bishop Geddes, in his 'Historical Account of Scalan', records that, after the failure of the Jacobite rebellion of 1715, the 'ensuing Calamaties' forced the Loch Morar seminary to close.[16] Since not only the MacDonalds, but also MacIntoshes, Camerons and many others had taken part in the rebellion, the West Highlands, in 1716, were thoroughly searched by government soldiers, and Loch Morar no longer seemed safe. The seminary was therefore transferred to Scalan in Glenlivet, probably without any significant break.

On 1st June 1716 Bishop Gordon wrote to Mr Thomas Innes in Paris:

> ... nev. Geo. [George Innes] is pretty well, but has not been able to do much for the stirr of folks about him, yet the shope [seminary] is kept in some manner, at least some of the prentices [students] together; ...[17]

Mr George Innes is known to have been in hiding in Glenlivet in 1716, and Bishop Gordon's letter suggests that he had brought at least some of the students with him from Loch Morar, and was continuing to teach them under what must have been difficult circumstances.

The site for the new seminary, at Scalan, had originally been chosen as a safe retreat by the priest in Glenlivet, Mr John Gordon of the family of Cairnborrow. Mr Gordon had been living further down the glen, somewhere about Minmore or Castletown, but, in 1716, when General Cadogan and other Hanoverian officers came north with their soldiers, he thought it would be safer to move to a more remote area. Accordingly he came up the glen to Scalan, where he lived in a barn until he had built a house, made almost entirely of turf, beside the Crombie.[18] It was here that the refugees from Loch Morar found shelter. The seminary was to remain at Scalan for over eighty years.

Scalan was an ideal place for a Catholic seminary at a time when Catholicism was forbidden by law. It was in a remote, wild spot, almost entirely surrounded by hills, in a staunchly Catholic district, and on the estate of the powerful Catholic Duke of Gordon. It was also in Bishop Gordon's own shire. The Bishop had been born in 1665 at Glastirum in the Enzie. He was related through his father to the Gordons of Letterfourie, and he was a cousin of the Marquis of Huntly. He therefore had many connections in Banffshire and western Aberdeenshire. It is not surprising that it was the North-East in general and Banffshire in particular that was, for about the next hundred years, to provide the Lowland Vicariate with most of its priests.[19]

In the first forty years of its existence Scalan, despite its remote situation, was not without its problems. The ministers of the Church of Scotland made many attempts to close the seminary which were often foiled because magistrates were inclined to disregard the penal laws and turn a blind eye to Catholic activity, at least so long as there was no threat of a Jacobite rising. The ministers of the presbytery of Kincardine O'Neil voiced a typical complaint in 1718 when they reported to the General Assembly that

> ... we find our shirriffs and Baillies take very good care of hares, wild fowl and black fish and strayed cattle, but priests and their adherents, masses, murders and adulteries etc are never

lookt after. If a man in this Country keeps the eighth Commandment he is reputed a good man though he regard not the other nine.[20]

Mr John Thomson gives the Catholic viewpoint on the same question under the year 1724:

But they [Catholics] still had a domestic persecution to suffer from the implaccable hatred of the Presbyterian ministers whose hearts would not be softened. For as they always found some magistrates and judges favourable to them and ready to join in their violent attempts they perpetually urged them to put in execution the penal laws against the Catholics and Missioners and in a particular manner instigated them against the Seminary and the Schools; nay this very year they obtained an order from Court to all Sheriffs to make strict search for priests and to cast them into prison . . . But the missioners were not much alarmed by this order which was given merely to please the ministers but not designed to be put into execution.[21]

Several times the Duke of Gordon and some 'unprejudiced Protestant gentlemen' managed to avert attempts to close Scalan, but in 1726 the ministers succeeded in having the seminary closed for several months while parties of soldiers were stationed in Glenlivet and Strathaven. By the following year, however, the seminary had reopened, thanks to the intervention of the Duke of Gordon.[22] In 1728 the seminary was twice dispersed in the space of two months by parties of soldiers, but little damage was done and it soon reopened.[23]

The Church of Scotland was zealous in waging war against Catholic schools and seminaries. In 1760, however, the General Assembly heard a report which made it wonder if it had perhaps exaggerated the importance of Scalan. The Assembly had sent out two ministers to enquire into the state of religion in Scotland. In due course the ministers arrived at Scalan where Mr Grey, the principal, invited them inside. The ministers, however, refused to dismount from their horses. Having spoken for a few minutes with Mr Grey:

. . . they rode off expressing surprise that so great a noise should have been made about a place that made so poor an appearance to them and seemed of so little consequence.[24]

In 1729 the seminary lost its most powerful protector with the death of the second Duke of Gordon. The third Duke was brought up an Episcopalian by his mother. However, on attaining his majority, he continued to maintain a friendly relationship with the priests on his estates, visiting Scalan when on hunting trips in that area, and frequently inviting the priest at Auchinhalrig to dinner at Gordon Castle. In spite of the Duke's continuing friendship, however, it may be that the decision to remove the seminary in 1799 to the estate of the Catholic Leslie of Balquhain was influenced by the fact that the Duke of Gordon was not a Catholic, and that his sons might be less tolerant than their father. Perhaps there still lingered the memory of the time when, in 1739, while still a very young man, the Duke had been persuaded to threaten to destroy the seminary, and only the united efforts of Bishop Gordon and his friends had succeeded in pacifying him and averting that disaster.[25]

1745 saw the start of the Jacobite Rebellion under Prince Charles Edward Stuart which was to end so tragically the following year on Drumossie Moor. In 1745 Bishop Gordon paid his last visit to the little seminary he had founded. He did not live to witness the burning of Scalan by a party of Cumberland's soldiers on 10th May 1746. Scalan was reduced to a smouldering ruin, but Mr Duthie, the superior, had had sufficient warning of the soldiers' approach to enable him to disperse the students, and to carry away to safety most of the moveables of the seminary including its vestments, chalice and books. Having sent his students home, Mr Duthie returned to Scalan, where he tried to save what he could of the harvest on the seminary's small farm. By 1747 he had had a lean-to erected, and, later, another building, but in 1748 the establishment of a garrison at Corgarf in Strathdon forced him to leave Glenlivet.[26] In 1749 the Bishops reported to Propaganda that both Scalan and its Highland counterpart at Guidal had been destroyed after Culloden, and that it had not yet been possible to rebuild them.[27] By the summer of 1749, however, Mr Duthie and a few students had returned to Scalan, and in 1750 Bishop Smith had a new, if makeshift and primitive, house built to accommodate them. In 1753 there were still soldiers stationed at nearby Denichmore, but they were, by now, if suitably rewarded, prepared to warn the seminary of any impending raids in time for priest and students, with their valuables, to make their escape into the surrounding hills.[28]

Apart from the fear of being forced to close, one of the main problems which Scalan had to face was the problem of lack of finance. Rome was frequently petitioned to send aid to Scalan, and, when it existed, to its fellow seminary in the Highlands. Some assistance was granted in 1735, and again in 1737. In 1735 Cardinal Falconeri, a particular friend of James VIII and of the Scottish Mission, died, leaving 4,000 crowns to be divided between the two seminaries.[29] In 1737, thanks to James VIII's intervention, Pope Clement XII granted the seminaries a further 2,000 Roman crowns.[30] This money was received by the Mission in 1738, and, in the same year, Mr Alexander Gordon, the superior of Scalan, replaced the turf house with a more substantial building of stone and lime.[31]

1745 was a disastrous year financially for the Scottish Mission in general. The French government brought out new regulations in an attempt to remedy the scarcity of money in France. This meant that the Mission's income from money invested in French funds was reduced. At the same time German wars were preventing Ratisbon and Wurzburg from sending the usual allowance to their monks who were serving in Scotland. Mission funds, reduced on the one hand by French policy, were, on the other hand, required to support extra priests. All this meant that there was even less money than usual to support students at Scalan.

In 1755 the Scottish bishops wrote to Cardinal Spinelli begging for financial assistance for their seminaries which were so important for the maintenance of a supply of priests for Scotland, and which had suffered so severely from the failure of Prince Charles's ill-fated expedition:

> Spinelli answered their letters with his usual kindness, told them that they must by no means drop the thoughts of their seminaries; that he would assist them as much as was in his power and desired they would inform him what would be the yearly expenses required to maintain a student in their seminaries. The good Bishops were modest in estimates they sent him, making the whole expenses amount to six pounds sterling only.[32]

In 1758 James VIII granted to Cardinal Spinelli 10,000 crowns, to use as he saw fit to help the Scottish Mission. Most of this gift was apportioned to the Scots College at Rome, but Spinelli added enough from it to Pope Clement XII's fund in the Luoghi di Monte (government bonds) to give the two Scottish seminaries together a total income augmented to 100 crowns per annum.[33]

In spite of this additional income, it was not until 1762 that Scalan began to show any real signs of recovery. In that year Mr John Geddes was sent as superior to the seminary, and he immediately set about rebuilding, gradually transferring the students from their makeshift accommodation to the new stone house. In 1767 the new house was completed and the lease of the farm renewed for a further seventeen years.[34] After eleven years of danger and discomfort, students and masters could begin to feel secure again. In 1769 Scalan was the place chosen for the consecration of Mr George Hay as coadjutor to Bishop Grant.[35] In 1780 Mr John Geddes became Bishop Hay's coadjutor.

Both Bishop Geddes and Bishop Hay were to return to Scalan in later years. Before he was consecrated, Bishop Geddes had spent nine years in Spain, placing the Scots College at Valladolid on the same sound footing as he had done with Scalan. He returned to Scotland in 1780 as Bishop Hay's coadjutor. In 1793, in failing health, he was persuaded by Bishop Hay to retire to Scalan in the hope that the change of air might benefit him. After a few months, however, feeling that he was too ill to be anything but a burden to the seminary, Bishop Geddes retired to Aberdeen, where he died five years later. Bishop Hay himself spent five years at Scalan between 1788 and 1793, only leaving when it became necessary for him to take the place of Bishop Geddes at Edinburgh. He always retained a great affection for Scalan, and after the seminary was moved to Aquhorties in 1799, he returned to his life among the students whose company he enjoyed so much.

During the eighty-odd years of its existence Scalan was faced with many problems, but, in spite of its difficulties, it saw over a hundred priests ordained from among its former students. Five of these priests later became bishops. Bishop Hugh MacDonald had been one of the very first boys to study at Scalan, and he was one of the few to have received all his subsequent education there, never going abroad to any of the colleges.

The memorial presented to the General Assembly in 1720 is a good summary of the role played by Scalan between 1716 and 1799:

> ... there is a famous Popish school in the forsaid Scalla in Duke Gordon's countrey under the inspection of one Father Innes, who still resides there, and keeps a correspondence with fforeign Popish colleges; to this nursery are sent children from the Isles and many other places, and such as Father Innes judges promiseing are educated and maintained here, and after [some time of] study at his school sent abroad, and when they have been a competent time at Popish Universities are returned in orders to Scotland, and by those means the nation is furnished with Priests suited to the Genious and Language of every Countrey, and with such as have friends and Blood Relations to Countenance and Shelter them.[36]

In 1760 the two ministers who visited Scalan and commented on the meanness of the place, nevertheless published an account of their visit in the *Scots Magazine* in which they credited the 'College' of Scalan with a staff of three priests — there was at that time only one master at Scalan, and he was only a Deacon. At about the same time the Presbyterian minister who lived only six miles distant was strenuously asserting that there were over thirty boys in the seminary when there were in fact only five.[37] It is hard to imagine how he could have thought that thirty boys could be housed in the temporary buildings that had been erected after Scalan was burned in 1746 — that number could not have been accommodated in Bishop Geddes's stone building. Exaggerations such as the above do indicate, however, that the Presbyterian ministers were well aware of the importance of the seminary at Scalan to the continuance of the Catholic religion in Scotland.

However important Scalan was to the Scottish Mission, it was always hampered by lack of funds. It sent many boys to the Scots Colleges abroad, but often the boys had not reached the standard hoped for by the Colleges. The whole problem of educating boys for the priesthood throughout most of the eighteenth century can be summed up by quoting the following extract which occurs under the year 1731 in Thomson's 'History of the Scottish Mission':

> Cardinal Falconieri, not knowing the circumstances and the difficulties the Bishops and Missioners had to struggle with, had been making grievous complaints that the boys sent to Rome were too young and too little advanced in their studies. Bishop Gordon wrote him to satisfy him on that head and to apologise for his conduct. He told his Excellence that necessity obliged him to send them off at that age, that among the children of Catholics few were fit for their purpose, their parents being so poor that they were not in a condition to give them any education to qualify them for the Colleges; that as the lowness of their birth and the poverty of their parents made them be despised when they returned priests, hence he made it his business to chuse children of the better sort, but that he found it difficult to find even such, as the Benedictines in Germany, and the Jesuits after usurping the College of Madrid, were always on the watch and picked up the best subjects and sent them to their seminaries at the age of ten or twelve years or even below it though little advanced in their studies; that he was obliged to do the same and either send them to the colleges abroad when there was a vacant place or to keep them four or five years in his schools or seminary which his poverty did not permit him to do.[38]

It is easy to understand, too, the difficulties under which Scalan operated, when one considers that one master had to teach as many as twelve boys who might have to be divided into three or four classes according to how advanced they were in their studies. In addition to teaching, the master had to attend to the spiritual welfare both of the boys themselves and of the Catholics who lived in the neighbourhood of Scalan. He also had to see to the management of the small farm attached to the seminary. Indeed, one of the criticisms of Scalan was that the boys were being employed too much on the farm to the detriment of their studies.[39]

Scalan was of great benefit to the Scottish Mission, but for many years it was really less than adequate. In spite of all its difficulties, however, it was not until 1793 that any suggestion arose of replacing it by a larger establishment. Indeed in the years immediately preceding 1793 various attempts were made to upgrade Scalan itself. In 1787 the buildings were improved and enlarged, and in 1788 the little seminary was even being considered as a possible replacement for the Scots College at Rome, which was being badly managed by its Italian rector.[40] In 1790 Bishop Hay wrote from Scalan to Mr Thomson at Rome:

> Since ever I came to this place I have thought it might be turned out to much better acct. than it has been and that if we could get its income sufficient for twelve or upwards we might both supply foreign shops [i.e. colleges] and bring up some here also to the highest step. I am daily more and more of this opinion and find that by good management and a small addition ... that number might be kept here always, and I am setting about it accordingly.[41]

In 1793 Bishop Geddes, who had by now replaced Bishop Hay at Scalan, wrote to the latter:

> We had a visit of the Duke [of Gordon] last week ... he expressed his being pleased with the appearance of the place, on which I observed that as so much money had been laid out on it we hoped his Grace would give us a long lease.[42]

In spite of their attempts to improve the seminary, it seems likely that the Lowland Bishops had for some time considered Scalan inadequate, because in October 1794 Bishop Geddes expressed his opinion that

> It is very desirable that we have as soon as possible a proper place for education.[43]

Certainly Scalan was hardly situated in a convenient place once the 1793 Relief Act made concealment unnecessary. Lying at the head of Glenlivet, surrounded by hills, it was extremely difficult of access — as indeed it still is. Monsignor MacWilliam, who was the priest at Chapeltown in Glenlivet in the 1940s, can remember one winter when from New Year's Day until the end of March the only way out of the glen was to walk across snow which lay deep enough to cover all the fences.

Not only was Scalan inaccessible, it was a small house incapable of accommodating many boys, and its small farm could barely produce enough to feed them, let alone produce a surplus that might be sold to supply much needed cash for books and clothes.

The passing of the Relief Act in 1793 must have provided the bishops with an incentive to look for a more convenient site for the seminary. The closing of the Scots Colleges of Douay and Paris in the same year made it imperative that the Scottish seminaries be enlarged to provide the extra places for students which had been lost in France. In 1794 the Duke of Gordon offered the Lowland Bishops the farm of Oxhill, which lies about four miles north of Fochabers. Bishop Geddes was enthusiastic and pressed Bishop Hay to buy Oxhill,[44] but Bishop Hay was more pessimistic. He pointed out that the purchase price of £2,500 was high; that a house would have to be built; that the increased number of masters and students would be an additional expense as would be the supplying of extra servants and furniture. To raise the capital, they would need to borrow at five per cent interest, while they could only hope to get a return of three per cent on their investment in the form of rents and so forth.[45] In spite of much opposition, by the end of December 1794 Bishop Hay had turned down the offer of Oxhill, pointing out:

> ... our intentions being known, other places have been proposed, perhaps no less to our purpose that it [Oxhill] was, so we must not give over our endeavours to procure the means if possible, and more time will be allowed us to do so.[46]

Almost exactly a year later Bishop Hay's hopes were realised. In October 1796 he concluded a bargain with Leslie of Balquhain for the farm of Aquhorties which lies about four miles west of Inverurie in Aberdeenshire. The farm was taken on a ninety-nine year lease at a moderate rent. The only initial capital outlay necessary would be the building of a house and the plenishing of the farm. There were few Catholic families, apart from the Leslies of Balquhain and of Fetternear, in the neighbourhood, but this was no longer a disadvantage. Communications, on the other hand, were good, and would be further improved with the building of the Aberdeen-Inverurie canal.

It was to be in the much larger building at Aquhorties that several masters would work together to take the students right through all the necessary studies for the priesthood in an environment where farm work no longer intruded on lessons.

Perhaps the best epitaph for Scalan is the one written by its former pupil, and former principal of the Scots College at Douay, Mr John Farquharson:

> Old Scalan's approaching dissolution affects me much for the sake of old long syne; next summer [when the move to Aquhorties takes place] I intend — God willing — to shed a few tears over it.[47]

NOTES

1 Paul MacPherson, 'History of the Scots College, Rome,' edited by W. J. Anderson, *Innes Review* 1961, p. 16.

2 Ibid., p. 19.

3 Ibid., p. 24.

4 Thomson, Vol. I, p. 532.

5 Thomson, quoted in Forbes Leith, Vol. II, pp. 239-240.

6 Thomson, quoted in Forbes Leith, Vol. II, p. 275.

7 MacPherson, 'History of the Scots College, Rome,' p. 61.

8 Ibid., p. 530.

9 Ibid., p. 530.

10 Thomson, Vol. I, p. 531.

11 'The Highland Seminaries: Loch Morar and Arisaig,' *St Peter's College Magazine*, December 1950, p. 133.

12 Thomson, Vol. II, p. 33.

13 'Scalan 1719-1799' — 'Glenlivatensis', *St Peter's College Magazine*, December 1946, p. 155.

14 Thomson — quoted in Forbes Leith, Vol. II, p. 232.

15 'The Highland Seminaries: Loch Morar and Arisaig,' p. 134.

16 Bishop Geddes, 'A Brief Historical Account of the Seminary of Scalan', *Innes Review* 1963, p. 94.

17 Bishop Gordon to M. Jacob Bayard, Merchant, Paris [but intended for Mr Thomas Innes], 1 June 1716, B.L.

18 Bishop Geddes, 'History of Scalan', *Innes Review* 1963, p. 95.

19 'Glenlivatensis', 'Scalan 1719-1799', *St Peter's College Magazine*, December 1946, p. 155.

20 'Encreasce of Popery', Document NLS MS 976 ff 147-9; *Innes Review* 1966, pp. 99-100.

21 Thomson, Vol. II, pp. 103-4.

22 Ibid., pp. 128, 141.

23 Ibid., p. 158.

24 Bishop Geddes, 'History of Scalan', *Innes Review* 1963, p. 101.

25 MacPherson's continuation of Thomson, Vol. II, p. 142.

26 'Scalan 1719-1799', *St Peter's College Magazine*, December 1946, p. 158.

27 MacPherson's continuation of Thomson, Vol. II, p. 223.

28 'Scalan 1719-1799', *St Peter's College Magazine*, June 1947, p. 28.

29 MacPherson's continuation of Thomson, Vol. II, p. 61.

30 Ibid., p. 106.

31 'Scalan 1719-1799', *St Peter's College Magazine*, December 1946, p. 158; Bishop Geddes, 'History of Scalan', *Innes Review* 1963, p. 98.

32 MacPherson's continuation of Thomson, Vol. II, pp. 189, 259.

33 Ibid., p. 265.

34 Bishop Geddes, 'History of Scalan', *Innes Review* 1963, p. 104.
35 Ibid., p. 105.
36 'Encreasce of Popery', Document NLS MS 68 ff 31-32, p. 107.
37 Bishop Geddes, 'History of Scalan', *Innes Review* 1963, pp. 101-102.
38 Thomson, Vol. II, p. 190.
39 *Scotichronicon*, p. 354.
40 Ibid., p. 280.
41 Bishop Hay, Scalan to John Thomson, Rome, 26th October 1790, B.L.
42 Bishop Geddes, Scalan to Bishop Hay, Edinburgh, 29th July 1793, B.L.
43 Bishop Geddes to Bishop Hay, 8th October 1794, B.L.
44 E.g. Bishop Geddes to Bishop Hay, 19th November 1794, B.L.
45 Bishop Hay to Bishop Geddes, 3rd November 1794, B.L.
46 Bishop Hay to Bishop Geddes, 27th December 1794, B.L.
47 Mr Farquharson to Abbé MacPherson, 19th October 1798, B.L.

9

The Highland Seminaries, 1732-1803

IN 1731 Mr Hugh MacDonald was consecrated Vicar Apostolic of the newly created Highland Vicariate. His most immediate and urgent task was to ensure that there would be, for the future, an adequate supply of Gaelic-speaking priests for his District. With this in mind he wrote to Propaganda in 1732:

> . . . the number of labourers amongst us who are versed in the Highland tongue is so scanty . . . Accordingly, when I considered what remedy could be applied to so deplorable an evil, the most efficacious means appeared to me to be that a seminary should be established in our Highland district, for the education of boys suitable for the ecclesiastical state. It will thus come about that there will be a supply of students, more advanced and better tested, to send to the foreign colleges, whilst others, ordained here in [this?] country, will supplement the scanty number who come from abroad after their ordination. Out of the many young Highlanders who, after as careful selection as possible, have been sent to the Continent, various adverse circumstances have caused a large number to abandon their studies and the idea of ecclesiastical life, to return to the vanities of the world, and so belie the hopes which had been formed of them. But if only after due probation in the seminary, and progress in their studies, they are sent to the colleges, it is to be hoped that more will bring their studies to a successful issue, and adhere to their proposed manner of life, . . . But as our Highlanders are for the most part poor, we shall have no means of undertaking so pious, useful and necessary a work, unless your Eminences give us a helping hand.[1]

Bishop MacDonald also pointed out that the boys who were sent abroad too young often forgot all their Gaelic. This misfortune, too, would be avoided if they were able to study at home until they reached the age of seventeen or so.

Without waiting for Propaganda to reply to his report, Bishop MacDonald took immediate steps to found his seminary. For a site he chose Eilean Ban on Loch Morar, the site of the little seminary where he himself had begun his education in 1715. Helped by contributions from Bishop Gordon, Mr Lewis Innes at Paris, Mr Stuart in Rome, and other friends, Bishop MacDonald began building as soon as the weather would permit it. Before the end of June 1732 there were at the seminary five lay boarders as well as several boys intended for the colleges abroad and ultimately for the priesthood.[2]

The problem facing the seminary at Loch Morar was one that was to dog the Highland seminaries over the next century: the problem of finance. In 1735 Bishop MacDonald and Agent Stuart were again begging Propaganda for assistance.[3]

Sometime before 1738 the seminary was transferred to Arisaig, to a site which has been identified as Guidal,[4] where it remained for the next eight years. In 1746, after Culloden, the Guidal seminary, like that at Scalan, had to be abandoned. For the next twenty-four years there was no seminary at all in the Highlands.

In 1765 Bishop Hugh MacDonald wrote to Mr Peter Grant, the Scots Agent at Rome, that he had sent his youths to Fochabers in Banffshire, where they were boarded out in private homes, attending the common schools, and receiving some instruction from Mr Godsman, the priest at Auchinhalrig.[5] It is uncertain for how long Bishop MacDonald had been relying on the parish school at Fochabers to educate his ecclesiastical students, but it may have been for a number of years. Bishop Geddes, in his 'History of Scalan' mentions that

> On the 4th of August 1764 . . . Lewis MacDonald . . . son of Mr MacDonald of Morar who had been at the School of Fochabers joined them [three Scalan boys] here [i.e. at Scalan] and went with them to Paris, being likewise to enter the College there.[6]

In 1739 Bishop Hugh MacDonald, desperately short of money, had begged Propaganda for financial assistance for his seminary. All he had received was fair promises. In 1758, however, thanks to Cardinal Spinelli, the Scottish seminaries were at last assured of a joint annual income of a hundred crowns. This grant was made on the assumption that the Highland seminary would soon reopen, Spinelli urging the bishops not to abandon their aim of maintaining a seminary for each Vicariate. Bishop Hugh and Mr Lewis Innes had supported the seminary at Guidal largely out of their own pockets;[7] any future seminary would at least have an assured minimal income from Rome. It was not until 1766, however, that Bishop John MacDonald, Bishop Hugh's nephew and coadjutor, was able to write from Glenfinnan to the agent at Rome that plans for a new Highland seminary were under way.[8]

In 1768 the new seminary was opened in Glenfinnan at the head of Loch Shiel, about twenty miles east of Guidal. Bishop Hugh, in a letter to Rome, explained that he had opened the seminary because maintaining boys at Fochabers was both expensive and educationally unsatisfactory.[9] By 1769 he was finding that the seminary itself was expensive to run, and he was considering returning the boys to Fochabers. In the following year, however, it was decided that a more practical solution to the problem would be to move the seminary to a larger house on the coast, where supplies could more easily be obtained. The possibility of finding a suitable farm on Loch Morar was discussed, and ultimately, in June 1770, Buorblach, on the north-west coast of Loch Morar, was chosen as the site for the new seminary. By October Bishop John MacDonald, at considerable expense, was building up its farm.

The seminary at Buorblach, instead of solving the financial problems which had dogged the Glenfinnan establishment, only increased them. By the end of 1772 Bishop John was so short of funds that he begged to be allowed to send two boys abroad as soon as there was a vacancy at any of the colleges. The factor refused to give him a long lease of the farm, and by 1774 he was weighed down by a load of debts, with no prospect of paying them off, and with no security of tenure. In September of that year he was forced to close the seminary at Buorblach although he continued to lease the property there.

After Buorblach closed, Bishop John hoped that the Highland and Lowland seminaries might be amalgamated, but he met with opposition from the Lowland

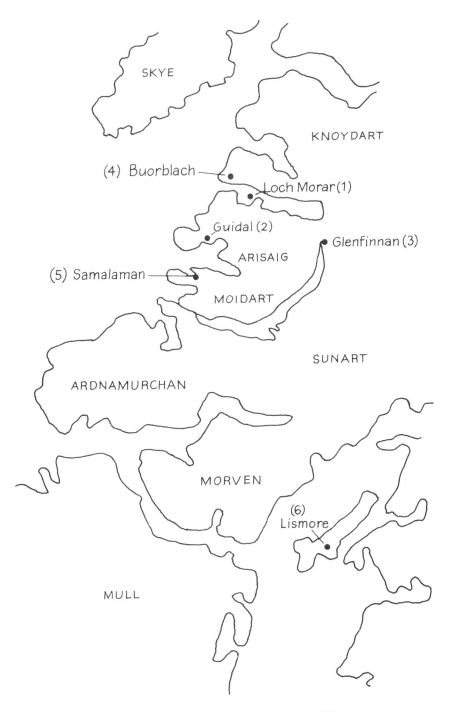

Map 1. The Highland Seminaries: 1732-1829

bishops. As Bishop Grant pointed out to Bishop Hay in March 1775, Scalan was on the estate of the no longer Catholic Duke of Gordon, and so was no longer protected as it had been when there was a Catholic Duke. It would therefore be unwise to draw attention to Scalan by increasing its size to accommodate the Highland boys. Moreover, it would take time to enlarge Scalan, and in the meantime the boys would be very overcrowded. Thirdly, Bishop Grant alluded to

> ... a very great difference there visibly is between the natural disposition of our country boys and that of the Highlanders, which often occasions disagreement and quarrels and jars, to the great detriment of regular discipline.[10]

Such an attitude on the part of the Lowland bishop suggests an uncharitable discrimination against the Highland District which was at least as badly in need of priests as his own Lowland Vicariate. The real reason for Bishop Grant's vehement stand against the union of the two seminaries is spelled out in the letter he wrote to Bishop Hay on April 1st, 1775. A great deal of money had been spent on the Glenfinnan seminary, which had then been abandoned, and now the same thing had happened at Buorblach. Bishop Grant, with some justification, did not think it right that the Highland District, having squandered so much of the slender resources of the Scottish Mission on two abortive seminaries, should now be allowed to add to the financial problems of the Lowland seminary at Scalan. The Lowland bishops refused to agree to a permanent union of the seminaries. They did, however, consent to take two of the Buorblach students at Scalan, on a temporary basis, on condition that they paid for their board at an economic rate.

Bishop John now had the offer of a farm near Fort Augustus for a seminary, but the appointment of the Catholic MacDonald of Sandaig to help with the management of the Morar estate persuaded him to stay on at Buorblach where he might now expect to be given more security of tenure. In October 1776, after a closure of two years, Buorblach reopened.

Troubles continued to plague the Buorblach seminary. Bishop John had hoped to lease a farm for the seminary, but its tenants were assured of their right of possession by General Frazer, and took a delight in mocking the bishop and the superior of Buorblach, Mr James MacDonald. By 1777 Bishop John was again deep in debt with no prospect of being able to extricate himself. Finally, in 1778 it was rumoured that the land on which Buorblach stood was about to be feued, the Bishop having no security of tenure.[11]

Bishop John's first idea was to obtain money from the Scottish Mission to buy Buorblach and its adjacent lands. He also attempted, again unsuccessfully, to have the Lowland and Highland seminaries united. On this occasion, Bishop Hay, with characteristic meticulousness, drew up a list of the 'Costs and Inconveniences that the proposed union of seminaries would bring on the Highland Vicariate'. These included the extension of Scalan, the cost of which would have to be met by the Highland Vicariate; the terms on which Lowland boys were admitted to Scalan and with which Highland boys would need to comply; the fact that the Highland boys would forget their Gaelic, that they would not like the frugal meals served up at Scalan, and that Highland and Lowland boys did not get on well together when youngsters — though when older and at the colleges abroad they formed warm friendships.[12]

By January 1779 Bishop John had decided to purchase land and five small farms at the lower end of Loch Morar. In the end he never did.[13]

Ultimately it was not the Bishop who decided the fate of Buorblach. In May of 1779 Bishop John died. He was succeeded by Mr Alexander MacDonald, the priest on Barra. MacDonald of Sandaig, who had expected his brother to be chosen as the new bishop, resented this appointment, and determined to take Buorblach away from the Mission.[14] After a faltering existence of nine years, the seminary at Buorblach finally closed. Five boys were sent, as a temporary expedient, to Scalan, and the Highland Vicariate was once again without a seminary of its own.[15]

The loss of Buorblach had been a sad blow to the Highland Vicariate, particularly as a good deal of money which the Mission could ill afford had been laid out on the house and farm there, without the usual compensation being given when the lease terminated. For four years there was once more to be no Highland seminary. Scalan, in view of the reluctance of the Lowland bishops to accept Highland boys into it, could only be regarded as a temporary stopgap. Without a seminary the future supply of priests for the Highland Vicariate was in jeopardy.

It was not until 1783 that Bishop Alexander MacDonald was able to inform Bishop Geddes that he hoped to have a house ready for a seminary by the autumn of that year. At a meeting at Scalan that August, in response to a complaint from Rome that two Highland boys sent there had proved unsatisfactory, Bishop Alexander expressed the hope that his new seminary would put an end to such problems.[16]

The site chosen for the new Highland seminary was Samalaman, by the shores of Loch Ailort in Moidart, where the loch met the sea, and just across the sound from the old seminary at Guidal. Its proprietor, Clanranald, gave the bishop a long lease of the farm of Samalaman at a fixed rent.[17] By December 1783 two houses were ready. They were intended eventually to be used as 'offices' — i.e. kitchen and servants' quarters — when the principal house was built, but in the meantime they were to be used to accommodate the first few students.

Once again money was to prove a problem. There had been no way of recovering any of the capital that had been invested in improvements at Buorblach, and in June 1784 Bishop Alexander was beginning to wonder whether he could keep his new seminary going till the next harvest. A constant fear of incurring debts kept him from maintaining more than four or five boys at a time. He complained repeatedly that he had not been sent the Spinelli income, without which he could not contemplate undertaking any improvements.[18] In 1789 he finally decided to go ahead:

> I am getting the necessary articles for building my house next summer to this place; they come very high, and the little house I propose, God willing, to build, I see will amount to much more money than I at first thought, but tis too late now to give up — were they at Rome willing to send me the Spinelli rents retained most unjustly during these four years past they would make things easy for me . . .[19]

By September the money had arrived from Rome, and the shell of the house had been built and the roof completely slated,[20] although it was the following summer before the inside of the house was begun.[21] In a letter to Mr Thomson, Bishop Alexander explained why he had gone ahead with the building in spite of the problem of finance:

> Since ever I was made Bp. I always lamented the distress of this Highland District for want of anything of a decent house, wherein some of the Clergy and I could convene from time to time in order to deliberate about matters regarding the good of Religion in these parts . . .[22]

The extension to Samalaman, in other words, was to provide a more fitting episcopal residence rather than better accommodation for the seminary.

On 9th September 1791 Bishop Alexander MacDonald died. In February 1792 Mr John Chisholm, priest in Strathglass, was consecrated as the new Vicar Apostolic, and inherited Samalaman with all its problems. In 1794 Bishop Chisholm wrote to Bishop Hay, lamenting the wretched state of the seminary:

> such has been my predecessor's economy that he has left it deprived of real necessaries in order to lay some money by of which it is now totally deprived by what went by his will to the mission and by the mismanagement of some things after his death.[23]

Some idea of the problems Bishop Chisholm faced can be gathered from letters he wrote in 1793:

> . . . Scalan . . . is more able to support an odd number [i.e. an extra boy] than this place where everything is almost wanting, and where am oblig'd for the present to have my boys and my few stirks under the same roof.[24]

And again:

> This house, unfinish'd, takes in water through the walls and if not repair'd will fall, and any houses we have on the small farm want thatch which must be got from other countries. In order to carry the necessaries to the Farm I have got a pretty large Boat built . . . [25]

In 1797 Bishop Chisholm wrote two letters to Bishop Hay from which it is clear that, however much he economised, he was finding it impossible to make ends meet:

> Between the havock of the stormy season, my last jaunt from home, and provisions for the family which this year were extravagantly dear and some of them brought the distance of between thirty and fifty miles, I have been . . . at very considerable expense.[26]

And again:

> . . . I have eight [boys] here . . . some of whom since I came here more than five years ago cannot provide themselves in any cloaths which with the high price of victuals for last year you may easily suppose must be heavy in spite of economy.[27]

The financial problems of Samalaman were reflected in the calibre of the boys it sent to the colleges abroad, about whose abilities there were frequent complaints. In 1786 Cardinal Albani voiced his dissatisfaction, and in 1793, when there were four vacant places at Rome, Abbé MacPherson wrote to Bishop Hay:

> I hope you will strive to fill them all this summer, but I should be sorry they were filled all by his [i.e. Chisholm's] people. That would be too great a number at once of raw boys from the Highlands.[28]

In 1794 Abbé MacPherson wrote to Scotland that Cardinal Antonelli had been complaining about the bad choice of boys sent from the Highlands for many years past. Bishop Chisholm replied:

> . . . you must be satisfied with such subjects as you get from the Highlands till such time as I can get above water.[29]

In 1797 there were eight boys at Samalaman, about twice the number that had even been there under Bishop Alexander.[30] It was in this year that Bishop Hay's new seminary was built at Aquhorties. Conceived on a much grander scale than Scalan, it was built to take twenty boys and three masters. Bishop Chisholm asked whether Aquhorties might not serve as a college for both the Highlands and the Lowlands. When Bishop Hay turned down this suggestion, Bishop Chisholm wrote again:

> Your arguments . . . weigh much upon me relative to separate foundations, but still I can scarecely be reconciled to a separate interest. What think ye of this plan? Let Scalan and Samalaman remain as they stand just now and send jointly students to Aquhorties from each of them till there is a college built in the Highlands which will be as soon as possible . . .[31]

Although Bishop Hay turned down this suggestion too, Bishop Chisholm continued with his plans for a Highland college which, like Aquhorties, would be capable of taking boys through all their studies for the priesthood. Such colleges were urgently needed by this time. In 1793, Douay and Paris had closed, and by 1797 it seemed likely that Rome would soon follow, as it did in 1798. After 1798, there was only one Scots College left, the Scots College at Valladolid, so good colleges in Scotland were necessary if enough priests were to be trained.

By October 1797 Bishop Chisholm had raised £200 in subscriptions from among the Catholic Highland gentry,[32] though he was afraid that emigrations from Strathglass would seriously affect his prospects of obtaining the rest of the money needed.[33] In March 1798 he decided that Samalaman was useless for the site of the proposed college, being 'susceptible of very little improvement and by far too small'.[34] Over the next few years several sites were considered[35] — the Isle of Muck, the Isle of Canna, and an estate on Mull. In 1801, Bishop Chisholm purchased the farm of Kilcheran on Lismore. The seminary was transferred from Samalaman to Lismore in 1803.

The seminary at Samalaman had survived for twenty years, much longer than any of its predecessors. Like its predecessors, it had been chronically short of money. Indeed the problem of financing the education of Highland boys for the priesthood would not be solved satisfactorily until the united College of Blairs opened in 1829. Samalaman, however, like the seminaries before it on Eilean Ban, at Guidal, at Glenfinnan and at Buorblach had played a vital role in the provision of Gaelic-speaking priests for the Highland Vicariate of Scotland.

NOTES

1 Report of Bishop Hugh MacDonald, Vicar Apostolic of the Highlands, to Propaganda, March 18th, 1732 — translation in Bellesheim, *History of the Catholic Church of Scotland*, translated by D. O. Hunter Blair (Edinburgh, 1840), Vol. IV, pp. 390-391.

2 MacPherson's continuation of Thomson, Vol II, p. 2 *et seq.*

3 Ibid., p. 61.

4 'The Highland Seminaries: Loch Morar and Arisaig', *St Peter's College Magazine*, December 1950, p. 138.

5 'The Highland Seminaries: Glenfinnan and Buorblach', *St Peter's College Magazine*, June 1951, p. 20.

6 Bishop Geddes, 'History of Scalan', *Innes Review* 1963, p. 104.

7 MacPherson's continuation of Thomson, Vol. II, p. 141.

8 'The Highland Seminaries: Glenfinnan and Buorblach', *St Peter's College Magazine,* June 1951, pp. 20-21.

9 *Ibid.,* p. 21.

10 *Ibid.,* p. 22.

11 *Ibid.,* p. 23.

12 These notes are written on the back of a letter dated 26th June 1778 to Mr William Reid, Aberdeen, contained in a folder marked 'Some Letters Relating to Scotch Colleges', no. C3(14), Columba House.

13 'The Highland Seminaries: Glenfinnan and Buorblach', *St Peter's College Magazine,* June 1951, p. 24.

14 *Ibid.,* p. 24.

15 'The Highland Seminaries: Samalaman,1783-1803', *St Peter's College Magazine,* December 1951, p. 54.

16 *Ibid.*

17 *Ibid.,* p. 56.

18 *Ibid.,* pp. 57-58.

19 Bishop Alexander MacDonald, Samalaman to Bishop Geddes, 2nd January 1789, B.L.

20 Bishop Alexander MacDonald to Bishop Geddes, 13th September 1789, B.L.

21 Bishop Alexander MacDonald to Bishop Geddes, 5th March 1790, B.L.

22 Bishop Alexander MacDonald to John Thomson, Rome, 20th July 1789, B.L.

23 Bishop John Chisholm, Samalaman to Bishop Hay, 5th May, 1794, B.L.

24 Bishop John Chisholm to Bishop Geddes, 7th May 1793, B.L.

25 Bishop John Chisholm to Bishop Hay, 25th July 1793, B.L.

26 Bishop John Chisholm to Bishop Hay, 9th January 1797, B.L.

27 Bishop John Chisholm to Bishop Hay, 5th May 1797, B.L.

28 Abbé MacPherson to Bishop Hay, 28th December 1793, B.L.

29 Bishop Chisholm to Abbé MacPherson, 18th September 1794, B.L.

30 Bishop Chisholm to Bishop Hay, 5th May 1797, B.L.

31 Bishop Chisholm to Bishop Hay, 30th January 1798, B.L.

32 John Farquharson to Abbé MacPherson, 14th October 1797, B.L.

33 Bishop Chisholm to Bishop Hay, 30th January 1798, B.L.

34 Bishop Chisholm to Bishop Hay, 28th March 1798, B.L.

35 Various Letters of Bishop Chisholm, 1798-1803, B.L.

10

Catholic Schools before 1793

IN 1560 the Scottish Reformers compiled a document which set out the doctrine, policy and discipline of the Reformed Kirk. This document, known as the first Book of Discipline, dealt among other things with the subject of education.[1] The reformers attributed many of the abuses which had grown up in the Catholic Church to an over-powerful if ill-educated clergy who preyed on the ignorance and superstition of their often illiterate congregations. They were determined, therefore, that in the Reformed Kirk not only would the ministers be well educated but also their congregations would be sufficiently educated and instructed to be able to play an active part in Church government. To this end they proposed that there should be a school in every parish, a grammar school in every town, a system of colleges, and finally the existing universities, which were to be reorganised along Protestant lines.

The establishment of parish schools was commanded by successive Acts, from the Privy Council Act of 1616 onwards, throughout the seventeenth century, and by 1700 the central lowlands at least were well provided with schools, though in the larger parishes of the more remote and mountainous areas the coverage was still less than adequate. In the parish schools the schoolmaster was appointed by the kirk session, and had his house, school and salary provided out of the parish funds. In 1646 the heritors were made responsible for the erection of schools and the payment of schoolmasters. The heritors worked in close conjunction with the kirk session to ensure that suitable schoolmasters were chosen. The schoolmasters were required to teach reading, writing and arithmetic. Many of them also taught Latin. They were also required to give the children religious instruction and to make them learn the Protestant catechism. It was this last item, the Protestant catechism, which worried Catholic parents and priests.

Between 1560 and 1700, although Catholic schools were not specifically forbidden by Act of Parliament, the Catholic faith was proscribed. In 1572 it was enacted that a list of all 'obstinate papists' be prepared. Subsequent Acts ordered all priests and Jesuits to leave the country under pain of death.[2] Such Acts of Parliament can have left Scottish Catholics in no doubt as to the dangers they would face if they were discovered setting up Catholic schools. The Act of 1700 finally spelled out what previous Acts had merely implied:

> ... no persons professed or suspected to be papists shall be capable to be imployed in the education of youth or the trust or management of their affairs: And especially that none such shall be capable to be Governours Chaplains Pedagogues or School-masters, Tutors or

Curators, Chamberlains and Factors, and that none presume to imploy papists or such as are suspect of popery in any of the said trusts under pain of ane years valued rent or one thousand merks . . . neither shall it be allowed to any professed or suspect papist to teach any art science or exercise of any sort either in families or out of them to young or old.[3]

Although in many parts of Scotland it became dangerous, after 1560, to profess the Catholic faith, there were some areas, notably in the West Highlands and in the more inaccessible areas of the North-East, where Roman Catholicism continued in strength. It is in these areas that there is some evidence of the existence of Catholic schools. There are two types of Catholic schools which must be considered: those run by the Scottish Mission and those run by private individuals. The Mission schools are comparatively well-documented; the private schools have left virtually no record.

There were no Catholic schools in Scotland financed by the Church until the second half of the seventeenth century. In 1657 Mr Alexander Winster or Dunbar, a newly ordained priest, set off from the Scots College in Rome for Scotland. He had been instructed by Propaganda to report fully on the possibility of establishing a Catholic school in the Highlands. In 1675 Propaganda made provision for two schools, one in Glengarry and the other in Barra. The master of each school was allowed fifty crowns per annum, the same allowance as was made to each priest serving in Scotland. To begin with, Propaganda tried to insist that Catholic children should be sent to these schools from all parts of the country, but it was informed that Catholic parents in Scotland would as soon send their children to Jamaica as to the Island of Barra.[4]

Mr James Gordon's report to Propaganda, made in 1703, traces the progress of these schools. Initially they had not been as successful as had been expected, owing to the 'difficulty of the times', but they had been put on a better footing by Bishop Nicolson after he arrived in Scotland in 1697. Thereafter they had succeeded very well until the 'Late Persecution' when they had been broken up and dispersed:

... for the Ministers persecuted with greater spite the School-masters than the Missioners as they saw how much these schools contributed to confirm the Catholic faith in the Highlands where the people out of a certain instinct or by some seeds of the Catholic religion which remained in their minds were well disposed towards it.[5]

The ministers themselves had established a school in the Highlands in 1702 to counter the effect of the Catholic schools, but had been able to persuade few people to attend it.

Mr Gordon was at pains to point out to Propaganda the great benefits that would accrue from the encouragement of the Catholic schools. Not only would they help to safeguard Catholicism in Scotland by instructing children in the faith, but they would also afford an opportunity to discover boys who might have a vocation for the priesthood.

Mr Thomson's 'History of the Scottish Mission', which derives its information from contemporary letters and documents, gives further information about the Church schools. In 1701 there were schools in Uist, Barra and Arisaig. The school in Arisaig had that year 'above thirty scholars of the best Gentlemen's children in the Highlands'.[6]

In 1702, the year of the 'Persecution' mentioned by Mr Gordon, the soldiers stationed in the Highlands were ordered by the Privy Council to search out and apprehend priests and Catholic schoolmasters. The schools were therefore shut down completely or were forced to move from place to place.[7]

In 1703 the schools seem to have reopened, as three schoolmasters were receiving salaries from the Scottish Mission. Two of the schools were in the Highlands, as before, in Uist and in Barra; the third was in Strathbogie, in the North-East.[8]

In 1707 Bishop Gordon paid his first visit to the Highlands, sailing to Barra on the 30th June:

> [He] spent the first second third and fourth of July in it [i.e. Barra] and the little island of Watersay . . . the laird and the principal inhabitants spoke to the Bishop about erecting a school on that Island as it was inconvenient for them to send their children to other countries, which he agreed to.[9]

It is not clear from the context which island — Barra or Watersay — wanted a school. If, as seems likely, it was Barra, then the school that had been there in 1703 must have closed down. This would, however, appear to be contradicted by Mr Thomson's entry under 1708:

> Notwithstanding the persecution, the schools in the Highlands continued to prosper; and the schoolmasters stood firm in spite of the threats of the ministers.[10]

In 1710 a new threat appeared:

> The ministers had collected immense sums to establish their new society for planting Protestancy and expelling Catholicism, out of the Highlands especially, and had opened many schools in those parts.[11]

The impact of the new Protestant schools in the Catholic areas of the Highlands was not at this time very great, although undoubtedly the threat which they presented urged the bishops to greater efforts in promoting their own schools.

In 1711 there were three thriving Mission schools in the Highlands, and the bishops were considering the possibility of establishing two more, as it was judged advisable to have a greater number of schools spread over different parts of the country rather than have a few larger and therefore more conspicuous establishments. Also it would be more likely that Catholic parents would send their children to a local school than to one situated at a great distance.[12]

In 1714 Bishop Gordon was in the Highlands, where he

> . . . settled proper orders in his schools, both for educating Catholic children and furnishing foreign Colleges.[13]

It was in this year that the first Scottish seminary opened on Loch Morar. In 1716, after the failure of the Jacobite rebellion, the seminary was forced to close and reopened in Glenlivet. It is likely that the Mission schools were also forced to close in 1716, but they were soon reopened. In 1720 there was a Catholic school in South Uist to which even Protestant children were sent, there being no Protestant school in the area.[14] In 1732 George Duncan, a priest, was sent to the Highlands to teach, presumably in a Mission school;[15] and, between 1734 and 1742, Mr Allan MacDonald, before his ordination, seems to have been similarly employed.[16]

It must have been a source of anxiety for the Scottish Mission that it was unable for so long to establish schools in the North-East, as this area was a major stronghold of Catholicism. In 1780 it was estimated that 65% of the Catholics of the Lowland Vicariate lived on the Duke of Gordon's estates, and that a third of all the Lowland Catholics lived in the Enzie district of Banffshire.[17]

There was a Mission school in Strathbogie in 1703. Under 1712 Mr Thomson records:

> [The bishops] had even ventured to begin a school . . . in the low countries but in a very private manner so as to escape public notice.[18]

This entry probably refers to the Strathbogie school, which must have been very small. After the seminary moved to Scalan in Glenlivet in 1716 it is likely that Mission schools were also opened in Banffshire. There must have been schools in the area by 1728 when Mr Thomson records that 'the seminary and some of the schools'[19] were twice dispersed by soldiers. Again, in 1730, he records that Bishop Gordon visited 'the low country, Glenlivet, Strathavin, his schools and seminary'.[20]

Both seminaries were forced to close in 1746 after Culloden. The Mission schools, too, must have been forced to close at this time, but they, unlike the seminaries, do not seem to have reopened. After 1745 the Mission was short of funds and short of priests, and many of its chapels had been destroyed by Hanoverian soldiers. There can have been no resources to spare for schools when the Mission itself was so overburdened. In the bishops' reports to Propaganda of 1763 and 1764 no mention is made of any schools being supported by Mission funds. It was not until 1778 that the Mission once again possessed a school, this time in Edinburgh.

Before 1745 the Mission schools seem to have been financed largely, if not entirely, by Propaganda. The schools which were opened from 1778 onwards were financed by the efforts of the priests in whose mission stations they were. It was individual priests rather than the Vicars Apostolic who were responsible for opening schools, and the priests financed them partly from money raised in their chapels, and partly from subscriptions raised both among their own congregations and further afield. In addition, the Catholic schoolmasters, like the masters in the parish schools of the Presbyterian church, charged a small sum for each pupil, and, in the country areas, kept a cow or two on the few acres that went with the school.

It is clear that the few schools which the Mission managed to establish in the first half of the eighteenth century could teach only a very small percentage of the Catholic children of Scotland. Mr Gordon's report of 1703 indicates other methods which were used to instruct Catholic children:

> Sometimes every Missioner took two or three boys and instructed them in his own house quietly without being observed. At other times they endeavoured to gain the goodwill of the Protestant schoolmasters and gave them a trifle of money not to plague the Catholic Children about Religion. Then they appointed one discreet layman to watch over the Behaviour and studies of the youths. Sometimes they employed many schoolmasters who had but very few boys each and by proper precautions escaped the Notice of the Ministers and other Protestants.[21]

Under 1708 Mr Thomson records:

> In the Lowlands the Catholics were in great difficulties and anxieties about the education of their children, for there were no schools there [i.e. Catholic schools]. The priests, however, supplied as well as they could this defect.[22]

In general it would seem that Catholic children attended the parish schools unless they were subjected to anti-Catholic teaching, and that any defects in their religious education were corrected by their priests. In addition many of the priests seem to have taught a few children in their own homes; probably these children were boys who seemed likely to have a vocation for the priesthood.

Protestant sources reveal that by 1720 there were several private Catholic schools in Banffshire:

> ... the papists have erected two popish Schools more than formerly in that countrey, one of them is taught by Mr ffarquharson at Glenlivet, and the other by Mr MacDonald in Auchriachan ... There are other two considerable schools in the ... Duke's [i.e. Duke of Gordon's] ground taught by nottour Jacobites viz Mr Alexander Mitchell at ffochabers ... and Mr Alexander Cheyn at Huntly besides many smaller ones ... .[23]

Bishop Geddes, in his 'History of Scalan', mentions one of these schools:

> There was indeed much about this same time [1735], a boarding school for Catholic young Gentlemen kept at Strands in Strathavin by Mr Gregory Farquharson who had Mr Archibald Anderson for some time to assist him. At this school some of Glengary's, Scotus's and Belfinlay's sons with many other Highland young Gentlemen, as also the late Mr Gordon of Munmore, some Stuarts from Deeside and the sons of Mr Gordon of Letterfurie received at least part of their education.[24]

The presence in Strathaven of boys from such a wide area is an indication of the scarcity of good Catholic schools in Scotland — and perhaps of the scarcity of good schools of any sort in the Highlands.

Presbyterian sources indicate the presence of several more Catholic teachers: a Catholic schoolmaster was teaching in Fochabers grammar school in 1714,[25] a good indication of the influence of the Duke of Gordon. Three 'popish schoolmasters and mistresses' were teaching within the bounds of the presbytery of Kincardine O'Neil.[26] Overall, however, private Catholic schools, and Catholic schoolmasters, like the Mission schools, can have contributed to the education of only a small minority of children. As the private schools relied entirely on fees paid by their pupils, it is likely that they benefited only the better-off families, families like those mentioned by Bishop Geddes.

Bishop Geddes, himself, was the son of a small tenant farmer. He was born at the Mains of Curridoun in the Enzie in 1735. His autobiography gives some indication of the sort of education a poor Catholic boy might receive in the Enzie which, in spite of its large Catholic population, had no Mission school. In 1739, when he was four years old, John Geddes learned to read; two years later he started writing. In the summer of 1742, when he was seven, he began to go to the 'School of Rathven' — presumably the Presbyterian parish school — where he was 'immediately applied to the Latin'. During the winter he lodged with his uncle, going home only at weekends.[27] At the beginning of November 1743 Geddes started going to Cairnfield where he was taught with Mr Gordon of Cairnfield's two sons, John and James. Since Gordon of Cairnfield was a Catholic, it is possible that the tutor he employed, Mr James Shearer, was also of that persuasion. John Geddes continued to study at Cairnfield until Martinmas 1745 when John and James Gordon were sent to Litchiestown to be taught with 'Buckie's' children [i.e. Gordon of Buckie].

Under 1745 Bishop Geddes notes: 'During the confusion of that winter at no school, studied at home, copied poems'.[28] This is the only reference he makes to the Jacobite rebellion of that year. His autobiographical notes continue:

> 1746: some time after Christmas went to the charity school below Litchiestown taught by Mr Grant of Ringoran, companions: Cosmo Reid, John Reid, Sandy Weir etc. In Summer returned to the school of Rathven. Mr Anderson still master, Mr Charles Hay there.
>
> 1747: Continued at school of Rathven until June. Went to school at Litchiestown, companions: Buckie's and Cairnfield's sons, also Mr Alexander Geddes . . . James Shearer went to Aberdeen to the college, William Wilson master in his place . . .
>
> 1748: Continued at the school of Litchiestown. William Wilson departed in spring and Mr Shearer returned; that school was given up at Martinmas. Mr Alexander Godsman came to Preshome, frequented that place, studied some Latin and French. John Reid, Sandy Geddes, Sandy Gordon of Landend and Jamie Paterson came there to study likewise.[29]

In 1749 John Geddes was sent to the Scots College, Rome to study for the priesthood.

Another example of the sort of education a priest might receive before entering a seminary is the case of Abbé Paul MacPherson. Born in 1757 near Scalan in Glenlivet, he first went to a 'Catholic school at Clashnore'. Clashnore, or Clashnoir, was a farm in Glenlivet whose tenants were Catholic Gordons. The 'school' that Paul MacPherson attended must therefore have been simply classes given to the Clashnoir boys and a few of their friends by a private tutor. This 'school' was closed in 1763, after MacPherson had attended it for about a year. He was sent next to a school run by an old woman who could read but not write.[30] The only Protestant schoolmaster in the area was hostile towards Catholics, and MacPherson's father preferred that his son should remain uneducated rather than that he be perverted from his faith. In 1767 Paul MacPherson was at last admitted to Scalan, where he began to study in earnest.

Although there is no evidence of Catholic schools other than those mentioned above, there may well have been other small private schools in existence at various times. It seems unlikely that they were educationally satisfactory. Outside the West Highlands and Banffshire, anyone opening a Catholic school would run a grave risk of imprisonment. In 1704, however, the General Assembly, in an address to the Queen, did protest that

> . . . at Edinburgh a French Papist kept a dancing school and . . . a Scotchwoman, a papist, taught young ladies to sew and draw.[31]

The Relief Act of 1793, although it gave Scottish Catholics many legal rights, was ambiguously worded in the clause which dealt with Catholic education, and seemed to imply that Catholics should not be allowed to teach even those children of their own persuasion. Such an ambiguity was undoubtedly the unintentional result of careless draughtsmanship, and its implications were disregarded. The Relief Act, in any case, did not alter existing trends in Catholic education. Of far greater immediate impact was the French Revolution. The Revolution brought an influx of French priests to Britain, and it was they, more than anything, who made Catholic schools and Catholic schoolmasters respectable, and indeed respected, in Scotland. In the widest sense the French Revolution demonstrated that Scottish

Catholics were no longer a political threat but instead were wholehearted supporters of the British Government.

NOTES

1 Gordon Donaldson, *Scotland: James V — James VII*, (Edinburgh, 1971), pp. 262-265.

2 *General Index to the Acts of the Parliaments of Scotland*, p. 924 *et seq.*

3 *Acts of the Parliaments of Scotland*, Vol. X, p. 218.

4 *Scotichronicon*, pp. x, xi.

5 Thomson, 'History of the Scottish Mission', Vol. I, pp. 528-529 (summary of Mr Gordon's report).

6 Thomson, Vol. I, p. 510.

7 Ibid., pp. 512, 516.

8 Ibid., p. 549.

9 Thomson, quoted in Forbes Leith, Vol. II, p. 233.

10 Ibid., p. 239.

11 Ibid., p. 274.

12 Thomson, Vol. II, p. 4.

13 Ibid., p. 39.

14 'Encrease of Popery', Document NLS MS 68 ff 31.32; *Innes Review* 1966, p. 107.

15 'Clergy Lists of the Highland District', *Innes Review* 1966, p. 135.

16 *Ibid.*, p. 140.

17 *Scotichronicon*, p. 181.

18 Thomson, Vol. II, p. 30.

19 Ibid., p. 158.

20 Ibid., p. 183.

21 Ibid., Vol. I, p. 529.

22 Thomson, quoted in Forbes Leith, Vol. II, p. 239.

23 'Encrease of Popery', Document NLS MS 68 ff 31-2; *Innes Review* 1966, p. 107.

24 Bishop Geddes, 'History of Scalan', *Innes Review* 1963, pp. 97-98.

25 'Encrease of Popery', Document NLS MS 976 f 143; *Innes Review* 1966, p. 92.

26 'Encrease of Popery', Document NLS MS 976 ff 147-149; *Innes Review* 1966, p. 98.

27 'Autobiographical Notes of Bishop John Geddes', ed. W. J. Anderson, *Innes Review* 1967, pp. 40-41.

28 *Ibid.*

29 *Ibid.* The 'school at Litchiestown' (now spelled 'Leitcheston') (1747-1748) was another private Catholic house in which Catholic children were taught by a tutor. Mr Alexander Godsman (1748) was the priest at Preshome.

30 *Scotichronicon*, p. 595.

31 Thomson, quoted in Forbes Leith, Vol. II, p. 218.

11

The French Revolution and Catholics in Scotland

ON 14th July 1789 the Bastille fell: the French Revolution had begun. Its outcome had a profound effect on Britain. In the years before 1793 there was, in Britain, a growing demand for Parliamentary reform. In Yorkshire, in 1780, the Rev. Christopher Wyvill urged the freeholders to demand a correction of the abuses in parliamentary elections. In the same year the commissioners of supply of Inverness-shire, the freeholders of Moray and the justices of the peace of Caithness all condemned the use of fictitious votes. At the meeting of reformers, in Edinburgh, which followed, freeholders of twenty-three out of the thirty-three Scottish shires were represented. Burgh reform, too, was called for by men like Thomas MacGruger, who published his 'Letters of Zeno' in the winter of 1792-1793.[1] None of the reforms demanded by these people could be described as revolutionary. Their aim was, in the government of the country, at local and at parliamentary level, to give a voice to the growing middle classes — merchants, doctors, lawyers and professors. They did not seek to implement anything approaching universal suffrage.

To begin with, British reform movements felt themselves to be in sympathy with the Revolution in France, while men like William Robertson, Dugald Stewart and Henry Erskine, together with most politicians, saw it as a means of curbing the power of the despotic Bourbon dynasty. As Ferguson points out:

> . . . the great doctrines of the Revolution made a strong appeal to the egalitarian values which had long co-existed in Scotland with feudal institutions.[2]

It was not long, however, before the French Revolution deteriorated into scenes of appalling violence and bloodshed.[3] By 1791 the French king was in prison, and fears were growing for his safety. In September 1792 news of the Paris massacres shocked Britain. From now on the British government was to regard any demands for even moderate reform as seditious, and a threat to its individual members.

At a time when the British government was thoroughly alarmed by events in France, and equally alarmed by what it saw as the threat of sedition at home, it might, as Abbé Paul MacPherson suggests, have been forgiven for disregarding the plight of that small and insignificant minority, the Scottish Catholics:

> The situation of the kingdom was such about the end of 1792, and the beginning of '93, that no Catholic could have expected any alteration in their favour of the laws. French principles had gained great influence with the lower class of people, and with the bad of every rank; and Government, however steady it was, had enough ado to guard the Crown and subjects from the

machinations of the deceived multitude and their malicious leaders. The making any relaxation of laws in favour of Catholics at such a critical period might be an additional source to those evil-designing men of exclaiming out against Government, and the deluded multitude, as former times had often shown, might soon become as great enemies as ever of Catholics. Government knew that the Scotch Catholics were as well affected to the Crown as they could wish them to be; but their number was so small in comparison of the enemies of Order in that part of the British Empire, that their utmost exertions could be but of little avail.[4]

The Scottish Catholic Relief Bill was, however, passed without any problem in June 1793. Indeed the French Revolution, far from causing renewed hostility towards Catholics in Britain, was to win for them and for their religion a widespread sympathy. Thousands of French priests fled to Britain rather than submit to a Revolutionary government, which insisted that they profess themselves servants of the state by an oath which Pope Pius VI had declared to be unlawful.[5] Abbé MacPherson described the situation regarding these émigré priests as he found it when in England in 1793:

> I was astonished at the attention and civility shown to them [the emigrant French priests] at London where there were on the first of this month [August 1793] 1,500 of them. Nor is less regard paid to them at Dover where, if you were to judge of the inhabitants by the people you see on the streets, you would think the one half were French Priests. Not only no insult is offered to them, but everyone of every rank pays them the greatest attention. While here at Bruges they can scarcely appear on the streets without being hissed. Generous Britain. Heaven must reward such eminent charity. They pass and repass between Dover and Ostend without paying a farthing. Government pays their freight; the English passengers, if there be any, their victuals, if not, the honest Tars — 'damn their eyes, would they allow a poor French priest to pay for a meal or two'.[6]

Britain was indeed generous towards the French Catholic refugees, laymen as well as priests, who flocked to her shores. By 1792 there were over 3,000 of them in Britain, and a subscription was opened for their support: £33,775 was collected within a few weeks, and was used to give each priest £2 a month, and each bishop £10. The government provided housing at Gosport and at Guildford, and, when these buildings proved insufficient, provided the large 'King's House' at Winchester. In April 1793, following an appeal which was issued by the king and read out in all Protestant churches, a further £41,303 was raised for the refugees. But funds raised by subscription could be adequate only in the short term, and Parliament voted to provide the French refugees with £200,000 annually from the public purse. Bishops were to receive £10 a month, priests £1.15.0; important laymen were to receive from £3 to £8 a month according to their rank, while ordinary laymen were allowed £1.11.6.[7] This was an extremely generous gesture for a British Government to make towards foreign Catholics at a time of national crisis.

A few of the thousands of French priests who had arrived in England made their way to Scotland, where their presence was welcomed, particularly in the towns. A few French laymen, too, made their mark in Scotland. Most of the refugees who came to Scotland found employment as teachers: in Greenock, in Paisley, in Glasgow, in Ayr, in Edinburgh, in Inverness, in Banff, in Dundee, in Perth and in St. Andrews. Many had been distinguished scholars and professors in France. A few found employment in the Scottish universities; most of them became teachers in the grammar schools and academies of the towns. Their contribution to Scottish education was considerable.[8]

Many of these priests continued to exercise their religious faculties with the blessing of the Scottish bishops. But for their efforts, the growing Irish Catholic population in the manufacturing towns in the West would have been destitute of the service of any priest.[9] They filled a gap in the West which the Lowland Bishops, for many years, were unable — and perhaps rather reluctant — to fill with Scottish priests. In places like Montrose, where there were too few Catholics to warrant more than an occasional visit from the hard-pressed Scottish priests, their French counterparts, supported as they were by government funds, could afford to open small chapels in their houses and say Mass for the few local Catholics.[10]

To Edinburgh, in particular, came some very distinguished French refugees. The Comte d'Artois held court at Holyroodhouse for a number of years; Holyrood Chapel was restored to Catholic worship for the first time since the flight of James VII in 1688; and eminent divines like the Bishop of Arras and the Abbé de Latil said Mass there, using the silver thurible and soleil of James VII's day, restored to Holyrood by Bishop Hay for that purpose.[11]

It was inevitable that one or two Scottish Catholics, at least, would support the French Revolution. These men, however, were the exception rather than the rule. Scottish Catholics before 1793 had no place in politics, and so it was unlikely that the agitation for parliamentary reform would have aroused much interest among them.

As early as 1789, when many people were still viewing with approval the French Revolution, many of the Scottish priests were viewing it with considerable alarm. In August of that year Bishop Geddes expressed to Mr Thomson at Rome his fear that the Revolution would hurt the Catholic Church:

> I should be glad to know whether or not at Rome they dread any bad consequences to Religion in France, from the present Revolution. I am much afraid that in that respect it will do harm.[12]

Mr Alexander MacDonald, priest in Keppoch, expressed the same fears.[13] Mr Thomson, for his part, prophesised that the French king would soon, like Charles I of Britain, lose his head.[14] He explained his reasons in a letter to Bishop Geddes:

> This revolution has been preparing for some time, and I consider it in great part owing to the pernicious principles with regard to civil and religious government contained in the numbers publications of the Infidels of the Age which have poisoned people's minds and have prepared them to throw off all subjection, both Civil and Religious.[15]

The only Scottish priest who expressed any sympathy for the French Revolution was Dr Alexander Geddes, and he can hardly be regarded as typical. He had left the Scottish Mission in 1779 after twelve years' service, during which time he had often been a thorn in the side of his bishops, and had settled in London. Although he continued to correspond with his cousin, Bishop Geddes, he neither worked for, nor was supported financially by, the Scottish Mission. He could, perhaps, afford to have revolutionary leanings; his counterparts in Scotland, who depended on French funds for much of their income, could not.

There were, in France, Scottish Catholic laymen, some of them prominent figures, who supported the French Revolution.[16] In Scotland only one Catholic was found guilty of revolutionary behaviour, and that was the Edinburgh goldsmith, David Downie. Downie, along with Robert Watt, was charged with High Treason in 1794, following the discovery of the Pike Plot. Watt was hanged, but Downie's sentence, after several respites, was commuted to banishment for life.[17] Father Anderson has suggested that Downie escaped the death penalty because he was a Catholic, and because the government, at that time, was carrying on secret negotiations with the Scottish bishops, negotiations aimed at buying Scottish Catholic loyalty with an annual payment of money.[18] These arguments simply do not hold water. The Scottish Catholics were almost all loyal to the Government — thousands had served in the British Army; they had reason to be grateful to the Government for the lately granted Relief Act; they were, moreover, far too insignificant a minority to be worth bribing. Negotiations for a government grant did not begin until after Downie's sentence had finally been decided, and they were set on foot at the instigation of Bishop Hay and not of the government. The first payment of the grant was not made until 1799, and subsequent payments were only reluctantly and belatedly made after repeated requests from the bishops.[19] Finally the grant benefited only the Catholic clergy, whose loyalty to the government was never in question. Indeed, the significance of Downie's trial as regards the Scottish Mission is that it produced the following letter from Bishop Geddes, which outlines the conditions with which Downie would have to comply if he were to receive absolution:

> . . . the one [condition], that he declares in private and in public also his disapprobation of all Jacobinical practices, which are really criminal before God as well as before man; The other condition is, that he discover the whole plot, if he really was engaged in a plot, and this to the utmost of his knowledge. This discovery he owes to his Country, which they were endeavouring to bring to ruin; and he is obliged to prevent the evil in so far as he can. He is not indeed obliged to this declaration untill after his trial or at the point of Death from Sickness; but if condemned, or being about to die of sickness, I do not think he can be excused from it. He may however very lawfully make any advantage he can to save his life, either before or after his trial, by offering this declaration of the whole affair.[20]

This letter declares unequivocally that revolutionary activities are 'criminal before God'. This being the official attitude of the Catholic Church in Scotland, it does not seem likely that the fate of one aging goldsmith could be sufficient to upset the relations between the Catholic Church and the British government. Indeed the Scottish bishops were fully convinced of the justice of harsh measures being taken against Downie:

> Several murdering instruments have been discovered at Edinburgh, and the unhappy Downie, notwithstanding all the good advices that you [Abbé MacPherson] and others gave him, is accused of having ordered and paid for them. He is in close confinement . . . Government seems determined to use vigorous measures, and will I hope be successful.[21]

In short, Downie owed his life neither to his religion nor to the intervention of the bishops. It is far more likely that he escaped hanging because he was an old man, an inept plotter, and the treasurer of that highly respected and reactionary body, the Edinburgh Goldsmiths' Association.

To the Scottish bishops, Jacobinism and the French Revolution were abhorrent. For this, if for no other reason, their support for the British Government was wholehearted. In the words of Bishop Hay:

> At present [April 1793] our Country is engaged in a war which, if ever any one was just and necessary, must be acknowledged without all hesitation to be so. To stop the progress of a set of furies, open and professed Enemies to God and man and to prevent the spreading of their contageous and diabolical doctrines, which carry devastation and misery wherever they go, is surely a common cause of humanity, and a duty which every man owes to his own Country in particular, and to mankind in general.[22]

One of the reasons why Bishop Hay was so violent in his condemnation of the French Revolution was that it had robbed the Scottish Mission of two of its colleges and much of its income, besides endangering the lives of Scottish priests and their students who were living in France at its outbreak. In order, therefore, to understand why Scottish Catholics in general, and the priests in particular, were so bitterly opposed to the French Revolution, it is necessary to turn to events in France in order to establish how great was their immediate impact upon the Scottish Mission.

NOTES

1 For a general account of demands for reforms, see William Ferguson, *Scotland: 1689 to the Present* (Edinburgh, 1968), Chapter 8.

2 *Ibid.*, p. 249.

3 For a general account of the progress of the French Revolution, see Franklin L. Ford, *Europe 1780-1830* (London, 1976).

4 Abbé Paul MacPherson, 'Repeal of the Penal Laws', in Forbes Leith, Vol. II, pp. 386-387.

5 Bernard Ward, *The Dawn of the Catholic Revival in England, 1781-1803*, Vol. II, Chapter I, describes the situation of French priests who fled to England.

6 Abbé Paul MacPherson, Bruges to Bishop Geddes, 24th August 1793, B.L.

7 Bernard Ward, *The Dawn of the Catholic Revival*, Vol. II, pp. 8, 20-31.

8 James MacGloin, 'Some Refugee French Clerics and Laymen in Scotland 1789-1814', *Innes Review* 1965, pp. 28-55.

9 E.g. Mr Farquharson to Abbé MacPherson 26th May 1795, B.L. (many other references in Blairs letters).

10 Charles Gordon to Bishop Cameron, 16th September 1803, B.L.

11 Bishop Hay to Bishop Cameron, 22nd December 1802, B.L.

12 Bishop Geddes to Mr Thomson, 25th August 1789, B.L.

13 Alexander MacDonald, Keppoch to Bishop Geddes, various letters 1789, B.L.

14 Mr Thomson to Bishop Geddes, 1st August 1789, B.L.

15 Mr Thomson to Bishop Geddes, 15th August 1789, B.L.

16 W. J. Anderson, 'David Downie and the "Friends of the People"', *Innes Review* 1965, p. 169.

17 *State Trials*, edited by T. B. and T. S. Howell, vol. XXIV, p. 1 *et seq.*

18 W. J. Anderson, 'David Downie and the "Friends of the People"', *Innes Review* 1965, p. 167.

19 See Chapter 16, which deals specifically with this grant.

20 Bishop Geddes to Alexander Cameron, scroll letter, Summer 1794, B.L.

21 Bishop Geddes to Abbé MacPherson, 19th June 1794, B.L.

22 Bishop Hay to George Mathison, 4th April 1793, B.L.

12

The Revolution in France

FROM June 1789 to 30th September 1791, France was governed by the National Constituent Assembly; and from 1st October 1791 to September 1792 by the Legislative Assembly. The monarchy was not completely abolished until September 1792. During the period of limited monarchy fundamental changes were made regarding the position of the Roman Catholic Church in France. By November 1789 the National Assembly was faced with a financial crisis. It ruled, therefore, that ecclesiastical property could be disposed of for the good of the nation, and church lands were seized. The assembly agreed to support the secular clergy, but it urged members of religious orders to renounce their vows and leave their monasteries and convents. On 12th July, 1790 it went further. It terminated all papal jurisdiction in France. Under the 'Civil Constitution of the Clergy' priests were henceforth to be selected by district electoral assemblies; the old episcopal dioceses were to be scrapped in favour of new ones which corresponded to departmental boundaries; and the government was to take over the payment of bishops and priests. In short, the Catholic Church in France was to be a national church controlled by the state.[1] All priests were to swear an oath of loyalty to the state, an oath which Pope Pius VI declared to be unlawful. Priests who refused to conform were classed as enemies of the state. In November 1790 all those who refused to take the oath were deprived of any offices or benefices they possessed. On 26th August 1792 all priests who refused to take the oath were ordered to leave the country within two weeks on pain of deportation to South America.[2] From now on, in all the Catholic countries of Europe, Jacobinism was to be identified with religious dissent. In Spain, for instance, foreign residents were compelled to swear allegiance to the Crown and the Roman Catholic Church.[3] It is not surprising, therefore, that at this time the British government was favourably disposed towards Catholics in Scotland, and that the Scottish Mission was opposed to the French Revolution.

When the French Revolution broke out in 1789, the rector of the Scots College at Douay was Mr John Farquharson. Under his care fourteen Scots boys were pursuing their studies at the University. By January, 1790 Mr Farquharson was beginning to wonder for how much longer that state of affairs could continue:

> Hitherto universities and colleges have not merited the attention of our all-informing states general; a thorough reformation in them must necessarily take place. I am credibly assured that foreign establishments are in great danger.[4]

By July the situation had further deteriorated. The following letter from Mr

Farquharson gives some idea of the nightmare in which he must have felt he was living:

> Since I wrote you last our situation here has been singularly curious; the most tyrannical government is preferable to none at all; better live under a Nero than be daily exposed to all the wild horrors of anarchy. Since the middle of May we are fairly at the mercy of our Military; they hold court martials, dismiss whom they please, insult openly their Officers and Clergy; for three days and four nights on end this town exhibited an image of hell; 4,000 armed drunken soldiers impunely rioted all over, entered Communities, forced Nunneries, made their quarters good everywhere; yet to their honour be it said, no indecencies were committed; our good Nuns were greatly frightened at such Nocturnal visits, some Seminarists were roughly handled; one in particular for making difficulty in joining the rioters received a thrust which should have proved mortal had not the point of the sword met with a rib. The English students were repeatedly dragged through the streets; my youth happily escaped; similar disagreeable scenes have been since repeated, tho in an inferior degree; the students have in a great measure abandoned the town. During these last ten days, owing to the great exertions of our Municipal officers we have enjoyed peace, but are much affraid of the approaching 14 of July. At present about 1200 Electors for the Assemblée du departement (fixed at Douay) are in Town; upon their choice our happiness greatly depends. Our future legal existence is still a problem; in 7ber [i.e. September] the fate of Universities, Colleges etc will be ultimately decided; each Department with a Bishop is allowed only one large Episcopal seminary; this University is to be suppressed; foreign Establishments expect to be excepted, but if no mercy be shown to National Foundations what have not foreign ones to dread? . . . scarce even can I think of the french Nation capable of seizing on the property of those to whom they gave shelter; yet my ideas are gloomy, all principles are a late overturned, nothing henceforth can surprise me . . .[5]

Mr Farquharson's main fears were that the proposed reorganisation of French education would affect his college, and that the college's landed property would be taken over by the French authorities in exchange for an equivalent in money. On 28th October his fears were temporarily abated with the passage of a decree whereby foreign establishments were to be left alone by the French authorities.[6] In November he was further reassured when the Assembly agreed to continue the College's pension of 2000 livres on the royal treasury.[7] In December 1790 two new Highland boys arrived at Douay, and in January 1791 they were followed by two Lowland boys,[8] a sign that neither Mr Farquharson nor the Scottish bishops had yet given up the hope that the Scots College at Douay would be allowed to continue untouched by the French.

By the end of January 1791 Mr Farquharson was again giving way to depression. Letters to and from Rome were being regarded with grave suspicion, and he was afraid that his correspondence with Mr Thomson would soon be stopped:

> The world is mad all over, nor can the days of anti-Christ be far distant.[9]

In April, however, he was able to send Mr Thomson a further report:

> Last week we had bloody scenes in this town: two worthy citizens were hung to our lamp irons by our lawless Military, without any form of trial, and the most shocking barbarities exercised upon their dead carcases . . .
>
> Of the numerous clergy of this town, only two complied and took the vile oath, and one of them has since been recompensed with the mitre of this department.[10]

In July changes took place which directly affected the Scots students at the college:

> Last week successors were appointed to our worthy Professors who hitherto have successfully fought their battles with the new-modelled time-serving masters. What am I to do with our

youths? Our present Patents force me to send them thither, and I greatly question if . . . I can obtain new ones. Conformity in Religious sentiments will not be insisted on, yet there are other impediments, and as my Boys make a conspicuous figure in said school, their absence will be resented and expose me.[11]

By the beginning of 1792 Mr Farquharson had removed all his boys from the public schools and was teaching them in the Scots College itself. In this he was aided by the former principal and another professor, both of whom had been deposed from Anchim College and had found refuge with Mr Farquharson.[12]

Although to continue the boys' education at the public schools became undesirable if not impossible after July 1791, there was still a chance that the Scots College itself might be saved for the Mission. In April 1791 Mr Farquharson decided to press for a new administration for the College. He proposed that the whole administration of the College should devolve on the Scottish bishops as heads and trustees of the Scottish Mission, to which the College properly belonged.[13] In this way the College would be recognised officially to be Scottish property and as such inalienable. For a time he was hopeful of achieving this solution to the problem of securing the continuation of the College.

The opening months of 1792 saw Mr Farquharson using all his diplomacy to keep on good terms with his district officials. He and other British priests in Douay were accused of having refused to take the oath of civil obedience. They pointed out that, as they were foreigners, they could not be bound by French oaths. Then the town council tried to overturn the administration of the Scots College, which was connected with Anchim College — the council was annoyed that the Scots boys had been withdrawn from Anchim College.

Wrangles with French bureaucrats continued; Mr Farquharson, in spite of the terrors of the Revolution, was determined to save his College. One cannot help but admire his courage and tenacity when one reads the reports he was sending home:

> *February 1792:* The present wild system cannot possibly hold, and as the old one is reduced to atoms I despair of seeing it revive; hence our future fate is highly problematical; our constitutional prelates are busy ordaining whosoever presents himself to make up the vast deficit; the refractory clergy are shockingly used and sanctifying our prisons; our once peaceable peasants are metamorphosed into furies; a mad cap or two, well paid and fully armed, force a whole village to what they please, for if the least opposition is made, armed soldiers are let loose from the neighbouring towns . . .[14]
>
> *July 1792:* I have been obliged to change the dress of my boys; none dare stir without doors but in secular Cloaths and with a flying tricolor cockade to his hat . . .[15]

Andrew Scott, who was a student at Douay, and who was destined to become a bishop, wrote, in August 1792, to Mr George Mathison, the priest at Auchinhalrig:

> . . . besides the extraordinary expenses laid out in procuring us a new kind of dress, the Ecclesiastical habit which we formerly wore being now proscribed, the College rents are all paid in paper money, on which the loss is never less than a third. If the present miseries continue for any time it is probable that some more will be obliged to leave the College which is already in great straits . . .
>
> . . . The Jacobin or republican party has now got the upper hand in the Assembly as well as most parts of the kingdom. Their project is either to assassinate the king or to deprive him of the little authority they have left him. . . . Not a day passes on which some horrid scene is not acted in some part of the kingdom; and the king is blamed for everything . . . The king has as yet

protected the unhappy clergy and hindered them from falling a prey to their enemies; but when he is no more they will be hunted like wild beasts and butchered wherever they are found. If any such thing happens our College runs a great risk for we pass for the greatest Aristocrates in the town, and we have so much liberty in this free country that we cannot go to walk without a passport from the magistrates.[16]

A month after Mr Scott wrote the above letter the September massacre took place. Hundreds of French priests lost their lives. Mr Farquharson wrote:

No news from Paris since my last. I have not been able to learn as yet whither or not the good Bp of Rhodez has escaped. Both the Irish houses of Paris have been sent adrift; within a limited time all were ordered to leave the kingdom; the Eng. monks mean to follow, and I question not, but they're off ere now. This is rather alarming for us others, yet hitherto we're left unmolested. A new oath is to be tendered . . . Against the royal authority, (which now is no more) it seems particularly aimed; many worthy persons even Eccles. have swallowed it rather than lose all and leave the kingdom. . . . I detest oaths as much as any quaker alive yet dare not condemn those who so far conform. You have surely heard of the fatal edict of the 26th ult. against Eccles: within 8 days all refractory fontionnaires publics viz curates, vicars, professors and superiors were sent off; next week 14 others were denounced and expelled; last week 52 more were added to the black list; scarce remains there a non-conforming Eccles. amongst us; foreigners have been hitherto spared, yet they ly equally under the lash of the law and at the mercy of the first informer . . .[17]

On 1st February, 1793 war was declared between Britain and France. In a long letter to Bishop Geddes, Mr Farquharson expressed his sorrow that after over two hundred years France had withdrawn its protection from the Scots Colleges within its domains. He commented on the irony of his situation:

It is an unlucky circumstance for us that Britain upon account of some turbulent individuals, should think of suspending its palladium of liberty, the habeas corpus act; what should the french be tempted to retaliate? Our case it must be owned is widely different from that of other particulars, yet to this in the present ferment little attention would be paid. Our situation will prove singularly curious, if expelled from this [word missing, letter torn] land, on account of our Native Country, which still deems us disaffected [and has not] as yet relaxed one iota of its absurd and barbarous laws; the most enthusiastic Bigot [would] blush to put them in execution, still however they disgrace our National Code.[18]

On 18th February, 1793 all British property in Douay was sequestered; seals were put on all the doors and chests containing anything of value; and the inmates of the British seminaries and religious houses in the town were kept under what amounted to house arrest.[19] At last, at the end of February, Mr Farquharson bowed to the inevitable and set about procuring, from London, passports to allow himself and his students to enter Britain. Thanks largely to George Chalmers, the passports were in Mr Farquharson's hands by March 23rd.[20] On April the first eight Douay students landed safely in England. They were sent to Scalan, and, after a few months, six of them set out for Valladolid. In June Mr Farquharson and the remaining students were evicted from the College:

Upon the 11th ult. the leading members of our Department, District or Municipality, paid me a visit and read me an arrete, the purport of which was, that the public stood in immediate need of a state prison for suspected persons, that french community could not answer, being so ruined, that troops could not be lodged therein, that after having narrowly inspected the British establishments mine was unluckily but unanimously pitched upon on account of its having but one issue, one staircase, and high walls all around; that they did not in the least mean to encroach on property which as belonging to foreigners was sacred, that as a proof of their respect for it all damage should be paid, and a considerable house rent paid; that in consequence of allum dominum they could equally seize for a time the property of any other individual.[21]

Even Mr Farquharson, for all his determined optimism, cannot have believed such empty promises. He and his students were given three hours to vacate the College. Mr Farquharson still refused however to admit defeat. His story is told by Abbé MacPherson who was at Bruges on his way to Rome when the Scots boys arrived there:

> On Friday 16th [the four Douay boys] were turned out of their House together with all the English and ordered so many leagues from town, there to remain till further orders. Mr Farqn with his Boys came to a village near their country house, where they rested for that night. Next day he got intelligence that all the English Benedictines were imprisoned, and that search was making for every British subject. He for 100ll procured a guide for the Boys, accompanied them himself till within a few leagues of the confines [of the convent at Bruges] whence he turned back to try if possible to meet some of the people whom he had intrusted with the moveables of the College that he got conveyed out of the House. The Boys arrived here without incurring any great danger, and we anxiously look out for the Principal every hour . . .

The convent at Bruges proved to be a gathering point for Catholic refugees. When the Scots boys arrived, it was sheltering some English Franciscans who had had to lie in a ditch, covered with mud and water, for several hours while the French searched the area, always within hearing, and often within sight of them.[22]

For almost two months no word of Mr Farquharson reached Scotland, and his friends began to fear the worst. By November, however, thanks to an incredible stroke of fortune, he was safe in Scotland. As he explained to Abbé MacPherson:

> . . . it was not in my power to rejoin you at Bruges without sacrificing our establishment and all which I could not in honour do, as we were at that period legally secured and constitutionally guaranteed. The whole of September I passed with Mr Alexander Innes at Paris; saw there mischief brooding against us, which made me return to Douay; upon the 9th of October the all destroying decree was passed; extraordinary carriers were everywhere sent and upon the 12th at midday the gates of Douay were shut that none of us might escape. Most luckily and accidentally I went out of town that morning to dine with a farmer, and on my return towards 4 o clock was met by some of my good french friends, who on finding me out of town, started in time to give me notice. The fatal decree (made in consequence of one of their deputies being hung at Toulon by Lord Hood, which Im assured by all here and at London is absolutely false) ordered all British subjects to be arrested immediately and sent into the interior; their goods confiscated, 10 years' imprisonment to any magistrate who is dilatory in putting said decree into execution; same penalty against any one who conceals any of our effects or lodges us for any short time without declaring us or giving us up. On seeing the decree and on hearing some other particulars from my friends, with their advice and assistance I made off, lay that night and next day concealed on the frontier; got two guides and ensueing night made good my escape, passed without being perceived the French and Austrian lines and arrived safe and sound but much fatigued at Orchie, where I was kindly welcomed by the Austrian garrison. All our British subjects at Douay were arrested, and imprisoned there for three days and then sent 40 miles into the interior to a place called Dourlery to be kept as Ostages whilst the war lasts; twelve of the English students made their escape out of the open carts whilst they were conducting them and joined me at Tournay. The Nuns of our English Convents have been treated in a like manner. I have had no accounts yet of my friend Mr Innes. Most luckily for me, I previously sent off all my boys, for had one of them been arrested I must have stayed.[23]

The English students were released from prison in 1795.[24] To find out what happened to Mr Innes, we must ascertain what happened to the Scots College at Paris during the French Revolution.

In 1788 Mr James Cattanach arrived in Scotland from the Scots College in

Paris. He was the last student to be ordained at Paris before the outbreak of the French Revolution. Indeed, in 1789, there do not seem to have been any students from the Scottish Mission training for the priesthood there, although there may well have been some lay students whose families were domiciled in France. There is, in the Blairs Letters, reference to only one student other than Mr Cattanach returning to Scotland from the College:

> Another youth from Grisy [i.e. Paris], of the name of MacLeod, after having applied himself to medicine for a couple of years, returned last summer [1789] to the Highlands in quality of Physician.[25]

The indications are that by the end of 1789 there were no boys from Scotland studying in the Scots College at Paris. The Principal of the College was Mr Alexander Gordon. In 1789 the prefect of studies of the College, Mr Henry Innes, left to become the chaplain to a Mrs Chichester in the south of England. He was replaced at Paris by his brother, Mr Alexander Innes, who sent the following report to Bishop Geddes in December 1789:

> Since the affairs of Versailles 5 and 6 of October everything has been quite here under the ——————— of the National Assembly which carries everything ——————— it and continues to settle the constitution in an entire new ——————— without control in the present situation of things the Royal sanction follows the decrees of the Assembly as the shadow follows the body.[26]

The College at Douay was threatened by mob violence and by the proposal of educational reform in France. The College at Paris faced a further threat, a threat from within. Principal Gordon was determined to act independently of the Scottish Mission. Mr Thomson spelled out the problem in a letter to Bishop Geddes:

> Have you taken no course with Compys [i.e. the Mission's] funds in town house at Paris as yet? Do you still leave it in Mr Gordon's power to stop or retain what part of them he pleases? I would sell them for two reasons: first because I don't consider them as perfectly secure, there, especially in the present distracted and Bankrupt Situation of the Nation, and I wish you may not suffer on that account, and secondly to put it out of the power of Mr Gordon or anyone else to stop the Mission money when the whim strikes them. The money could be settled in british funds or in any other way it would be more secure and you would get better interest for it.[27]

What particularly perturbed Mr Thomson was that Principal Gordon, in addition to running the Scots College at Paris, also controlled the funds of the Scottish Mission which were invested in French funds at Paris.

In June 1790 Principal Gordon sent a reassuring letter to Bishop Geddes:

> What will be the final result of our public funds here I cannot determine, and to give my conjectures is needless. One thing you may depend upon is that I shall take the same care of your property as I shall do of our own . . .[28]

In October he sold the Mission's five East India Actions because, having fallen very low, they suddenly rose 'by a mere trick'[29] to what was reckoned to be a good price. The Mission received £320.6.3d. for them. This small sum was virtually all that was salvaged of the funds of the Scottish Mission invested in France.

If the Mission funds invested in France were threatened by the Revolution, so too were the valuable archives deposited in the Paris College. The situation was complicated when the French government dissolved the Carthusian House in Paris. The Prior of the Carthusians had been the superior of the Scots College;

now that he was no longer prior, on whom should the superiority devolve? In Bishop Hay's words:

> The Prior of the Carthusians is now no more; are the present masters to become the only Superiors and be under no Controul? This doubtless deserves our serious attention. If it were to be put on the same footing as Douay, so that the nomination of its superiors at least should belong to the VVAA [i.e. the Vicars Apostolic] it might turn out yet a Benefit to Religion and the Mission, but this I suppose the present Superiors would not be fond of, and it is not impossible but they may be contriving to get it settled in a way that they may be as independent of VVAA as formerly, that is that they may be the sole masters, in which case I am perfectly persuaded that it never will be of much service to this Mission.[30]

Of one thing Bishop Hay was sure, and that was that the papers deposited at the College were outwith the control of Principal Gordon:

> ... might it not be proper to let him [Mr Andrew Stuart] know that the Papers in Grisey are not the Property of that house, but a deposit, and belong to the Scotch Catholics as a body. Its present superiors cannot appropriate it to themselves, nor to the house, nay those left by the Archbishop of Glasgow, as I have heard, are ordered to be returned to Glasgow if ever religion should be restored. Could not some steps then be taken to get part at least of the Price allotted to the mission etc.[31]

Bishop Hay hoped to sell some of the Paris archives as the Scottish Mission stood much in need of extra funds. By November 1791 such a sale seemed likely. Bishop Geddes wrote to Bishop Hay from London:

> ... I have learned that the king wishes to purchase King James' papers, and the only difficulty appeared to arise from a Doubt whether the price should come from the Privy Purse or from the public money.[32]

Bishop Geddes, while he was in London, also had talks with Sir Joseph Banks and other trustees of the British Museum regarding the Parish archives.[33]

Needless to say, Principal Gordon was implacably opposed to any such negotiations on the part of the Scottish bishops:

> You will do well to tell such people in Scotland as talk of petitioning the National Assembly that the Mss belonging to the College may be sent them, that such petition on their part will only serve to defeat the very purpose of such petition, that I will take very ill any such measures, that I will counteract them, if carried into execution without my previous consent, and that I can counteract them effectually were the whole kingdom of Scotland to sign the petition.[34]

In the end, the question of who had the right to dispose of the Paris archives was largely academic. Most of the deposits, including King James VII's original memoirs, were lost in 1793. Only a few of the more valuable manuscripts ultimately found their way home to the Scottish Mission.[35]

It was perhaps because of its valuable archives that Principal Gordon was able to persuade the British Government to intervene on behalf of the Paris College. On 5th March 1790 the Duke of Leeds instructed Lord Robert Fitzgerald, the British Minister at Paris, to present to the French government, should it become necessary, a memorial stating the particular circumstances surrounding the Paris College, and requesting that it be allowed either to remain unmolested and unchanged, or to sell out and remove from France with all its property.[36]

Mr Thomson, in Rome, learned of the result of this application to the French government and informed Bishop Hay:

What I wrote you about Mr Gordon's having applied to the British charge d'affairs in behalf of the College at Paris, and of the latter having applied to the National Assembly by order of the Court of Britain is very true. It has been written here from Paris . . . The Assembly has deliberated upon it, has taken it amiss, and put a wrong construction on the application, but notwithstanding the high hand with which they are carrying on matters in France, they will be obliged to pay some regard to the Interposition of the Court of Britain in behalf of its subjects and their property.[37]

Principal Gordon had applied directly to the British Government for help, without mentioning his intentions to the Scottish bishops. His refusal to discuss anything with them forced Bishop Geddes, in the autumn of 1791, to make the long journey to Paris because, as he informed Mr Thomson:

Principal Gordon maintains that we have no Right to interfere with his College and has plans of his own . . . which he does not choose to communicate fully; but they appear to be very dangerous.[38]

When he arrived in Paris, Bishop Geddes found that Principal Gordon, perhaps influenced by an old quarrel he had had with Bishop Hay, was determined to go his own way. He believed that, in the interest of maintaining Catholic principles, the College should be removed from France. So far the bishops might have agreed with the Principal, had the latter not insisted that he had the right to take the necessary steps to re-establish the College outside France without consulting the Scottish bishops in any way.[39] This Bishop Geddes was determined to prevent. By February 1792 he had persuaded Principal Gordon to meet with the Prior of the Carthusians, and two arbitrators chosen by himself, to ascertain with whom authority over the College should now be vested. Following this meeting, Principal Gordon reluctantly agreed to consult the Scottish bishops in any plan he might formulate for selling the College.[40] The meeting had agreed that the College had been founded for the education of Scottish Catholics by Scottish priests, and that it was therefore the responsibility of Scottish Catholics, whose representatives were the Scottish Vicars Apostolic and their coadjutors. The College was not the responsibility or the property of any individual, not even of the Principal.[41]

By the end of August 1792, Principal Gordon had decided that it was no longer safe for him to stay in Paris. He planned to leave the College in the care of a lawyer and tried to make Mr Alexander Innes leave France along with him. This Mr Innes resolutely refused to do. The Prior of the Carthusians disapproved of Mr Gordon's plan and immediately named Mr Innes procurator of the College. To this appointment Mr Gordon ultimately agreed.[42] By 15th October, Principal Gordon was safe in England. Mr Innes was left in charge of the Scots College in Paris.

In February 1793 Mr Innes sent an alarming report to Bishop Geddes:

. . . you see we are at this moment in a very critical situation. In consequence *apparently* of this decree of the 14th inst.[43] Mr Farquharson wrote me that on the 18th the Department there put these elles in form on the archives, papers etc of all the British Houses at Douay, clapping a couple of Sentinels on each under the state pretence of protecting them from the mob, but in fact to prevent secreting of effects etc. In this they certainly exceeded their Commission as the Decree authorises no such proceedings but this is an instance among a thousand others of our L-b-ty which is nothing else but the despotism of the Million. A question occurs — what are they likely to do with respect to us. It is not easy to say, but we may form some judgment by what they propose with respect to their own colleges. A member of the Conven. told us that they are going to seize upon all the funds and possessions of colleges (the Colleges themselves and dependencies excepted) and put them up to sale. They are to pay the Professors and bourses out of the Nat. Treasury and establish their new systems of education.[44]

In April Mr Innes wrote to Scotland that he believed that the property of the College would be respected.[45] Six months later, on 15th October 1793, Mr Innes was arrested. It was not until 15th April 1795 that he was at last able to write from Rouen to his mother in Scotland to reassure her of his safety and to tell her of his imprisonment:

> . . . to describe half of what passed before our eyes in these days of terror and revolution would far exceed the bounds of a letter; scenes so very different from anything I would ever have formed any idea of meeting with in my retreat that it seems to me more like a dream than a reality — in effect what could be more extraordinary than to see the chief Nobility of fame entering our gates, not with pomp nor honour, but guarded like criminals and subjected to all the miseries of a prison, under the caprice of a female tyrant, one of the most complete viragos that ever existed who was appointed our Concierge – cette Etre Nationale had served several years as a solder in his Majesties horses and retained all the manieres of that profession, along with an air of Insolence which she was instructed to assume in regard of all the prisoners, more especially the Noblesse whom she tyrannised over with the greatest audacity, not allowing them to see a friend or servant nor to receive any other service than such as we could render them, and often not even that, saying she took pleasure to see them perform the meanest offices for themselves . . . such lessons are perhaps from time to time necessary to the great ones of the world least they should place too much confidence in their riches and nobility, both which at that time served only to render them more hateful in the eyes of the people. *We* as less guilty in that respect, were on several occasions more favourably dealt with, especially in that last and cruel transition they underwent, when things were at the greatest violence; with what intention God knows, that a sudden separation was made between the secular and religious, the former on an hour's warning were ordered to quit this house, where they had at least tollerable accommodation, and were conducted by companies guarded through the streets to our house at Graveline which in repair could not well contain above 80 persons, but was then, tho much demolished, thought sufficient for more than 300 noblesse and other persons [including a Scotswoman, Mrs Goldie] . . . The religious were exempt from that trial. We remained here, about 400 in number, well enough lodged and had a very humain concierge — the Creature we had before accompanying the unfortunate noblesse to exercise their patience.[46]

Mr Innes spared his mother's feeling by omitting to tell her that he and some other prisoners were unexpectedly saved from the guillotine, after their graves had been dug in the garden, by the downfall of Robespierre on 27th July 1794.[47]

In view of the alarming reports which were being sent to the Scottish Mission from France from as early as 1780, it is not surprising that the Scottish Catholic clergy condemned the French Revolution right from the start. Many Catholic families in Scotland also became personally involved when boys whom they knew well were in danger of imprisonment or perhaps even of the guillotine. The students who came home from Douay in 1793 had families respectively in the Enzie, in New Abbey, in Kinmore, in Glengairn, in Keith and in the West Highlands. Mr Farquharson had served as missioner in Glenlivet. He had been born in Strathaven. Mr Alexander Innes had been born at Balnacraig on Deeside. Many Catholics in Scotland must have known one at least of these students or priests, especially as each individual congregation was small enough for its members to know one another. This must surely have been one reason why the British Government never had to doubt the loyalty of the Catholics in Scotland.

NOTES

1 Franklin L. Ford, *Europe, 1780-1830* (London, 1976), pp. 114-5.

2 Bernard Ward, *The Dawn of the Catholic Revival in England, 1781-1803,* (London, 1909), Vol. II, pp. 2-6.

3 Franklin L. Ford, *Europe, 1780-1830*, pp. 152-3.

4 John Farquharson to Bishop Hay, 25th January 1790, B.L.

5 John Farquharson to Bishop Hay, 5th July 1790, B.L.

6 John Farquharson to Bishop Geddes, 1st November 1790, B.L.

7 John Farquharson to John Thomson, 26th November 1790, B.L.

8 Bishop Geddes to Bishop Hay, 10th February 1791, B.L.

9 Mr Farquharson to Mr Thomson, 29th January 1791, B.L.

10 Mr Farquharson to Mr Thomson, 1st April 1791, B.L.

11 Mr Farquharson to Bishop Hay, 25th July 1791, B.L.

12 Mr Farquharson to Mr Thomson, 22nd February 1792, B.L.

13 Mr Farquharson to Bishop Hay, 21st April 1791, B.L.

14 Mr Farquharson to Mr Thomson, 22nd February 1792, B.L.

15 Mr Farquharson to Bishop Geddes, 26th July 1792, B.L.

16 Andrew Scott to George Mathison, 3rd August 1792, B.L.

17 Mr Farquharson to Bishop Geddes, 26th September 1792, B.L.

18 Mr Farquharson to Bishop Geddes, 14th February 1793, B.L.

19 Mr Farquharson to Bishop Geddes, 28th February 1793, B.L.

20 Mr Farquharson to Bishop Geddes, 23rd March 1793, B.L.

21 Mr Farquharson to Bishop Geddes, 5th July 1793, B.L.

22 Abbé MacPherson, Bruges to Bishop Geddes, 24th August, 1793, B.L.

23 Mr Maxwell and Mr Farquharson to Abbé MacPherson, 5th and 17th December 1793, B.L.

24 Bernard Ward, *The Dawn of the Catholic Revival,* Vol. II, p. 105 (pp. 73 *et seq* give the story of the fate of the English College at Douay).

25 John Farquharson to John Thomson, 22nd October 1789, B.L.

26 Alexander Innes to Bishop Geddes, 13th December 1789, B.L. (letter torn).

27 John Thomson to Bishop Geddes, 15th August 1789, B.L.

28 Principal Gordon to Bishop Geddes, 1st June 1790, B.L.

29 Principal Gordon to Bishop Geddes, 18th October 1790, B.L.

30 Bishop Hay to Bishop Geddes, 26th December 1790, B.L.

31 Bishop Hay to Bishop Geddes, 23rd November 1790, B.L.

32 Bishop Geddes to Bishop Hay, 11th November 1791, B.L.

33 Bishop Geddes to Bishop Hay, 14th November 1791, B.L.

34 Principal Gordon to Bishop Geddes, 1st June 1790, B.L.

35 The story of these archives is told in David MacRoberts, 'The Scottish Catholic Archives', *Innes Review* 1977, pp. 87-94.

36 The Duke of Leeds to Lord Robert Fitzgerald, 5th March 1790, B.L.

37 Mr Thomson to Bishop Hay, 10th July 1790, B.L.

38 Bishop Geddes to Mr Thomson, 1st September 1791, B.L.

39 Bishop Geddes to Mr Thomson, 4th December 1791, B.L.

40 Bishop Geddes to Bishop Hay, 29th February 1792, B.L.

41 'Proposals regarding the Scotch College of Paris made to its Principal Dr Alex. Gordon by JG', 1792, B.L.

42 Bishop Geddes to Bishop Hay, 24th September 1792, B.L.

43 This decree put the future of the British Colleges under review, meanwhile freezing their assets.

44 Alexander Innes to Bishop Geddes, 28th February 1793, B.L.

45 Alexander Innes to Bishop Geddes, 15th April 1793, B.L.

46 Alexander Innes, Rouen to his mother at Balnacraig in Scotland, 15th April 1793, B.L.

47 David MacRoberts, 'Scottish Catholic Archives', *Innes Review* 1977, p. 90.

13

The Effect of the Napoleonic Wars: Rome

THE Scottish Mission, in 1793, lost its property and funds in France. By the end of 1793 Rome was being threatened by the French. Over the next five years Abbé MacPherson was to endure the same fears and uncertainty for the future which had so undermined Mr Farquharson's health at Douay.

In January 1793 Peter MacLachlan, one of the students at the Scots College, Rome sent Bishop Hay a long account of the French threat to Rome, of the murder of a French Admiral by the mob in Rome, and of the Pope's refusal to fly the French 'Arms of Liberty' from any flagpole in Rome.[1]

The French threat to Rome moved the Pope to ask for British protection. This gave the Scottish bishops fresh hope that they might be able to obtain National Superiors for their College: the British Government could be asked to request the granting of National Superiors for the three British Colleges at Rome.

Bishop Geddes had already suggested, in 1792, that such an approach be made. In February 1793 he raised the subject again with Bishop Douglas,[2] who sent the following report to Scotland:

> ... Rome has thought proper to employ [me] ... to obtain the protection of Great Britain in the imminent danger to which Rome was exposed etc. The Cardinal Antonelli pledged me his word that there was nothing which would be denied me at Rome, if I would exert myself and did succeed in procuring the protection of this Court, and now, it having pleased Almighty God to grant success to my intreaties and to incline the hearts of our Ministry to protect the Temporalities of his Holiness, I advised with Mr Smelt [the English agent at Rome], and have directed him to claim the Cardinal's promise and to ask for National Superiors to our *two* Colleges as soon as he should see a proper opportunity for making the application ... and in his last letter to me which I received on the 6th of June, he told me that he should wait till Lord Hood's fleet appeared in the Mediterranean; his application, he thought, would be much enforced by the sight of the Fleet.
>
> Should this application fail of success, it is my intention to pray Lord Grenville to support my petition ... Should I stand in need of requesting Lord Grenville's good offices I shall previously desire Bishop Geddes to send me a letter [for] Dundas with whom he is acquainted, requesting that Gentleman's interest with Lord G[renville] and with Rome. As I shall, very probably, have to send our Missionaries to the East Indies, where Mr Dundas is so powerful, his intercession will have a powerful weight with the Propaganda.[3]

This letter demonstrates clearly how religion and politics could be made to work together for mutual benefit.

In August 1793, when Abbé MacPherson was in London, on his way to Rome, he had several conversations with George Chalmers, author of *Caledonia*. Chalmers was sure that Mr Dundas and Lord Grenville, if properly applied to, would have no hesitation in helping the Scottish Mission to obtain National Superiors for their College at Rome. He suggested that Abbé MacPherson should draw up a memorial, promising that he would present it personally to them.[4] Abbé MacPherson passed on this suggestion to Bishop Geddes:

> ... you should write an ostensible letter to Mr Chalmers about the unhappy College, insisting particularly on the advantage that would accrue to Government by having that House under National Superiors. That is the light in which men in power must consider it, else they'll do nothing in the matter.[5]

Abbé MacPherson was doubtful whether co-operation with the English Mission would be of much advantage, especially as Bishop Douglas was not an active man, and because he was too involved in disputes with his own priests to have time to fight to obtain National Superiors. By the beginning of 1794, as Abbé MacPherson had predicted, Anglo-Scottish co-operation had broken down. Bishop Hay received no further communications from Bishop Douglas and concluded that the English preferred to negotiate independently of the Scots. However, as he shrewdly pointed out:

> In case our friends in England make the application by themselves, and do not succeed, it will be so much the better for us not to have had a hand in it, ... and if they do succeed we will undoubtedly reap the same benefit and perhaps with greater cordiality at Hilton [i.e. the Scots College, Rome] that we did not join in the Application. Whilst at the same time our friends in England could not blame us, as they will not accept of our aid, and to make an application to Ministry by ourselves would I am afraid have worse consequences.[6]

On 1st March 1794 Abbé MacPherson confirmed Bishop Hay's suspicions. Bishop Douglas had already antagonised the Papal Curia by opposing Monsignor Erskine. He then made matters worse by writing to Cardinal Antonelli and to the Pope, assuring them that the British Ministry was going to demand National Superiors for the British Colleges. No demand was forthcoming, and so Bishop Douglas lost credibility in Rome.[7]

In August Bishop Douglas wrote to Bishop Hay explaining that he had been warned that a demand by the British Government might offend Rome; on the other hand, if Rome refused the demand, this might offend the British Government. It was therefore in the interest of good relations between the two countries that the British Ministry should avoid the subject of National Superiors.[8]

The British Ministry might decline to interfere officially in matters relating to the Scots College at Rome, but early in 1795 Sir John Cox Hippisley, the agent of the British Government at Rome, wrote to Cardinal Zelada on the subject of National Superiors.[9] He pointed out that the Italian rectors had long proved unsatisfactory; that Britain and Ireland were short of priests; that British parents were reluctant to allow their sons to go to Rome as long as they were placed under foreign rectors. He explained that the British Secretaries of State had been approached on the subject of National Superiors. The Secretaries, though they thought it would be difficult for the British Ministry to intervene, at the Court of Rome, on behalf of religious establishments, were nevertheless agreed that it was harmful for British priests to receive their education under foreigners whose character and political outlook were necessarily different from their own. The

British Secretaries of State, though they could not intervene officially, would be very glad to hear that National Superiors had been appointed.

The argument that British priests should be educated under British superiors, and preferably in Britain rather than on the continent, was one that was used with some success throughout this period. With Britain at war with France, and with France in control of so much of Europe, it was natural that the British Government would prefer priests to be educated in colleges remote from the influence of French revolutionary ideals. Also, if the colleges on the continent came under French control, the students might be educated to act as French agents in Britain.

At about the same time that Hippisley wrote to Cardinal Zelada, Abbé MacPherson made a similar appeal to Monsignor Erskine, stressing the harm that had been done to the Scots College through bad administration, and pointing out how crucial to the Scottish Mission was its College at Rome now that the two Colleges in France had been lost.[10]

A few months later the campaign for National Superiors received a severe setback with the death of Cardinal Campanelli, who had been favourably inclined to the proposal.[11] The Pope was in favour of granting National Superiors but he was opposed by the powerful Cardinals, Albani and Antonelli, and, as he was old and in poor health, it was unlikely that he would risk offending such influential men.[12] However, thanks to Hippisley's exertions, Abbé MacPherson was hopeful that some advantageous reforms would be introduced soon. Three months later, in September 1795, the Scottish bishops sent a letter to the Pope himself, in which they stressed the urgent need for the speedy granting of National Superiors.[13] In January 1796 it seemed likely that their request would be granted, and Abbé MacPherson warned them that it would be undiplomatic for them to nominate him as first rector.[14] By April, however, it had become obvious that there would be no speedy reform of the Scots College. Abbé MacPherson, who had intended to delay sending for more boys until the reform should be accomplished, saw no point in delaying any further and asked the Scottish bishops to send him two students.[15]

Two months later, in June 1796, Abbé MacPherson, far from wanting more students, was wondering whether he should send his two existing students to safety. Bologna had been taken by the French, and Rome no longer seemed safe:

> I think its full time for me to provide for the safety of my two dear boys. It is with the deepest regret I think of parting with them . . . Prince Augustus went off two nights ago. I saw him before his departure. He advised me to flee with my charge. Flee I cannot, and will not, while there is a probability of my being of any use to you here. The Irish agent is gone, Mr Smelt departs for Naples one of these days. They can do it — their constituents do not depend for their maintenance on this place as mine do. The [Scots] boys can be got to Naples or Tuscany in two days' time . . .[16]

Abbé MacPherson was more courageous than many people. Nobles and cardinals fled the city; when Abbé MacPherson visited Cardinal Brancadoro, he found him 'dressing in his robes, and in such a panic that it was useless to talk to him'. Among the common people, too, panic spread:

> Such noise and confusion as there was in town, such dejection, and despair surpasses conception. Not a House but resounded with the cries of women and children; not a

countenance but expressed terror and dismay. Many entirely lost their judgments, and parents tried to make away with their daughters by a violent death, to preserve them from insult. If the courier [bringing the news that Rome was not in danger] had delayed for 24 hours more, scenes would have happened here that would have equalled anything that is barbarous in history, and it is too probable that this day Rome would be a mass of ruins.[17]

Throughout the panic Abbé MacPherson and his students remained in Rome, and by 2nd July the former was able to reassure Bishop Hay that the danger had passed and that a peace treaty was to be concluded. The treaty was to include provision for the establishment of French garrisons and for the removal of some statues and pictures to France along with about a hundred manuscripts from the Vatican library.

In August an edict was published in Rome whereby

... any Frenchman may insult with impunity every individual, while it is, in the strongest terms, declared a capital crime punishable by certain death, on the part of the Romans, to resent any injury from them, farther than to complain to impotent magistrates.[18]

The French were 'still greater enemies to Religion than to civil order'.

By February 1797 the French were again massing at Bologna, and an attack on Rome seemed certain. Again Rome was spared by a treaty. On 11th February Abbé MacPherson wrote:

Rome has sued for peace, it is a question if it will be granted, and if granted the terms must be such as the brave Bonaparte pleases. My two pupils are so terrified that they will not stay here if the French should come, and I must fall on some method to send them back to you. For my own part the humanity and generosity of the French has been such since they entered Italy that I see no danger I can fear by remaining and I am determined to keep my ground while I can get bread, and can be of any use to our poor mission.[19]

Cardinal Albani refused to provide any money to help the two Scots students to get away from Rome to safety. He did, however, order the rector of the Scots College to hand over to Abbé MacPherson the College's money and church plate. The Abbé then discovered that the students of the English College were relying on him to provide for their escape as well. He succeeded in procuring passports and hired carriages which conveyed the two Scots boys and the fifteen English boys to Civita Vecchia.[20] There they were befriended by Mr Sloane, business agent of the British Resident, Mr Graves. Mr Sloane, who had himself been a student at the Scots College, Rome, was to prove an invaluable friend to the Scottish Mission after Abbé MacPherson returned to Scotland. For the moment, however, the danger receded and the students were soon able to return to their Colleges, Napoleon having marched his army north again to fight against Archduke Charles of Austria.[21]

Rome had been spared twice from occupation by French troops. It faced nevertheless the inevitable consequence of Napoleon's invasion of Italy — a tottering economy. The Scottish Mission had funds invested in the Luoghi di Monte for the support of its College at Rome. In November 1793 Abbé MacPherson suggested that the Mission should sell its Luoghi shares. The Pope, however, refused to allow this,[22] and in 1798 these shares were lost to the Mission when the French finally occupied Rome. But even before this final blow had fallen, Abbé MacPherson was experiencing financial problems. A general scarcity of money had led to the imposition of new taxes and to a proposal that all lands belonging to religious establishments should be sold. Propaganda, as well as suffering from these general problems, was facing unprecedented financial demands. Its overseas missions in China and other parts of the east had formerly been financed largely by France. These French funds had been withdrawn. In addition, French foreign policy had lost Propaganda much of its capital. Faced with growing demands on its dwindling resources, Propaganda was no longer able to help the Scots College or the Scottish Mission.[23]

Even against this background of political uncertainty and financial chaos, Abbé MacPherson never lost sight of his aim to obtain a National Superior for the Scots College. Sir John Cox Hippisley also continued to involve himself in the campaign. In October 1797 he wrote — presumably to Bishop Hay:

> You may as well both to the P[ope] and the C[ardinal] Protector take notice that when Mr J.H.
> 'represented to the king's ministers the steps he had taken with respect to national superiors they highly applauded the measure and the Hereditary Honours since conferred by His Majesty on Sir J.H. are a proof how acceptable his conduct was during his residence at Rome.'
> This will be gratifying to H.H. [His Holiness] and is supported by the fact and you may say the same to Card. Albani.[24]

Sir John Cox Hippisley's intervention in the matter of National Superiors persuaded the Italian rector of the English College to tender his resignation. This made the granting of an English Superior there much more likely and Abbé MacPherson urged the Scottish bishops to grasp the opportunity to press for a Scottish superior for the Scots College. The Cardinal Duke of York had already promoted the English cause with the Pope, and would be pleased, if asked, to do the same for the Scots.[25]

Unfortunately the English cause collapsed on the eve of success, due to a dispute as to who would be the first rector. The English bishops nominated the English agent, Mr Smelt, in December 1797. The Cardinal Duke opposed this nomination.[26] In February 1798 Bishop Douglas was still determined on Mr Smelt, while Monsignor Erskine had added his voice to that of the Cardinal, proposing Dr Gregory Stapleton for rector.[27] In the face of such an impasse it seemed unlikely that an English rector would, after all, be appointed. By this time, however, the question of National Superiors had lost much of its relevance, the French having entered Rome.

In December 1797, during an attempted revolution, a French general had been killed just outside the French Embassy in Rome. The French ambassador had left Rome the following day, and General Berthier had been ordered to march on the city.[28] In February 1798, French troops entered Rome. Four cardinals and as many prelates were taken as hostages to Monte Cavallo. Abbé MacPherson sent an alarming report of what followed to Bishop Hay:

> On [the] 13th all Regular Troops belonging to H.H. except 500 left as a guard to his person were disbanded. On the 14th an edict was published, signed by the Treasurer commanding under very severe penalties everyone having in trust or otherwise goods of whatever nature belonging to British, Portuguese or Russians to give note of them at an appointed place within 24 hours after the publication of the Edict. This will hurt many . . . and it will ruin us, for I fear every article belonging to the mission and college will be confiscated.[29]

Abbé MacPherson's fears were justified. A week later he wrote again:

> On 20th current the Pope left this City and is gone to Tuscany . . . Yesterday our college with everything belonging to it was taken possession of in the name of the French Republic. Every civility was shown to us, and more would have been shown if a French Commissary had executed that business in place of a Roman. We are still here, and have every reason to hope that the generosity and humanity of the French nation will not suffer us to be turned out on the street without subministrating what will bring us decently to our own country.[30]

By the beginning of March the French had issued Abbé MacPherson with a series of passports[31] allowing himself and his students to travel home. Once again Abbé MacPherson was forced to take charge of the English and Irish students as well as his own two Scots boys. His loyalty and courage, and his extreme reluctance to leave his post, had matched that of his confrères in France, Mr Alexander Innes and Mr John Farquharson. Unlike them, Abbé MacPherson had only to face the well-disciplined armies of Napoleon, and not the bloodthirsty rabble of the early Revolutionary period. Nevertheless it must have been quite an ordeal conducting a party of boys right through a country which was at war with his own.

On 21st March Abbé MacPherson wrote a final letter to Bishop Hay:

> I with all the youths of our three establishments here am now ready to set off. The French, having confiscated the whole property of these houses, and of the respective missions, have generously been pleased to allow us so much as with good economy will, I hope, bear our expenses to Britain. We have likewise obtained ample Passports to go through France etc . . . and we have resolved to try it. We are 22 in all, a number too great if I could have settled otherwise with propriety and humanity. Mr Smelt fled in time, is now in Tuscany, and will take no charge of his youth; the poor Irish lads have had none to look after them for some time but a Dominican Friar, who now in the day of danger looks to himself alone. Both these colleges recommended themselves to me in a way it was impossible I could do otherwise than I have done . . . Propaganda is totally suppressed and all its funds appointed to the French Republic.[32]

By the beginning of June Abbé MacPherson's party had landed safely in England. Among the students was a little boy, William Sloane, the son of the Mr Sloane who had befriended the students the previous year at Civita Vecchia. William Sloane and another Scots boy from Rome, John Gordon, were among the first boys to be admitted to the new College at Aquhorties. John Gordon was the first priest to be ordained there.

Throughout the time that Abbé MacPherson and Sir John Cox Hippisley were trying to obtain National Superiors for the British Colleges at Rome, Great Britain and Rome were moving towards a political alliance against France. Such a radical swing in British political attitudes gave British Catholics fresh hope of emancipation.

In 1793 the British Government agreed to send its fleet to protect Rome. By June 1794 a commercial treaty between Britain and the Pope seemed likely. Abbé MacPherson believed that this would mean Sir John Cox Hippisley's being appointed British Minister at Rome. He therefore wrote a letter to Hippisley on which he obtained the signatures of all the Catholic clergy belonging to the British Dominions who were then at Rome.[33] In this letter, parallels are drawn between Britain's attitude to the Pope and its attitude to British Roman Catholics.

The letter [34] acknowledged Mr Hippisley's exertions in promoting 'a perfect conciliation and correspondence' between Britain and Rome, and spoke of the great advantages that would accrue to British Catholics from such a conciliation. It reminded Mr Hippisley that British Catholics were still

> ... often necessarily obliged ... to offer a constructive violence to Laws yet existing, though the Spirit of them has been long since dead

and hoped that an 'open, liberal Communication' between Rome and Britain would be a prelude to a repeal of all Penal Laws against Catholics.

The letter dwelt on the generosity of Pope Pius VI in supplying the British fleet with food at a time when food was scarce, and on the gratitude of the fleet for this kindness. It went on to mention the presence of a British regiment of cavalry, stationed for three months in the Papal States, and the presentation of a gold medal to each officer of the regiment in the name of the Pope.

The visit of Monsignor Erskine to England and his kind reception there by the British Royal Family and by the Ministry were mentioned. Attention was drawn to the fact that since Monsignor Erskine's arrival in England, a law had been passed discharging English Catholics from the burden of double taxes. Another Bill, which would have given British Catholics emancipation, had even been considered but had been shelved for the moment as the Ministry had not considered it prudent to advance such a measure at that time.

Jacobitism, too, was mentioned, and reference was made to the preparation by the Scottish Mission of authentic documents which would prove that Rome preached not rebellion but obedience to established governments.

This letter deliberately stressed the growing co-operation and friendliness between the Pope and the British Government. It emphasised, for instance, that a British fleet had been despatched to protect the Pope — although undoubtedly this had been a strategic manoeuvre rather than one with charity as a motive. Similarly, the Pope's kind reception of British soldiers must have owed at least as much to diplomacy as to benevolence. However, the inference to be taken from such references is clear: British Catholics should receive the same consideration from the British Government as British troops had received from the Pope.

The letter also indicates the new political significance of British Catholics in the light of Britain's resumption of diplomatic relations with the Pope. No longer could they be so easily dismissed as second-class citizens on the grounds that they were politically dangerous, although the British Government was at first cautious about openly acknowledging this. In April 1794 Sir John Cox Hippisley wrote on this subject to Abbé MacPherson:

> ... it may be extremely material that our Government should have before them Copies of the Orders of Benedict 14 ... to the Mission and such letters of Propaganda of different periods say for a century backwards which inculcate submission and even support of the established Government of Great Britain.
>
> I would wish you to examine the letters as near the Periods of the two Rebellions of 1715 and 1745; if you can find any extractions of those dates, for if they are conceived in the usual state they will be doubly valuable to prove the conclusion we wish to establish ...
>
> The Advantage of this measure is obvious because when the measure comes before Parliament their letters ... may be moved for by any member and ordered to be presented by the House.[35]

H

The question referred to in the above letter was one that was to be raised time after time as Parliament debated the granting of Catholic emancipation. It was the same question which had always caused problems from the twelfth century onwards: how far were priests and prelates accountable to their own governments, and how far must they first answer to the dictates of Rome? In 1794 Propaganda offered the services of its archivists to secure evidence that it had always advocated obedience to national governments.[36]

Abbé MacPherson, in his long letter to Sir John Cox Hippisley, mentioned the visit of Monsignor Erskine to London: in September 1793 Monsignor Erskine left Rome, ostensibly to see to some personal affairs in Scotland, but in reality on Papal business. The Pope, believing that the allied powers were shortly to hold a congress in London, wished Erskine to attend it as Papal delegate.[37] The arrangement for the visit owed much to Erskine's friend and fellow-lawyer, Sir John Cox Hippisley; as Abbé MacPherson informed Bishop Hay:

> You will have heard of the great civility Mr Erskine has received at court. It is believed a very strict commercial union will soon take place between this [i.e. Rome] and it. Mr Hippisley M.P. who is married to a sister of Madame Cicciaporci and has been here for this year past, has done a great deal to bring about this amicable intercourse. It was he who first planned out, and all along has supported Mr Erskine's Embassy. He is a man of great parts . . . there is none in Rome has such influence at this court as he.[38]

In the event, Monsignor Erskine's stay in England did little to influence Catholic affairs there, but his reception demonstrates how far attitudes towards Catholics had changed in the last decades of the eighteenth century. As for his influence in the diplomatic relations between Rome and Britain, it has been stated that

> Monsignor Erskine did not succeed in bringing the reopening of diplomatic relations between England and the Holy See any nearer.[39]

It is worth noting, however, that in October 1797 Sir John Cox Hippisley wrote:

> . . . had not the eruption of the French into the Pope's territories taken place a more frequent and direct communication could have taken place between the two Govts. and a British Resident from our Govt. was actually named tho' not sent. He was later changed to a mere Resident on the part of the British Merchants in the person of Mr Graves.[40]

While Monsignor Erskine was being kindly received at the British Court in London, one of Britain's princes, Prince Ernest Augustus, was achieving popularity in Rome. In 1793 Peter MacLachlan, one of the Scots Students, sent the following account to Bishop Hay:

> Prince Ernest Augustus the king's son has been in Rome about two months and intends to stay till towards the end of April. Yesterday Jany 13th he came to the Academy of the languages at Propaganda, where he was treated with as much respect and distinction as they could have done the Pope himself, the hall being most superbly hung with rich tapestry and a throne erected for him in the middle . . .
> P.S. This evening I have been informed that when the King's son left Propaganda last night, and having occasion to pass through the mob that was assembled . . . as soon as they perceived him they flocked round him, and began to cry out 'Viva il Re. La familia reale d'Inghilterra, Viva l'Inghilterra, Viva il Papa et Inghilterra', and could by no means be prevailed upon to depart till they had kissed his hand, as is the custom here in Italy. So much reputation has England gained here by reason of the decent and becoming behaviour of the English who resort here in vast numbers.[41]

With Britain and Rome on a friendly footing, British Catholics could no longer be regarded as a political threat. On the contrary, the British Government was able to use as agents priests whose education at the various Colleges abroad had made them proficient in European languages. For instance, in 1804 Father Alexander Horn, a Scots Benedictine, could boast of being

> ... quite alone, the only diplomatic agent of Govt. between Dresden and Naples, and between the Rhine and Vienna ... I have received indirect assurance of how pleased Govt. is with my services and this is the more agreeable to me as I am the first Roman Catholic employed in this line since the Reformation.[42]

Another Scots Benedictine who acted as a British agent was Father James Gallus Robertson, who was for many years a priest in Scotland. Before war broke out between Spain and France, 14,000 men, the cream of the Spanish army, were acting as a garrison force for Napoleon in Denmark. In 1808 Father Robertson was sent to Denmark by the Duke of Wellington. His mission was to enlist the aid of these Spanish troops in the Peninsular War against Napoleon. Posing as a German cigar merchant, Robertson made his way to Nyborg, where he disclosed his mission to the Spanish commander, the Marquis de la Romana, conveying the British Government's offer of ships to transport the Spaniards south. The offer was accepted; Romana escaped with nearly 10,000 men. Father Robertson made his way south through Europe to Linz in Austria. There he obtained copies of Wellington's despatches telling of British victories in Spain, translated them into German, and printed them as handbills which he scattered in the streets of Munich. In 1809, closely pursued by the French, Father Robertson made his way home to Britain.[43] A year later Mr William MacDonald, a secular priest, was sent secretly to France.[44]

The Revolutionary and Napoleonic Wars turned the Scottish Roman Catholic clergy into British agents as well as allies of the British Government. Men like Sir John Cox Hippisley in Rome, and Cardinal Erskine in England, helped to forge closer links between the Papacy and Britain. The same co-operation was reflected at home in the relationship between Catholics in Scotland and their Government in London.

NOTES

1 Peter MacLachlan, Rome to Bishop Hay, 14th January 1793, B.L.
2 Bishop Geddes to Bishop Hay, 7th February 1793, B.L.
3 Bishop Douglas, London to Bishop Hay, 3rd July 1793, B.L.
4 Abbé MacPherson, London to Bishop Hay, 15th August 1793, B.L.
5 Abbé MacPherson, Bruges to Bishop Geddes, 24th August 1793, B.L.
6 Bishop Hay to Bishop Geddes, 3rd January 1794, B.L.
7 Abbé MacPherson to Bishop Hay, 1st March 1794, B.L.
8 Bishop Hay to Abbé MacPherson, 16th August 1794, B.L.
9 Sir J. C. Hippisley to Cardinal Zelada, scroll letter, 15th January 1795, B.L.
10 Abbé MacPherson to Mgr. Erskine, 20th January 1795, B.L.
11 Abbé MacPherson to Bishop Hay, 7th March 1795, B.L.
12 Abbé MacPherson to Bishop Hay, 11th April 1795, B.L.
13 Bishops Hay, MacDonald and Geddes to the Pope, scroll letter, 11th September 1795, B.L.

14 Abbé MacPherson to Bishop Geddes, 2nd January 1796, B.L.

15 Abbé MacPherson to Bishop Hay, 9th April 1796, B.L.

16 Abbé MacPherson to Bishop Hay, 25th June 1796, B.L.

17 Abbé MacPherson to Bishop Hay, 2nd July 1796, B.L.

18 Abbé MacPherson to Bishop Hay, 6th August 1796, B.L.

19 Abbé MacPherson to Bishop Hay, 11th February 1797, B.L.

20 Abbé MacPherson to Bishop Hay, 18th February 1797, B.L.

21 Franklin L. Ford, *A General History of Europe, 1780-1830*, pp. 155-6.

22 Abbé MacPherson to Bishop Hay, 7th December 1793, B.L.

23 Abbé MacPherson to Bishop Hay, 17 June, 24 June, 15 July, 24 August, 1797, B.L.

24 Sir John Cox Hippisley to (?) Bishop Hay, 11th October 1797, B.L.

25 Abbé MacPherson to Bishop Hay, 26th August 1797, B.L.

26 Abbé MacPherson to Bishop Hay, 16th December 1797, B.L.

27 Abbé MacPherson to Bishop Hay, 10th February, 1798, B.L.

28 Bernard Ward, *The Dawn of the Catholic Revival in England*, Vol. II, p. 183.

29 Abbé MacPherson to Bishop Hay, 17th February 1798, B.L.

30 Abbé MacPherson to Bishop Hay, 24th February 1798, B.L.

31 These passports all survive among the Blairs Letters of 1798 in Columba House.

32 Abbé MacPherson to Bishop Hay, 21st March 1798, B.L.

33 Abbé MacPherson to Bishop Hay, 28th June 1794, B.L. encloses copy of this letter.

34 Abbé MacPherson and others to Sir John Cox Hippisley — scroll letter, 17th June 1794, B.L. enclosed in letter to Bishop Hay, 28th June 1794.

35 Sir John Cox Hippisley to Abbé MacPherson, 30th April 1794, B.L. (letter torn).

36 Abbé MacPherson to Bishop Geddes, 3rd May 1794, B.L.

37 Mr Smelt to Bishop Hay, 30th September 1793, B.L.

38 Abbé MacPherson to Bishop Hay, 1st March 1794, B.L.

39 Bernard Ward, *The Eve of Catholic Emancipation* (London, 1911), Vol. I, p. 49.

40 Sir John Cox Hippisley to Bishop Hay, 11th October 1797, B.L.

41 Peter MacLachlan to Bishop Hay, 14th January 1793, B.L.

42 Father Alexander Horn to Bishop Cameron, 20th October 1804, B.L.

43 James Robertson, *Narrative of a Secret Mission to the Danish Islands in 1808*, ed. Alex. C. Fraser (London, 1863).

44 James Kyle to Donald Carmichael, 22nd June 1810, Kyle Letters, S.C.A.

14

The Effect of the Napoleonic Wars: Valladolid

THE last of the Scots Colleges on the Continent to be affected by the Napoleonic Wars was the College at Valladolid.

In 1789 the Vice-rector of the College, Mr John Gordon, sent to Scotland an account which included mention, among other things, of the educational innovations at the University, and of Spanish attitudes towards the French Revolution:

> Every article of life is exorbitantly dear at present in Spain, and a great deal of money is necessary to buy even the few things I stand in need of . . . Compomanes has at last been made Governor of the Council. The nation in general has been happy at this promotion . . . The coronation of the King was celebrated with all possible ceremony . . .

> Few students have come to the University this year and, unless things take a change, the number must become very insignificant in a short time. Good taste is advancing fast in this country. In this University we have now got a chair of Mathematics, and it is expected that in a few years Modern Philosophy will be publickly taught all over the Kingdom. In Salamanca, Madrid and other places greek and hebrew are encouraged. Who knows but some years hence we may have our Newtons, Bradleys, Gregories and the like. The talents of the Spaniards are certainly equal to those of any other people; what is wanting is an application to useful studies and good taste.

> Our Papers have never mentioned the disturbances of France, and every precaution has been taken to hinder people from speaking of them. Our Inquisition is actually employed in gathering up any papers that have made their way into the Kingdom relative to them. It is credibly told that severals in different places have been shut up in prisons for having ventured to speak of them, as was imagined, with too great freedom.[1]

It was not until 1794 that Mr Gordon began to have any fears for the safety of his College. Spain was experiencing stirrings of unrest and Mr Gordon began to wonder if the bloody scenes of the Revolution in France were about to be repeated with even greater barbarities. In his opinion:

> The convulsions of the state would be terrible beyond expression and the madness of the rabble would run to extremities unknown even in France. We are more ignorant than our neighbours, and our breasts would easily catch the flame of liberty and equality . . . [by 'we' he means the Spanish].[2]

Another letter written by Mr Gordon in 1802 reveals some at least of the reasons why the Spanish peasants were likely to harbour revolutionary sentiments:

> It is impossible for you and others to form an idea of our present system of government. Every means is made use of to raise money to supply the luxury of our court. Almost all the pious foundations of the nation are destroyed and the funds annexed to the crown.[3]

An impoverished people who were being bled white to satisfy the rapacious demands of an extravagant court were the stuff of which the French Revolution had been made. It was little wonder that the Spanish government had tried to prevent the news of the Revolution from reaching Spain.

By 1796 French revolutionary principles were rapidly gaining ground in Spain. Not only that, but there was now talk of war breaking out between Spain and Britain.[4] Anti-clerical feeling was also increasing: French priests who had taken refuge in Spanish monasteries were being turned out and many of them were reduced, as a result, to abject poverty.[5]

It was against this background of financial difficulties and of political unrest that Mr Gordon fought to keep the Scots College going. After 1798, when the College at Valladolid was the only Scots College on the Continent that was still open, it became more important than ever that Mr Gordon should succeed in maintaining it, and of this responsibility he was well aware. In 1794 he wrote to Abbé MacPherson:

> We shall stand our ground as well and as long as we can, and if things come to the last extremity, we shall save what we can and try to find our road to Scotland.[6]

By 1796, in spite of financial problems, Mr Gordon had finished building a country house for the students at Boecillo. His main fear at this time was that if war broke out between Britain and Spain, it would be impossible for students to travel between Scotland and Valladolid.[7]

In 1802 Abbé MacPherson, who had by this time returned to Rome to try to re-establish the Scots College there, suggested that the College at Valladolid should be united with his at Rome to provide one large College. Mr Gordon turned down this proposal on the grounds that he would not be permitted to send out of the kingdom the money he received from property owned by the Scottish Mission in Spain.[8] By 1802, in any case, Mr Gordon was finding it difficult, with rising prices, to make ends meet, especially as the king had not paid the College 27,000 reals of its annual income that year.[9] Mr Gordon, however, had his own brand of insurance:

> I have at present nine students from Scotland . . . I have besides ten Spanish Children who pay pensions for their maintenance and education. They are all of our best families and in time of need their parents will befriend us.[10]

As late as January 1803, Mr Gordon was so optimistic about the future of his College that he wrote asking Bishop Cameron to send him eight more students. By April, however, he was forced to amend this request to six, as he had incurred heavy expenses in repairing the houses in Madrid which belonged to the College.[11] Even six places in Valladolid would be of great benefit to the Scottish Mission, whose only other educational institutions by now were the new, small colleges at Lismore and at Aquhorties. In October 1804 seven boys arrived at Valladolid from Scotland, unannounced and unexpected. Mr Gordon, who was by now facing unprecedented price rises for every necessity of life, was understandably annoyed at having to pay the viatics of seven boys from Scotland to Valladolid via the expensive route through Portugal.[12]

The English bishop, Bishop Douglas, was, by 1804, apprehensive about the prudence of sending more students to Spain; his fellow bishops were even more cautious; as Bishop Douglas informed Bishop Cameron:

I have sent some boys thither. My confreres have not followed my example, apprehensive that a Revolution will take place in that Kingdom; . . . the parents of those I sent thither were made acquainted with the dangerous state of the kingdom of Spain, and notwithstanding, they wished their Children to be sent.[13]

By 1806 religious communities in Spain were under threat. A Bull was published authorising the king to 'secularise the goods of Communities to a great amount',[14] and it was feared that friaries and nunneries would soon disappear altogether. One might have expected the Scots College at Valladolid to feel apprehensive that its property, too, would soon be seized. This was not the case. Mr Gordon, buoyed up with the same optimism which had prevented Mr Innes in Paris from admitting defeat, suggested that another priest be sent out from Scotland to assist in the teaching at the College. This drew a strong protest from the priest who was stationed at Tomintoul:

I am sorry to understand that the Spanish College is at such a low ebb, but in these circumstances I cannot see the propriety of asking or granting an additional master. Don Juan [Mr Gordon] has already two assistants . . .[15]

It was not until 1808 that Mr Gordon finally admitted defeat. During the late winter of 1807 and the early spring of 1808 more and more French regiments, ostensibly on their way to Portugal, remained in Spain, effectively occupying the northern half of the country. In March 1808 a dynastic crisis in the Spanish royal family resulted in Charles IV's handing his crown over to Napoleon, who bestowed it on his brother Joseph.[16] The people of Madrid, in a brave but foredoomed gesture of defiance, rebelled against the French. Mr Cameron, six years later, recalled the occasion:

The fray began in the Court of the Palace but soon it extended itself over all the town; men, women and children fought in despair; the Ladies hurled death from their windows, and children attacked the french batteries with their daggers; the streets were covered with the slain . . . At last Murat made all the Consigos go out in their robes to appease the people; when this was effected, the french seized perfidiously all they met on the Streets; a mock council of war took its seat at the fountain in the Prado, and in the style of the Revolutionary tribunals sentenced all to be shot. The fusilading continued all that night and the following day.[17]

When the Spanish king returned in 1814, after the expulsion of the French, he decreed the 2nd of May to be kept as a day of remembrance each year for all those who had fallen in Madrid in 1808.

In December 1808 Mr Gordon at last decided to send his students home. Four boys left for Scotland under the care of Mr William Wallace, who had himself as a student in 1793 been forced to leave the Scots College at Douay. The five were given a free passage to England by the English Admiral.[18] Two of the boys continued to become priests in 1815: Duncan MacKenzie for the Highland District, and John Forbes for the Lowland. Mr Gordon, Mr Cameron and one student, Sandy MacKenzie, elected to stay on in Valladolid to try to keep safe the College and its property.

NOTES

1 John Gordon, Valladolid (probably to Bishop Geddes) 16th November 1789, B.L.
2 John Gordon, Valladolid to Abbé MacPherson, Rome, 1st October 1794, B.L.

3 John Gordon, Valladolid to Abbé MacPherson, 28th September 1802, B.L.
4 John Gordon, Valladolid to Abbé MacPherson, 1st August 1796, B.L.
5 John Gordon, Valladolid to Mr Bagnall, 19th August 1796, B.L.
6 John Gordon, Valladolid to Abbé MacPherson, 1st October 1794, B.L.
7 John Gordon, Valladolid to Abbé MacPherson, 1st June 1796, B.L.
8 John Gordon, Valladolid to Abbé MacPherson, 28th September 1802, B.L.
9 John Gordon, Valladolid to Thomas Bagnall, 7th February 1802, B.L.
10 John Gordon, Valladolid to Abbé MacPherson, 29th January 1804, B.L.
11 John Gordon, Valladolid to Bishop Cameron, 29th April 1803, B.L.
12 John Gordon, Valladolid to Bishop Cameron, 11th January 1804, B.L.
13 Bishop Douglas to Bishop Cameron, 4th April 1804, B.L.
14 Mr Reid to Bishop Cameron, 4th August 1806, B.L.
15 Alexander Badenoch to Bishop Cameron, 22nd August 1806, B.L.
16 Franklin L. Ford, *Europe 1780-1830*, pp. 208-209.
17 Mr Alexander Cameron, Valladolid, 20th June 1814, B.L.
18 William Wallace to Bishop Cameron, 29th December 1808, B.L.

15

The Effect of the Napoleonic Wars:
Ratisbon and Wurzburg

THE four Scots Colleges were the most important establishments on the Continent in Scottish hands to be lost during the Revolutionary and Napoleonic wars. Other foundations, however, also suffered, notably the Scots Benedictine monasteries of Wurzburg and Ratisbon.

In 1793, after the Scots Colleges in France had been lost, Bishop Hay considered the possibility of sending boys to Wurzburg and Ratisbon to train as secular priests. Both monasteries already had seminaries for educating boys for the Benedictine order. The only problem attendant on such a scheme was that of the expensive and dangerous journey that students would have to make between Scotland and Germany.[1] The monasteries themselves were in favour of the scheme, as Father John Ingram of Wurzburg wrote, in January 1795, to Abbé MacPherson:

> ... a union and mutual intercourse, more than has ever yet subsisted, ought to be entered into and firmly cemented, for the preservation of this House and the propagation of Religion in our own native country.

He made a further, less practical suggestion:

> ... considering the Emperor's connection with Britain, and in some degree his dependence upon it, it would only cost the British Court a single request to obtain the restoration of the Scotch House in Vienna, or some foundation equivalent to it, that would maintain six or eight alumni at least.[2]

If Austria was hardly a practical proposition for the founding of a Scots College, Bavaria was soon to prove equally impossible. By March 1795 the French were approaching and the old Prince had died. The new Prince expressed a desire to turn the monastery at Wurzburg into a boarding school.[3]

In the spring of 1796 Peter MacLachlan was sent to Wurzburg from Rome because he was consumptive, an indication that the monastery was still considered safe.[4] Later that year the French occupied Wurzburg for a time, but the monks suffered little — perhaps, it has been suggested, because they could speak French.[5] After the Austrians arrived the French shut themselves up in Wurzburg Castle and canonaded the town night and day for four days before surrendering.[5]

In 1803 the Scots Benedictine monastery of St James at Wurzburg was finally secularised and its monks pensioned off. The monastery became a military hospital. The monks continued to live privately in or near Wurzburg, the last of their number dying in 1839. At the time of its secularisation there had been seven monks resident in the monastery itself, and an eighth, Father William Pepper, serving on the Scottish Mission at Munshes, near Dumfries.

Ratisbon, the mother house of Wurzburg, was the only German monastery which was not secularised in the first decade of the nineteenth century. At the end of the eighteenth century it seems to have been in a more flourishing state than the Scots monastery at Wurzburg. Throughout the eighteenth century its monks had distinguished themselves as professors at Erfurt University.[6]

In the spring of 1800 Father James Gallus Robertson, who had left the Scottish Mission that year, was aked by the monastery to send over some boys from Scotland.[7] Mr Robertson recruited four youngsters in the North-East and sailed with a convoy from Leith to Hamburg on the 18th of June.[8] These four were the last boys to be sent to Ratisbon for many years.

On 18th July, 1800, French troops entered Ratisbon. The monastery was obliged to contribute towards the maintenance of French officers and men, and to furnish hay, straw and oats for their horses.[9] Financial ruin, if not secularisation of the monastery, must have been dreaded by its abbot, Abbot Arbuthnot, who described conditions at Ratisbon in a letter dated March 1802:

> ... we had been allmost ruined by the french, whose contributions and requisitions had no end; after their departure began the exactions of the elector, and now after all we live in a very precarious position. In bavaria they have begun to abolish religious communities. The capuchins and franciscans and other mendicant orders are reduced and put together in a few monasteries, where they must stay till they die; the rest of the monasteries are to be sold. In the upper palatine they have attacked also the founded monasteries, which are to be also abolished and their estates sold ... God only knows how far this will go ... we here in this town, not being under the jurisdiction of the Elector, our property has not been attacked as yet ...[10]

Nine months later, Father Alexander Horn wrote to his mother in Scotland, telling her of the decree of the Elector of Mainz: the monks at Ratisbon might either remain *in situ*, enjoying their revenues during their lives, but forbidden to take any new members; or they might surrender their property in return for a life pension.[11]

In 1803 Father James Robertson journeyed to Paris, where he succeeded in obtaining an order to the French Minister at Ratisbon to ensure the preservation of the Scots Benedictine Monastery there.[12]

In 1805 Father Peter Sharp sent the following account to his cousin, Mr James Sharp, priest at Scalan:

> The late secularisations have had hitherto no other remarkable effect upon our house than we the present surviving members, 9 in number with Mr Robertson, are the last of the Scotch nation who shall have any share or reap any benefit thereof. After our demise it devolves for ever on the Elector of Maynz and his successors. Two of our fathers, Messrs Hamilton, not counted to the nine above, are at Erford and provided for during life by the King of Prussia. One of our house, Mr James Moir, brother to John Moir, bookprinter at Edinburgh, has been sick of a tertian ague this whole summer, and also Mr Deasson from Huntly has been very indisposed ... the rest of us, thank God, are all well. In our Seminary we have at present only two boys viz one James Cruickshank from Aberdeen, and another, Thomas Carmichael, from Havre de Grace. When these two take leave of it, it will undergo the fate of our Abbey and be abandoned to our Elector.[13]

The monastery was permitted to enjoy all its estates and properties as hitherto, so long as it gave the Elector a monthly account of its income and expenditure, and so long as it accepted no more novices.[14]

By 1808 there was only one student, James Cruickshank, left in the monastery's seminary. There was, however, no more thought of suppressing the monastery as its assets would release insufficient capital to pay for its administration as well as for pensions for its monks. Of the monks surviving in 1808, the Superior was in his nonage, and his second-in-command a 'malade imaginaire'; Father Alexander Horn had been exiled for his political involvement as a British agent and his brother was employed as confessor to the 'Prince of Toura Taxis'; Angus MacIver, newly ordained priest, had gone to act as preceptor to a nobleman.[15]

Although it seemed to be in a moribund state in 1808, the monastery at Ratisbon escaped secularisation. In 1817 there was even a proposal afoot to re-establish the seminary as soon as the Government formally reassigned the building to the monastery, enabling its then occupiers to be evicted. By this time the monastery desperately needed young recruits, but its finances were such that it could barely maintain and educate four boys.[16]

In spite of its financial difficulties, Ratisbon did succeed in reopening its seminary, and in 1828 was able to send home to Scotland James MacNaughton, an Aberdeen boy, who was ordained shortly after his arrival and served the Scottish Mission as a secular priest.[17] In 1836 six boys from Scotland were sent to Ratisbon in the company of a secular priest, Mr James MacHattie. Mr MacHattie, whose health was bad, was permitted by the Scottish bishops to enter the monastery, where he became a Benedictine in 1832, dying there three years later on 18th June, 1835.[18] In 1862 the Scots Benedictine monastery at Ratisbon was finally dissolved but, as Mark Dilworth has pointed out, its traditions were transferred to Scotland:

> Its last monk, Anselm Robertson, having returned to Scotland, took a hand in the founding of the monastery at Fort Augustus in the 1870s. The last student of the seminary, Donald Mackintosh, was a parish priest in the Western Highlands until his death in 1927.[19]

The monastery at Ratisbon had maintained to the last its close connections with the Scottish Mission.

Bishop Cameron was perhaps influenced by sentiment rather than by practical considerations when he wrote, in 1804, to the Lord Chief Baron, Robert Dundas:

> The seizure of various houses we had in Germany, where youth was educated and old age had a decent retirement and asylum, is a heavy blow, and we shall feel the effects of it for many years.[20]

Nevertheless it is true to say that, although the monasteries of Ratisbon and Wurzburg had never supplied a great number of priests for the Scottish Mission, those whom they had sent were doubly welcome both because they supplied a chronic need, and because they were supported by their monasteries whenever possible, freeing Mission funds to support more secular priests.

NOTES

1 Bishop Hay to Abbé MacPherson, 11th October 1793, B.L.
2 Father John Ingram to Abbé MacPherson, 5th January 1795, B.L.
3 Father John Ingram to Abbé MacPherson, 15th June 1795, B.L.

4   Bishop Hay to Abbé MacPherson, 9th February 1796, B.L.
5   Father John Ingram to Abbé MacPherson, 7th December 1796, B.L.
6   Mark Dilworth, *The Scots in Franconia* (Edinburgh, 1974), p. 268.
7   Abbot Charles Arbuthnot to Bishop Hay, 14th April 1800, B.L.
8   Father James Robertson to Mr Charles Maxwell, 14th July 1800, B.L.
9   Abbot Arbuthnot to Bishop Hay, 18th August 1800, B.L.
10 Abbot Arbuthnot to Charles Maxwell, 24th March 1802, B.L.
11 Bishop Cameron to Bishop Hay (quoting Mr Horn's letter), 27th December 1802, B.L.
12 Alexander Innes to Bishop Cameron, 30th April 1803, B.L.
13 Father Peter Sharp to James Sharp, 18th August 1805, B.L.
14 Father Peter Sharp to John Sharp, 18th August 1805, B.L.
15 Father James Robertson to Abbé MacPherson, 30th November 1808, B.L.
16 Father MacIver, 1st July 1817, B.L.
17 James Kyle to Bishop Paterson, 21st November 1828 (Kyle Letters).
18 'Alphabetical list of Aquhorties Students' — W. J. Anderson, *Innes Review* 1963, p. 193.
19 Mark Dilworth, *The Scots in Franconia,* p. 269.
20 Bishop Cameron to Robert Dundas, 13th November 1804, B.L.

16

The Government Grant to the Scottish Catholic Clergy

THE French Revolution dealt the Scottish Mission a severe blow. By 1793 it had lost not only two of its four colleges, but also much of its income. It was therefore faced with the problem of having to set up colleges in Scotland to compensate for those lost, while, at the same time, it had an even smaller income than hitherto to meet the expense thereof. Two possibilities were open to the Scottish bishops: to obtain compensation for the property they had lost in France, and to apply to the British Government for assistance. Initially they determined to try to obtain compensation for their French property. An opportunity for this arose in 1795 when, Robespierre having fallen, the Government of France was taken over by the Directory. Under the Directory the religious climate in France became more favourable; some French priests returned home; and a peace treaty seemed likely.[1]

In June 1795, encouraged by the more favourable climate of affairs in France, Mr Farquharson wrote from Glasgow to Abbé MacPherson:

> ... I intend writing him [Bishop Hay] a long letter, requesting that he and his fellow BBs may concert matters in time to send a proper *memorial* of losses at Douay College to his Majesty's ministers. I shall furnish them proper materials, for since my coming over I have extricated out of the hands of French Harpies authentic legalised copies of all our landed property, with all the proper documents of whatever else we possessed in that infatuated land. The English BBs have taken the start of us, made known their claims, and, it's confidently expected, however soon a peace of any kind is patched up some compensation on either side will be granted us; ministry will be warmly applied to, nor can they well refuse their support ... .[2]

It is worth noting that it was the English bishops who were first to pursue a claim for compensation for their losses in France, even though the Scottish bishops had lost far more. The English Colleges in France had relied for their income on fees paid by boarders; the only property they possessed was the college buildings themselves. The Scots Colleges, on the other hand, relied for their income on rentals from property they owned in and around Paris and Douay and on money invested in public funds in Paris.

On 9th August, 1796 Bishop Hay wrote a letter to Sir John Cox Hippisley, illustrating how he was following the lead of the English and Irish bishops:

> About the time of your late return to Britain our chief sollicitude was how to get a succession of our Clergy kept up, having lost our two Colleges in France. Our friends in England and Ireland were in the same predicament with us. But the Catholicks in England being numerous and generally very wealthy, could easily supply their want at home, which we with pleasure see they are doing; and it gave us no less satisfaction to see the generous attention of Government to

make a most ample provision for those in Ireland. We in Scotland had not the means of supplying that want among ourselves; and considering of how little importance we are, both on account of the smallness of our number in comparison to those others, and of the poverty of by far the greater part of our people, we could not think of giving any trouble to Government, by applying for assistance, especially in these distressing times, in which Government itself has so much to do. Considering however that if we possibly could get redress for the loss of our Colleges, when it shall please God to restore peace in Europe, this would fully enable us to get a place of education among ourselves. With this view Bishop Geddes and I wrote a conjunct letter to Mr Secretary Dundas, requesting his assistance on this head when the proper period should arrive, to which he was pleased to give us a most satisfactory answer.[3]

In April 1796 Mr Alexander Innes regained possession of the Scots College building at Paris, though most of the furniture had gone. He also seems to have regained possession at this time of the other properties belonging to the College.[4] In November 1796 Mr Farquharson managed to have some letters smuggled over to France, as a result of which a stop was put to the sale of the property belonging to the Scots College at Douay.[5] By 1797, however, any hope of peace being concluded between Britain and France had vanished. The Scottish priests were forced once again to surrender their property in France. When peace negotiations were resumed in 1802, hope revived in the Scottish Mission, but it was not until Napoleon had been defeated at Waterloo in 1815 that the question of the Mission's property in France could finally be settled. In the interim the Scottish bishops had been forced to turn to the British Government for financial assistance.

In 1795 Mr Sone, a rich miller from Bedhampton, gifted £10,000 for a Catholic college to be built in England to serve either the whole country or, failing that, to serve the London area. The college was to be for the education of boys for the priesthood.[6] Bishop Hay could expect no such munificence from the Scottish Catholics. In Ireland, however, the Government had, in 1795, founded Maynooth College, endowing it with an annual grant of £8,000.[7] In England, too, there were rumours that the Government would support Catholic colleges: in January 1796 Abbé MacPherson heard that the English Vicars Apostolic were to receive a considerable allowance for their college,[8] and in March Bishop Douglas confirmed that Mr Pitt had promised the college financial assistance.[9] It was, therefore, reasonable to suppose that the Government might agree to help the colleges of the far more impoverished Scottish Mission, even though the Scottish Catholics were far and away the most insignificant both politically and numerically.

In April 1796 Bishop Hay wrote to Abbé MacPherson telling him that he had been promised reimbursement for the Scots Colleges of Paris and Douay once peace was restored. He continued:

It is upon this that our expectations of getting a proper one at home are grounded.[10]

Almost exactly a year before, however, Bishop Hay had made the first tentative enquiries as to whether the British Government would give financial assistance to a Scottish Catholic College. In March 1795 he had written the following to Mr Mathison, the priest at Auchenhalrig, near Fochabers:

On seeing in the newspapers that Government was allowing considerable sums for erecting Catholick schools in Ireland it was suggested that on proper application some help might perhaps be got from that quarter. But two reasons kept me back from thinking of this. Considering the enormous expenses Government is obliged to be at, in the present calamitous times, I could not think of giving any additional trouble to my Country on our account, and besides, by what means could application be made? I have no friends that could have any weight in making such application; I am but a nothing myself in the Eyes of Government and can be of no essential service to my country, further than by prayers and good wishes, which is my bounden duty at any rate, but what title could that give me to make such an application? If a person of Mr Brodie's influence and interest would take our case to heart and patronize it perhaps something might be done; but in a matter of such magnitude I could not have face even to propose it to him.[11]

This letter, ostensibly written to Mr Mathison, was, from its tone, undoubtedly intended to be shown by Mr Mathison to Mr Brodie, his local Member of Parliament. On 2nd April Bishop Hay wrote again to Mr Mathison asking him whether Mr Brodie might sound out the Ministry on the possibility of granting money for a college in Scotland.[12]

Mr Mathison consulted the Duke of Gordon, who approved of the idea of applying for Government aid, and then wrote to Mr Brodie giving details of the financial circumstances in which the Scottish Mission found itself. He outlined the investment of money in French public funds; the losses these funds had incurred with the collapse of the Mississippi scheme; and the final loss of all funds in France with the French Revolution, a loss which forced the Mission to rely almost entirely for its income on shares purchased in the Bank of Scotland. He went on to describe the loss of the Scots Colleges at Douay and Paris, pointing out that, whereas the English were able to finance the building of colleges in England to offset the loss of their colleges in France, the Scottish Catholics were too poor to do likewise.[13] Mr Brodie enclosed Mr Mathison's letter with one of his own addressed to the Lord Advocate dated 7th July 1795:

Permitt me to offer to your perusal the accompanying letter from a worthy priest who, strange to tell, on an income of 12£ per annum not only LIVES respected by his own floke but by all descriptions of people in the district in which he resides. The letter will speak for itself and it would much oblige me if when you have the leizure you would have the goodness to let me know how far you think the case would be likely to meet with attention from Government. It would indeed afford me sencible gratification could I derive the information from you personaly in the corner where the priest has his residence and where I should feel happy to make the good man known to you . . .[14]

In January 1796 Bishop Hay sent Mr Brodie, at the latter's request, more information on the Scots Colleges in France, stressing their former importance in maintaining a supply of priests for Scotland. He estimated that the yearly income of the two colleges together, exclusive of the college buildings themselves, had been about 30,000 livres. He went on to outline the steps he had taken, through the mediation of the Lord Advocate, to ask the Duke of Portland and the Secretary, Mr Dundas, to procure reimbursement from the French government once peace should be made. He pointed out that, whatever happened in France, it would not be practical to try to re-establish the Scots Colleges there, and suggested that it would be far more satisfactory to establish colleges in Scotland with any compensation received. Indeed, only such compensation could enable the Mission to found colleges in Scotland.[15]

By August 1796, Bishop Hay was tentatively enquiring whether the British Government might be willing to finance, not only colleges in Scotland, but also the

Scottish priests themselves. In a letter to Mr Hippisley, having reiterated the problem of financing colleges in Scotland, Bishop Hay continued:

> But now matters are materially changed indeed! The question now is not about getting a supply for the loss of our Colleges, but how we shall get the means of subsistence for ourselves . . . From the disturbances in France we have lost about £130 of our yearly rents from that country, and now from what Mr MacPherson writes . . . it is much to be feared that we have little more to expect from Rome . . . In this situation, Kind Sir, what shall we do? Our people in general are far from being in a condition to maintain their Clergymen, and only three of our families, who are able, keep a chaplain. To apply to Government, I shall be at a loss what to allege in our favour; our situation and our most sincere attachment to our gracious Sovereign and the Constitution, is all I could say; but in times like the present something more substantial than these would be required to entitle us to any favour. Besides, I have been assured that Ministers are determined to give no more pensions for the present, and I am not surprised at it. Our gracious Sovereign has given proof of his humane and benevolent heart to those in distress, though foreigners; perhaps if he knew our situation he would extend his charity to a handful of his own most faithfull and loyal subjects.[16]

The 'foreigners' to whom Bishop Hay referred were the French émigré priests in Britain, who had been given pensions by the British Government.

When the question of Irish Catholic emancipation came to be discussed in the early nineteenth century, the British Government suggested that it pay the salaries of the priests and have some say in the election of bishops. This the Irish condemned as bringing the Catholic Church in Ireland under the control of a Protestant Government.[17] In the case of the grant to the Scottish Catholic clergy, such questions never arose.

Bishop Hay, in his letters to Sir John Cox Hippisley and others, stressed that without receiving either compensation for the losses sustained in France, or else some sort of Government grant, he and Bishop Chisholm would be quite unable to open colleges in Scotland. In 1794, however, long before there was any hope of money from either of these sources, Bishop Hay had considered purchasing Oxhill. In 1797 he leased Aquhorties, still without having received any compensation or grant. This move placed the Bishop in urgent need of capital, and prompted him to write again to Hippisley to explain how he had been offered the lease. Building a college at Aquhorties, he continued, would require considerable capital, but:

> . . . as we could never expect such an offer from any other, and if refused, might never get it again, as others would have stept in, at the persuasion of friends I was induced to accept of it, and was lately in the north and concluded the bargain. How to procure the means of accomplishing this business must depend chiefly upon the benevolence of friends and well-wishers; but as little can be expected of our own people here, who are generally poor, I take the liberty of laying the case before you, and of proposing two expedients which, if approved by you, might be tried. I have been informed from London that there are many staunch friends to Government who, knowing our attachment to our King and Country, if our case were known to them, would be willing to assist us by a subscription, and I flatter myself if you think this adviseable, that you will take the trouble to see if anything could be done in this way. If not, as a few hundred pounds would be a great relief to us, perhaps Ministry, if the case were laid before them, would not refuse their assistance.[18]

Hippisley, in reply, suggested that an appeal should first be made to Parliament, and urged Bishop Hay to ask Mr Dundas to raise the subject with the Duke of Portland, under whose department it would come.[19] The Bishop's letter and Hippisley's reply suggest that Mr Brodie's approach to Mr Dundas had failed.

Hippisley himself prepared a memorial for Government in which he suggested that each bishop should receive £50 per annum, and each priest £10. He urged that some immediate interim relief be granted because he dreaded 'the effects of the distresses of the poor Clergy of such a Season'.[20]

On 4th January 1799, Bishop Hay furnished Hippisley with further arguments in favour of a Government grant.[21] One argument took advantage of the fact that the British Government had, for some time, been very concerned to put a stop to the flow of emigrants from the Scottish Highlands to Canada. As he pointed out:

> There has been for some years past a pretty general disposition among our people in several places of the Highlands to emigrate to America; they were much encouraged to this by the invitations of their friends who are already there, and even by some of our priests, who saw no other way of being relieved from their present hardships; and matters have gone so far that they only waited for peace to put their design in execution.

The agent of the Trustees on Clanranald's estate had asked Bishop Hay to use his influence to prevent the priests from emigrating, but the Bishop had said that it was only extreme want that had made them plan to emigrate:

> ... I am perfectly persuaded that none of our priests would ever think of leaving his native country and much less would he encourage others to do so if he could get a comfortable subsistence in it.

In other words, a Government grant which would provide the Highland priests with an adequate salary would do much to prevent Catholic emigration.

Bishop Hay further argued that, although the Scottish priests were already loyal to Government, a grant which would help them in their present financial difficulties would 'confirm and secure their fidelity and allegiance for ever'. Furthermore, such an act of charity on the part of the British Ministry would comfort Pope Pius in the midst of his afflictions by assuring him that the Ministry was providing the Scottish priests with the financial support which he himself could no longer offer.

Finally Bishop Hay outlined the Mission's financial position: its funds had arisen partly from benefactions given by pious people to support the priests, because their congregations were generally too poor to support them themselves; and partly from an annual payment made by the Holy See. He continued:

> The difficulties in former times of securing our money in this country, and some considerable losses our Predecessors had met with, made them judge it prudent to send as much of our money as they could to Paris and invest it in the public Funds there.

The money invested in Paris, together with the income from Rome, had been lost.

Before the French Revolution each Vicar Apostolic had received a pension of about £45 from Rome, and each coadjutor a small pension from the same source. Funds invested in Scotland gave each Vicar Apostolic a further £40 yearly. Now this Scottish money was all that was left to support all the bishops.

Bishop Hay sent further details of the Mission's funds to the Lord Advocate:

> ... the funds of the Roman Catholic Clergy in Scotland ... are divided into three classes: viz Those that belong to the Missionaries, those belonging to the Bishops, and those that are allotted for the support of two small schools ...
>
> The funds belonging to the Missionaries are settled partly in the Bank of Scotland, and partly in private hands. ... In [the] Bank the Missionaries have 50 shares, which at present yield £250 yearly. They have also a capital of £4,333 settled in private hands, which at legal interest give

£216-13-0, and these together make the whole income £466-13-0 per annum. But from this must be deducted £9 yearly for charitable purposes, according to the intentions of the Donors. And there remain for the maintenance of the Missionaries £457-13-0. . . .

The number of Missionaries now in Scotland is 50. Of these five are in Gentlemen's families, and of course taken off the common funds. But of the 45 who remain those that are in towns are allowed one half more than those in the country, as they are exposed to more expenses. There are at present five in towns, and one, who, having been deprived of his judgment, requires that additional allowance to have him properly boarded. . . . The above sum . . . gives only £9-10-8 to each of the 40 who are in the country, and £14-5-10½ to the other six, and nothing is left for accidental expenses of any kind. The one who is deranged is considered as super numerary.

There are commonly four Bishops in Scotland: two Apostolic Vicars and two Coadjutors, one for each Vicar. In this Country their whole Capital is £1720 stg. which is settled in several private hands and yields at legal interest £86 stg. But out of this, £4 yearly is allotted for charitable purposes, according to the intention of the Donors, and of the remaining £82 each Vicar has one half or £41 stg. The two Coadjutors had nothing but what they got from Rome, and what their respective Principals could spare them . . . As to myself, I informed your Lordship the other day that I had some personal property in the Bank of Scotland. . . . after paying all the incumbrances I had contracted, there remains, for my own use, £23-11-6.

We have two schools, one in the highlands, and one in the low country. Their funds were benefactions from Friends both at home and abroad. What was given by those abroad, was settled abroad, and is now lost with the rest. The intention of these schools is to maintain a few boys, under the care of a priest, to initiate them in the rudiments of the Latin language, to try their genius and dispositions, and to accustom them to the practice of virtue and to regular discipline before they be sent abroad to our foreign Colleges . . . [of which only Valladolid by now remained open] to prosecute their education.

Their funds in this country are settled partly in the Bank of Scotland, where they have thirty shares of the capital of that Bank, and a capital of about £800 settled in private hands. The produce of these belonging to each school is nearly the same; and upon that, from betwixt eight to twelve boys, with masters and servants, are maintained in each school . . . [22]

Bishop Hay went on to repeat once again the story of the loss of the Scots Colleges in France and his consequent leasing of Aquhorties to provide a new college. The college at Aquhorties had by now been completed, but the expenses incurred had far outstripped subscriptions raised. The Bishop considered that it would be unwise to have both Highland and Lowland boys educated in the one college. The Highland Vicar Apostolic, Bishop John Chisholm, was therefore determined to build a college in the Highlands. Finally, Bishop Hay stressed that such colleges would ensure that boys destined for the priesthood in Scotland would be educated in

> . . . the principles of Government and loyalty, which are congenial to the constitution of our Country, which they could not have easily got elsewhere.

On 27th August, 1797, over four years since Bishop Hay had first approached Mr Brodie, Sir John Cox Hippisley was at last able to inform the Scottish bishops that Mr Secretary Long of the Treasury had received orders to pay the Scottish Catholic clergy £1,600.[23] The decision had been taken at a meeting at Wimbledon on 2nd January, 1799, between Henry Dundas, Lord Melville; William Dundas, Secretary at War; Sir John Cox Hippisley and Mr Ferguson of Pitfour,[24] but the first payment was not finally made until December 1799.[25]

The £1,600 was to be divided as follows: each Vicar Apostolic was to receive £100 per annum, and each Coadjutor £60. Each priest was to receive sufficient to augment his Mission quota to a total income of £20 per annum.[26] Aquhorties and the proposed Highland College were each to receive £300 in 1799 and a further £300 in 1800 to help defray building costs. Over and above these specific payments, each college was to receive £50 per annum.[27]

Sir John Cox Hippisley felt that such a settlement, which gave the priests only a very small total salary, merited some explanation:

> Some apology seems to be due from me in recommending a provision so very inadequate to the pressures of the times, but when the pressure also of the public opinion is considered, and the fact also is — that great numbers of the established Clergy and their families, particularly in Wales, are living on £20 per annum, I thought I could not press at present a greater allowance in the apprehension if I did so I might wholly fail in my object.[28]

Ultimately, each coadjutor was allowed £50 per annum, and each priest £12.[29]

Sadly, the extra money which Bishop Hay had fought so hard to procure aroused feelings, not of gratitude, but of bitterness, among the priests of the North-East, who banded themselves into what became known as the 'Northern Confederacy'. They were understandably annoyed that the Vicars Apostolic, who already had a relatively generous income from Mission funds, should receive such a large percentage of the annual grant of £1,000, while they, as priests, received so little that they would still have great difficulty in making ends meet.[30] They felt sure that the Government must have been unaware of their plight when it made the award. Mr Mathison, the priest at Fochabers, voiced the general opinion:

> I cannot help thinking that an address from the Body to the Bishop, and by him conveyed to Sir John Hippisley would have the desired effect. Can it be expected that Government will assist us unless it knows our situation and straits?[31]

The Northern Confederacy demanded of Bishop Hay a salary of £50 per annum for each priest, a sum for which, as the Bishop pointed out, an extra £1,500 would have to be found. Bishop Hay patiently pointed out that such a sum could not be obtained: the Scottish Catholics would never contribute so much, and Catholic congregations could not be asked to contribute to the upkeep of priests in a Protestant country. He dismissed the demand for £50 as a 'romantick scheme' which was not practicable.[32] Interestingly, he did not use the argument put to him by Hippisley that Catholic priests could not hope to receive more than the salary received by many established ministers.

In spite of Bishop Hay's well-reasoned arguments, resentment continued to fester. In 1801 Mr William Reid demanded that each priest be given a minimum of £13 from the grant, making a total annual salary of £22.3.0. He criticised the bishops' large salaries and the fact that they kept for themselves the allowance made for a Highland Coadjutor, there being none at that time. Lastly, he complained:

> Why make the Masters in the Colleges who have bed, board and washing, equal with poor labourers [i.e. mission priests] who have bed, board, washing, and every other necessary expense to take out of their scanty allowance.[33]

Bishop Hay had not made matters any better by admitting that it cost £27 per annum to keep a boy at Aquhorties.[34] The depth of feeling aroused against him by the distribution of the grant can be deduced from the following extract from a letter written by Mr Reid:

> I find the brethren in general are in the full persuasion that you have laid down a Maxim to keep

your Clergy always Poor, in a state of Dependence and Starvation, and in proof of this they adduce some instances wherein you acted accordingly, when you had it in your power to meliorate their circumstances. It is even asserted, that you deny the clergy to have any right, from the Mission, or from those who employ their labours, to a decent and sufficient maintenance.[35]

Mr Reid wanted the Scottish, English and Irish bishops to act together to get a 'decent and permanent settlement' sanctioned by Parliament, particularly as he had heard rumours that the Irish were to receive such a settlement in the next Parliamentary session. (The Irish settlement, tied as it was to fears of Government control of the Catholic church in Ireland, did not in fact take place).

It is interesting to note that Mr Reid and others were still grumbling about the distribution of the Government grant in 1801, a year after Bishop Hay had put all the facts about both the Mission funds in general, and the grant in particular, before the annual meeting of those priests who held office as administrators of the Mission's affairs.[36] The continuing discontent illustrates how badly the priests had been affected by the general rise in the cost of living over the preceding ten years. It is also significant that in 1809 Mr Scott, appealing for money from the Catholic Chapels of Glasgow, Paisley and Greenock, assured the readers of his pamphlet that

No Missionary employed in serving the Irish Catholics on that West coast receives at present, or will receive more than a yearly salary of Fifty Pounds Stg till all the necessary chapels be erected.[37]

In other words, in 1809 Mr Scott considered £50 per annum to be the minimum salary on which a priest could live.

In the event, all the resentment engendered by the distribution of the Government grant proved to have been a mere tilting at windmills. It was not long before payment of the grant was discontinued, or, to be more accurate, was gradually allowed to fall by the wayside. The 1799 instalment was made in December 1799; the 1800 instalment in February 1801;[38] the 1801 instalment in March 1802;[39] the 1802 payment in August 1803;[40] and the 1803 payment not until the summer of 1805.[41] No further payments were ever made. Even the few that had been made had been made only after repeated requests by the Scottish bishops and their friends.

In 1812 hope revived that the grant might be resumed, although there was no prospect of any arrears being paid.[42] In 1820 Sir John Cox Hippisley raised the subject with Lord Liverpool.[43] In 1824 Bishop Alexander MacDonell, a Canadian bishop and former chaplain of the Glengarry Fencibles, pointed out to members of the British Government the hardships which the Scottish priests had undergone since the grant had been dropped. His comment caused surprise, those to whom he spoke having thought that the grant was still being paid.[44] In spite of these various attempts, the Government grant was never paid again after 1805. It was politically expedient for the Government to continue to subsidise Maynooth College; it saw no such necessity to continue to subsidise the politically insignificant Scottish Catholic clergy.

The payment of the Government grant to the Scottish Mission can be related directly to the careers of the Dundas family, and in particular to that of Henry

Dundas, Viscount Melville. In 1783 Henry Dundas committed himself to support William Pitt the Younger, and when Pitt won the general election in 1784, Dundas followed him to power. During this period of Pitt-Dundas ascendancy Scottish Catholics were granted relief, and the Scottish Mission obtained its grant. In 1801 Pitt resigned, not returning to power until 1804. In 1804 Dundas was appointed First Lord of the Admiralty. In March 1805, a commission of enquiry brought to light malpractices in the office of the Naval Treasurer, and Dundas was impeached and forced to resign. He was acquitted by his peers in 1806, but the damage had been done.[45]

The letters of the Scottish Catholic clergy show how much they felt themselves to be in Henry Dundas's debt. In 1803 Mr Maxwell wrote to Bishop Hay:

> The present turn that affairs have taken in the House of Commons between Mr Pitt's party and the Prime Minister fortify me in my suspicion [that the grant will not be continued].[46]

In November 1804, Mr Gordon, teacher at Aquhorties, wrote to Abbé MacPherson:

> . . . we ascertained great hopes for the return of Pitt and Dundas to power. Application has been made [for the grant]; some hope and others are confident.[47]

In April, 1805, when word of Melville's impeachment reached the Scottish Mission, Mr Farquharson wrote to Bishop Cameron:

> With the Dundas interest (whose fate I greatly deplore) our Govt. allowance, I am apprehensive, is done away with, as it was in a manner charitably smuggled over to us.[48]

In May 1807 Mr Reid asked Bishop Cameron:

> What do you think of the late changes in the Cabinet? Will they be favourable to our pretensions [ref. the grant]? I should think Lord Melville will have it in his power to do something if he pleases.[49]

The conclusions to be drawn from this evidence are inescapable. As far as Ireland was concerned, religion could not be divorced from politics. Since the vast majority of the people of Southern Ireland were Catholic, measures such as the Government financing of Maynooth College were politically expedient. Scottish Catholics, on the other hand, were numerically and politically insignificant. The concern shown by men like Viscount Melville for the plight of the Scottish priests may have stemmed from a disinterested benevolence, as well perhaps as from some sense of shared nationhood. In no way can the grant, as has sometimes been suggested, have constituted a bribe calculated to buy the loyalty of the Scottish Catholic clergy.

The grant, although it was shortlived, was important to the establishment of the new colleges at Aquhorties and Lismore. It had another no less important, if less obvious, result, as was pointed out by Sir John Cox Hippisley:

> By this arrangement a regular communication is constructed with Government, which will go far in the end to place you in a more comfortable situation than at present.[50]

The grant, though it afforded the Scottish priests some financial help over a period of about five years, did little to improve their situation in the long term. They were forced to find other ways of compensating for the loss of their income from France and Italy.

NOTES

1 Franklin L. Ford, *Europe 1780-1830,* pp. 128-130.
2 John Farquharson to Abbé MacPherson, 7th June 1795, B.L.
3 Bishop Hay to Sir John Cox Hippisley, scroll letter, 9th August 1796, B.L.
4 Bishop Geddes to Bishop Hay, 26th April 1796, B.L.
5 John Farquharson to Abbé MacPherson, 27th June 1797, B.L.
6 Bernard Ward, *The Dawn of the Catholic Revival in England,* Vol. II, p. 108.
7 *The Catholic Encyclopaedia* (London, 1911), Vol. X, p. 87 (under 'Maynooth').
8 Abbé MacPherson to Bishop Geddes, 2nd January 1796, B.L.
9 Abbé MacPherson to Bishop Hay, 6th April 1796, B.L.
10 Bishop Hay to Abbé MacPherson, 16th April 1796, B.L.
11 Bishop Hay to George Mathison, 19th March 1795, B.L.
12 Bishop Hay to George Mathison, 2nd April 1795, B.L.
13 George Mathison to Alexander Brodie M.P., 5th May 1795, printed in the 'Report on the Laing MSS, University of Edinburgh', Vol. II (Historical MSS Commission, London 1925), pp. 576-7.
14 Alexander Brodie to the Lord Advocate, 7th July 1795, Laing Mss, Vol. II, p. 576.
15 Bishop Hay to Alexander Brodie, 19th January 1796, B.L.
16 Bishop Hay to Sir John Cox Hippisley, scroll letter, 9th August 1796, B.L.
17 Gearoid O Tuathaigh, *Ireland Before the Famine,* Gill History of Ireland (Dublin, 1972) Vol. 9, pp. 42 *et seq.* gives details of the fight for Irish Catholic emancipation.
18 Bishop Hay to Sir John Cox Hippisley, scroll letter, 14th March 1797, B.L.
19 Sir John Cox Hippisley to Bishop Hay, 9th April 1797, B.L.
20 Sir John Cox Hippisley to Bishop Hay, 29th December 1798, B.L.
21 Bishop Hay to Sir John Cox Hippisley, scroll letter, 4th January 1799, B.L.
22 Bishop Hay to the Lord Advocate, scroll letter, 26th February 1799, B.L.
23 Sir John Cox Hippisley to Bishop Hay, 27th August 1799, B.L.
24 Bishop Cameron to William Dundas, scroll letter, 1804, B.L.
25 Bishop Cameron, scroll letter, 8th June 1809, B.L.
26 Robert Dundas, Lord Advocate, to Bishop Hay, 2nd May 1799, 14th May 1799, B.L.
27 Bishop Hay to George Maxwell, 14th September 1799, B.L.
28 Sir John Cox Hippisley to Bishop Hay, 25th June 1799, B.L.
29 'Present Settlement Wrote by the Lord Advocate in presence of Bishops Hay and Chisholm', 1800, B.L. (among Bishop Hay's letters).
30 Andrew Scott, Huntly, to Charles Maxwell, Edinburgh, 13th December 1800, B.L.
31 George Mathison, Auchinhalrig, to Charles Maxwell, 3rd November 1800, B.L.
32 Bishop Hay to Messrs Scott, Paterson, Stuart etc., 20th March 1801, B.L.
33 William Reid to Bishop Hay, 10th August 1801, B.L.
34 Bishop Hay to Abbé MacPherson, 26th October 1800, B.L.
35 William Reid to Bishop Hay, 10th August 1801, B.L.
36 Bishop Hay to Charles Maxwell, 9th February 1800, Preshome Letters, S.C.A.
37 Andrew Scott: Printed Pamphlet: 'Roman Catholic Chapels for the Emigrant Irish on the West Coast of Scotland', 1809, B.L.
38 Sir John Cox Hippisley, 3rd January 1801, B.L.
39 Charles Maxwell to Bishop Hay, 17th March 1802, B.L.
40 Charles Maxwell to Bishop Hay, 10th August 1803, B.L.
41 Bishop Hay to Bishop Cameron, 18th May 1805, B.L.
42 Sir John Cox Hippisley to Bishop Hay, 27th June 1812, B.L.
43 Sir John Cox Hippisley to Bishop Cameron, 5th June 1820, B.L.
44 Bishop Alexander MacDonell to Bishop Cameron, 13th March 1824, Preshome Letters, S.C.A.
45 William Ferguson, *Scotland: 1689 to the Present,* pp. 266, 269.
46 Charles Maxwell to Bishop Hay, 18th June 1803, B.L.
47 John Gordon (Junior) to Abbé MacPherson, 16th November 1804, B.L.

48 John Farquharson to Bishop Cameron, 24th April 1805, B.L.
49 William Reid to Bishop Cameron, 11th May 1807, B.L.
50 Sir John Cox Hippisley to Bishop Hay, 25th June 1799, B.L.

17

The Lowland Vicariate, 1793-1829: its Priests and their Lives

UNDER the year 1734, in his continuation of Thomson's 'History of the Scottish Mission', Abbé MacPherson, writing in about 1815, noted:

> They [the Lowland priests] then and even till of late had no means of procuring the necessaries of life, but the miserable pittance they received from the Mission funds, and that pittance was already greatly inferior to their necessities.[1]

The Lowland priests may have received only a pittance, but their lifestyle was gradually changing. As Mr William MacDonald, priest at Dufftown, pointed out in 1805:

> The days are not, as formerly, when the Pastor was always welcome in his turn to any of his hearers' houses. Besides my hearers are all exceedingly poor save one, and he lives altogether at an outside of the Mission.[2]

Mr MacDonald was referring to the practice of priests staying with various members of their congregations by turn, rather than having their own houses. The practice had long been discontinued in the Lowlands, but still continued in the Highlands, where the priests served large areas and scattered congregations. The first houses that were obtained for the Lowland priests provided only very basic accommodation. The priest for the Keith area, for instance, lived in a but and ben on the small farm of Kempcairn. His chapel was a small straw-thatched building adjoining his house.[3] The priest for the Huntly area lived on the farm of Boghead in a house which was not built with 'stone and lime'[4] and which consisted of two rooms furnished with box beds, a few small closets, and a kitchen.[5]

Times, however, were changing, as Bishop Cameron wrote to Bishop Hay in 1804:

> I am glad Mr MacDonald is reconciled to Auchindown. I slept a night there last year with Mr Davison. The house, it must be allowed, is not equal to those of most of our brethren; but ten pounds sterling would have made it equal or superior to any country priest's house twenty or thirty years ago. I cannot help observing that what we now call a decent home associates too closely with furniture and expences which our predecessors would not perhaps have thought becoming our station any more than our income.[6]

Bishop Hay answered that he was in complete agreement:

> What you say about the great change you observe in certain novelties among our Brethren, both in houses and furniture, has *often, often* given me, and every time I think about it never fails to give me, the greatest distress.[7]

Certainly the house at Tombae in Glenlivet, which Mr James Gordon described to his mother in 1814, bore little resemblance to the but and ben at Kempcairn.

Downstairs it consisted of a dining room and another room with two bed closets off it. Upstairs were two more rooms. This part of the house was slated. From the north end of the house a passage door led to the kitchen quarters, which were roofed with black divots. The kitchen, where the maidservant slept, contained a bed, two presses, a dresser, a bench and a rack. A door from the kitchen led into a close off which were a barn, a kiln, four byres, a stable, and cartsheds.[8]

It was from about the middle of the eighteenth century that people in Scotland, thanks to an improved economy, were becoming able to live more comfortably than in former years. By the early nineteenth century the nobles, influenced by the customs of their English counterparts, were deserting their old draughty castles in ever-increasing numbers in favour of gracious mansion houses, of which Hopetoun House is the most splendid example. The gentry of Edinburgh were moving from their cramped flats in the tenement buildings which clustered thickly round the smelly closes of the Old Town, to live in large houses among the wide streets and squares of the New Town. Improving landowners were housing their tenants in new villages. Farmers were building larger, more comfortable houses. The Catholic priests were determined not to be left behind. One priest, in 1804, expressed what must have been the feelings of many:

> At a former period, still fresh in the remembrance of some here present, when a certain plainness and homliness was observable in the dress and manners of our Rustic gentry, a country priest could have supported the dignity of his character with less expense than a town priest; and therefore did our former Administrators very justly allow more to the clergy residing in towns, especially as they had nothing to depend upon, but their mission quota, no contributions being yet made by the people for their support. But circumstances have now changed. That plainness and simplicity of manners unhappily no more exist in most country places, and the man with the coarse coat and blue Bonnet would at present be accounted a companion only for Clowns. Now you very well know that a priest, in order to do good, must dress and appear in such a manner as to be accounted an unexceptionable companion for the high as well as for the low, for the Rich as well as for the poor; else we should imitate the Quaker who renders himself singular by the old-fashioned make of his clothes, and the cock of his hat . . . [9]

Such an attitude can hardly have found much sympathy with Bishop Hay, who, having been complimented by an old lady on the fashionable colour of his lilac suit, never wore that suit again.[10]

Mr MacDonald was not the only priest who believed in the importance of keeping up appearances. Mr John Sharp, a priest at Deecastle, described his life there in a letter written to Bishop Cameron in 1805:

> The first winter I was here I lived mostly on Potatoes, alternately boiled and roasted by way of a change, which had this farther advantage that being scarce of fire they generally served to warm my hands whilst I was taking my frugal repast. This likewise occasioned very little consumption of meal. I had no cow and could afford no malt, but then I had abundant supply of water from a neighbouring well, which nearly served the same purpose. Milk or Bear were luxuries of diet, to which I could then by no means aspire . . . Thus by observing the most rigid Economy I gradually got in my necessaries, I procured several articles of genteel furniture and endeavoured to keep myself in decent clothes.[11]

When Mr Sharp left Deecastle later that year, an inventory was made of the contents of the house. It included such items as a mahogany dining table, twenty-three green-edged plates, thirteen glasses, several decanters, a writing table, a mahogany breakfast table, a mahogany easy chair covered with red silk, two crystal goblets, and seventeen yards of London carpet. The total value of the contents of the house was estimated at £36.12.3.[12]

At the college of Aquhorties, too, the purely practical business of farming the land was carried on side by side with improvements to the policies immediately surrounding the college building. In 1808, long before all the farm land belonging to Aquhorties had been enclosed and improved, Mr Reid offered the following advice:

> The moor (rig and baulk) towards the Lint Mill on the west side of the road leading to the Mansion house, should also be attended to, and broke in without loss of time, not so much for the sake of the soil itself; but because in its present state it hurts the view from the house, and is disagreeable on the approach to it, and when improved it will serve to beautify both . . . [13]

The Scottish priests were struggling against heavy odds in their fight to keep up appearances. In 1793 their funds invested in France had been lost, and by 1798 their income from Rome had also ceased. Meanwhile, in Scotland, times were hard. In 1798, for instance, following a bad winter, the price of cattle fell disastrously, causing grave hardship in those parts of Scotland which depended on the sale of cattle to pay rents.[14] In 1803 the Duke of Gordon set his farms at inflated rents.[15] In 1806 many sheep died following a bad winter and a worse spring.[16] In 1808 Mr Reid, Preshome, wrote to Mr Maxwell:

> This has been rather a calamitous year for me, and still more so for many others in this north country. In some places a scarcity exists bordering on an absolute famine. No one is able to give assistance to his neighbour. A want of provender and a close winter have proved fatal to our farmers. Thousands of their sheep and cattle have died of hunger . . . [17]

A bad harvest or a severe winter not only caused a general distress among the farming communities of Scotland, it also had a direct effect on the priests themselves. By the end of the eighteenth century almost all the priests stationed in the North-East of Scotland had small farms attached to their houses, generally just a few acres, enough to support a few cows, and perhaps a horse, but sometimes large enough to show a cash profit over and above supplying the priest with meal and milk. These farms were the primary means by which country priests supplemented their inadequate Mission quotas.

Priests varied in their enthusiasm for farming. Mr Charles Maxwell, who lived on the farm of Boghead, outside Huntly, from 1775 to 1798, was famous for his enthusiastic application of gunpowder to the blowing up of rocks which impeded his plough.[18] Mr William Reid, who lived on the farm of Park, near Stobhall, when the leases were renewed in 1805, took on an extra acreage of unimproved land which, under the terms of the new lease, he undertook to 'improve and to bring into good arable ground'.[19] He sent Bishop Cameron weekly reports on the progress of his improvements.

Bishop Cameron was the most enthusiastic farmer of all, though forced to farm by proxy from his house in Blackfriars Wynd, Edinburgh. His stream of letters to Mr James Sharp at Aquhorties, full of instructions on the conserving of dung and on the housing of cattle, exhibit a passion for farming that almost makes the reader

Map 2. The Scottish Mission in 1790

wonder why he chose the priesthood as a career. His attitude towards improvements in agriculture was typical of a time when improving landowners were beginning to change the face of Scotland:

> I am happy . . . that your bear is secured and that you have used the scythe for cutting down your corn. You surely see, by experience, the very great and essential importance of various modern improvements in every branch of farming. We may not have talents, knowledge etc for taking the lead; but ignorance of what is done and of the reasons on which anything new rests, is not pardonable in us *as men of letters*.[20]

Bishop Cameron, though he found time to send letter after letter to Mr Sharp about the Aquhorties farm, was notably negligent in answering the queries of his priests regarding Mission affairs, such as the granting of dispensations. There are numerous letters still extant begging Bishop Cameron for an answer to queries which had sometimes been outstanding for over a year. It seems ironic, therefore, that Bishop Cameron should write to Mr Sharp:

> I shall never keep a priest in a station for the sake of his enjoying the benefit of a farm . . . [21]

Bishop Hay, unlike his successor, relegated farming to its proper place. In 1799 Mr Reid, the priest at Kempcairn, who was already the tenant of a small farm, took the lease of a second farm at some distance from his house. Bishop Hay deemed this to be an infringement of the Canon Law which prohibited priests from engaging in secular pursuits, and informed Mr Reid that, since he had taken the lease of the second farm, he had been living in mortal sin. He gave Mr Reid two weeks to give up the lease.[22] Whether Bishop Hay was aggravated principally by the fact that the second farm was at quite a distance from Mr Reid's house, or simply by the fact that the priest had increased his acreage, it is clear that he felt that Mr Reid had taken on more land than was necessary for his subsistence, and that he might, as a consequence, neglect his duties.

Some priests were in broad agreement with Bishop Hay. Mr James MacLachlan remarked:

> I know that to have a farm is inconvenient, but I feel it more inconvenient to want it . . . [23]

Other priests went further in their condemnation of farming. Mr Andrew Scott, when accepting a change of station from Boghead to Glasgow, wrote:

> I am now heartsick of farming to which I never had any inclination.[24]

Mr William Thomson, priest on Deeside in 1808, echoed those sentiments:

> I have no notion of managing a farm; nay I hate and detest it from the bottom of my heart; indeed my sole inclination is to employ myself in studying, praying, reading, and in exercising other offices of charity to my neighbours.[25]

However much some priests might object to having to combine farming with their ecclesiastical duties, the tradition persisted in the North-East. When the new station of Eastlands was set up in 1808, it was provided with a farm to help maintain its priest. Indeed the long line of priest-farmers in the North-East ended only in 1950 with the death of Canon Donald Mackay at Preshome.[26]

A farming tradition was not peculiar to the Catholic Church in Scotland. The ministers of the parish churches in the established Church were provided with glebes which they either farmed themselves or leased out. Some of the ministers in the North-East, in the eighteenth and early nineteenth centuries, were just as dependent on this source of support as were the Catholic priests.

Many Church of Scotland manses still possess glebes today, although there is beginning to be a tendency to sell them off. The Catholic Church, however, by about 1830, was beginning to view less favourably the farms that were attached to Mission stations. In 1829 Bishop Kyle, Vicar Apostolic of the newly formed Northern District, wrote to Mr Forbes:

> It certainly gives me extreme pain that our northern missionaries are left by their people in circumstances so despondent, and are obliged in so many instances to eke out the scanty means of subsistance that they draw from the proper source, by farming . . . [27]

Bishop Kyle's attitude towards farming as a necessary evil, to be abolished as soon as possible, was shared by most of the younger priests in 1829. Such an attitude was incomprehensible to their older colleagues, who had accepted their small farms with gratitude. In 1828 Mr Alexander Grant, a newly ordained young priest, gave up the lease of his farm at Auchmully, near Portsoy, on the grounds that it took up too much of the time that he should have been spending on his duties as priest.[28] Commenting on this, Bishop Paterson, who had been a priest in Scotland for thirty-five years, wrote:

> . . . as I had some little experience myself of the advantage of a farm in days of yore, and as Auchmully was a central place, I thought I had conveyed a favour on the incumbent of Banff and Portsoy by closing with George Low . . . and also by becoming bound for the rent . . . I find that I was mistaken. When I was younger I found farming a rational amusement and relaxation of mind, but I am sorry to see from Mr Grant's letter that he has found it a trouble and vexation before he begins; no doubt he is horrified at the very thought.[29]

Irrespective of whether or not the country priests were involved in farming, theirs was a hard life, particularly in winter. In 1809, Mr William Thomson of Deecastle described the effects of a severe frost:

> I was obliged to put my ink bottle in the fire, when I wrote, to get it thawed. It [the frost] burst the bottles with beer in my press and at a few feet's distance from the fire.[30]

Hard winters and the need to cover large distances, often on foot, were the greatest hardships which a country priest had to face. When Abbé MacPherson was stationed in the Cabrach district he was called out one day to visit a dying man. His guide warned him to be careful where he walked in case he fell down the chimney of a house over which they were walking, the house having been completely buried in snow.[31]

One of the most evocative letters to have survived was written by Mr Lachlan MacIntosh, priest in Glengairn, a station which stretched from the Dee to Corgarf, as well as taking in eleven miles on Deeside and nineteen miles on Donside.[32] In June 1829 Mr MacIntosh wrote to Bishop Kyle:

> . . . I have been here forty six years out under very great difficulties, amidst these stormy mountains, which I had dayly occasion to transverse, and besides in wants of every kind. I was blessed with a robust constitution, but this late winter has given it a severe shock and I find myself therefore much disabilitated. This was caused principally by calls to the sick during storms, which some years past I would have made very light of. I hope then you will now consider my decayed condition and appoint me to some easier a situation for the poor remains of my life, which cannot be long.[33]

Mr MacIntosh wrote the above letter when he was in his seventieth year. For the first time in his life he was afraid to face the cold of a winter in Glengairn. In spite of his plea to his bishop he was not moved, and spent the rest of his life in

Glengairn, dying there in 1846 aged eighty-eight.

Priests who lived in towns were unable to supplement their incomes by farming. They were, therefore, given an additional allowance. By 1804 Mr William MacDonald felt that paying country priests less than town priests could no longer be justified:

> ... one in my situation, whose people are so far scattered, must keep a horse. And as for the table expenses of country priests, I do not see how they can be much less than those of our Brethren in towns. For if their farms afford them meal and milk, with some other necessaries, it is not for nothing. With rent and men servants' wages, of which our town clergy are free, they are dearly purchased. It is also evident that whatever is bought from towns costs the additional expense of carriage while everything may be had in towns at prime cost ... [34]

Mr MacDonald need not have complained about such discrimination. Only two months previously, Bishop Hay had informed Bishop Cameron:

> ... none in towns have any more than those in the country; for this reason, that having lost all our funds abroad, what remains in this country scarcely allows the £11 for each.[35]

Mr MacDonald had, of course, wanted country quotas to be increased to the same amount as town quotas, instead of which the town quotas had been reduced to the same level as country ones.

Even with the reduction in quotas there were still, at the beginning of the nineteenth century, certain advantages attached to the town missions. In general the Catholic congregations were small, and so the priest had fewer sick calls to make, while those he did have to make were generally fairly close to his house. In 1804, for instance, Mr Reid estimated that there were in Dundee forty adult Catholics and fifteen children, and in Forfar six Catholics.[36] In this year Mr Donald Stuart was moved from Strathavon to Dundee. He considered the change to be most advantageous to one of his infirm constitution. Even in summer he found the life there much easier, while in winter the difference, he anticipated, would be even more pronounced.[37]

Two events were to alter the life of the town priest out of all recognition. Firstly, there was the advent of Irish regiments to Scotland from about 1800 onwards. Many of these Irish soldiers were Catholics, and the town priest, used to a small congregation, was suddenly faced with large numbers of Catholics for whom his chapel was quite inadequate. There were Irish regiments in Glasgow and Dumfries in 1805, in Ayr in 1806, at Edinburgh and Perth in 1809, at Dundee in 1811, and again at Dundee and Perth in 1820.[38] As the regiments were generally stationed only for a short time in any given place, the priests tried to hire halls or to acquire barracks buildings for use as temporary chapels, building new chapels being generally out of the question.

Secondly, there was the growth of the Irish immigrant population in the West of Scotland, in the Glasgow area and in Galloway, and to a lesser extent in eastern towns like Edinburgh and Dundee. These immigrants changed the whole pattern of Catholicism in the towns. For one thing, their sheer numbers were something quite new. In 1822, for instance, there were an estimated twelve hundred Catholics in Glenlivet, and an estimated fifteen thousand Catholics in Glasgow.[39]

Although the Scottish priests did their best for the new Irish congregations, there is a great deal of evidence, from the letters they wrote, that they viewed the

Irish with some consternation. This is understandable; the priests who had to cope with such immigrants had themselves been born and raised in the settled Catholic communities of the North-East, where the priests could ensure that their congregations were well-instructed. By contrast the Irish Catholic population of the South-West was a shifting one made up of poor, often illiterate, people who had left Ireland in the hope that they might find work in Scotland. In 1813, for instance, Mr Scott, priest at Glasgow, remarked that most of his congregation had never had any instruction in the Catholic faith before they reached Scotland.[40] Other priests complained of the superstitions and sometimes corrupt practices of the Irish Catholics:

> . . . the Irish Catholics hold, at least practically, part of the Presbyterian doctrine and seem to think that while they stick to the *true faith* they may safely neglect every other moral and religious duty which it prescribes. They are not only wretchedly ignorant of their duty, but seem perfectly careless about using the means of attaining the necessary knowledge of it.[41]

> The paddies or Irish people here apply often for gospels to hang about the necks of their children to preserve them . . . from all evil. I have given much offence to persons for refusing such gospels . . . Another thing by which I have offended persons is by refusing to give blessed earth to be put into the coffin with a dead person.[42]

> . . . the great bulk of Catholics in this quarter are Irish of the lower classes. They come over poor, tattered, ignorant, and partly pious and partly vicious. They come over, not with a view to settle here, but either out of frolic, or to make some little money, or to escape the just punishment of their crimes. This last-mentioned class, which is by no means inconsiderable, carrying with them here their vicious dispositions, are commonly soon compelled to quit this country also, after giving great scandal to their holy Religion and to their native land. Many, however, generally of the better sort, contrary to their original intention, consider at length their residence as fixed here, either because they are prosperous more than they could expect to be at home, or because they or some of their children intermarry with natives of this country. But the great bulk of them here are merely birds of passage; and no sooner have you got those of them whom you can induce to attend, instructed and brought into some degree of order, than away they go . . . Even amongst [the truly pious] there is one melancholy circumstance not at all uncommon. It is their inconsistency. After restraining their passions, and frequenting the sacraments most devoutly for years; the next thing you hear of them is, that they have been concerned in some scandalous scenes of drunkenness, rioting, etc. But they soon repent as heartily as they had sinned; and will not be condemned for lukewarmness. For they are hot or cold, saints or divels . . . [43]

Although the Irish Catholics settled in Scotland in ever-increasing numbers, they were not readily assimilated into the indigenous Catholic community. In spite of the fact that Catholics of Irish extraction had come, by the 1820s, to represent so large a percentage of the Catholic population of Scotland, Bishop Cameron was notably reluctant to accept any of them to train for the priesthood at Aquhorties. In 1815, however, he did admit to Aquhorties a boy by the name of Peter Dougherty, who came from Ireland but had been living for several years in Crieff. Peter was expelled six months later for using bad language.[44] This did nothing to endear Irish boys to Bishop Cameron. In 1821 another Irish boy, George MacNally, from Glasgow, was admitted to the College, but he left almost at once when he found he would not immediately be sent abroad.[45] In 1821 an Edinburgh Catholic of Irish extraction, Charles Ralston, applied to be admitted as a Church student to Aquhorties. Mr Reid, in a letter to Mr Kyle, outlined the dilemma in which he was placed by this application:

> I could not refuse it, without losing the confidence of Ralston [i.e. the boy's father] and all the Irish part of this extensive congregation . . . In truth I must say that the boy has several good qualities though not more than many others of Irish parents, but I know that Bishop Cameron is against receiving more Irish children . . . [46]

Bishop Cameron, ten months later, finally agreed to accept Charles Ralston into Aquhorties, adding: ' . . . but he shall be the last of the generation [i.e. Irish] in my time'.[47] Charles Ralston was ordained priest in 1832.

Mr Alexander Paterson, for many years priest at Paisley, was more realistic than Bishop Cameron and, when he was consecrated bishop in 1816 and became Cameron's coadjutor, he made strenuous efforts to have Irish priests, or priests of Irish extraction, admitted to the Scottish Mission. His first attempts were made in Paris where, in 1818, he had succeeded in establishing bursaries in French colleges for Scots boys, out of what he had managed to salvage of the wreck of the Scots Colleges there. In September 1824, he wrote to Bishop Cameron:

> We have only ten students here, and, as we can have sixteen, the Archbishop of Rheims' opinion [is] that we would do well to admit two or three Irish students who are now studying Theology at St Sulpice and [are] highly recommended by their Bishops.[48]

Bishop Cameron's reply was soon forthcoming:

> . . . I must formally and solemnly protest against your receiving any Irish students upon any account whatever; nor can I help expressing my astonishment that such a measure should be submitted to my opinion for my approbation.[49]

Bishop Cameron's attitude towards the Irish was coloured by the fact that the Scots Colleges at Valladolid in the 1760s and at Paris during the Napoleonic wars had come under Irish control to the detriment both of the colleges and of the Scottish Mission.[50]

In spite of Bishop Cameron's attitude, Bishop Paterson did accept some Irish students on the Scots funds at Paris. They were all theology students nearing the end of their training, and therefore they were of proven character and ability. In 1825 two of them were ordained. Bishop Cameron refused to accept them for the Lowland District, so they were sent to the Higlands. One of them proved unsatisfactory and soon left for Ireland; the other, Terence MacGuire, served the Scottish Mission faithfully until he died at Fochabers in 1869 aged seventy-nine.

On the whole, Bishop Paterson's experiment with Irish boys in Paris was unsuccessful. One of his protégés, in particular, highlights the whole problem of the Irish Catholic population in Scotland: the Scottish priests were adamant that no Irish priest should serve the Irish Catholic congregations of the South-West. Bishop Paterson's idea was that Irish priests should serve in the North-East of Scotland, while priests from Banffshire and Aberdeenshire should serve in towns like Glasgow in the West.[51] Mr Scott, priest in Glasgow since 1805, spelt out the problems of having an Irish priest in Glasgow:

> I am quite convinced that the Glasgow mission in particular would be most seriously injured by bringing an Irishman to it, even for only a few months, and that you would put prejudices against yourself in the minds of the most respectable protestants which would never be eradicated . . . It is natural even for Scotchmen in a foreign land to draw together. Irishmen

have the same feelings, but less prudence. There has been a cry to get Irishmen to Glasgow, and most certainly an Irish priest would soon associate with his countrymen and naturally fall, into all the habits he was accustomed to see between his own country priests at home and their flocks. He would appear to have all their hearts, which might flatter too much a young mind, and if he had not extraordinary prudence, all Episcopal authority would soon be set aside. This has happened elsewhere. He would also impart to them everything that passed, and many things that he ought not to do . . . I should fear the total ruin of the Glasgow mission in its present circumstances from such a step. I beg leave also to mention to you that Kirkman Finlay Esq when he subscribed for the chapel, and when he became president of the School Society, asked me very seriously whether there was any intention of bringing *Irish priests* to Glasgow or to that country. Knowing Bishop Cameron's ideas on the subject, and supposing you were of the same mind, I assured him there was no such intention and that it would never be the case. I perhaps went too far. He said he hoped they 'would never be allowed to come to this country' or words to that effect, and mentioned in very strong terms how disagreeable it would be to the local authorities of the Country and to every respectable protestant in Glasgow; and the great prejudices it would excite and keep alive against Catholics in this Country. Many other respectable protestant Gentlemen have expressed themselves in the same strong language on the subject.[52]

Mr Gibbons, an Irish priest from Paris, confirmed Mr Scott's worst fears. He arrived in Scotland in 1826 and for two years served the Mission well, first as professor at Aquhorties, and then for a short time at Huntly. In 1828 he was sent to Tombae, where his drinking caused a scandal. Removed from Glenlivet, Mr Gibbons drifted between Aberdeen and Edinburgh before finally turning up in Glasgow. From Glasgow Mr Scott reported:

[Gibbons] denies everything laid to his charge, declares that he is sent away by a combination among the Scotch Bishops and Priests, merely because he is an Irishman. He says that the Irish Catholics, being the most numerous body of Catholics in all the South of Scotland, have a right to be served by Irish priests and governed by Irish bishops . . . [53]

In short, Mr Gibbons, because of his dismissal from Tombae, stirred up the Irish Catholics of Glasgow against the Scottish bishops and priests, urging on them the idea of separatism, of establishing an 'Irish Catholic' Church in Scotland.

Since the Irish immigrants to Scotland came in the main from Ulster, there were as many Protestants as Catholics among them. The Protestant ministers, like the Catholic priests, had to cope with enormous congregations which needed larger churches and more clergymen than were available. The old educational and poor relief systems, based on the parishes of the established Church, were no longer able to cope. The priests did what they could to help the Catholics by setting up schools and by encouraging Catholic Friendly societies. Priests and ministers encountered the problems of overcrowded slums, of dirt, and of disease. In 1847 alone, three priests, one in Greenock and two in Paisley, died of typhus fever. In 1856 Glasgow lost three priests to the same disease. The Irish Protestants, however, unlike their Catholic countrymen, were relatively easily assimilated into the indigenous population, and it was the Irish Catholics who, set apart by their religion, engendered the anti-Irish feeling which still exists today.

By the middle of the nineteenth century Irish priests were being posted to the West of Scotland, but while Bishop Cameron was alive, it was left to men like Mr Scott and Mr Paterson, both from the Enzie district of Banffshire, to cope with the change caused by Irish immigration. In 1790 Edinburgh was the only town in

Scotland with a significant Catholic population. By 1830 Catholic chapels had been founded in Glasgow, Paisley, Greenock, Ayr, Dumfries and Newton Stewart. The priests attached to these chapels also served Catholics in Girvan, Irvine, Kilmarnock, Hamilton, Airdrie, Stranraer and many other towns in the South-West of Scotland. No longer were town priests more comfortably placed than those in the country stations.

The mushrooming of mission stations in the South-West of Scotland caused a split between the priests who served there, and those who served in the North-East. Those in the North-East considered that their confrères in the Glasgow area, since they had much larger congregations, must be proportionally better off financially. They forgot to take into account the enormous initial capital outlay that had to be spent in building the much larger chapels needed there like, for example, the magnificent chapel, later cathedral, of St Andrew in Glasgow, completed in 1816. The priests of the South-West, for their part, considered that those of the North-East did not know what hard work was. As one of them put it:

> Since I came to the South I have found that you are not missionaries at all in the North. Here we are employed day and night in visiting the sick, in administering the sacraments, in reclaiming sinners, in making up the peace of families etc, but in the North you scarcely know what it is to labour in the vineyard.[54]

The split between North and South became what amounted to open warfare, in 1827, when Bishop Paterson decided that Scotland should be split into three Vicariates in place of two. Bishop Cameron had, by this time, resigned all his authority into his coadjutor's hands but, when the question of the three Vicariates was raised, he denied that he had done so, and violently opposed the measure. The priests of the North-East acknowledged their allegiance to Bishop Paterson, and those of the South to Bishop Cameron. Even the death of Bishop Cameron in 1828 failed to heal entirely the breach between North and South, between town priests and country priests.

In both town and country the Mission quota, by the beginning of the nineteenth century, was no longer sufficient to maintain a priest in any degree of comfort. The neediest priests were allocated funds that had been bequeathed for the saying of specific masses, but even that was not enough.

In 1765 Bishop Hay estimated that a priest received about £10 from Mission funds, out of which he had to pay for bed, board, washing, clothes; and for the keep of a horse if he lived in the country. He believed that this was insufficient, that country priests should receive £15 per annum and town priests £20. He looked forward to a time when each priest should have a house of his own, however humble, where he could study and meditate in private.[55]

By 1790 Bishop Hay's hopes had been realised in that each priest of the Lowland Vicariate had a house. As regards quotas, however, country priests never received more than £12 per annum except for the few years when the Government grant was paid.

Since the Mission quotas were insufficient, other methods had to be found of supplementing the incomes of the priests. One method, already discussed, was to attach a small farm to each country station. Such a method, however, could not be applied to a town. The problem of supporting priests from Mission funds was compounded by the need to open new stations in towns like Paisley, Greenock and Ayr, to serve the growing Irish Catholic population. The quotas, which were already insufficient, would be reduced to an intolerable level if Mission funds had to be stretched to support many extra priests for these new stations. One obvious solution to the problem was to ask each congregation to contribute something towards the support of its priest.

In 1781 Bishop Hay had informed Propaganda that nothing at all was asked of the people; in a few places in the Highlands, the better-off Catholics would make the priest a present of food if he officiated at a baptism or a marriage, but everywhere else the priests performed their duties free of charge, partly to prevent Protestants from accusing the Catholic Church of greed, and partly because the vast majority of Scottish Catholics were too poor to be able to pay anything.[56]

By 1791 the Mission was in danger of losing all the money it had invested in French funds, and the bishops, in their annual letter to Propaganda, revealed that they had begun to induce the people to contribute to their priests' support, but that such an innovation required both time and great prudence.[57]

Bishop Hay might hope that people could be induced to contribute; he was adamant that they could not be forced to do so. He made this quite clear in 1801 in answer to a petition for higher pay presented by some of the priests. Referring back to a previous petition which had suggested that congregations be asked to contribute, he wrote:

> . . . the application made to the Bishops to have recourse to their people for assistance . . . was found inadmissible, because they did not think themselves authorized by the laws of the Church to adopt it. Wishing to settle my own mind upon this last point I have of late been examining proper authorities concerning it, and I have every reason to be persuaded that, whatever may be the case in places where the Catholic religion is settled and the Hierarchy established, in Missions the Bishops have no authority to have recourse to the people for the support of the Missionaries.

Bishop Hay had consulted with the English Vicars Apostolic to see how matters stood relative to people's contributions in England. The English bishops agreed that:

> (1) . . . we have no authority to lay on Burdens upon the people for the support of their Pastors; everything of that kind must come from the voluntary act of the people themselves; all that we can do, if necessary, is to let the people know that they are in straits.
>
> (2) . . . such applications made by the Bishops and enforced by their authority are apt to cause complaints and murmurings which are very dangerous matters.
>
> (3) . . . the Bishops have a full power to restrain, change or annull all such contributions as have been made by the priests themselves, if such murmurs and complaints should appear.[58]

The English bishops added that many of their priests were short of money and that many charged a rent for the seats in their chapels. Occasionally a bishop had to intervene if the rents were thought to be too high. Nobody, however, was compelled to take a seat by paying for it.

The charging of seat rents was common practice in the Church of Scotland. It was also practised, to a certain extent, by 1800, in the Catholic chapels in Scotland. Seat renting was, however, in no way compulsory. In 1791, according to

Mr William Pepper, only eight of his congregation paid seat rents, and furthermore:

> ... the circumstances of my congregation's poverty neither does nor can afford but so small a relief [i.e. collection] that it scarcely keeps the Chapel in candles, wine and washing of the Chapel linnings [linens].[59]

In Edinburgh sufficient money was made from seat rents in 1791 to pay the salary of a schoolmaster. In the same year it was suggested that in future the seat rents should be put instead towards the building of a new chapel.[60]

Seat rents appear to have been paid by some members at least of the congregations of a number of chapels in the North-East by about 1800. In September, 1806, for instance, Mr James Carruthers, priest at Preshome, suggested to Bishop Cameron that seat rents should be organised under the bishop's authority, in order to accustom the people to obeying episcopal directions. This would have the additional effect of placing seat rents on a uniform basis. He went on to suggest that, if the seat rents amounted to more than the bishop judged to be necessary for the priest, the surplus should be put into a fund to be used for chapel repairs and improvements.[61] This letter suggests that seats had been rented for some time at Preshome, if on a somewhat haphazard basis.

A letter from Mr Badenoch, priest at Tomintoul, illustrates one of the problems that could be caused by charging for seats. When Mr Donald Stuart had built the chapel at Tomintoul, he had sold some of the seats to help defray building costs. The purchasers had come to regard these seats as their personal property, and some of them had subsequently double-let them, causing disputes. Mr Badenoch pointed out that the only way to sort things out was for the Mission to take over the ownership and the letting of all chapel seats.[62]

Mr Carmichael inherited Mr Badenoch's problem. He consulted Bishop Cameron, and was told:

> It is indeed contrary to the discipline of the Catholic Church, by which no layman has or can have any property in the house of God. This reflection has made the people give up the property of the seats in all the principal Catholic congregations in Scotland; and when individuals do not make a present of their seats to the Chapel, they are either paid the original value of them, or they are allowed to carry them away.[63]

Mr Carmichael faced another problem regarding the seats in the Tomintoul chapel; he upset many members of his congregation when he tried to reduce the size of each individual seat. At that time a 'seat' in his chapel, presumably an allocation on a long pew, occupied twenty-nine or thirty inches of space. Mr Carmichael, finding that there were insufficient seats to go round all those who wanted them, proposed to reduce each seat size to twenty-six or twenty-seven inches. In that way he would be able to increase the seating capacity of the chapel.[64] Some of his congregation clung obstinately to their extra two inches, and prevented the necessary alterations from being carried out. By the following year, however, everyone had agreed to co-operate.[65]

It is clear that some at least of the chapel seats were being rented out at Preshome and at Tomintoul by about 1800. Probably the other chapels in the North-East were doing likewise. In most cases the income from seat rents can have amounted to very little. Probably only a few seats were rented because few people would have been in a position to pay for them. Those who did pay cannot have paid very much, judging by the description written by Mr Reid, priest at Preshome in 1804, of the lot of the Banffshire priests:

> Our present quotas are scarce sufficient to keep decent clothes on our backs, and most of our little farms produce nothing now but loss. The Tenantry on the Gordon Estate must soon be ruined, and the Catholic part of them rendered totally unable to furnish any effectual support to their needy clergy.[66]

Seat rents may not always have been the answer to priestly poverty in the North-East, but they were crucial to the economy of the new chapels that were springing up in the South-West. If one bears in mind that each priest's yearly Mission quota amounted to £12, the amount of money raised by the renting of chapel seats will be seen to have been very large indeed by comparison.

In 1805, when Mr Farquharson was on the eve of giving up the Glasgow chapel to retire to Elgin, he reported to Abbé MacPherson that Glasgow soon would be

> . . . perhaps the most numerous and certainly the most independent station we have; with ordinary attention it will afford (as a pattern for other places) £50 a year to [its] incumbent, in clearing over and above the £50 annually of the chapel debt . . . Mr Scott, on replacing me, on being insured in £50, gives up his quota for the good of others . . . [67]

Mr Farquharson, in short, estimated that Glasgow chapel would have an annual income of over £100. This income would arise from seat rents and from collections.

In 1810 Mr Scott wrote, of Glasgow, that, in spite of hard times and business failures:

> I will always be able to make £250 stg. per annum, and I think if there was a sufficiently large chapel that sum could be doubled in ordinary times.[68]

In 1816 Mr Scott realised his dream of a really large chapel. The seat rents brought in a large income — £600 in 1826[69] — but this income was all swallowed up, for many years after 1826, in paying off the huge debt incurred in building the chapel.

Other places with an expanding Irish Catholic population were also able to take substantial sums in seat rents. In 1808 Mr Rattray obtained a hall in Paisley for the use of the Catholics there. He commissioned seats, which he proposed to let as being the only way of getting his congregation to pay anything. Mr Scott estimated that the seats should bring in £50 – 60 per annum, and that Sunday collections should bring in £30, making a total of at least £80 income per annum.[70] In November 1808, building started on a chapel and priest's house for Paisley, and in November 1810 Mr Rattray informed Bishop Cameron that over the previous six months the seats in the new chapel had raised £55-2-6 in rents, while collections had amounted to £29-2-10. He feared, however, that with the decline in trade, many of his people who worked in the cotton mills would be unable to pay much during the following six months.[71]

In 1808 Greenock, which had previously been served from Glasgow, obtained its first resident priest. A hall was rented to serve as a chapel, and Mr Scott estimated that the seat rents should produce £50 per annum for the priest, the collections being sufficient, he hoped, to cover the rent of the hall.[72] In 1810, however, the priest, Mr Davidson, collected only £20 for six months' seat rental.

In spite of this he believed that, had he large enough premises to seat all his congregation, he could raise more than enough money to support himself.[73]

In Dumfries, where a growing Irish population had necessitated the building of a chapel in 1813, Mr William Reid was able to report that the first letting of the seats had brought in £60 for the half-year. Seat rents and collection money were to go towards paying off the debt on the chapel, as Mr Reid was provided for as chaplain at Terregles.[74]

In general the chapels of the South-West were making at least £100 per annum in seat rents by 1810. By contrast Mr Paterson, priest in Glenlivet, collected just over £13 in seat rents for the year 1810 to 1811.[75] Seat rents may have been a solution to the provision of an adequate salary for priests in the South-West; they were not the solution in the North-East. One reason why seat rents raised so much more in the South-West was that congregations in the cities were far larger than those even in the largely Catholic areas of the North-East. Prices on seats, too, varied from place to place. In 1829 Mr James Gordon, Glenlivet, was charging from one shilling to three shillings rent for the half-year, depending on where the seat was situated in the chapel.[76] In 1815, by contrast, when Edinburgh's new chapel was opened, the priests were able, since the Edinburgh congregation included a number of very wealthy people, to charge much larger sums for some of the seats. As Mr John Cameron somewhat inelegantly put it: 'In the front seats the doup-room rents at £5.'[77]

In 1811 Mr Paterson, Glenlivet, collected £13 in seat rents, and received the Mission quota of £12. His salary for that year, therefore, amounted to £25, exclusive of what he made from his farm. In 1809 Mr Scott estimated that the minimum salary for a priest in the South-West should be £50. In 1814 the Catholics of Wigtown petitioned for a priest, guaranteeing that they would provide him with a salary of £50 per annum.[78] In 1813 the Catholics of Ayr, in a similar petition, guaranteed a salary of the same amount.[79]

It is little wonder that Mr John Gordon attached so much importance to the farm attached to his Mission station at Eastlands in Aberdeenshire,[80] or that Mr Thomson, with only a small, poor farm at Deecastle, was unable to make ends meet.[81] Neither priest could expect much in the way of seat rents from his small, scattered congregation.

Seat rents supplemented the incomes of priests and helped to finance the building of chapels, but they did have some quite serious disadvantages. They produced a tendency for chapels to cater for the more well-to-do Catholics at the expense of the very poor. Mr Scott, for instance, in 1811, said that, in spite of the trade recession, he had had no trouble letting all his seats because there were far more Catholics in Glasgow than there were seats in the chapel.[82] Obviously the seats went to those who could afford them, leaving the very poor with no place to sit.

In 1808 Mr Davidson of Greenock wrote to inform Bishop Cameron that, although many of the seats in his chapel were not rented out, they were all occupied on Sundays:

> ... some of my elders, upon this account, proposed to adopt the violent measure of excluding

everyone who either had not payed or would not consent to pay for a seat. I own I was half tempted to agree to this measure . . . [83]

In 1812 Mr Rattray wrote from Paisley that he had been so strict with people who had not paid their seat rents that many had renounced all religious exercises and were now refusing to come to Easter communion, for shame at coming forward when they had no seats in the chapel.[84] The Paisley chapel had incurred a large debt when it was built in 1808 and Mr Scott of Glasgow, who was involved in paying off the debt, was adamant that the people of Paisley must pay seat rents for this purpose. He went so far as to write in 1812:

> As to the threat I mentioned of placing men in the passes [i.e. passages] after a few Sundays to prevent those who do not take seats from occupying them, I should think it essentially necessary (from the experience I have of the Irish character and of the fertility of their genius in framing plausible excuses for not doing what is disagreeable to their passions) I should think it, I repeat, essentially necessary to put it in execution . . . The Irish must be treated in a different manner from our Scots people, or they never can be helped on the way to salvation.[85]

Mr Scott appears to have applied strict rules about seat-letting in his own chapel in Glasgow, if the following anonymous letter addressed to Bishop Cameron can be believed:

> I request you to be so good as to write and admonish our Pastor, the Revd. Andrew Scott as he has of late used several Expressions tending to hurt the Feelings of the Irish, a people naturally proud and rather easily offended when their relative Poverty has been made the subject of their Reproach also it would be well if the seats that has been appointed for the Poor that was unable to pay for their seats was Returned to them and Not to keep them standing up as a gazing stock during the sermon that Every Person present may know their Poverty and your Reverence knows best the Reason why the Morning Service is totally omited and I humbly presume that this is a wrong time for any bitter Reflections concerning Religious Difference of opinion when Roman Catholics Dare scarcely acknowledge the Name of their profession and that there is Every Appearance of a Severe Persecution in this City and that Every thing appears both Dark and gloomy in the present time.[86]

It was Mr Scott who concerted the most ambitious scheme to obtain contributions from his congregation towards the building of a new chapel in Glasgow. He outlined his plan to Bishop Cameron in August, 1813:

> We have resolved ourselves into one general society including men and women, and as all public works pay their people once a fortnight the payments are to be once a fortnight from all without exception. Men give one shilling a fortnight, or more if they please. Women, from a penny to a shilling as they can afford. It is optional to them. To make it practical every street or so has a collector who calls on every individual when they receive their pay, once a fortnight, receives their money, marks it in his book, and brings his book and money to me, to be copied into the books kept by me . . . I have got already about fifty districts appointed and upwards of thirty will begin to collect on Sunday first.[87]

Mr Scott hoped to collect £100 a fortnight — £2,600 per annum. It is not surprising that, with a trade recession, and considering the poverty of his congregation, such an ambitious target proved impossible.

Besides the priests who served in the town missions, and in the country missions, there was a third group. This was the group of priests employed as chaplains to the Catholic families of Traquair, Kirkconnell, Munshes and Terregles. A chaplain was maintained completely by the family with which he lived; he therefore drew nothing from Mission funds. Although he was expected to serve the Catholic families of the neighbourhood, his duties were generally far less onerous than those of his confrères. A chaplaincy was an ideal post for an old or infirm priest. Mr MacGillivray, for instance, after serving on the Mission for twenty-seven years, seventeen of them in Glenlivet and Mortlach, retired to Traquair where he ended his days, pottering happily about, binding books and carving egg-cups out of wood.

Even for a chaplain, however, there were problems. Mr Bagnall, chaplain at Kirkconnell, for instance, mentioned to Bishop Cameron:

> ... no banns are ever published in our chapel, as it is a private one. To publish them would be an encroachment upon private property.[88]

This was the basic problem which faced a chaplain. He was employed by a private family, but at the same time the Mission expected him to serve the surrounding Catholic families just like any ordinary priest. Generally speaking, the laird whom the chaplain served made no objections to the general public attending services and instruction in his private chapel. There was inevitably, however, some friction inherent in such an arrangement. In 1804 Mr Maxwell of Kirkconnell complained to Bishop Cameron:

> I consider this chapple at Kirkconnell as a private one. Consequently that no Missionary would Reasonably take upon himself to Establish any new Rules or Regulations in Regard of Examination of children one Sunday in the month and having forty or fifty Children Running about till called into the chapple one by one. One other thing I think that our Congregation are not a little Encouraged in making themselves very busy about my family and why and wherefore they do not attend in the chapple. . . . I should certainly be very sorry to prevent any of the congregation being as much in this chapple as they please, or as is thought proper but I must confess I do not think they have any business to meddle with any arrangements in my family.[89]

In 1822 matters came to a head between Maxwell of Kirkconnell and his chaplain, Mr Bagnall, who was then sixty-one years old and had been chaplain at Kirkconnell for twenty-seven years. Mr Bagnall explained the circumstances to Mr Kyle:

> You'll no doubt have heard of the fatal blow given to Religion, in this corner of Galloway, where the Catholic priest and Catholic people had ever found an assylum even in the most troublesome times, since the Pretended Reformation. From the politics which, of late years, especially since the year 1818, have prevailed in this house, everyone in this neighbourhood, Protestants as well as Catholics, saw the storm gathering, which threatened destruction to me and my flock, and this storm was to have burst over us, at Martinmas next, at latest, with a tremendous crash. For on the day of the 24th of July last, a Decree passed in full Council here: 'That very soon, at Martinmas next at latest, I and my family (says the Laird) and this Congregation shall have to attend Dumfries Chapel in place of the convenience we have hitherto had, because from the unforeseen pressure of the times, and other unexpected circumstances, I am no longer able to support this mission.' Because, a great fortune, I may add, must, at any rate be accumulated for our young Heiress, whom God may, ee'r long, call to a much richer inheritance.[90]

Mr Maxwell pleaded poverty as a reason for dispensing with a chaplain; but he seems to have had a personal grudge against Mr Bagnall. In a letter to Bishop Cameron he complained:

> Ever since Mr Bagnall has been here something or other has always occurred which did not agree with his ideas, and particularly within these three years past in which I have been obliged to reduce my expenses and did not find it convenient to keep a poney for his use as formerly and which has been the cause of many serious and disagreeable consequences. So much so that

should I ever find it convenient to support this mission I should not wish him for the incumbent.[91]

Mr Bagnall left Kirkconnell in 1823 and founded a new Mission station at New Abbey, where he saw a chapel and priest's house built before he died in May 1826.

Mr Constable Maxwell of Terregles was the cause of quite a different problem for the Mission. At one time the Terregles Chapel had been large enough to accommodate all the Catholics in the Dumfries areas, but Irish regiments and Irish immigrants swelled the congregation in the first decade of the nineteenth century to such an extent that the Chapel was no longer large enough. By 1810 it had become obvious that a chapel would have to be built in the town of Dumfries. It was completed in 1813 and was served by Mr Reid, the chaplain at Terregles. When Mr Maxwell and his family were, as they often were, in England, this arrangement worked very well, as Mr Maxwell paid for Mr Reid's maintenance at Terregles, while Mr Reid was free to say Mass in Dumfries. In the summer of 1813, however, Mr Maxwell wrote to Bishop Cameron from London, informing him that he was bringing his family to Terregles for a holiday. He insisted, with some justification, that Mr Reid should put his duties as chaplain first as it would be a great inconvenience to him to take his 'numerous family' to Dumfries on Sundays and holy days.[92] As a result Mr Reid reverted to the duties of domestic chaplain, leaving the aged Mr William Pepper to cope as best he could at Dumfries. The Catholics of Dumfries were understandably annoyed that, having paid their seat rents, they were deprived of the services of their priest.[93]

Although it was useful to have chaplaincies in which old and infirm priests could live in semi-retirement at no expense to the Mission, there must have been many times when the Scottish bishops echoed Mr Sharp's sentiments:

> I would most cheerfully undergo a little more fatigue in order to maintain a total Independence upon all these great folks . . . [94]

By 1829 only Traquair kept a permanent chaplain. On the rare occasions when Mr Maxwell of Terregles was in Scotland, the Mission supplied him with a temporary chaplain, but the Mission station had moved to Dumfries by 1813. Maxwell of Kirkconnell, after 1823, employed as chaplain a Mr Witham, a cousin of Mrs Maxwell, who was an English priest with no connections with the Scottish Mission. The Mission station had moved to New Abbey in 1823. At Munshes the last Catholic Maxwell died in 1810, and in 1814 the Mission station moved to Dalbeattie. Chaplaincies which had been crucial in the seventeenth century and in the first half of the eighteenth century in the preservation of Catholicism had, by 1829, become almost completely a thing of the past.

So far we have considered, as ways in which priests could augment their quotas, farming and charging seat rents. There were two other ways in which they could augment their incomes. They could teach; and, in cases of real need they, or at least those of them who served in the Lowland Vicariate, could apply for relief to their Friendly Society.

The 1793 Relief Act forbade Roman Catholics to teach the children of Protestant parents. In spite of this clause many Catholic priests eked out their quotas by teaching modern languages to Protestants. This the priests who had studied at the Scots Colleges abroad were singularly well qualified to do. A priest who had spent six years in, say, Douay, would be, by the time he returned to Scotland, as fluent in French as in his own native tongue. Even priests who had studied only in Scotland knew French well.

In 1803, for instance, Mr Badenoch was teaching French at Elgin.[95] Mr Forbes, although he had been educated at Aquhorties and Valladolid, taught French in Banff and in Elgin, from 1818, for many years.[96] Mr James MacLachlan, Mr Forbes's predecessor at Banff, had also taught 'a pretty numerous school'.[97] Mr Rattray taught Spanish at Paisley; Mr Davidson taught at Greenock,[98] as did Mr Gordon after him;[99] Mr MacGuire was teaching French to the children of a Church of Scotland minister in 1829.[100] All the priests taught Protestants rather than Catholics because it was the Protestants who could afford to pay them.

Friendly Societies were quite a common phenomenon in the nineteenth century. A group of people held together by a common bond, whether of religion or because they worked at the same trade, would form themselves into a Friendly society. Each member was required to make a stipulated annual contribution to the Society's funds. This money was invested and the income so derived was used to help any members of the Society who were in real financial difficulties.

The priests of the Lowland Vicariate of Scotland founded their Friendly Society in 1809. Their annual contributions to it varied between £2 and £3 per annum, but the society's initial capital was augmented by various gifts. Grants to priests began to be made in 1814 when the Society's capital reached £1,000 for the first time. By 1819 the funds exceeded £2,000 and by 1823 they amounted to just over £3,000. In 1826 they exceeded £4,000.

In 1814 a total of £20 was granted to priests; in 1829 £78. Individual grants varied between £5 and £20, £10 being the usual amount. In only one instance was a grant of over £20 made: in 1823 Mr Bagnall was given £30 to help him establish his new Mission station at New Abbey. In 1821 the practice began of allowing each new priest a grant of £20 to help him equip himself with the necessary books, vestments and so on which he would need when he took up his duties as priest.

The distribution of grants is revealing. Mr Alexander MacDonald, priest at Crieff, received an average of £10 a year between 1814 and 1829. Mr William Thompson received about the same for each year that he was stationed at Deecastle. Mr Bagnall received yearly help after he was forced to leave Kirkconnell for New Abbey. Mr Forbes, wherever he happened to be stationed, asked for money every year, and was occasionally awarded something. In no instance was any money granted to any of the priests in the struggling new Mission stations of the South-West. In 1823 three priests were awarded grants because of illness and old age, although in no instance had a grant been applied for by the recipient.

Generally speaking, a priest who thought he merited help from the Friendly Society would apply either in writing or in person to the annual meeting of the administrators of the Society's funds. The administrators would discuss his case and vote on whether to make a payment to the applicant. Although the sums granted were never large, they represented large additions to the incomes of priests who received only £12 Mission quota per annum.

In July 1830 an extraordinary general meeting of the Society was held to decide how to divide up the funds now that the old Lowland Vicariate had been replaced by the new Northern, Western and Eastern Districts. The priests of the old Highland Vicariate had been refused admittance to the Society, so they could have no claim on its funds. At this meeting it was resolved, after lengthy discussion that:

> ... the Society, as to its present form, be dissolved, and do terminate, in consequence of the new ecclesiastical division of Scotland, and that its funds be divided into three parts proportional to the number of members actually belonging to the three districts of Scotland.

The Society had then thirty-two members: nine belonging to the Eastern District, eight to the Wetern District, and fifteen to the Northern District.[101]

Today the Northern is by far the smallest numerically of the three districts, but, thanks to the division of Society funds made in 1830, it is wealthy enough to be able to maintain some of the most beautiful chapels in Scotland.

NOTES

1 MacPherson's Continuation of Thomson's 'History', Vol. II, pp. 59-60.

2 William MacDonald, Auchindoun, to Bishop Cameron, 20th January 1805, B.L.

3 *Scotichronicon*, p.609.

4 Andrew Scott to Bishop Cameron, 26th February 1805, B.L.

5 *Scotichronicon*, p. 315.

6 Bishop Cameron to Bishop Hay, 23rd May 1804, B.L.

7 Bishop Hay to Bishop Cameron, 9th June 1804, B.L.

8 James Gordon to his mother, 1814, B.L.

9 William MacDonald to the Bishops and Administrators of the Scotch Mission, 31st July 1804, B.L.

10 *Scotichronicon*, p.360.

11 John Sharp to Bishop Cameron, 22nd March 1805, B.L.

12 Inventory of Mr Sharp's furniture etc left at Deecastle, 10th June 1805, B.L.

13 'Report made by the Rev. William Reid to the Right Rev. Dr. Cameron of the Operations proper to be carried on on the farm of Auqhorties during the summer 1808', B.L.

14 Bishop Chisholm to Bishop Hay, 10th April 1798, B.L.

15 Donald Stuart to Bishop Cameron, 16th November 1803, B.L.

16 Alexander Badenoch to Bishop Cameron, 21st May 1806, B.L.

17 John Reid to Charles Maxwell, 30th May 1808, B.L.

18 Abbé MacPherson to Charles Maxwell, 21st December 1798, B.L.

19 'Conditions of Let for Park, held formerly by Paul MacPherson and now by Mr William Reid', 1805, B.L. (under 'Hay').

20 Bishop Cameron to James Sharp, 14th September 1813, B.L.

21 Bishop Cameron to James Sharp, 10th June 1807, B.L.

22 *Scotichronicon*, p. 417.

23 James MacLachlan, Deecastle, to Bishop Cameron, 6th April 1807. B.L.

24 Andrew Scott to Bishop Cameron, 12th February 1805, B.L.

25 William Thomson to Bishop Cameron, 29th May 1808, B.L.

26 Alexander MacWilliam, typescript on Aquhorties, Columba House, (S.C.A.) p. 299.

27 Bishop Kyle to John Forbes, 3rd April 1829, Kyle Letters, B.L.

28 Alexander Grant to Bishop Paterson, 25th January 1828, B.L.

29 Bishop Paterson to Captain Grant, scroll letter, 7th March 1828, Preshome Letters, S.C.A.

30 William Thomson to James Kyle, 6th February 1809, B.L.
31 *Scotichronicon*, p. 598.
32 Lachlan MacIntosh to Bishop Kyle, 12th November 1829, Preshome Letters, S.C.A.
33 Lachlan MacIntosh to Bishop Kyle, 30th June 1829, Preshome Letters, S.C.A.
34 William MacDonald to the Bishops and Administrators, 31st July 1804, B.L.
35 Bishop Hay to Bishop Cameron, 6th May 1804, B.L.
36 William Reid to Bishop Cameron, 18th April 1804, B.L.
37 Donald Stuart to Bishop Cameron, 9th July 1804, B.L.
38 John Farquharson, 17th February 1805; Thomas Bagnal, 26th April 1805; M. Nicolas, 12th October 1806; McDonagh and McDonell, 13th May 1809; Reid, 11th January 1809; Stuart, 27th December 1811; Rattray, 23rd March and 7th June 1820; B.L.
39 Bishop Kyle's Report to Propaganda, 1822, in 'Life of Kyle', typescript, S.C.A.
40 Andrew Scott to Bishop Cameron, 23rd June 1813, B.L.
41 John Davidson, Greenock, to Bishop Cameron, 25th April 1809, B.L.
42 James MacLachlan, Glasgow, to Bishop Cameron, 25th April 1809, B.L.
43 William Rattray, Paisley, to Bishop Hay, 24th February 1809, B.L.
44 John Bremner ('Lindorf') to John Forbes, 13th January 1816, B.L.
45 James Kyle to Bishop Cameron, 26th March 1821, Kyle Letters, B.L.
46 William Reid, Edinburgh, to James Kyle, 22nd July 1821, B.L.
47 Bishop Cameron to James Kyle, 6th May 1822, B.L.
48 Bishop Paterson to Bishop Cameron, 18th September 1824, B.L.
49 Bishop Cameron to Bishop Paterson, 24th September 1824, B.L.
50 Bishop Cameron to Bishop Paterson, 11th October 1824, B.L.
51 Bishop Paterson to Andrew Scott, 10th December 1827, B.L.
52 Andrew Scott to Bishop Paterson, 15th January 1826, B.L.
53 Andrew Scott to James Kyle, 15th October 1829, B.L.
54 Charles Stuart to James Sharp, 9th January 1817, Preshome Letters.
55 *Scotichronicon*, pp. 50 and 51.
56 *Ibid.*, p. 210.
57 *Ibid.*, p. 316.
58 Bishop Hay to 'Messrs Andrew Scott, Alexander Paterson, Donald Stewart etc who signed the reply to their answer to my address' — copy — 20th March 1801, B.L.
59 William Pepper, Dundee, to Bishop Geddes, 16th March 1791, B.L.
60 Bishop Geddes to Bishop Hay, 2nd May 1791, B.L.
61 James Carruthers to Bishop Cameron, 6th September 1806, B.L.
62 Alexander Badenoch to Bishop Cameron, 26th February 1806, B.L.
63 Bishop Cameron to Donald Carmichael, 17th August 1810, B.L.
64 Donald Carmichael to Bishop Cameron, 10th July 1810, B.L.
65 Donald Carmichael to James Kyle, 21st January 1811, B.L.
66 John Reid, Preshome, 5th June 1804, B.L.
67 John Farquharson to Abbé MacPherson, 12th March 1805, B.L.
68 Andrew Scott to Bishop Cameron, 11th October 1810, B.L.
69 Andrew Scott to Bishop Paterson, 8th November 1826, Preshome Letters, S.C.A.
70 Andrew Scott to Bishop Cameron, 23rd May 1808, B.L.
71 William Rattray to Bishop Cameron, 26th November 1810, B.L.
72 Andrew Scott [to Bishop Cameron], 17th November 1808, B.L.
73 John Davidson, Greenock, to Bishop Cameron, 22nd December 1810, B.L.
74 William Reid to Bishop Cameron, 18th June 1813, B.L.
75 Alexander Paterson, 'A list of money collected at Kandakyle in the year 1811', Tombae, 1811, B.L.
76 James Gordon, Tombae, to James Kyle, 6th April 1829, Preshome Letters, S.C.A.
77 John Cameron to James Gordon, 5th April 1815, B.L.
78 Mr Heal and others to Bishop Cameron, 1st January 1814, B.L.
79 Mr Quinn and others to Bishop Cameron, 13th June 1813, B.L.

80 John Gordon to Bishop Cameron, 6th December 1808, B.L.
81 Bishop Cameron to John Gordon, 24th October 1814, B.L.
82 Andrew Scott to Bishop Cameron, 24th June 1811, B.L.
83 John Davidson to Bishop Cameron, 30th December 1808, B.L.
84 William Rattray to Bishop Cameron, 31st March 1812, B.L.
85 Andrew Scott to James Gordon, Paisley, 10th September 1812, Preshome Letters, S.C.A.
86 Anonymous letter from Glasgow addressed to Bishop Cameron, 6th April 1820, B.L.
87 Andrew Scott to Bishop Cameron, 27th August 1813, B.L.
88 Thomas Bagnall, Kirkconnell, to Bishop Cameron, 18th February 1808, B.L.
89 James Maxwell, Kirkconnell, to Bishop Cameron, 3rd July 1804, B.L.
90 Thomas Bagnall to James Kyle, 7th October 1822, Preshome Letters, S.C.A.
91 James Maxwell to Bishop Cameron, 24th January 1823, Preshome Letters, S.C.A.
92 Mr Constable Maxwell to Bishop Cameron, 9th June 1813, B.L.
93 William Reid to Bishop Cameron, 26th October 1813, B.L.
94 John Sharp, Deecastle to Bishop Cameron, 9th January 1805, B.L.
95 John Farquharson to Charles Maxwell, 27th March 1803, B.L.
96 E.g. John Forbes to James Kyle, 15th September 1819, B.L.
97 James MacLachlan to James Kyle, 20th September 1817, B.L.
98 John Davidson to Bishop Cameron, 15th March 1810, Preshome Letters, S.C.A.
99 John Gordon to Bishop Cameron, 4th February 1818, B.L.
100 Colin Chisholm, Inverness, to John Forbes, 13th June 1829, Preshome Letters, S.C.A.
101 For all the foregoing information on the Friendly Society I am indebted to Monsignor Alexander MacWilliam of Aboyne, who has in his possession all the old minute books belonging to the Society, and who kindly furnished me with relevant extracts.

18

Post-Reformation Catholic Chapels

THE main capital outlay of the Scottish Mission was the provision of chapels. After the Reformation, although a few chapels in the more remote areas continued to be used by Catholics, while the houses of Catholic nobles and gentry continued to employ priests as chaplains, the vast majority of existing chapels fell into the hands of the Reformed Church.

Bishop Geddes' account of the Jacobite rebellion of 1745 indicates that, by that date, the Scottish Mission had acquired a number of buildings which served as chapels. The account mentions, for instance, that in Fochabers and Tombae the chapels were not burned by Cumberland's soldiers because of the risk of fire spreading to other properties. The chapels at Keithock, at Tulloch near Tynet, at Huntly and at Preshome were not so lucky; they were all burned, as were all the chapels in the Highlands.[1]

The chapels at Tombae and Fochabers were probably simply converted rooms in existing buildings in which Catholics could meet. They must have been in the centre of small settlements or ferm-touns. The chapels which were burned were probably barns attached to more isolated farms, or perhaps, in the Highlands at least, pre-Reformation chapels which had never become Protestant. It is unlikely that any chapels outwith the more remote glens bore any exterior resemblance to a church building; the poverty of the Scottish Mission, and the penalties imposed by the Penal Laws, would have made that both impractical and dangerous.

In the years immediately following 1746 the priests were forced to say Mass in private houses, or in barns, and usually late at night to avoid detection. Mr Scott, although referring to his own, much later, experiences, has left us a description of the problems to be met with in saying Mass in private houses:

> Had he [Mr Rattray] been obliged, as I have been, to say Mass in a place where the pot was boiling over, and the child sometimes crying in the cradle, had he been obliged in a damp shop to get a canopy of leather above him to keep the drops from the altar, and a load of Shillenseeds below his feet to keep the water from going in at the mouths of his shoes, he would then have better known what want of room and inconvenience was.[2]

Mr Christopher MacRa, a Highland priest, although again referring to a later period, described the problems of saying Mass in Ardentoul, with no chapel and winter approaching:

> I do not know in the world how to act for want of a place for the congregation. During the warm season I had different shifts, such as Barns, the open air, etc. but now I scarcely have any at all — so that it is entirely necessary to be relieved some way or other. I dare say there will be nearly

to the amount of 300 souls of Catholics in this quarter, and I think it hard that such a number should want a place where they can assemble properly.[3]

By about 1770 the worst of the anti-Catholic feeling in Scotland had died down, and in 1773 a house and chapel were built for the Aberdeen priest, who had previously said Mass either in his lodging or in a garret hired for the purpose. The new building consisted of a chapel which occupied the whole of the ground floor, and a priest's house on the floor above.[4] The Aberdeen chapel was the first new building of its kind to have been completed after 1745. Mr Alexander Geddes had started work on a new chapel at Tynet in about 1769, but it was only completed in 1779.

The Tynet chapel was enlarged in 1787 but even today it resembles, on the outside, a but and ben with adjoining byre and barn, being a long low, very plain single-storey building. The next new chapel to be built was at Shenval in 1780. Although it no longer survives, it was undoubtedly similar to those which were built a few years later at Kempcairn and at Auchindoun.[5] The chapel at Kempcairn, built in 1785, was a one-storey thatched building adjoining the but and ben where the priest lived. The Auchindoun chapel, built in 1793, was also single-storeyed and thatched. Chapels were built at Huntly in 1787, at Tombae in 1786 and at Tomintoul in 1788.

In 1790 a new chapel was built at Preshome. This chapel, which is still in use today, was the first Catholic Chapel to have been built since the Reformation which was recognisably a church building.

Thus, by 1790, three years before the Relief Act had been passed, all the chapels in the North-East which had been destroyed after the '45 rebellion had been replaced with new buildings.

In the Highlands rebuilding was not accomplished so quickly. Indeed many Mission stations there remained without a priest for thirty years or more after 1746. By 1790, however, most stations again had priests, and some at least of the chapels had been rebuilt. Mr Angus Chisholm, who was the first priest to be stationed at Crochel in Strathglass since 1746, had built himself a house and chapel by the end of 1789.[6] Two chapels had been built in South Uist by 1790. There was at least one chapel on Barra where, according to the *Old Statistical Account*:

> The number of Protestants has always been so small that it was thought unnecessary to put the heritor to the expense of building a church.[7]

Aberdeen had been the first place to build a new chapel after 1746; it was also the first town to build, in 1803, a chapel which was a recognisable church building. The chapel was built in the garden of the old house, whose ground floor had previously served as a chapel, but was now converted to provide extra accommodation for the priest.

The next town to replace its old chapel with a purpose-built church was Edinburgh, in 1814. For some time before 1767 the Edinburgh priests had lived in Chalmers Close. In 1767 Bishop Hay moved to Blackfriars Wynd where the chapel was situated on the floor above the priest's house, in Robinson's Land. The house in Chalmers Close was sold. In 1777 work started on building a new house and chapel in Leith Wynd. This building was burned in the anti-Catholic riots of 1779,[8] and its priest moved to Dickson's Close. In 1783 a new tenement was bought on the opposite side of Blackfriars Wynd from the existing chapel there, and Mr Thomson moved there from Dickson's Close.[9] For the next thirty years these were the two chapels, with their attached houses, which served Edinburgh's Catholic congregation. The old chapel was completely renovated in 1785 and served the Gaelic-speaking Catholics who had moved to Edinburgh from the Highlands. The new chapel, which was on the fifth floor of the building opposite, was reached by a turnpike stair. This must have caused its congregation, which consisted of gentry and of visiting foreigners as well as tradesmen and servants, considerable inconvenience.

The siting of Edinburgh's main chapel on the fifth floor was not the only drawback to the set-up in Blackfriars Wynd. By 1800 the street itself was not the most desirable in which to live. As Mr Farquharson wrote to Bishop Cameron in 1805:

> ... your constantly breathing the *stinking air* of your *abominable close* is tantamount to your being *buryed alive*.[10]

In 1800 it was decided to build a new chapel in Edinburgh, and Mr Rattray made a series of expeditions to collect subscriptions towards the cost.[11] The Lord Advocate, although he felt it would be unwise to put his name to the subscription list, gave the project his approval.[12] Arguments, however, developed over which of two possible sites would be the more suitable, and Bishop Hay was forced to make the long journey from Aquhorties to try to sort things out.[13] By 1802 £800 had been raised,[14] and, by January 1803, over £1,000.[15] In April 1804, in response to the petition of some of his congregation that the new chapel should be built that year, Bishop Cameron replied that, while he was fully sensible of the need for a new chapel, he had to act prudently. Only £1,000 had been subscribed while a total of £4,000 would be needed. The plan to build a new chapel in Edinburgh must therefore be shelved for the moment.[16]

At about this time Bishop Cameron bought a house in High School Yards.[17] He himself continued to live in Blackfriars Wynd, and used the new house for boarders, mainly English Catholics who came to Edinburgh to attend classes at the University.

In 1812 Mr Menzies of Pitfoddels provided £2,000 to purchase a site for a new chapel in Edinburgh at the head of Leith Walk.[18] By September 1813 the building was ready to be slated, and it opened for worship in 1814. It had been designed by James Gillespie Graham, and was much admired by all the priests. Mr Kyle, for instance, wrote from Edinburgh to Mr Carmichael in Tomintoul:

> On the outside it is elegant beyond description. Its front is unquestionably the first in Edinburgh.[19]

Mr Farquharson, whose letters at the beginning of the nineteenth century were full of the unhealthy situation of the chapels in Blackfriars Wynd, was, ironically, at that time serving in Glasgow, a city which would soon surpass Edinburgh in its proliferation of teeming, filthy slums. For most of the eighteenth century the Catholics in Glasgow had been served at irregular intervals by one of the

Edinburgh priests. Towards the end of the century, when Highlanders began to settle in Glasgow, the Gaelic-speaking priest at Crieff made occasional journeys to hear their confessions and to say Mass. By 1790 there were enough Catholics in Glasgow to necessitate the hiring of a hall, and in 1791 the Mitchell Street tennis court was pressed into service. In 1797 Mr Farquharson built a chapel and priest's house — the house on the ground floor, and the chapel above, reached by an outside stair. By 1799 he had cleared all the debts incurred on building costs.[20]

Mr Farquharson's chapel soon became too small. In June 1806 Mr Scott wrote to Bishop Cameron that at eleven o'clock Mass the chapel was filled to capacity, while many of the congregation were forced to stand outside in the pouring rain.[21] In 1813 Mr Scott decided that, whatever the cost, he would have to build a new chapel.[22] The new building was slated by December 1815[23] and was officially opened on December 22nd, 1817.[24] Again the architect was James Gillespie Graham. The building was a magnificent Gothic structure, surpassing in its decoration the new chapel at Edinburgh, but the cost had been crippling. In October 1819 Mr Scott estimated the total cost to have been £20,000.[25] In 1826 he was still paying interest on the money borrowed for the building at a rate of £600 per annum.[26]

Although the chapel at Glasgow was far and away the largest and most magnificent chapel to have been built in the South-West by 1830, it was not the only one to have been built there in the early nineteenth century. It was preceded by Paisley (1809) and Greenock (1814-1816) and was followed by Ayr (1827) and Dumbarton (1828). All these chapels were designed to look like churches, partly because there was, by now, no need for secrecy, and partly because the old-style buildings consisting of chapel on one floor and priest's house on the other were of necessity far too small to accommodate the growing Irish Catholic populations of the towns of the South-West.

It was not only in the towns of the South-West that new Mission stations were opened after 1793. In the rural North-East, too, new stations were opened and provided with chapels. These chapels, however, unlike their counterparts in the large towns, continued to follow the traditional pattern of a two-storey building in which chapel and priest's house were combined. Examples are Deecastle, built in about 1796,[27] and Banff, completed in 1801.[28] As late as 1806 Mr Farquharson bought a house in Elgin, one room of which he converted for use as a chapel.[29] Further south, a house was bought in Dundee in 1790, part of which was converted into a chapel.[30]

It was not until the 1820s that the Banffshire priests began to build proper churches to accommodate their congregations. By this time many of the old chapels were in poor repair, while most of them were too small. The trend towards building new chapels in the North-East was often accompanied by a move from farm steading to town. In 1826, for instance, the thatched chapel at Auchindoun was replaced by a beautiful church in Dufftown; and in 1831 a church in Keith replaced the little chapel on the farm steading of Kempcairn. Between 1827 and 1829 Catholic Churches were built at Fochabers and in Portsoy, and at Chapeltown and Tombae in Glenlivet. The new chapel at Tombae was completed

L

just in time, for, in 1829, the River Livet flooded its banks, sweeping away the old chapel.[31] By 1840 only Elgin in the North-East still retained its traditional house-cum-chapel. In 1844 it, too, was replaced by a proper church. Only at Preshome does the chapel today still stand hard by the old farm steading that used to support the incumbent.

Generally speaking the new chapels built by about 1830 followed the same pattern as that of St Mary's, Edinburgh, and comprised a fairly simple Gothic front which masked a plain rectangular chapel with a shallow apse at one end, and a small entrance hall surmounted by an organ gallery at the other. This pattern was dictated by the desire for an elegant facade coupled with the need for economy.

Just as old-style chapels gave way to churches, so too did private chapels. In Galloway private chapels gave way directly to churches in neighbouring towns. In the North-East many private chapels gave way in the first instance to chapels on farm steadings. The best example of such a development occurs not in the North-East, however, but in Perth.

From about 1690 until 1777 the Catholics of the Perth area were served by successive chaplains to the Dukes of Perth. These priests lived at Stobhall, saying Mass in the beautiful little chapel with its painted ceiling which still survives today. In 1777 the titular Duchess of Perth died, and the Mission was forced to make new arrangements for the accommodation of the priest. Bishop Hay succeeded in leasing the farm of Park, which lies about a mile from Stobhall. Between 1783 and 1791 Abbé MacPherson was stationed at Park. During his incumbency there he built a two-storey house for himself, and he converted an existing barn into a chapel by the simple expedient of inserting a Gothic window into one of the walls[32] and furnishing the interior with seats and an altar. This barn continued to serve as a chapel until 1831, although latterly it was considered to be less than adequate.

In 1816 Mr Forbes, newly appointed priest at Park, sent Bishop Cameron the following description of his house and chapel:

> The dwelling house, which is evidently not of solid workmanship, is, I am told, in so ruinous a condition that Mr Wallace [the previous incumbent] and his domestics were afraid every windy day of its falling; and, it is added, that on more than one occasion, terror compelled them to leave their beds and take shelter elsewhere . . . A professed man belonging to the Congregation says that none of the walls of the dwelling house are perpendicular, and that one of the Gables is inclined inwards more than eight inches, and supported solely by the strength of the roof. A great part of the timber is rotting and some of it crumbling into dust. The floor of the room below stair is sunk and decayed, and that one of the apartments above could not bear even a sack of corn in Mr Reid's time [1792-1812] except at a corner . . .
>
> The Chapel presents a very poor appearance. The floor is eaten, and it is complained that, in winter, it resembles a sink, the mud and water coming past the shoes. The drain from the dunghill running alongside is in a great measure imbibed and produces in the interior a green crust which cannot fail to be offensive.[33]

Even allowing for Mr Forbes's customary exaggeration of his problems, the chapel at Park must have been both dirty and uncomfortable. Quite possibly many of the old chapels of the North-East, built on farm steadings, suffered from similar inconveniences.

As early as 1813 plans were being made to remove the Mission station from Park to the town of Perth.[34] Various possible houses were considered, the matter assuming some urgency as Irish regiments were occasionally stationed at Perth. Owing, however, to financial difficulties, no positive steps were taken to acquire any property. When the priest at Dundee died in 1818 the two stations were combined,[35] and, from 1819, Perth was served from Dundee. By 1822 the Catholic population of Perth was increasing rapidly and it was obvious that a large chapel would have to be built there, and the station separated off again from Dundee.[36] Finally, in 1830, a young priest, Mr John Geddes, was sent to Perth. He immediately set about building a chapel. The work, however, was brought temporarily to a halt when Mr Geddes died in 1832, aged only twenty-six. The chapel was finally completed in 1833, by which time the congregation numbered several hundred, almost entirely Irish.[37]

It has been suggested that the Relief Act of 1793 and the Emancipation Act of 1829 were the two main stimuli in the building of Catholic chapels. Such a hypothesis is not borne out by the facts. The main rebuilding programme, following the devastation of 1746, was completed by 1790. The second phase of building, which arose from the opening of new mission stations in the South-West, got properly off the ground in 1809, and continued fairly uniformly well into the second half of the nineteenth century. What might be considered as a third phase — the replacing of the old chapels in the North-East by church buildings, was well under way before 1829, collections having been made and plans being drawn up in many instances where the chapels themselves had not yet been built.

In the Highlands the main building programme got under way after 1829. It was not triggered off by the Emancipation Bill, but rather by the split-up of the old Highland Vicariate, part of it being incorporated in the new Northern District, and most of it in the Western. This gave the Highlands greater financial resources, which, together with the enthusiastic efforts of Bishop Kyle and Bishop Scott, ensured that the Highlands were supplied with adequate, well-built chapels.

There were four main stimuli to the building of Catholic chapels between 1746 and 1830. Firstly, there was the need to build chapels either where the old ones had been destroyed or where a new Mission station was being opened; in other words there was the need to build a chapel where there was no existing building. Secondly, there was the need to replace chapels which had became too small, or too ruinous, to serve their congregations adequately. Thirdly, there was the need to move the chapel either from a farm-steading or a private house, to the nearby town. Finally, there was a growing desire that Protestants should be made to respect the Catholic faith. It was difficult to respect a congregation which met in a barn situated beside the farmyard midden. The desire for respectability crops up time after time in correspondence between priests. In 1821, for instance, Mr John Cameron wrote from Valladolid to Mr James Gordon in Glenlivet:

There is nothing which gives me greater joy, nothing certainly can be a juster motive of joy to any friend of religion, than to be informed of the pious zeal which at present prevails over all the Mission of building new Chapels and of labouring to restore religious worship in general to the splendour which it had among our forefathers.[38]

In 1826 Mr Mathison wrote about his new chapel:

> The new chapel in Fochabers is roofed, and the slating is going rapidly on, and will if the present mild weather continues, be finished by Christmas. The expense of this work far exceeds what I was induced to suppose, but still I trust in Providence I shall be enabled to compleat it without incurring much debt. It will be an ornament to the town, and I hope draw respect to Religion.[39]

There might be unanimity as to the need for a splendid chapel building in a place like Glasgow, where it could be seen and admired by many people; there was less agreement when it came to a small North-East glen like Glenlivet. Bishop Paterson, who had studied at Scalan and retained a great affection for the area, wrote to the priest in Glenlivet about his proposed new chapel for Tombae:

> The front must be and shall be what a chapel in Glenlivet, the ancient Granary and nursery of Religion in Scotland ought to have, and the altar a commanding appearance. All the rest just such and no more than will accomodate all the Congregation.[40]

With Bishop Paterson, as regards Glenlivet, economy had to blended with visual splendour; with Mr Scott economy alone was the key word: he disapproved of Mr Gordon's spending so long in Ireland collecting money merely to ornament a chapel in Glenlivet which would never be seen by any strangers.[41]

In the eighteenth century the buildings which were either converted or erected to serve as chapels were small and unpretentious. Chapel and priest's house together cost only a few hundred pounds. In 1790, for instance, Mr Pepper, the priest at Dundee, bought a property which would provide a chapel, priest's house, cellars, and something of a garden, for £155.[42] The money for such purchases came mainly from the collection of subscriptions from wealthy Scottish Catholics like Menzies of Pitfoddels, and from the better-off members of the congregation. Any debts that were incurred in such a purchase could genrally be paid off, from seat rents or collections, within a year or two. It was always the responsibility of the priest in whose station the chapel was to be built to ensure that sufficient money would be forthcoming to make the building possible.

When priests began to build churches, rather than houses or 'barns', to serve as chapels, costs escalated. In 1789, for instance, Mr Reid, who was building a new chapel at Preshome, admitted that he owed £300 over and above the £300 which he managed to collect, and that he did not know how he could raise such a sum.[43] In 1803 the new Aberdeen chapel cost £1,100.[44]

In Paisley the building of the chapel ran into problems when it was discovered that the site was marshy, necessitating the driving of piles deep into the ground to provide a solid foundation. Not only that, but, when the chapel was half-built, it was discovered that one of the walls was off the plumb and had to be rebuilt.[45] The debt incurred in the building of Paisley chapel was a constant source of worry for many years to come.

When the first really ambitious post-Reformation chapel was built at Edinburgh, the cost was enormous, and the debt in 1829 was still over £8,000.[46] Edinburgh, being Scotland's capital, and the home of a Catholic bishop, could expect to receive donations towards its chapel from wealthy and important Catholics, and even Protestants, in both Scotland and England. Glasgow, with a far larger Catholic population, had none of Edinburgh's advantages. Mr Scott was therefore forced to fall back on his congregation. On paper it looked as if a small, fortnightly donation from each of the several thousand Catholics of Glasgow could easily finance the magnificent chapel which Mr Scott had planned. In fact trade depression, bringing with it lower wages and massive unemployment, meant that Mr Scott's scheme largely failed. In 1819 he put the cost of building his chapel at £20,000.[47] In 1821 he admitted that the debt on the Glasgow chapel was still £10,000.[48] For the next decade and more Mr Scott lived under a dark cloud, constantly worried about raising money, afraid that the loans that had been made to him might be called in, generally irritable, and jealously trying to prevent any other priests from collecting money in Glasgow for chapels in other parts of Scotland.[49]

As more and more chapels were built in the nineteenth century, and at a much larger cost than twenty or thirty years before, many priests began to cross the Irish Channel and go on begging expeditions through Ireland. This movement began among the priests of the South-West who felt, not unreasonably, that, since it was for Irish immigrants that they were forced to build large and expensive chapels, it was only right that Ireland should help to finance them. By the 1820s priests from Banffshire, none of whom had a single Irishman in his congregation, began to jump on the bandwaggon, because they found that Catholics in Scotland were unable to meet the escalating demands made on them as chapel after chapel was planned.

By 1830 most of the existing Mission stations in the old Lowland Vicariate had been, or were on the way to being, provided with the chapels which still serve them today. Between 1830 and 1900 the old Highland Vicariate was similarly provided for. But the period after 1830 was characterised principally by the mushrooming of chapels in the urban areas of Scotland: at Dunfermline (1846), Falkirk (1839), Haddington (1853), Kirkcaldy (1865), Renfrew (1877), Barrhead (1841), Lanark (1859), Coatbridge (1848), Carluke (1849) and many others. The distribution of Catholics in Scotland had changed radically from the predominantly rural congregations of the eighteenth century to the predominantly urban congregations of the nineteenth and twentieth centuries.

NOTES

1 Bishop Geddes, "Some Account of the state of the Catholic Religion in Scotland during the years 1745-6-7", printed in Forbes Leith, Vol. II, pp. 336-338.

2 Andrew Scott to Bishop Cameron, 21st February 1808, B. L.

3 Christopher MacRa to Bishop Geddes, 23rd October 1789, B.L.

4 Alexander MacWilliam, *St Peter's Church, Aberdeen* (Aberdeen, 1979), pp. 1-2.

5 Odo Blundell, *The Catholic Highlands of Scotland* (Edinburgh and London 1909) Vol. I, pp. 21 and 20 respectively.

6 Angus Chisholm to Bishop Geddes, 27th January 1790, B.L.

7 Quoted in Odo Blundell, *The Catholic Highlands of Scotland* (1917) Vol. II, p. 21.

8 *Scotichronicon*, pp. 58, 136, 150, 158-60 gives details of all the various buildings.

9 *Scotichronicon*, p. 221.

10 John Farquharson to Bishop Cameron, 27th February 1805, B.L.

11 William Rattray, various scroll letters begging for subscriptions, 1802, B.L.

12 Lord Advocate Hope to William Rattray, 31st October 1801, B.L. (copy letter).

13 See various letters from William Rattray, Charles Maxwell and Bishop Hay, 1800, B.L.

14 William Rattray to Thomas Bagnall, 11th May 1802, B.L.

15 Bishop Cameron to Alexander Innes, 29th January 1803, B.L.

16 Bishop Cameron to William Rattray, 13th June 1804, B.L.

17 Alexander Badenoch to Donald Carmichael, 19th December 1808, B.L.

18 Mr Menzies to Bishop Cameron, 8th May 1813, Preshome Letters, S.C.A.

19 James Kyle to Donald Carmichael, 17th May 1814, Kyle Letters, B.L.

20 Alexander MacWilliam, "The Glasgow Mission 1792-1799", *Innes Review*, Vol. IV, 1953, pp. 84-91.

21 Andrew Scott to Bishop Cameron, 30th June 1806, B.L.

22 Andrew Scott to Bishop Cameron, 27th August 1813, B.L.

23 Andrew Scott to Bishop Paterson, 23rd December 1815, B.L.

24 Andrew Scott to Bishop Cameron, 1st December 1817, B.L.

25 Andrew Scott to Bishop Paterson, 29th October 1819, B.L.

26 Andrew Scott to Bishop Paterson, 8th November 1826, Preshome Letters, S.C.A.

27 *Scotichronicon*, p. 465.

28 James Carruthers to Charles Maxwell, 4th May 1799, B.L.

29 John Farquharson to Charles Maxwell, 15th June 1806, B.L.

30 Bishop Geddes to Bishop Hay, 18th February 1790, B.L.

31 James Kyle to his mother, 18th August 1829, Preshome Letters, S.C.A.

32 The chapel at Park was pulled down several years ago, but the present Lord Perth saved this window, and had it incorporated in the new library which he was building at Stobhall. A well at Park is still known locally as the "Priest's Well".

33 John Forbes to Bishop Cameron, 22nd October 1816, B.L.

34 E.g. William Wallace to Bishop Cameron, 16th January 1813, B.L.

35 E.g. William Caven to John Forbes, 2nd May 1818, Preshome Letters, S.C.A.

36 William Rattray to Bishop Cameron, 14th February 1822, B.L.

37 *Catholic Directory*, 1831, 1832, 1833 — entries under "Perth".

38 John Cameron, Valladolid to James Gordon, Tombae, 7th May 1821, B.L.

39 George Mathison to Charles Gordon, 15th December 1826, Preshome Letters, S.C.A.

40 Bishop Paterson to James Gordon, 24th April 1826, Preshome Letters, S.C.A.

41 Andrew Scott to Bishop Paterson, 22nd February 1827, Preshome Letters, S.C.A.

42 Bishop Geddes to Bishop Hay, 18th February 1790, B.L.

43 Bishop Hay to Bishop Geddes, 30th April 1789, B.L.

44 Charles Gordon to Bishop Cameron, 20th February 1803, B.L.

45 William Rattray to Charles Maxwell, 2nd November 1808, B.L.

46 Bishop Paterson to James Gordon, 28th December 1829, Preshome Letters, S.C.A.

47 Andrew Scott to Bishop Paterson, 29th October 1819, B.L.

48 Andrew Scott to Bishop Cameron, 22nd February 1821, B.L.

49 E.g. Constantine Lee to Bishop Paterson, 27th June 1829, Preshome Letters, S.C.A.

19

Music and Ceremony

ON 15th June, 1793 Mr Smelt, the English Agent at Rome, sent the following letter to Bishop Geddes:

> I congratulate you on the late Act of Parliament with regard to Scotland. I presume your chapels will now be publick like those in London with High Mass and Vespers. It is proper your Boys should learn the Gregorian note and be instructed in Church Ceremonys. I have desired them to attend the Singing Master at Propaganda.[1]

At this time two types of music might have been heard in the London chapels. Firstly, there was the singing of hymns by the congregation. Secondly, there was the sung or High Mass in which the whole text of the Mass was sung or chanted by the officiating clergy — a priest, a deacon and a sub-deacon. Parts of the High Mass might be sung by a choir, the music involving difficult part-singing. All singing in Scottish chapels, contrary to Mr Smelt's expectations, was still expressly forbidden by Bishop Hay in 1793.

The ban on singing in Scottish chapels had originally been a matter of prudence; Catholics had had no wish to draw attention to themselves or to their chapels. It must be remembered that, in the Church of Scotland, until the second half of the nineteenth century, the only music allowed was the unaccompanied singing of psalms, where the precentor sang a line at a time, the congregation answering it. Hymn-singing and the use of organs were forbidden. Indeed, as late as 1859 the Reverend Robert Lee, minister of Greyfriars Church in Edinburgh, was admonished by the General Assembly for allowing organ music in his church.[2] Had the Catholics sung High Mass or even hymns in their chapels in the seventeenth and eighteenth centuries they would have made themselves very conspicuous.

Towards the end of the eighteenth century one or two priests began to allow music to creep back into their chapels. One of the first was Mr Menzies, priest to the Highland Congregation in Edinburgh. There is a story that it was thanks to Mr Menzies and his congregation that the Christmas carol, 'Adeste Fideles', was popularised in Edinburgh, with apprentices whistling it in every street.[3] In May 1789 Mr John Gordon, priest at Aberdeen, wrote to his uncle, Bishop Geddes, who was at that time living in Edinburgh:

> I have heard that Mr Menzies has begun singing in his Chappel some time ago. I have lately begun to make a trial of the same nature; the success hitherto has surpassed my expectations, but we are at a great loss for Music, and as I suppose Mr Menzies will have some good pieces I would take it as a favour if he would send me a Copie of any of the Hymns, or any other Church

> Music . . . I will be glad to have your approbation of my introducing singing, and wish you would give me your opinion of what you think the best method of bringing it to perfection.[4]

Two months later Mr Gordon wrote again to his uncle:

> Mr MacGillivray delivered to me a letter from Bishop Hay which gave me a good deal of surprise, it was regarding the use of Church Music in our Chapel at Aberdeen; in this letter he says: 'There is a necessity of putting an immediate stop to it everywhere' but he has not been so good as add any of the reasons for so general and absolute a command, although it is nothing less than a prohibition of one of the most ancient and universally approved practices of the Church . . . [5]

Bishop Hay had told Mr Gordon, by way of excuse, that he would be delighted to see Church music reintroduced, could it be done with propriety and decency. Mr Gordon considered that the singing in his chapel was unexceptionable. He pointed out that he had only followed Mr Menzies' lead, and that he had assumed that Bishop Geddes, who was living in Edinburgh, had known of, and approved, the introduction of singing by Mr Menzies.

Mr Gordon was not the only priest in the North-East to have reintroduced singing. Mr Mathison, the priest at Fochabers, himself a keen amateur instrument maker, had also reintroduced the practice, and was equally indignant at Bishop Hay's summary veto. In a letter to Bishop Geddes he pointed out that much good had come of the reintroduction of singing in his chapel:

> I have found that since the time we had singing, many more of the people attend at Christian doctrine than formerly. I find also that since singing took place on the Holy Days the chapel is crowded whereas I had, before that time, reason to complain of the people's slackness on such days. I know that the people in general are edified with singing: There are, to be sure, persons everywhere to be found who make it their practice to find fault with everything (be it ever so good) that does not humour their fancy, from motives best known to themselves . . . One of the chief objections I have heard against singing is the fear of exciting a jealousy in our Neighbours against us; this you know better than I do can have little weight, as our Neighbours seem rather surprised at our having neglected it so long. For my part I consulted previously the sentiments of my Neighbours of different denominations. I have found them unanimous in approving and recommending it . . . Why should we not embrace the means which Divine Providence puts in our power to render our Holy Religion respectable as well in the eyes of its enemies as of its friends.[6]

As Mr Gordon and Mr Mathison suspected, Bishop Geddes was in favour of reintroducing singing in chapels. In July 1789 he informed Mr Thomson that he had hoped to persuade Bishop Hay to relent towards the Edinburgh Catholics who were willing to pay the cost of singing lessons themselves.[7] In December he returned to the subject with a well-reasoned argument which would have convinced anyone but Bishop Hay:

> In one of my late letters I just mentioned that I thought you might allow some hymns to be sung in our Chapels here and at Aberdeen on the Sunday's Afternoons after the Christian Doctrine. I shall now give the Reasons, which I beg you will take into Consideration. I need not say anything on the Advantages that accrue to Religion from proper Music: the Church in all Ages has been agreed on this; singing is mentioned as a Part of the divine Worship by St. Justin even when the Christians were meeting in the Catacombs. From all that I can judge, there does not appear to be the least Danger from our beginning to have some Music. The generality of our People seem to wish that we had it, and cannot well be made understand why it should not be encouraged by us. Had not the late Prohibition been obeyed with Prudence, it would certainly have occasioned some Scandal. But what has the principal Weight with me, especially with

regard to these two towns, is that the Sundays afternoons and evenings are the most dangerous time for youth and therefore it is a matter of no small importance to draw them to the Chapels to the Christian Doctrine and other Devotions, to which some Music would contribute greatly. This would likewise be a Preparation at a Distance for our having a High Mass sung on some Festivals to the great edification of the faithful, when we shall see it expedient. Your Predecessor was very desirous of seeing this; and what he said to me on the Subject was one of the Reasons I had for making Church Music be taught at Valladolid, which I wish were done in all our Houses abroad. I beg you will consider this and I hope you will give a favourable answer to our Petition.[8]

In spite of Bishop Geddes's persuasive arguments, Bishop Hay saw no reason to change his mind. He had seen too much violence in his time to want to risk anything which might bring Catholics into the public eye. He had seen the havoc that had been wrought on chapels in 1746; he had witnessed the looting and burning of his own Edinburgh chapel in 1779; and the recent setting fire to the chapel at Park by a Protestant had only served to strengthen his determination to stamp out all singing in chapels.[9] The discovery that the Protestant who had set the thatch of the Park chapel alight had done so merely because of a domestic quarrel with his wife did nothing to alter him in his determination.[10]

Bishop Hay's ruling was unpopular both with the priests who had introduced singing and with their congregations. The Edinburgh Catholics, for instance, had engaged Giambattista Corri as choirmaster, and about twenty people had been practising for some time. After the prohibition of singing in chapels they continued to practise under Mr Corri's tuition. By the beginning of 1790 they felt themselves to be ready to sing in public and asked permission to be allowed to sing some hymns on Sunday afternoons in the chapel.[11] Bishop Hay again refused. By 1791 even the Catholics in remote Glengairn were begging to be allowed to have singing in Chapel,[12] all to no avail.

Even after the passing of the Repeal Bill in 1793, which Mr Smelt was sure would result in singing in Scottish chapels, Bishop Hay refused to relax his ruling. Perhaps he felt that the Relief Bill had already drawn sufficient attention to Scottish Catholics without their doing anything to make themselves even more conspicuous. If the Protestants felt that the Catholics were interpreting the Relief Bill too liberally too quickly, it might rekindle any latent fires of anti-Popery that were still smouldering. It would therefore be prudent to be even more careful just after the passing of the Bill than it had been before.

This, if it was indeed Bishop Hay's reasoning, may have been sound and prudent, but it was incomprehensible to at least one of his priests, Father James Robertson, who tried in vain to get permission to reintroduce singing in Munshes in Galloway in 1798:

If you had prudential reasons to prohibit it at Edinburgh and before the Repeal, I was confident you had none now, at least for Munshes, and I am at a loss to conjecture any, since our meetings are not only regarded now as tolerated but lawful . . . I assure you our neighbours would not grudge, and that we might enjoy it here without inconvenience.[13]

By 1800 Bishop Hay's strength was beginning to fail him, though he lived for a further eleven years at Aquhorties. In 1802 his coadjutor, Bishop Cameron, arrived in Scotland from Valladolid,[14] and in the summer of 1803 Bishop Hay, now in his seventy-fourth year, asked permission from Propaganda to retire from all his episcopal duties. His petition was granted, and so, from 1803, Bishop Cameron was acting Vicar Apostolic for the Lowland District. Having spent twenty-two years as professor and rector at the Scots College, Valladolid, Bishop Cameron was accustomed to the music and ceremony with which Mass in Catholic Spain was celebrated. It is therefore not surprising that 1805 saw, at Aberdeen, the first public High Mass to be celebrated in Scotland since the Reformation — King James VII, when in Edinburgh, had heard High Mass in his private chapel at Holyrood. It was not, however, until 1810 that singing by congregations as opposed to priests was reintroduced into Scottish chapels.

In 1803 Mr Charles Gordon, priest at Aberdeen, started work on his new, large chapel. In August 1804, when the chapel was nearing completion, he wrote to Bishop Cameron, asking permission for High Mass to be celebrated when the chapel was consecrated.[15] Permission was granted. High Mass was celebrated again in Aberdeen in 1807 and 1810, when Bishop Cameron came north to confirm members of the congregation.[16] Nowhere else but in Aberdeen does High Mass appear to have been sung before 1814, with the exception of the college at Aquhorties. The reason for this was simple: High Mass required the services of three priests to act as priest, deacon and sub-deacon. Each priest required the proper vestments. In addition, a small choir was needed. Mr Gordon was singularly fortunate in that he had Aquhorties close by, as his letter to Bishop Cameron in 1807 illustrates:

> I have consulted the gentlemen at Aquhorties and they have sent me the vestments and everything necessary for High Mass . . . How shall we get a choir formed? Messrs George Gordon and Davidson [priests at Blairs, outside Aberdeen, and at Aquhorties, respectively] have promised to be here, but they would need some others to join them. Would there be a possibility of getting two or three of the young Gentlemen from Aquhorties? There are three divines [i.e. students in theology] there, and, they being candidates for the Church, should certainly as much as possible be made acquainted with everything that relates to the public service of the Church. Now they can, at present, if you think proper, assist at the Celebration of High Mass. Two of them can sing and could join Messrs Gordon and Davidson. The other would look on. They perhaps, poor fellows, will never have an opportunity of seeing the like again.[17]

Mr Gordon was being unduly pessimistic when he referred to the slim chance of Aquhorties students seeing High Mass celebrated, but, for some years to come, they would be able to see it only at Aberdeen. In most other parts of the country the task of finding three priests capable of singing the different parts of the Mass, which they had not heard since their student days, would have been a daunting one. In 1817, for instance, referring to the singing of High Mass at the opening of the Glasgow chapel — probably the first High Mass to be sung outside Aberdeen with the possible exception of Edinburgh — Mr Scott wrote to Bishop Cameron:

> Mr Reid spoke of the preparations for the opening of the chapel and said he would sing High Mass. He can get Mr Gordon and Mr Halley [a French priest] to assist him. I am as ignorant of all the ceremonies as the youngest boy you have at Aquhorties, and could do nothing at it.[18]

It took a considerable time for High Mass to become customary for special occasions throughout the Lowland Vicariate. It took less time for choirs to be formed from members of Catholic congregations.

It appears that, in 1810, Mr Rattray, the priest at Paisley, annoyed Bishop

Cameron by introducing singing in the chapel there without first having obtained permission. Mr Rattray excused himself as follows:

> As to the singing in the Chapel, it was begun at the request particularly of a young man, of an excellent character, who is well acquainted with Church musick, and had been leader of the band in a Chapel in Ireland. It is conducted, in the opinion of competent judges, with accuracy. It is authorised by example of Mr Scott's in Glasgow; whose example, as you taught me to look up to it, I considered, under all the existing circumstances, to be a sufficient warrent.[19]

There must, therefore, have been a choir formed in Glasgow by 1810. In 1812 Mr Scott apologised for having allowed singing to continue in the Glasgow and Paisley chapels:

> It was certainly very abruptly and rashly begun here, and I blame myself very much for doing so, and the moment you wish it, it shall be given up.[20]

Mr Scott had heard Mr Charles Gordon of Aberdeen mention that Bishop Cameron approved very much of singing in chapels, and so he had rashly introduced it at Glasgow, under the charge of a French priest, M. Nicolas, without having first mentioned his intention to Bishop Cameron.

In 1814 Mr Charles Gordon asked permission to introduce singing at Aberdeen.[21] In the same year, Mr Andrew Carruthers, priest at Munshes, wrote to Bishop Cameron:

> Understanding that your feelings go along with those of the Brethren in desiring to reintroduce into the Solemn Church Service the ancient and laudable custom of chanting, I have been, at the earnest sollicitation of my people, endeavouring during this season to form a young band of Choristers . . . may they to begin with start off on an English hymn before and after Mass — till they're ready to sing the Mass proper.[22]

In 1814 the new chapel at Edinburgh was completed. Bishop Cameron authorised a choir to sing in it. Singing in chapels had at last been given the episcopal blessing. By 1815 Greenock in the south, and Tynet in the north, had choirs, and by the end of 1817 choirs had been formed in almost all the chapels of the Lowland Vicariate, with the exception of Dumfries, Huntly and Perth.[23] By 1820 Braemar and Glengairn in the Highland Vicariate had followed suit. By 1820 High Mass had been sung in the chapels of Edinburgh, Glasgow, Paisley, Greenock, Aberdeen, Dumfries and Preshome. By 1820, therefore, singing was an accepted part of the service in Catholic chapels in Scotland.

With singing gaining popularity in the chapels of the Lowland Vicariate, the introduction of organ music was inevitable. St Mary's, Edinburgh was the first to have an organ installed, in 1814, by Messrs Wood and Company of Edinburgh.[24] The new chapel of St Andrew's, Glasgow followed suit in 1817. Its organ was installed by 'a man from Muir and Wood'[25] and proved to be a great success. Other chapels opened subscriptions to raise money for organs: Paisley and Aberdeen in 1815, Greenock in 1816, Auchindoun in 1817, and Preshome in 1818. By 1820 most chapels in the Lowland Vicariate either had organs already installed or were in the process of purchasing them. Even Mr Forbes at Park, who had held out for so long against introducing a choir into his chapel, and who had given Mr Gordon of Glenlivet a lecture against organs, had, by 1820, an organ set up in his chapel and playing on Sundays.[26]

The installation of organs at Edinburgh and Glasgow had been simplified by the fact that these were new chapels and could therefore be designed from the start to accommodate an organ and a choir. In the North-East, however, old chapels had to be altered and adapted. In general this was done by building a gallery at the back of the chapel, facing the altar, and large enough to hold both organ and choir. Aberdeen, for instance, added a gallery in 1815, over a newly constructed entrance hall.[27] At Preshome in 1822 Mr Badenoch took down the existing singing gallery, cut the wall, formed a 'very large and elegant recess for the organ' and then extended a gallery which had originally been built to give extra seats before choirs had been introduced.[28]

Although organs were the obvious musical instruments to accompany the newly formed choirs, one or two priests did have recourse to other instruments until they were able to afford an organ. Mr Mathison made his own double bass, with which he accompanied the choir.[29] The double bass, however, was only a temporary expedient. Mr Mathison had also built an organ which he had sold to Mr Charles Gordon for the Aberdeen Chapel. Mr Gordon found this organ unsatisfactory and returned it to Mr Mathison, ordering a new one for himself from London. In 1817 Mr Mathison was busy improving and tuning his organ before installing it in his own chapel. He ordered organ pipes from a Mr Bruce. Mr Bruce, however, had contracted to finish an organ for Newcastle by a certain date, and had to use Mr Mathison's pipes in order to meet the deadline. Mr Mathison's order had to be delayed until another set of pipes was completed.[30]

Mr Mathison's double bass was not the only instrument to be used as a temporary expedient. In 1817 Mr Gordon of Glenlivet asked Mr Kyle if he could borrow his harpsichord.[31] In 1819 Mr Bremner wrote to Mr Mathison:

> I should like to know whether there be any intention to bring into the choirs other musical instruments besides the double bass and organ. Perhaps the people of Scotland, accustomed to see the violin so much used on every occasion would not like to see it in the Church.[32]

When a priest had installed his organ, his next task was to find, or to have trained, an organist. Mr George Gordon, priest at Auchindoun, who had been, in his professors' opinion, too interested in music when he was a student at the Scots College, Valladolid,[33] had himself trained six organists by 1819.[34] In 1821 he offered to train an organist for Mr Forbes, priest at Park, under the following conditions:

> ... you will have no expense except my own charges; at any rate they must be but trifling anything besides that. He will be lodged in the house of one of my own organists, (John MacIntosh — Coppersmith — Dufftown) where he will have the use of the Piano, Bed, Board and washing for five shillings per week. The diet is understood to be common country fare. A few steps from his Quarters a Cooper lives who says he can give him as much work as he can hold his face to [to pay for his board] ... In the mean time let him learn what he can of his Notes on any Keyed Instrument, it will always be so much time gained. I shall keep him at first a couple of weeks or longer to teach him to move his fingers and ascertain whether he will answer your purpose. After that I may perhaps send him home to practise by himself for some time, unless I find that he had made such progress that he may remain here constantly till he finish with me.[35]

For his services in teaching an organist Mr Gordon charged £10.10.0 plus one quire of drafted music paper, plus five shillings for every sheet of music on which he wrote music and fingering for his pupil.

Not only did Mr George Gordon train organists; he also compiled and had printed two collections of sacred music scored for small choir and organ. These collections he sold in Ireland and England as well as in Scotland to help to raise funds for the new chapel he planned in Dufftown.[36] Other priests, too, interested themselves in the printing of hymns and of sacred music. Mr Kyle brought out a small hymn book which he had printed on the press he had set up at Aquhorties.[37] Mr Mathison enquired into the possibilities of engraving on stone, since he had heard that stone plates were much cheaper than copper ones while producing a finer print than wooden ones.[38]

All in all the letters written by the priests of the Lowland Vicariate of Scotland between 1814 and 1824 are full of a tremendous enthusiasm for the introduction of music into their chapels. Their enthusiasm was matched, not only by that of their congregations, but also by that of their Protestant neighbours. Protestant interest in organ music meant extra money for the Catholic chapels. In 1820 Mr Badenoch, priest at Preshome, wrote to Bishop Paterson:

> Our organ is doing very well and the choir is improving. Great numbers of Protestants are attracted and the collections on Sundays are double of what they formerly were. Mr Mathison is always tuning and improving his organ, but she is still in his own room, and his famous Fiddle has lost much of her renown by the superior powers of our Organ.[39]

Mr Scott in Glasgow considered his organ as an essential money-maker in the payment of his chapel debt,[40] because of the wealthy Protestants it attracted. Mr Rattray, priest at Huntly sent the following piece of news to Bishop Cameron:

> ... the Haldanite or Missionary Congregation here, who are numerous, and the most prepossessing of all the sects against Papists, have solicited Mr Davidson, a rank papist, to teach them singing for payment, and if possible to transfer his tunes to their Psalms, but if that cannot be done, to teach them to sing properly their own Psalm tunes.[41]

Mr Davidson was the choir master in Mr Rattray's chapel.

The popularity of sacred music was recognised by the magistrates of Glasgow and of Aberdeen. In 1818 the Board of Management for the Catholic schools of Glasgow, which was mainly composed of Protestants, met to decide how to raise funds. They proposed that Dr. Chalmers preach a sermon in his church for that purpose, and that, since the Glasgow chapel possessed an organ, there should be a concert of sacred music held there for the same purpose.[42] The concert proved to be very popular, though it involved Mr Scott in a libel suit, which he finally won in 1821.[43]

In 1819 Mr Charles Gordon, at the Provost's request, allowed an oratorio to be performed in his chapel in aid of the fever hospital. Tickets cost three shillings each;[44] Mr Ross and Mr Downie performed at the organ, and the choir of the chapel sang various pieces, all of which, Mr Gordon assured Bishop Cameron, were 'rigidly Catholic'. He added:

> It is not perhaps quite correct to open the chapel for such a purpose. But Charity is the motive and the end of the thing, and I have taken such an active part among the fevers, and the application was made in such a manner that I could not well get off otherwise.[45]

When so many Protestants obviously enjoyed music and the choral singing of sacred music, it is, perhaps, surprising that the General Assembly held out so long against the introduction of organs in their own churches.

As priests began to introduce music and High Mass into their chapels, they were forced to provide not just one suit of vestments as hitherto but a whole array. In 1791 Mr John Chisholm had written to Bishop Geddes:

> Bishop MacDonald told me long ago he wish'd there was a suit of good vestments in each of our chapels.[46]

In 1827 Mr Thomson mentioned to Mr Charles Gordon that he now had all five suits of vestments: black, purple, white, green and red, but that he could do with another white suit for very grand occasions.[47]

Just as priests were beginning to adorn their persons with splendid vestments, so too were one or two, by the 1820s, beginning to consider adorning their chapels with stained glass windows. In 1822 an anonymous writer petitioned Bishop Cameron for a stained glass window for the Edinburgh chapel.[48] In 1826 Mr Mathison, who was building a new chapel in Fochabers at the time, to a plan by Gillespie Graham, wrote to Mr Charles Gordon:

> I intend a transparency on the window above the altar. Do you think Mr Lamond could make it with taste? The subject might be a luminous Cross in the Clouds, surrounded with Cherubs. The space is 13 feet long by 8 feet wide . . . I have applied at London, but the terms are beyond our reach.[49]

In the event, lack of money prevented any stained glass windows being installed in Scottish chapels at this time. Mr Mathison, for instance, died in 1828, leaving the Fochabers chapel uncompleted and heavily in debt.

The final step in restoring to the Catholic religion in Scotland all the ceremony used in Catholic countries was taken, in 1816, by Mr Charles Gordon, priest at Aberdeen. This was the exposition of the Blessed Sacrament, followed by the service of Benediction. From 1816 onwards Mr Gordon performed this ceremony on special occasions.[50] Mr Mathison followed suit in 1820.[51] Once again it was only a matter of time before the practice became general.

If Bishop Hay had been able to return to earth in 1829, he would hardly have recognised his Vicariate. Chapels had been transformed into elegant church buildings; organs and choirs added music at Mass; and ritual and ceremony had been restored. Had he journeyed to the Highlands, however, he would have found that little there had been changed since his time.

NOTES

1 Mr Smelt, Rome, to Bishop Geddes, 15th June 1793, B.L.
2 William Ferguson, *Scotland, 1689 to the Present*, p. 338.
3 *Scotichronicon*, p.292.
4 John Gordon to Bishop Geddes, 17th May 1789, B.L.
5 John Gordon to Bishop Geddes, 25th July 1789, B.L.
6 George Mathison to Bishop Geddes, 18th July 1789, B.L.
7 Bishop Geddes to Mr Thomson, 5th July 1789, B.L.
8 Bishop Geddes to Bishop Hay, 21st December 1789, B.L.
9 Bishop Hay to Bishop Geddes, 27th August 1789, B.L.
10 Bishop Geddes to Bishop Hay, 25th September 1789, B.L.
11 Bishop Geddes to Bishop Hay, 18th February 1790, B.L.

12 Lachlan MacIntosh to Bishop Geddes, 15th March 1791, B.L.

13 Father James Robertson to Bishop Hay, 1st January 1798, B.L.

14 Bishop Geddes died in February 1799. Alexander Cameron was consecrated bishop at Valladolid in 1798, but remained in Spain until 1802.

15 Charles Gordon to Bishop Cameron, 3rd August 1804, B.L.

16 Charles Gordon to Bishop Cameron, 29th May 1807, 13th August 1810, B.L.

17 Charles Gordon to Bishop Cameron, 29th May 1807, B.L.

18 Andrew Scott to Bishop Cameron, 1st December 1817, B.L.

19 William Rattray to Bishop Cameron, 26th November 1810, B.L.

20 Andrew Scott to Bishop Cameron, 16th June 1812, B.L.

21 Charles Gordon to Bishop Cameron, 2nd October 1814, B.L.

22 Andrew Carruthers to Bishop Cameron, 29th March 1814, B.L.

23 E.g. James Gordon to John Forbes, 13th December 1817, B.L.

24 Messrs Wood & Co to Bishop Cameron, 26th May 1814, B.L.

25 Andrew Scott to Bishop Cameron, 18th May 1817, B.L.

26 George Mathison to James Gordon, 6th May 1820, B.L.

27 Charles Gordon to James Kyle, 9th May 1815, B.L.

28 Alexander Badenoch to Bishop Paterson, 26th August 1822, B.L.

29 James Gordon to James Kyle, 14th October 1816, B.L.

30 William Reid to George Mathison, 13th February 1824, B.L.

31 James Gordon to James Kyle, 9th September 1817, B.L.

32 John Bremner, Valladolid to George Mathison, 16th August 1819, B.L.

33 John Gordon, Valladolid to Bishop Geddes, 30th July 1794, B.L.

34 Alexander Badenoch to Bishop Cameron, 22nd January 1819, Preshome Letters, S.C.A.

35 George Gordon to John Forbes, 17th February 1821, B.L.

36 George Gordon to Charles Fraser, Dublin, 27th September 1829, B.L.

37 E.g. William Rattray to James Kyle, 3rd June 1819, B.L.

38 George Mathison to James Kyle, 28th August 1817, B.L.

39 Alexander Badenoch to Bishop Paterson, 22nd November 1820, B.L.

40 Andrew Scott to Bishop Paterson, 14th August 1823, B.L.

41 William Rattray to Bishop Cameron, 13th March 1818, Preshome Letters, S.C.A.

42 Andrew Scott to Bishop Cameron, 21st April 1818, Preshome Letters, S.C.A.

43 *Scotichronicon*, p. 468.

44 Charles Gordon to James Kyle, 14th April 1819, B.L.

45 Charles Gordon to Bishop Cameron, 15th April 1819, B.L.

46 John Chisholm to Bishop Geddes, 7th April 1791, B.L.

47 William Thomson to Charles Gordon, 11th June 1827, Preshome Letters, S.C.A.

48 Anonymous letter to Bishop Cameron, 12th June 1822, B.L.

49 George Mathison to Charles Gordon, 15th December 1826, Preshome Letters, S.C.A.

50 Charles Gordon to Bishop Cameron, 9th February 1816, B.L.

51 George Mathison to James Gordon, 6th May 1820, B.L.

20

Catholics in Scottish Society, 1793-1829

THE Relief Act of 1793 gave Scottish Roman Catholics a legality which they had not enjoyed for over two hundred and thirty years. It had, however, more immediate impact in the Lowland Vicariate than in the Highland. According to one Highland priest:

> ... in this country where the Catholics were very numerous without any mixture of Protestants till of late they seem to be less sensible of the indulgence granted.[1]

In the largely Catholic areas of the Highlands there had never been the same friction between Catholics and Protestants that had existed in the Lowlands. In the latter area, however, toleration had been growing before 1793, and the trend continued into the nineteenth century. Protestants, for instance, contributed to the cost of building chapels in the South-West.[2] Also the publishing of the Bishops' Pastoral letter of 1803 in papers such as the *Herald and Chronicle* was well received, the letter being described as showing the 'loyalty of Scotch Catholics *unimpeached* and *unimpeachable*'.[3]

The Relief Act allowed Scottish Catholics to find employment in the public service without being forced to take an intolerable oath. Menzies of Pitfoddels, for instance, in 1811, held the offices of deputy lieutenant of the counties of Aberdeen and Kincardine, and of convener of the county of Aberdeen.[4]

The Relief Act, however, did little to ease the situation of some Catholics. Mr Scott and Mr Davidson, priests respectively in Glasgow and Greenock, found that many members of their congregations were afraid to admit to their religion. Mr Scott found difficulty in estimating the number of Irish Catholics in Glasgow because

> ... many of the Catholics conceal themselves at first; there are instances of some of them working together for nearly a year before they know one another to be Catholics.[5]

A letter to Bishop Cameron from his sister, who lived in England, illustrates that it was not only the Irish who feared that Catholics in Scotland might still be persecuted:

> Did you live anywhere but Scotland I would direct my letters to you in a different Maner, but as it is I do not know how far it may be prudent.[6]

Bishop Cameron had recently arrived in Scotland, and his sister, in the above, her first letter to him after his arrival, addressed him as 'The Rev. Alexander Cameron', being afraid to give him any title which alluded to his new dignity.

One of the commonest problems with which the Scottish bishops had to deal was when a Catholic servant had a Protestant master. There was, for instance, the question of meagre days — days on which Catholics were forbidden to eat meat. In the spring of 1790 braxy killed off a considerable number of lambs in Braelochaber. This meant that there was an abundance of meat, and some Lowland shepherds dismissed their Catholic employees rather than provide them with a more expensive alternative to mutton on meagre days.[7]

In 1811 Mr Reid drew Bishop Cameron's attention to a similar problem regarding the Catholics of Dumfries:

> I find from my own experience that the abstinance on Fridays and Saturdays throughout the year proves a very common stumbling block to a great many particularly of the Irish, who in that and other respects are as harshly used in this country by their Presbyterian employers, as by the Orangemen in their own.[8]

Mr Reid wanted Bishop Cameron to grant a dispensation to allow Catholics to eat meat on meagre days. A similar dispensation was often applied for on behalf of Catholic farmers at harvest time when they might have both Protestant and Catholic workers, and did not want to have to provide two separate meals — the Protestants insisting on their entitlement to meat.[9]

Another cause of dispute between Protestant servants and Catholic masters was that of Holy Days when Catholics were expected to attend Mass. Bishop MacDonald wrote about this problem in strong terms to Bishop Geddes in 1789:

> I can easily forsee from the strict adherence you cause your Missionaries here [to] observe in regard to holy days, that it is like to turn out of bad consequences to the poor people in the first place, and of course to your Flock in general in the long run: for Instance the Superior [on South Uist] on that account of the holy days, will not take any of his own country people as servants, but people from North Uist, and threatens to turn off his poor tenants the same ways, for he was very much provoked last assumption day that he could get none of his people to ship his Kelp, tho' they were idle, and one of the finest days could be seen. It is so preposterous to set a whole Country idle on such days and especially when they make the worst use of it, drinking etc, ... no reasonable person would hinder any go hear prayers on these days, that were near the place of worship, but to set the whole Country idle does not look so well in the eyes of the world nowadays ... [10]

The problem of Holy Days must have been a continuing one, because in 1827 Mr James Gordon suggested that application be made to Rome to have the number of Holy Days reduced. He also suggested that Saturday should be dispensed with as a day of abstinence by Rome.[11]

Finally, there was the problem of Protestant masters insisting that their Catholic servants attend Protestant family prayers. Bishop Cameron, in 1802, suggested to Bishop Hay that, since such prayers generally consisted merely of a Scripture reading, a psalm, the Lord's Prayer and creed, all of which were acts of worship common also to the Catholic religion, it could do no harm for Catholics to attend them.[12] Bishop Hay's reply was typically uncompromising:

> I refer you to the first Titles both of Bishop Nicolson's statuta and those made lately; in the former they are nomination forbid, and in the latter lays down reasons which apply to those cases also. And if you and Mr Rattray think these can be evaded I would wish servants in that case (especially if their masters know that they are Catholicks) to tell them when they are engaging, to let their masters or mistresses know that they are obliged to say their own Evening prayers, at any rate, and hope they will allow them to take the time of family worship to say their own prayers by themselves. But if they be already engaged and must necessarily be present with the family, let them leave the place at next term.[13]

In 1813 Bishop Cameron received two letters from Catholic servants which illustrate vividly their problems. The first was written by Bell Burgess, a Scottish maidservant employed in London.

> I have never Been at my duties but once about a month after i came heir — I have every morning to make Breakfast for a dozen of Ladies at eight of the clock besides our own famely. I never get to Bed before one or two of the clock, and to get to my Duties in a morning or noon i cannot when i go at night their is none of the Cleargy at home and this is the way that i am.
>
> My misstres is for ever abusing me about my religion indeed my Lord it would very much offend your ear weir I to repeat what I suffer about it as my religion teaches me everything that is bad and had my Mistress known that i was a Catholic i should never have entered hir door — but i will encroach no longer upon your time an i hope you will pardon me for trublin you but have no other recourse.[14]

The other letter came from James Kelly, who was lodging at St Andrews, and who asked for a dispensation to eat meat on Fridays and Saturdays because

> I Dont Lik to Let them Know what I am as to my Religion as I know by the word of God and also by Experience the hatred and Ridicul that Catholics are Exposed to when they are among protestants therefore for the Sake of Bee at pace with all men I have troubled you . . .[15]

From such examples it is easy to see why Catholic servants preferred to be employed by members of their own religion, and why a Catholic complained bitterly in 1808 that he had been unable to get a job at Aquhorties while Protestants were being employed there.[16] Fortunately, most Catholic families who were in a position to hire servants much preferred to have Catholics — there are many requests among the Blairs Letters to priests to find Catholic servants from among their congregations.

The priests themselves experienced a certain measure of trouble with Protestants. In 1813 three 'Protestant ruffians' attacked Mr Charles Grant in the inn at Braemar.[17] In 1808 Mr Rattray, the priest at Paisley, found that he was in no position to argue about the rental charged for a hall which he wanted to lease as a chapel:

> Tho' a larger sum had been demanded, we should have been under the disagreeable necessity of agreeing to it, and that too immediately. For had the neighbourhood once heard of our attempt, they would have dissuaded the Landlady from suffering us to have it at any price.[18]

In 1814 two Glasgow Irishmen were condemned to be hanged. They were professed Catholics, and, during their last days, Mr Scott was assiduous in attending them. The ministers, however, insisted that it was their exclusive privilege to conduct prisoners to the gallows, because that was a public duty and no Catholic priest had any right to perform his functions in public. It was only after both Mr Scott and the two unfortunate Irishmen had protested vigorously that Mr Scott was allowed to mount the gallows.[19] In 1820 Mr James Carruthers had a similar experience in Dumfries. He described the event to Bishop Cameron:

> You will have heard of the disagreeable duty I had lately to perform, and its afflicting nature was yet more embittered by harassing circumstances. We were plagued by the officious visits of fanatical ministers and intruding zealots of every description. But when the time of execution approached, the Provost informed me that the custom of this town was, that the Magistrates and Minister assisted at the execution of a Criminal and that some devotions were performed. That this was principally intended to impress the spectators and to calm their own minds for the awful spectacle. I answered that, on this occasion, as the Criminal professed himself a Catholic, that devotion might be dispensed with, and, in other places such obtrusion had been rejected

and over-ruled. That, however, if they deemed such rites necessary for themselves and the crowd they had better finish them before the condemned person appeared on the scaffold as neither he nor I meant to partake of them. The Provost seemed satisfied but the Enthusiasts were not and the Doctor's prayer which was elaborately adapted to strike upon the head of the victim and thence to reverberate upon the listening throng would otherwise have lost its effect. The poor criminal's presence must therefore give the zest to the exhibition . . . Poor Ned and I knelt down and began our prayers, but were instantly drowned in Psalmody which was followed by a prayer which, it seems, for eloquence might have eclipsed Mr Brougham . . . [20]

Public hangings were vehicles, in some instances at least, for displays of religious intolerance; but other public institutions demonstrated a much more Christian attitude. Bishop Cameron, for instance, was one of the 'ordinary managers' of the Edinburgh Lying-in Hospital.[21] He was also connected with the Edinburgh New Town Dispensary, and was approached, in 1821 alone, by seven applicants for the post of medical officer then vacant.[22] In spite of the fact that Catholics were forbidden by law to have anything to do with the teaching of Protestant children, Bishop Cameron was also a member of the Edinburgh Education (Lancastrian School) Society, in which capacity he was invited to attend the Public Examination of its schools in 1820.[23] He was asked to attend a meeting of the Committee appointed to superintend the subscription for the distressed Irish in 1822[24] and to a public meeting, appointed to be held by the Lord Provost, in 1824, in which Dr Duffin illustrated by a series of engravings and drawings the diseases for the treatment of which a new dispensary was planned.[25] It was not, of course, a desire to do away with religious discrimination that led to Bishop Cameron's becoming so involved in charity work in Edinburgh. Bishop Cameron's large congregation was expected, along with all the other congregations of whatever persuasion in Edinburgh, to contribute to these charities. The charities appealed for Catholic subscriptions and donations; in return they promised to extend their help to Catholics in need of it.[26]

After the Relief Act had been passed, the Scottish priests believed that they should have complete religious freedom in accordance with the seeming intent of the Act. They were therefore upset when the Church of Scotland, as the established Church, still insisted that it had certain rights over Catholics, such as the right to dues when a Catholic marriage took place. In an attempt to find out exactly where they stood, several priests joined forces and sent the following list of queries regarding Scottish Catholics to the Lord Advocate:

(1) Are they obliged to proclaim their marriages in the Kirk, or will it suffice it to be done in their own chapels?

(2) Does the law oblige them to be married by the Minister of the place, or fine them if they don't?

(3) If one of the parties be a protestant, be satisfied to be married by a Catholick clergyman, can the Minister or Kirk Session take them to task, or fine them for so doing?

(4) Does the law oblige Catholick parents to registrate their children's names in the Kirk Session's books?

(5) If any Catholick gives public Scandal, for which they are severely reproved in their own chappels, has the Kirk any legal authority to punish them, or make them appear before their congregations for that purpose?

(6) Can any legal objections be made to Catholick clergymen for baptising unlawfull children of protestant parents, if the parents request it of them?

(7) Can the Kirk Session oblige Catholic parents, when their children are baptised by their own priests, to pay, besides the King's dues, so much for the Session Clerk, and so much for the Beddal [i.e. Beadle] for bringing in the water, an office which he never performs?

(8) Are the Masters of the Society Charity Schools authorised by law to cause the children of Roman Catholicks to learn the Protestant catechism, or expel them from the schools if they refuse? The practice is a very great loss to the children, they of course neither learn one nor the other to any purpose, and their minds are confused between them.

(9) Are not the Roman Catholicks by the late act in their favour, put upon an equal footing, at least as to all the above articles, with his Majesty's other subjects who are of a different communion from the established church?[27]

In due course they received the following answer from the Lord Advocate and the Solicitor General:

All marriages by the law of Scotland are either regular or clandestine. The first are those which are contracted for after publication of banns according to the rules of the established Church. Marriages of a different description whenever and by whomever celebrated excepting those celebrated by Episcopal Clergy in virtue of the act 10 Ann c 7 are termed clandestine and are liable to certain penalties and fines imposed by Act of Parliament.

In answer to the first three queries we are of opinion that the Memorialists in any of the cases therein put are liable in common with every other person who celebrates a clandestine marriage to the fines and penalties imposed in such cases. These are stated in the Acts of the Scotch Parliament 1661 c 34, 1695 c 12 and 1698 c 6.

query 4: We know of no obligation which parents of the Catholic or any persuasion whatever are under to registrate their children's names in the book of the kirk session of the parish in which they reside, unless they are so inclined, but we think the practice a very expedient and proper one which the Memorialists ought not to resist but to acquiesce in.

query 5: The established Church of Scotland has certainly full right to call before its proper judicatory, and to censure and reprove, all persons guilty of public scandal and such immorality as are the subject of ecclesiastical censures under the penalty of excommunication which is attended with no civil consequences to the excommunicated person, but merely excludes him from Church ordinances and privileges. Persons of the Roman Catholic persuasion may therefore refuse to appear before any Kirk judicatory as the penalty of their contumacy is only excommunication from a Church to which they do not belong.

query 6: We know of no legal objection to Catholic Clergymen baptizing children in any case where the parents chuse to present such children to them for Baptism.

query 7: The duty on Baptisms which we suppose is what is here alluded to by King's dues is now repealed by act of parliament. The session Clerks' and Beadles' dues depend not upon any positive law but are authorized and founded in practice and usage. In such parishes where these dues have been uniformly and immemorially levied we are of opinion that the exaction is legal, and that Roman Catholics in common with all other parishioners of whatever sect or description they be, will be liable in payment of them.

query 8: The schools established by the Society for propagating Christian knowledge are governed alone by the rules and regulations established by that society. If the Roman Catholics think they have reason to complain of the regulations at present observed and enforced in these Schools they must apply to the managers of that Society, with whom alone there lies to grant or refuse the favour which may be applied for.

query 9: Having given specific answers to all the above queries, an answer to this one appears almost unnecessary. The purpose of the late act of parliament is clearly expressed both in its preamble and enactment to have been merely this: to enable Roman Catholics to hold and enjoy property of all kinds without molestation on account of their religious persuasion, and to substitute, in place of the Formula by which they are obliged under the act of King William to renounce their religion, an oath of abjuration and Declaration sufficient to secure their allegiance to the king and to the Constitution of this Country.[28]

The above queries and answers give a good indication of the main causes of friction between Catholic priests and established Church ministers. The Lord Advocate's reply did not eliminate much of the friction because it was not generally known of among those who became priests after 1794, nor indeed was it known of by all of those who were already priests at that time. For instance, in 1804, Mr Badenoch, priest at Tomintoul, asked whether Catholics were bound to pay the schoolmaster, who was session clerk, when marriages and baptisms were performed by the priest:

> ... as this little man, who seems to mind his dues more than his duty, will probably put them to trouble. I do not think schoolmasters receive anything in the lowlands, except from those who wish to have their marriage or the baptism of their children registered. I am also somewhat at a loss with regard to the minister's dues.[29]

One or two interesting points emerge from the Queries of 1794. There is the question of clandestine marriages. Clandestine or irregular marriages were prohibited, in Catholic countries, under canon law by the Council of Trent in 1563. Scotland, by 1563, was officially a Protestant country, and so it was unaffected by the Council of Trent. Irregular marriages, therefore, were still legally recognised under Scots Law even though they were condemned by the established Church. Three forms of irregular marriage existed: 'Declaration de Praesenti' or the consent of the parties to present marriage; 'Promise subsequente Copula' or the promise of marriage, followed by intercourse permitted upon the faith of the promise; and 'Cohabitation with Habit and Repute'. The first two forms were removed from the statute book in July 1940; the third form still exists today.[30] It is the first two forms which concern us.

When a priest conducted a marriage ceremony, the marriage was recognised as valid by the Roman Catholic Church. It was not recognised as a regular marriage under Scots Law until the passing of the Marriage (Scotland) Act in 1834. It was, however, a perfectly legal marriage by Declaration de Praesenti. Thus both God and the Law were satisfied.

The second form of irregular marriage — Promise subsequente Copula — was to cause the priests of the South-West of Scotland some concern. They were frequently confronted with cases of Irishmen who had fathered children in Ireland after promising marriage, and who had then formed similar connections in Scotland. Which, if any, was a valid marriage? Presumably the second marriage was legally valid as the rulings of the Council of Trent applied in Ireland, but was the first not perhaps morally valid — or would it be recognised as such in Scotland? This was the sort of problem with which the priests had to cope, problems which had not occurred in Scotland before the Irish immigrations.[31]

Another interesting point to arise out of the 1794 Queries regards the calling of banns. The point of having banns called was to ensure that both parties to the proposed marriage were free so to contract. In a settled community a previous marriage or other impediment would probably be known by at least some of its members, and thus the proposed marriage could be prevented if invalid. The system, of course, broke down in a situation like that in the South-West of Scotland where the Catholic population was largely made up of immigrant and often migratory Irish.

The law regarding banns was quite clear. A marriage was regular only if the ceremony was performed by an established minister after the banns had been called in the parish church. Even after 1834, when marriage by a priest was recognised as a regular marriage, banns had to be called in the established parish church. It was not until 1878 that the Marriage Notice Act introduced an alternative to banns: the publication of a Notice of intention to marry in the Registry of Births, Death and Marriages.[32] Until 1977 banns still satisfied a legal requirement, but only if called in a Church of Scotland parish church. The Marriage (Scotland) Act 1977 made a notice submitted to the registrar the only legal prerequisite for marriage.

The law of Scotland laid down clearly and precisely what constituted a regular marriage up until 1834. This law, however, was imperfectly understood by many Catholic priests. In 1815 Bishop Cameron sent Bishop Chisholm of the Highland Vicariate the following advice regarding marriages:

> In the Lowland district our general rule is to marry none who do not present the certificate that the banns have been regularly published in the Parish Church. I believe however that in Country Parishes the Registers are not always attended to, and that the proclamations, as they are called, are very seldom required. But the Letter of the Law does certainly require them, at the Parish Church, and when they procede in due form, the marriage is neither clandestine nor irregular, of whatever persuasion or sect the officiating clergymen may be. I do not know how far Parish Ministers are legally authorised to dispense with the banns; but I know they do, sometimes, marry people without them. And I have known instances of their desiring priests to do so. Those cases happen however only where Parsons and Priests wish to live on good terms. A Parson who knows that marriage is accounted a sacrament among Catholics will never desire them to receive it from him.[33]

Bishop Cameron's letter suggests that parish ministers as well as priests were somewhat hazy about the law concerning regular marriages. It also suggests that, generally speaking, priests and parish ministers worked out together a compromise regarding Catholic marriages irrespective of what the law might dictate.

Whether or not priests had marriage banns read in the parish churches, they often had them read in their own chapels with a view to preventing bigamous marriages. A priest, however, might sometimes dispense altogether with the reading of banns, as when a servant with a Protestant master might lose her place if the marriage became known,[34] or where the woman was pregnant.[35] A certificate from their former priests that the parties were single was sometimes requested if the couple had recently moved into the district.

There were other areas where Catholics still had cause for complaint after 1793. In 1808 Mr Scott uncovered a legal anomaly in Glasgow's burgh laws. Nobody in the royal burgh of Glasgow could go into business as a merchant or shopkeeper without having first become a burgess. The burgess ticket was freely available to anyone who applied, and who paid the required sum of money. The burgess oath, however, contained the words ' . . . renouncing the Roman Religion called papistry . . . ' In 1808 a survey was carried out in Glasgow of all merchants and shopkeepers to find and summon to appear at the Dean of Guild's office all those who had not become burgesses. They were threatened with prosecution should they refuse to pay the customary dues and take the burgess oath. There were several

Catholics among those summoned. Mr Scott suggested to the Dean of Guild that Catholics should be allowed merely to pay the customary dues without having to take the oath which was contrary to the intention of the 1793 Relief Act. The Dean of Guild had been unaware of the existence of that Act but when Mr Scott showed him proof of its existence, he agreed that Catholics should not be required to take the burgess oath as it then stood. He said that the whole question would have to be referred to lawyers for a decision but that in the meantime no Catholics would be prosecuted.[36]

Another question, which was raised on several occasions by Mr Menzies of Pitfoddels, was that of praying by name for the King. Although Bishop Hay assured him, in 1795, that most chapels were already including such a prayer,[37] Menzies wrote to him again in 1797 asking that he make such a prayer obligatory in all chapels,[38] and in 1800 he returned to the subject, expressing concern that, because the prayer for the King was in the wrong part of the service, and was worded the way it was, it might not conform to the legal requirements laid down by Act of Parliament.[39] What was troubling Menzies was the implication of an Act of Parliament of 1746 which read:

> ... from and after the first day of September no person shall be capable of being elected, or of voting in any election of a member of Parliament for any shire or borough in that part of Great Britain called Scotland, or of being elected or of voting in the election of a magistrate or Counsellor for boroughs or of a Deacon of Crafts within the Burghs, or of a Collector or Clerk of the Land Tax, or Supply, who shall have at any time within one year preceding that election been twice present at Divine Service in any Episcopal meeting house or congregation in Scotland not held and allowed in pursuance of that act made in the 10th year of the reign of Queen Anne, or which shall not, after the first day of September be registered according to the directions of this act, or where the Pastor or Minister officiating did not in express words pray for his Majesty, his heirs or successors, by name, and for all the Royal Family ...[40]

Bishop Hay was able to assure Menzies that the Lord Advocate himself had approved of both the position and the wording of the Catholic prayer for the King.[41] At the same time he instructed all his priests to use this prayer in their chapels.[42]

The Roman Catholic Church in Scotland faced one major legal problem after 1793. It was not recognised as a legal corporation for the purpose of owning property. As a result chapels and houses were registered in the names of the priests attached to the individual stations, or perhaps of several priests who acted in capacity of trustees for the property. Such a situation naturally led to problems: priests regarded the houses they lived in, and the chapels they served, as their own property, on which they spent money which they themselves had raised, and on which they expected to receive melioration when they were moved to other stations. Bishop Hay wrote about the problem to Bishop Cameron in 1803:

> I am wholly of your opinion that both Chapels, houses and farms should be the property of the Mission; but I am affraid it will be difficult to get it done to the purpose. My reason is this. I had in view some time ago, to set that plan on foot, and began with the houses and furniture, and set up no less than five. I shall give you one sample of how I was treated. I built the house by myself with some small contributions; that then stands still to me; but for the furniture I gave £25 and got an obligation from the Incumbent to leave as much on his removal. In the small time of two years he was removed, and on valuing the furniture it was diminished to £17, but instead of

> making up the deficience by the outgoing client I was obliged to help him to the place he went to. What could I do? He had nothing.[43]

Generally speaking, an incoming priest agreed to take over the furniture, farm implements, standing crops and stacks at an independent valuation. After the Friendly Society was formed, many priests made over their chapels to it. Houses constituted the biggest problem. Mr Mathison, for instance, wrote in 1808:

> Several years ago I made over to Bishop Hay for the use of the Mission what houses I then possessed here. Some time thereafter part of them became so frail that I found it expedient to pull down that part, in place of which I built at my own expense the new addition, consisting of kitchen, passage, principal room with a garret above etc which cost between £40 and £50. I proposed to Bishop Hay to give up to him for the Mission this additional building, on condition of his bearing the half of the expence, as I could not well afford to bear the whole. The plan he proposed for paying his share was such as I did not think proper to accept of.[44]

In other words, Mr Mathison considered the priest's house at Auchenhalrig to be his own personal property, as indeed it legally was, being in his name.

Such a situation as this could cause grave problems for the Mission. In 1826 Mr Bagnall, priest at New Abbey, died. His relations claimed not only his house but also the chapel he had built at great cost to himself.[45] A lengthy lawsuit followed, which was finally won by the Mission in 1828, after two years of uncertainty and anxiety.[46]

This was the first time that the relatives of a priest had laid claim to a chapel as well as to house and chattels. Mr Bagnall had intended that all his posessions, as well as the buildings at New Abbey, should remain the property of the incumbent of that Mission station. The legal action resulting from his relatives' claim called in question the legality of bequests to the Mission itself, or to any particular organisation within the Mission. It was at this time that Mr Menzies was considering making over to the Mission his house and estate at Blairs, in Aberdeenshire. He was anxious that the conveyancing of his estate to the Mission be legally watertight, and suggested to the Solicitor General that, as Blairs was to be used to found a Catholic college for educating boys for the priesthood, the college might be classed as a charitable trust to which the gift of Blairs could be made. The Solicitor General thought that such a charitable trust, being Catholic, might not be immune should an heir wish to challenge a bequest made to it. He advised making Blairs over to named indiviuals. This, of course, raised the problem of what title the heirs of these individuals might have to the property should any of the named individuals die intestate. The only long-term solution, in the Solicitor General's opinion, was to ask Government to repeal the relevant Penal Laws.[47]

In 1829 the Catholic Emancipation Act made it lawful for Catholics to form themselves into corporations, and in 1832 a further act was passed ' . . . for the better securing the Charitable Donations and Bequests of His Majesty's Subjects in Great Britain professing the Roman Catholic Religion'.[48] Only then could houses, farms and chapels be properly secured to the Mission.

Between 1793 and 1829 Catholics and Protestants, on the whole, co-operated well, in spite of minor irritations such as demands for dues by the Church of Scotland. Ownership of property remained a problem until 1829, as far as the

Mission was concerned. As far as ordinary Catholics were concerned, they were deprived of the political rights which would only be granted with the Emancipation Act, but before the passing of the Reform Act of 1832 few Catholics would have had the franchise anyway. During the years 1793 to 1829 the main problems faced by the Mission concerned Irish Catholics and were of a social rather than a religious provenance.

NOTES

1 John Chisholm to Bishop Hay, 22nd July 1793, B.L.
2 E.g. John Davidson to Bishop Cameron, 21st September 1808, B.L.
3 Bishop Cameron to Bishop Hay, 14th September 1803, B.L.
4 James Gordon, Aquhorties, to his mother, December 1811, B.L.
5 Andrew Scott to Bishop Cameron, 17th March 1808, B.L.
6 Clare Hardy to Bishop Cameron, 30th March 1803, B.L.
7 Alexander MacDonald to Bishop Geddes, 22nd March 1790, B.L.
8 William Reid to Bishop Cameron, 18th February 1811, B.L.
9 Andrew Carruthers to Bishop Paterson, 18th August 1829, B.L.
10 Bishop MacDonald to Bishop Geddes, 13th September 1789, B.L.
11 James Gordon to Bishop Paterson — scroll letter — 23rd June 1827, Preshome Letters, S.C.A.
12 Bishop Cameron to Bishop Hay, 27th December 1802, B.L.
13 Bishop Hay to Bishop Cameron, 5th January 1803, B.L.
14 Bell Burgess to Bishop Cameron, 29th October 1813, B.L.
15 James Kelly to Bishop Cameron, 5th June 1813, B.L.
16 Alexander Badenoch to Bishop Cameron, 12th March 1808, B.L.
17 Donald Carmichael to Alexander Paterson, 23rd January 1813, B.L.
18 William Rattray to Bishop Cameron, 17th May 1808, B.L.
19 Andrew Scott to Bishop Cameron, 9th November 1814, B.L.
20 James Carruthers to Bishop Cameron, 4th November 1820, B.L.
21 A. G. Ellis to Bishop Cameron, 16th April 1821, B.L.
22 E.g. Robert Carnegy to Bishop Cameron, 21st December 1821, Preshome Letters, S.C.A.
23 G. Lyon to Bishop Cameron, 22nd November 1820, B.L.
24 Letter to Bishop Cameron from Edinburgh Council Chambers, 17th May 1822, B.L.
25 Dr Duffin to Bishop Cameron, 1st July 1824, B.L.
26 E.g. William Moffat, Edinburgh Public Dispensary to Bishop Cameron, 7th May 1817, B.L.
27 "Queries relating to the Roman Catholicks in Scotland in Consequence of the late Act of Parliament in their Favour," January 1794, B.L.
28 "Answer to the Memorial and Queries of the Roman Catholics in Scotland", Robert Dundas, Lord Advocate, and Robert Blair, Solicitor General, 1st August 1794, B.L.
29 Alexander Badenoch to Bishop Cameron, 6th November 1804, B.L.
30 Gloag and Henderson, *Introduction to the Law of Scotland* (Edinburgh, 1956), pp. 604-605.
31 E.g. Thomas Bagnall to Bishop Cameron, 1st May 1815, B.L.
32 Gloag and Henderson, pp. 602-603.
33 Bishop Cameron to Bishop Chisholm (presumably), 11th September 1815, B.L.
34 Charles Gordon to Bishop Cameron, February 1813, B.L.
35 Bishop Cameron to John Forbes, 28th November 1816, B.L.
36 Andrew Scott to Bishop Cameron, 28th April 1808, B.L.
37 Bishop Hay to Bishop Geddes, 5th January 1795, B.L.
38 Menzies to Bishop Hay, 3rd April 1797, B.L.
39 Menzies to Bishop Hay, 14th May 1800, B.L.

40 William Rattray to Bishop Hay, enclosing transcription of the Act, 13th August 1800, B.L.
41 Bishop Hay to Mr Menzies, 16th June 1800, B.L.
42 Bishop Hay to Charles Maxwell, 21st June 1800, B.L.
43 Bishop Hay to Bishop Cameron, 28th December 1803, B.L.
44 George Mathison to Bishop Cameron, 26th March 1808, B.L.
45 Andrew Scott to Bishop Paterson, 17th July 1826, B.L.
46 James Carruthers to Bishop Paterson, 29th December 1828, B.L.
47 Mr Menzies to Bishop Paterson, 18th August 1826, B.L.
48 *The Catholic Directory for Scotland*, 1835, p.69.

21

Recovery of the Scots Colleges Abroad: 1. France

THE college at Aquhorties in Scotland was established in the hope that it would provide most, if not all, of the education of future priests for the Lowland District. The Scots Colleges abroad, however, represented too large a capital investment to be abandoned without any attempt having been made to recover them.

The first hope of recovering the Colleges in France arose in 1802 with the signing of a peace treaty between Britain and France at Amiens.[1] Although there was little hope that the peace would be a lasting one, the Scottish bishops, as soon as a treaty seemed likely — in 1801 — set out to make the most of it.

In October 1801, at the instigation of Mr Farquharson and Mr Innes, Bishop Hay sent a memorial to Lord Hawkesbury, principal Secretary of State for the Foreign Department, in an attempt to persuade the British Government to intervene in France on behalf of the Scottish Mission. In his memorial Bishop Hay stressed the fact that the Scots Colleges in France were Scottish property, founded and endowed by Scots. He related what had happened to the Colleges during the preceding ten years, and requested that his claim for compensation be considered. He stressed the advantages, both to the Mission and to the British Government, of educating Scottish priests in the safe political climate of their own country. He added that Mary Queen of Scots, when she had founded the Scots College at Douay, had expressed the hope that it might one day be transferred to Scotland. If Bishop Hay were to receive compensation for his losses in France, he would be able to fulfil Mary's desire by using the money to help the colleges in Scotland.[2]

It is doubtful whether the wishes of Mary Queen of Scots can have carried much weight with Lord Hawkesbury; but the administration of the Scots College at Paris, as settled by a decree of Napoleon Bonaparte, now first Consul, must have made him aware of the desirability of severing the Scottish Mission's connection with France. Under this decree the Scottish clergy were totally excluded from every concern in the College, whether in the administration of the house, the education of the boys, or the appointing of the masters. All they were entitled to do was to hand over Scots boys to be educated by the French.[3] This was hardly likely to appeal to the British Ministry, which was aware that the peace was likely to be only temporary, as, under such regulations as these, the Scots College might well be transformed into a recruitment centre for French spies.

Lord Hawkesbury, who held no hopes of the Scots, English and Irish Missions recovering anything more in France than their college buildings,[4] referred all discussions on the subject of their property to Lord Cornwallis.[5] Memorials were sent and meetings arranged, but nothing had been accomplished when Mr Farquharson arrived in France, in 1802, in an abortive attempt to save the Scots College at Douay.

In March 1802, shortly after his arrival in Paris, Mr Farquharson sent to Abbé MacPherson the gloomy news:

> Mr Innes, having lost nothing, has no claims to make . . . but with regard to our Douay foundation the case is widely different; only the college walls remain unsold; all our landed property, amounting to near 500 acres of excellent ground, besides 5 houses, have been sold and resold; the loss is entire, . . . according to the present existing laws, for though the sale is avowedly illegal, yet a posterior sanction given precludes all redress; an equivalent of lands (of which a vast quantity remains as yet unsold, in the ci-devant Belgium) is what we want.[6]

Bishop Hay had hoped to obtain recompense for the Douay property rather than lands elsewhere on the Continent, but Mr Farquharson saw the impracticability of this, as the French government, whatever it might promise, had no funds with which to pay any recompense. Without its property the Douay College would have no income and would be unable to reopen.

By May Mr Farquharson was heartily sick of France. He had been to Douay, and was beginning to realise that it would be madness to think of settling there again. The college building, which was the least damaged part of the property, would require several years' revenue for repairs. The British Government refused to intervene in the matter — 'for fear of compromising its dignity' — and only the direct intervention of the British Ministry might obtain for the Scottish Mission the leave to sell out. Accordingly, having collected together all the original documents he could find relative to the College, and its finances, for use if any occasion arose in the future to pursue a claim for the College, Mr Farquharson returned home to Scotland in July 1802, leaving Mr Innes to do what he could to save the as yet unsold Scots College in Paris.[7]

Mr Innes's negotiations regarding the Paris property had been complicated by the arrival in Paris, in July 1801, of Principal Gordon, who was determined to protect what he regarded as his personal sinecure. Principal Gordon was connected to the Laws of Lauriston, one member of which family stood high in Napoleon's favour. In an attempt to counteract Principal Gordon's influence with this gentleman, who was a general in the French Army, Bishop Hay asked Sir John Cox Hippisley to present General Law with an account of Principal Gordon's deplorable behaviour in 1793 when he had, firstly, refused to obey the directive of the Scottish bishops, and, secondly, had abandoned the College to its fate.[8]

In 1802 Bishop Hay sent further exhaustive memorials — to Lord Hawkesbury,[9] and to Lord Whitworth, the British Ambassador in Paris[10] — requesting them to use their influence to help the Scottish Mission sell up its property in France and bring the money to Scotland. His memorial to Lord Whitworth was supported by the Bourbon heir to the French throne.[11]

By November 1802 hopes were fast fading in Scotland that anything could be salvaged out of the wreckage in France. The Scots College at Douay had long since been written off as lost, and there seemed little immediate chance of recovering anything worthwhile in Paris. It was at this juncture that Napoleon sealed the fate of, not only the Scots, but also the English and Irish Colleges in Paris. He was determined that the Colleges should resume their educational function, but under French jurisdiction, and, to this end, he issued a series of arrêtes;[12] the Scots and Irish colleges were the first to be affected. A previous arrête — in November 1801 — had placed the Scots and Irish Colleges in Paris under French control; now a new arrête united all the Irish and Scots Colleges still existing in France into one college. The superior of this united college was to be alternately Irish and Scots, with Mr Walsh, an Irish priest, as the first superior. Mr Walsh accepted the appointment, thus sanctioning the arrête.

The union of the Scots and Irish Colleges had been talked of in France for about two years, but the blow, when it fell, was no less serious for the Scottish Mission. Although Archbishop Troy wrote from Dublin to Bishop Cameron that he, too, was against the union,[13] the Scottish bishops remained suspicious. As Mr Innes, writing from Paris, put it:

> The Irish, as you know, have made more than one attempt upon our Colleges. They never had a better opportunity than the present crisis: you see by Mr W[alsh]'s proceeding that they are disposed to make the best use of it, — the union once effected they lay their account to drive us out and our property will become the fruit and reward of their complaisance and perseverance. This will be the upshot of all their fair professions if we do not get this last decree repealed.[14]

The union of the Scots and Irish Colleges prompted Bishop Hay to make a fresh appeal to Lord Hawkesbury who, although he could not requisition the Scottish property, could at least ask permission for the Scottish Mission to sell up as a favour from the French government. Bishop Hay had little hope, however, that this appeal would meet with any success. As Mr Innes shrewdly summed up the situation:

> . . . neither government is disposed at present to ask favours of the other, nor are they likely to be so for some time . . .[15]

Mr Innes did manage to gain one concession. Thanks to the help given by Mr Law, he was able to present a petition to Napoleon, as a result of which the affairs of the Scots College were placed in the hands of the Ministre des Relations Extérieures,[16] a tacit acknowledgement that the College was Scottish and not French property. Furthermore it was promised that the Scottish and Irish revenues would be separately accounted: there would be no financial union of the Scots and Irish Colleges.[17] The union as such, however, could not be repealed; on the contrary it was compounded when, in 1804, the English colleges were brought in as well.[18]

When, in September 1803, Mr Innes died in Paris, worn out by a struggle in which he had never felt that he had been adequately aided by the Scottish bishops, all attempts at recovering, and selling out, the property of the Scots College at Paris ceased. The Scottish Mission was not prepared, however, to have anything to do with the united college, and no students were sent to France. As might have been expected, Ireland, where many of the people, if not the bishops and priests, were in sympathy with Napoleonic France, continued to support the college. That the English should have anything to do with the college seemed inconceivable. As

Mr Farquharson expressed it:

> I truly cannot credit, that Bishop Douglas thinks of sending Boys to Walsh's heterogenous Shop, and if any, some Irish Street-runners of St Giles or Billingsgate, to save appearances and in the expectation of making spiritual and seasonable remonstrances in due time.[19]

In the event the united college in Paris came to have, as students, some Irish boys intended for the priesthood, and a large number of French boys, who were there to receive an ordinary education. The building belonging to the Scots College at Paris was rented out, in 1810, to a schoolmaster.[20] It was not until 1814 that the Scottish Mission saw any prospect of recovering any of their losses in France.

In July 1814, with Napoleon in exile on Elba, Commissioners, appointed to carry into effect some of the articles of the peace treaty, invited all British subjects who had claims upon the French government for the value of property illegally confiscated by the French authorities, to present those claims.[21] The Scottish and English Missions presented their claims for the property of their Colleges in France, and for ten years pursued those claims by the usual methods: writing memorials, beseeching influential friends to intercede on their behalf, and furnishing all the documentary evidence they could that this property was in fact British and not French. Finally, in February 1824, their claims were judged. Mr Riorden sent word of the outcome to Bishop Paterson:

> You were rightly informed as to the determination of the Commision to Reject the Ecclesiastical Claims — the Claim for Douay College, the seminary at Paris, that at St Omers connected with it, the Claim for the Scotch College, and one Claim preferred by the Religious Ladies have been rejected and published in the Gazette with a Recommendation that we should appeal to the discussion of the Commissioners to the Privy Council . . . [22]

In 1825 the English appeal was heard by the Privy Council and rejected on the following grounds:

> (1) Tho the members of these Establishments were British, tho the property was derived from funds constituted by British subjects, yet the Institutions were in the nature of French Corporations, under the control of the French Government, and to be deemed French Establishments.
>
> (2) That it was not, nor could have been, in the contemplation of the British Government to demand, nor of the French Government to grant, compensation for property held in trust for establishments in France and for purposes inconsistent with British laws and which were subject to the control of the French Government.[23]

Hence the Privy Council concluded that the English case was not within the meaning or spirit of the Treaties, and consequently it confirmed the Commissioners' rejection of the claim.

As a result of the English appeal, the Scottish Mission gave up all hopes of receiving indemnification for that part of its property in France which had been sold by the French Government during the Revolutionary and Napoleonic Wars. It was, however, more successful as regards its unsold property in France. The unsold buildings belonging to the Scottish Mission had been rented out by the French Bureau under whose control they had been placed. The income so derived had been allocated to help support the united college, The Scottish Mission, therefore, had two aims: to regain control of its property from the Bureau, and to extricate itself from the united college.

By January, 1816 Mr Farquharson was back in Paris. Shortly after his arrival the French king, by royal edict, put the British Missions in full possession of their respective properties. Mr Farquharson was named administrator general of the Scottish property in France.[24] In practice this meant that he acquired

> . . . the wrecks of our two establishments which, escaping the all overwhelming revolution [are] still worth looking after.[25]

Although the college building in Paris was leased out until April 1821, Mr Farquharson hoped to set up a 'sham establishment' in his lodgings, with two or three boarders to keep up appearances. By December 1816 he had managed to salvage much of the college's library.[26]

In 1817 Mr Farquharson died and Bishop Paterson was forced to travel to Paris to unravel his affairs, everything having been sealed by the French authorities on Mr Farquharson's death. He reported as follows to Bishop Cameron:

> I have procured an ordonnance from the Tribunal . . . to have the seals taken off, but so many ex officio men must be present . . . I am afraid I shall have to wait in my slippers.[27]

By 1818 Bishop Paterson was once more in possession of the Mission's property. In 1818 he requested that four Scots boys be sent to Paris because the united college had an excuse to hold on to the Scottish part of its income so long as there were no Scots boys in Paris to require it.[28] Accordingly, in the autumn, four boys were sent out from Aquhorties. They were given places in the French college of St Nicolas, Mr Desjardins, the administrator of the English, Irish and Scots funds in France, having agreed to support them there. Along with the four boys came James Gillis, later Bishop, whose parents preferred to pay for his education themselves.

Although the French Board of Administration continued to control the income derived from Scottish property in France, it proved to be quite helpful, agreeing in 1822 to accept ten Scots boys as bursars on the funds.[29] As Bishop Paterson pointed out to Bishop Cameron, the Scottish Mission fared better this way than if it had re-established an independent college. The Paris College building was leased out, and to recover it the Mission would have to buy up the lease and then carry out the expensive repairs and refurnishing before it could be opened. Then, if the College were to support two superiors and a number of servants, as it had done before 1793, the number of students in Paris would have to be reduced from ten to two or three.[30]

In 1824 the Scottish assets in France were separated from those of England and Ireland; the united college was disbanded; and Bishop Paterson regained control of the management of all the Scottish property and its income.[31] He did not, however, re-establish a Scots College as such, being content that Scots boys should attend the French seminary of St Nicolas and its college of St Sulpice as bursars, the number of bursars being increased to fifteen. The same practice continues today.

NOTES

1 Franklin L. Ford, *Europe 1780-1830*, pp. 198-199.
2 Bishop Hay to Lord Hawkesbury, scroll letter, October 1801, B.L.
3 Bishop Hay to Sir John Cox Hippisley, 10th November 1801, B.L.

 4 John Farquharson to Mr Maxwell, 9th November 1801, B.L.
 5 Sir John Cox Hippisley to Bishop Hay, 21st November 1801, B.L.
 6 Mr Farquharson to Abbé MacPherson, 5th March 1802, B.L.
 7 E.g. Mr Farquharson to Bishop Hay, 29th May 1802, B.L.
 8 Bishop Hay to Sir John Cox Hippisley, scroll letter, 10th November 1801, B.L.
 9 Bishop Hay to Lord Hawkesbury, scroll letter, 13th February 1802, B.L.
10 Bishop Hay to Lord Whitworth, scroll letter, May 1802, B.L.
11 Lord Whitworth to H.R.H. Monseigneur, 1802, B.L.
12 Bishop Cameron to Bishop Hay, 8th March 1803, B.L.
13 Archbishop Troy to Bishop Cameron, 22nd November 1802, B.L.
14 Alexander Innes to Bishop Cameron, 5th February 1803, B.L.
15 Mr Innes to Bishop Cameron, 30th March 1803, B.L.
16 Mr Innes to Bishop Cameron, 30th April 1803, B.L.
17 Mr Walsh to Bishop Cameron, 23rd February 1803, B.L.
18 Bishop Douglas to Bishop Cameron, 4th April 1804, B.L.
19 John Farquharson to Bishop Cameron, 12th February 1804, B.L.
20 Mr Smelt, Paris, to Abbé MacPherson, 29th October 1810, B.L.
21 "Office of the Commissioners appointed to carry into effect the 2nd and 4th additional articles of the Treaty of Peace; 19th July 1814", B.L.
22 Daniel Riorden to Bishop Paterson, 12th February 1824, B.L.
23 Bishop Poynter to Bishop Paterson, 28th November 1825, B.L.
24 John Farquharson to George Mathison, 12th February 1816, B.L.
25 John Farquharson to George Mathison, 25th March 1816, B.L.
26 John Farquharson to Bishop Cameron, 9th December 1816, B.L.
27 Bishop Paterson (under "Bringos") to Bishop Cameron, 28th August 1817, B.L.
28 Bishop Paterson to Bishop Cameron, 12 April 1818, Preshome Letters, S.C.A.
29 Bishop Paterson to Bishop Cameron, 22nd January 1822, B.L.
30 Bishop Paterson to Bishop Cameron, 17th September 1822, B.L.
31 Mr Menzies to Bishop Cameron, 20th March 1824, Preshome Letters, S.C.A.

22

Recovery of the Scots Colleges Abroad: 2. Rome and Valladolid

THE Scots College at Rome, though it suffered less than those at Douay and Paris, was also lost to the Scottish Mission for a number of years. The College was evacuated in 1798 and, for the next two years, Mr Sloane, the merchant who had befriended the Scots boys at Civita Vecchia, kept a watchful eye on it, sending reports to Abbé MacPherson who was, for the time being, stationed as priest at Huntly. In July 1798, for instance, he reported that an edict had been published, promising a hundred crowns a year to any priest or friar who married. To Mr Sloane's disgust several priests had not only married under the terms of the edict, but had also continued to say Mass.[1]

In December 1798 he had rather better news:

> I hope that long ere this you will have heard of our delivery from the Tyranny of the Cursed French, by the arrival of . . . Neapolitan Troops . . . I hope I will soon be able to tell you that I have recovered your College, Land etc. I have wrote to Naples to know if Sir William Hamilton will claim it in the Name of His British Majesty, as I would prefer that method to applying to Cardinal York or Albani who probably as before would think of providing [for] some of their hungry sincophants in preference of those that have an undeniable right to possess it in benefit of the mission.[2]

In March 1799 Abbé MacPherson learned of the siege of Civita Vecchia. The town had refused to allow the French to re-enter after the retreat of the Neapolitan army. Galley slaves had been freed to help to defend the town, and were reported to have drunk five hundred crowns' worth of Spanish wine out of Mr Sloane's warehouse.[3]

By October 1799 the French had removed from Rome and, as the result of a decree passed with reference to ecclesiastical property which had been alienated by the French, the Scots College had been placed under the directorship of Monsignor Connestabile. Mr Sloane went at once to Monsignor Connestabile and offered to provide any money necessary for the repair of the College building, or the cultivation of its vineyard. His offer was accepted, but a day or two later a new edict declared that all the ecclesiastical effects disposed of by the French were to be sequestered in the hands of their illegal possessors, and were to be administered on behalf of the Government, to defray public expenses, as an alternative to the imposition of heavy taxes on private individuals. There was therefore no hope of recovering the Scots College or its property for the moment.[4]

In June 1799 Abbé MacPherson expressed a hope that it might soon be possible for someone from the Mission to go to Rome to try to recover the College, but he was determined that he should not be the one to go.[5] Bishop Hay thought otherwise; to his mind Abbé MacPherson, who knew so many people in Rome, was the obvious choice. Until Abbé MacPherson could be sent, however, it seemed sensible to ask someone on the spot to take any necessary action on behalf of the Mission. Bishop Hay consulted Sir John Cox Hippisley, who suggested Mr Moir, a banker, who was held in esteem by Lord Grenville, and who had recently gone out to Rome.[6]

Abbé MacPherson was not happy at this choice. He wanted the affairs of the Scots College entrusted to Mr Sloane, who had already proved his friendship on so many occasions. Bishop Hay, however, was unwilling to offend Hippisley, whose influence with the British Government had been a great service to the Mission. Accordingly, Mr Moir was authorised to act as the agent of the Scottish bishops at Rome until Abbé MacPherson should arrive there himself.[7] On 9th May, 1800 Mr Moir sent the following letter to Scotland:

> ... upon the entry of the Neapolitan Army, Sir William Hamilton wrote to Mr Fagan, desiring him to lay claim to, and demand restitution of, whatever property belonged to British subjects in that part of the Ecclesiastical state occupied by the Arms of his Sicilian Majesty. In Consequence Mr Fagan obtained from General Masselli (the Neapolitan commander) restitution of the property belonging to the religious bodies of Britain and Ireland, and has continued to act for these bodies. In this capacity he has, I have been informed, appointed Persons to receive Payment of the Revenues of the Colleges, and has also directed the works of the Vineyards and whatever else he judged best for the interest of the Proprietors ... The Property being recovered ... I did not see I could be of any service.

Having heard that Mr Moir was in town, and that he had been appointed as agent of the Scottish bishops, Mr Fegin called on him:

> The object of his conversation was to induce me to take upon me the management of the property of the Scotch College, which he found troublesome and expensive; that he had been obliged to disburse one hundred pounds to have the works done at one of the vineyards, and that fifty more would be necessary; that the Vineyard was ruined; and that, being in want of Money, if I did not chuse to reimburse him and take the concern upon myself, he would be obliged to let the Vineyard.[8]

Mr Moir refused to have anything to do with the College property, while Mr Sloane, who had been anxious to help, was hurt at having had his offer refused.

By July, 1800 Abbé MacPherson was back in Rome. The Pope, too, had returned, cheered along his route by delighted crowds.[9] On 11th July Abbé MacPherson sent Bishop Hay his news:

> Our College and its Vineyards are in a deplorable state. The house is going fast to ruin. It is let out to almost as many different families as there are rooms in it; all wretched poor creatures, unable to pay the rent or keep the House in repair. I wished Mr Fegin to turn them out; he attempted to do so, and could have done it at pleasure a month or two back; but ever since Cardinal Albani returned to Rome they have got protectors enough among his creatures and laugh at Fegin. I have seen the Cardinal. He says till Fegin resigns all his assumed power he will do nothing ... In the meantime I am obliged to take up my quarters elsewhere, and if I ever get into the college, it will now be with difficulty and not on the terms you or I expected. The old Rector is returned, and has by far more interest in Albani's court than I, and I fear in spite of me he will enter Rector one of these days ... The Vineyards, already in a wretched state, will be in a

worse one before we have anything to do with them. They have been let by Mr Fegin till the end of this year for a hundred and a few odd crowns. Hence till autumn of 1801 though I get possession of the College I cannot touch a halfpenny of its revenues.[10]

In August 1800 Mr Fegin became involved in a quarrel with Cardinal Albani over which of them should administer the Scots College. They were both so wrapped up in their dispute that Abbé MacPherson was able to take possession of his old quarters in the College before either of them became aware of his intentions. Finding the Abbé actually established in the house, they allowed him to stay. Money now became the most pressing problem. Mr Fegin demanded of Abbé MacPherson payment for his expense during the time he had administered the College property. On top of this, immediate repairs to the College building were essential if it was not to fall into utter ruin. Cardinal Albani, seeing this state of affairs, devolved the whole charge of the College on the sympathetic Monsignor Connestabili. At this juncture Mr Sloane, magnanimously bearing no grudge against the Scottish bishops, intervened. He lent Abbé MacPherson 2,000 dollars free of interest, to be paid back when convenient. This money put the vineyards in order, assuring the College of at least a small annual income. But the vineyards alone would take years to pay off the debt on the College; the Holy See refused to help; and Abbé MacPherson told Bishop Hay that he might have to sell the College.[11]

The finances of the College received another blow in 1801 when a Papal Decree was issued which, though it finally granted National Superiors to the British Colleges, debarred them from the management of temporal affairs. Abbé MacPherson foresaw the hard-earned College earnings disappearing into the pocket of some Italian priest, and protested vehemently against such a measure.[12]

The Scottish Mission refused to send Abbé MacPherson any financial assistance. The only help he received from Scotland was the gift of a plough and a harrow, sent out by Mr Charles Maxwell, priest at Edinburgh, and one of the Abbé's closest friends.[13] The financial position of the Scots College at Rome received yet another setback when Mr Sloane died suddenly in January 1803. His heirs immediately recalled the loan he had made to the College. Abbé MacPherson, who had used the money to cultivate the vineyards and purchase new wine-making equipment, could not repay the money without ruining the vineyards, which were just beginning to show a profit.[14] Again Bishop Hay refused his appeal for help, and, in the end, Mr Farquharson and Mr Maxwell between them repaid the loan out of their own pockets.[15]

In spite of all those setbacks, Abbé MacPherson achieved considerable success in restoring the College to something like its previous state. In June 1803 the English bishop, Bishop Sharrock, wrote to Bishop Cameron:

I had the satisfaction to hear lately from my friend and agent in Rome, Mr Waters, that the Scotch College began to recover itself and that Mr MacPherson had a share in the administration.[16]

On 13th April, 1805 Abbé MacPherson wrote to the Scottish bishops:

I feel much satisfaction in informing you that, by the great attention and activity of the Cardinal [Erskine] this college will, in the course of this year, clear all its debts; and I am desired

> by his Eminence to tell you that, if no public misfortune intervenes, in the course of the next year he will call for four students.[17]

By 1806, however, the political situation had deteriorated. In December Abbé MacPherson wrote to Bishop Cameron:

> It is likely that in a few days we British subjects will be deprived even of pen and paper. H.H. [His Holiness, the Pope] has been required to arrest our persons and confiscate our property. A peremptuous refusal has been given to both demands. The question is now how far his own person and property will be respected.[18]

From 1806 onwards things got worse for the College. In 1807 it lost one of its greatest supporters with the death of the Cardinal Duke of York, son of the Old Pretender. In 1809, after a long series of encroachments on Rome and the Papal States, Napoleon annexed them to his Empire. Pope Pius VII, who had been forced to attend Napoleon's coronation in Paris in 1804, excommunicated the French who had seized his dominions. The French, in return, seized the Pope and took him, virtually a prisoner, first to Avignon, and then to Savona on the Italian Riviera. Rome, destined by Napoleon to be the seat of his heir, was designated a political and not a religious capital.[19] Propaganda closed its doors. Abbé MacPherson, frustrated in his plan to re-open the College, settled down to collect material for a history of the College from its foundation until the death of Mr Thomson, his predecessor.[20] From 1808 until 1810 virtually no news of Rome reached the Scottish Mission. In 1811 Abbé MacPherson returned to Scotland.

In 1811 Cardinal Erskine, another friend to the Scots College, died in Paris, and in 1812, fearing that without his presence the College might again be lost to the Mission, Abbé MacPherson once again undertook the long journey to Rome. The civil magistrates there were civil to him, assuring him that, though the College was all let, forcing him to seek lodgings elsewhere again, it would not be sold.[21]

In 1814 Abbé MacPherson returned to Britain on behalf of Monsignor Quarantotti, who, in view of the current lobbying of the British Government to pass a Catholic Emancipation Bill, sent letters authorising the British Catholics to accept any terms that the Government might offer them.[22]

By the beginning of November, 1914 Abbé MacPherson was back in the Scots College, and he had regained possession of the vineyards which, although they represented the whole of the College income, were again in a poor state.[23] By August 1815 the financial situation was improving; as the Abbé reported:

> The vineyards are the only part of our income as yet restored. Them I have let to advantage; and am paying off the debt left by the French. The Luoghi di Monte will soon begin to pay; and so, I hope, will the Dataria,[24] and then students must be called.[25]

In the spring of 1818 Abbé MacPherson wrote to Bishop Paterson to discover when it was intended to send some boys out to Rome. He also asked that another superior be sent, as he himself felt unable to cope with the College as well as with his duties as agent for the Mission. He continued:

> Until I officially am told that students and a superior are to be sent, and when, I can make no arrangement for their reception. I mean by this, besides providing the various articles of necessary furniture . . . I must get the College cleared of the tenants who do occupy it, and have done so for these twelve years past. According to the tenor of the lease, they cannot be removed but to give place to students, and by the laws of the Country they are entitled to six months' warning.[26]

By this time Abbé MacPherson had recovered the former allowance made to the College by Dataria, but he was afraid that it would be withdrawn again if no students were sent out very soon.

In 1819 Mr James McDonald was sent out from Scotland to assist the Abbé. He found that, although the College building had been vacated by its tenants, it contained nothing at all in the way of furniture — "not a chair, bed, stool, book or anything else" — and that the Abbé himself had been too ill to do anything to remedy this state of affairs.[27] Finally, in 1820, the College reopened with five boys: three from the Highland College at Lismore, and two from Aquhorties.

In 1815 Abbé MacPherson had written to Bishop Cameron concerning the re-opening of the college run by Propaganda:

> Some time ago I petitioned Cardinal Litta to admit as formerly two Scots students into Propaganda. The funds of that establishment are so much reduced that, for the present, he would only agree to receive *one*, paying 60 Roman Crowns for his journey hither; the rest must be made up by the Mission. Will you send one on these terms?[28]

In November 1817 the Abbé wrote to Bishop Paterson, complaining that he had never received a reply from Bishop Cameron in answer to his letter regarding the sending of a boy to Propaganda. This had caused the Abbé considerable embarrassment, as the Cardinal kept asking when the boy would be arriving.[29]

By 1823 two Highland boys, although in the Scots College, were being almost entirely supported by Propaganda, and in 1826 they were joined by a Lowland boy. These three boys lived in the Scots College, but attended the College of Propaganda, while the other boys in the Scots College attended the Roman College. Mr MacDonald compared the Propaganda College very favourably with the Roman one:

> In the latter [Propaganda] education is adapted to qualify students for the Mission in every part of the world and the utmost attention is paid to the choice of professors for that purpose, whereas in the former [Roman College] the professors are mere boys, and the [time] required for finishing studies is much longer, and many points treated of no wise to our purpose being obsolete mere scholastic questions.[30]

By 1828 the Scots boys supported by Propaganda were residing in that college instead of in the Scots College. This move was condemned by Mr MacDonald who commented:

> The Scottish Mission has received little benefit hitherto from keeping boys in Propaganda. Mr Norman and the late Mr James MacDonald are the only subjects for these fifty or sixty years that came to the Mission from Propaganda, and the latter was in bad health.[31]

Mr MacDonald petitioned Propaganda that the Scots boys be allowed to return to the Scots College to live. This, he asserted, would be better for their health. Also with more boys in the Scots College, that college would have "an additional degree of respectability".

Mr MacDonald's petition was not granted. The *Catholic Directory* for 1980 contains the following account:

> In the year 1772 the Cardinal de Bernis founded two bursaries for the Scottish Mission and since then the Scots students have regularly been allocated places in this college. There are no Scots students in Propaganda College this year.[32]

When the Scots College at Valladolid was evacuated in 1808, Mr Gordon and Mr Cameron remained behind with one student, Sandy MacKenzie. Mr Gordon died in 1809, in France, where he had gone in the hope of recovering his health.[33] In 1811 Sandy MacKenzie left to join a cavalry regiment.[34] Mr Alexander Cameron, Bishop Cameron's nephew, remained alone in the College throughout the Peninsular War, trying to keep everything safe against the day when the College would be able to re-open.

The French occupation of Spain met with unexpected resistance. Ever since the uprising in May, 1808 in Madrid, the Spanish had been engaged in guerilla warfare against the occupying army. In this they were reinforced by British troops. In 1808 Sir Arthur Wellesley — the future Duke of Wellington — landed in Portugal. In 1809 Napoleon forced a section of the British army in Spain to retreat to Corunna, where it was taken aboard the British fleet. He turned his attention to Austria and then to Russia. By the summer of 1811 he was preparing to march to Moscow with his army. He reached that city in September 1812. By the end of December he was back in Paris, leaving his army to face the horror of the winter retreat from Moscow.[35] Meanwhile Wellington had been making progress in Spain, defeating the French at Salamanca in 1812, and occupying Madrid itself for a time. Finally he crossed the frontier with his army into France. The war in Spain was over.

In September 1813 Mr Cameron wrote to Bishop Cameron about the French occupation of Valladolid between November 1812 and June 1813. Fortunately none of the houses belonging to the Scots College had been materially injured, though billetings and the levying of contributions had hit hard the College's dwindling resources. Mr Cameron went on to relate his own experiences:

> In the afternoon of the 29th July the French began to evacuate the city — [Valladolid] — with great haste . . . and disappeared all before morning . . . Lord Wellington, having forded the Duero below Herera, entered the city unexpectedly, at ten o' clock by the Tudela gate; the clocks and bells instantly announced his arrival; the streets were crowded in a moment; all hailed him with enthusiastic joy; young and old of all ranks and of both sexes crowded around him and embraced him with tears of joy. I saw he was sensibly affected with such unfeigned marks of gratitude; at first I kept aloof for reasons sufficiently obvious; but I was soon sought out by Ugarte, and requested by the Bishop to attend the Noble Lord, the hour and a half he remained in town. He invited me to dine at his headquarters in Boecillo, whither he was just returning. The day was excessively hot. I met the highlanders encamped on both sides of the Duero. On reaching Boecillo I found it full of general officers in the College [i.e. the summer house of the Scots College, Valladolid]. Your apartment was occupied by his Lordship, and the other rooms by his brilliant staff, composed of the Prince of Orange and numbers of the primo nobility. I took the liberty, next morning at breakfast, to congratulate myself and the College on having such illustrious guests, and mentioned the pleasure you would feel on learning that the house you had built had been so highly honoured.[36]

By 1814 the theatre of war had moved northwards. Mr Cameron, whose patriotic soul had been stirred at the sight of Wellington's troops, settled down to pick up the pieces: to estimate the financial position of the College, and to prepare it to receive students again. By the summer of 1815 he had acquired new vineyards in place of the old ones which were exhausted and no longer capable of being restored to fruitfulness. He had also tried to procure compensation for the losses he had sustained relative to the houses owned by the College in Madrid. His exertions had succeeded sufficiently for him to be able to ask Bishop Cameron to send some students to the College.[37] He was particularly anxious to receive the boys as soon as possible, as he had used the extreme need of the Scottish Mission as a reason for petitioning the Spanish Government for financial assistance, and for the clearing of the College of all those who had been billeted in it.[38] In October 1816 Mr Badenoch sent out to Valladolid an iron plough and an iron drill plough, together with some spare parts.[39] At the same time twelve boys set out for Valladolid under the care of Mr John Cameron,[40] who was to take the post of vice-rector in the College, and of Mr Wallace, who remained as professor in the College for two years, until he was forced to bring two of the students, who had become ill, back to Scotland.

Valladolid, the last Scots College to have been closed by Napoleon, was the first to recover. By 1820 Scots students were once again able to pursue their studies in the Scots Colleges of Valladolid and Rome; and as bursars at the French Colleges of St Nicholas and St Sulpice in Paris. The Revolutionary and Napoleonic Wars had jeopardised all the property of the Scottish Mission on the Continent. Much was irretrievably lost, but enough was recovered to allow roughly the same number of boys to study abroad again as had done so before 1793. The same Colleges and bursaries obtain today, taking about fifty students between them.

In the negotiations for the recovery of its property in France and, to a lesser extent, in Rome, the Scottish Mission had had numerous dealings with members of the British Government, all of which had opened channels of communication which were to play their part in the political integration of the Scottish Mission with Protestant Britain.

NOTES

1 Mr Sloane to Abbé MacPherson, 28th July 1798, B.L.
2 Mr Sloane to Abbé MacPherson, 1st December 1798, B.L.
3 Mr Smelt, Pisa, to Abbé MacPherson, 7th March 1799, B.L.
4 Mr Sloane to Abbé MacPherson, 26th October 1799, B.L.
5 Abbé MacPherson to Charles Maxwell, 4th June 1799, B.L.
6 Bishop Hay to Abbé MacPherson, 4th December 1799, B.L.
7 Bishop Hay to Patrick Moir, 13th December 1799, B.L.
8 Mr Moir to ?, 9th May 1800, B.L.
9 Mgr Charles Erskine to Bishop Cameron?, 31st July 1800, B.L.
10 Abbé MacPherson to Bishop Hay, 11th July 1800, B.L.
11 Abbé MacPherson to Bishop Hay, 21st March 1801, B.L.
12 Abbé MacPherson to Mr Sloane, 1st June 1801, B.L.
13 Charles Maxwell to Abbé MacPherson, 19th June 1802, B.L.
14 Abbé MacPherson to Bishop Cameron, 29th January 1803, B.L.
15 Charles Maxwell to Abbé MacPherson, 8th June 1803, B.L.
16 Bishop Sharrock to Bishop Cameron, 13th June 1803, B.L.
17 Abbé MacPherson to Bishops Hay, Chisholm and Cameron, 13th April 1805, B.L.

18 Abbé MacPherson to Bishop Cameron, 31st December 1806, B.L.
19 Franklin L. Ford, *Europe 1780-1830*, pp. 177-178.
20 Abbé MacPherson to Bishop Cameron, 15th August 1807, B.L.
21 Abbé MacPherson to Bishop Cameron, 30th January 1813, B.L.
22 Bernard Ward, *The Eve of Catholic Emancipation*, Vol. II, pp. 82-84.
23 Abbé MacPherson to Bishop Cameron, 3rd November 1814, B.L.
24 Office of the Roman Curia dealing with benefices, dispensations, etc.
25 Abbé MacPherson to Bishop Cameron, 25th August 1815, B.L.
26 Abbé MacPherson to Bishop Paterson, 23rd May 1818, Preshome Letters, S.C.A.
27 James MacDonald to Bishop Cameron, 25th November 1819, B.L.
28 Abbé MacPherson to Bishop Cameron, 25th August 1815, B.L.
29 Abbé MacPherson to Bishop Paterson, 29th November 1817, B.L.
30 Angus MacDonald, Rome, to Bishop Paterson, 1st August 1826, B.L.
31 Angus MacDonald to Bishop Paterson, 19th February 1828, Preshome Letters, S.C.A.
32 *The Catholic Directory for Scotland*, 1980, p.321.
33 Bishop Cameron to James Sharp, 3rd July 1810, B.L.
34 Mr Tidyman to Bishop Cameron, 15th December 1811, B.L.
35 Franklin L. Ford, *Europe 1780-1830*, p. 207 *et seq.*
36 Alexander Cameron to Bishop Cameron, September 1813, B.L.
37 Alexander Cameron to Bishop Cameron, 31st May 1815, B.L.
38 Alexander Cameron to Bishop Cameron, 5th December 1815, B.L.
39 Alexander Badenoch to Bishop Cameron, 30th October 1816, B.L.
40 John Cameron to Bishop Cameron, 4th December 1816, B.L.

23

The Lowland College of Aquhorties: Foundation and Financing

THE college of Aquhorties stands about four miles west of Inverurie and looks out over the valley of the River Don, which flows about a mile to the south. It is a solid granite building, three storeys high with an attic, eighty feet long by twenty-two feet broad, except at the north-west corner where a small, two-storey wing projects to the rear of the building. The economy which had to be practised in the construction of the building is reflected in its simple lines and lack of ornament.

The college chapel used to occupy the first two floors of the western end of the building. Any neighbouring Catholics who attended Mass there were seated on the ground floor, while the boys occupied a gallery which extended round two sides of the chapel and could be entered from the schoolroom. Behind the chapel is situated the two-storey wing which is perhaps the remains of what must have been extensive domestic offices — kitchen, wash-house and so forth. The rest of the ground floor was taken up by a dining room and a playroom. On the first floor the school-room adjoined the chapel, while across the landing were the library and Bishop Hay's room and bed-closet. All the rooms on the first two storeys stretch across the whole width of the house.

On the third floor the house is bisected by long dark corridors running down its length, off which are the long, narrow rooms each of which was originally divided into bed-closet and living area. These rooms were occupied by the procurator and professors of the college, and by any visitors. Above this floor are the attics, two small and two large, lit by dormer windows, which served as dormitories for all the boys.

Behind the house is a large, walled garden, first laid out under the supervision of Mr James Sharp in 1811; and behind that is the farm steading with its byres and stables, cartsheds and cottages, barns, waterwheel and stackyard. Round the steading lie fields which, in 1797, were largely undrained marshland. From the steading a grassy track leads northwards, up a fairly steep incline, between fields, and through a belt of coniferous forest, to emerge on a plateau of higher ground at the East Aquhorties Stone Circle. Round the Circle are cultivated fields which, in 1797, were heather-covered, boulder-strewn moorland. To the south and east lie the plains of the River Don, and its tributary the Urie, spread out like a map below the Circle.

When Bishop Hay obtained the lease of Aquhorties in 1797 the Scottish Mission had already lost its colleges in Douay and in Paris, and by the time the college at Aquhorties opened in 1799 the Scots College at Rome had also been forced to close. The Scots College at Valladolid followed in 1808. Valladolid reopened in 1816, Rome in 1820, and bursaries were obtained for Scots boys to study in Paris in 1818, but for eight years Aquhorties was the only college where boys could be trained for the priesthood for the Lowland Vicariate. Samalaman and Lismore were of corresponding importance to the Highland District.

It was obvious from the first that Aquhorties must provide not only a basic education, aimed at giving boys a proficiency in Latin, but must also teach the most advanced subjects of Philosophy and Theology. Bishop Hay expressed his own aims for Aquhorties in two letters which seem, at first sight, to contradict one another. The first letter was written, in 1802, in reply to a complaint from its professors about the running of Aquhorties. Bishop Hay, who refused to alter any of his regulations, defended himself by comparing Aquhorties unfavourably with the Scots Colleges abroad:

> The Colleges in foreign countries were founded by people possessed of great riches and some of them by crowned heads and by those in high rank in the World; who, suitable to their rank and abilities, took a complacency in raising Publick Establishments, so useful to Mankind, in a magnificent manner, and founded them with large revenues, both for the subsistence of the students and competent Salaries for the Masters and other superiors. In this respect Aquhorties does not deserve the very name of College. It is a private school or seminary intended only for educating a few youths in the knowledge necessary for Apostolic Missioners who may become fit instruments in the hand of God for preserving the small remains of religion in their native country.[1]

The other letter was written, in 1803, in response to a request that eight boys, ready to start studying Philosophy, be sent to the Scots College, Valladolid:

> ... if Don Juan's demand be laid down as a plan that must always be followed, we will scarcely have it in our power to carry anyone through their full education for by the time we have any ready for Philosophy, those sent before to Valladolid will be ready to come home and a new demand will be made for our farthest advanced. By which we shall be reduced to a Scalan, a seminary for preparing little boys for being sent abroad. I cannot help therefore being of opinion that the best plan would be to send little boys, that so they, at Valladolid, should have the whole charge of their Education from beginning to the end.[2]

Clearly Bishop Hay, however hampered he might be by lack of money, was determined to preserve the status of Aquhorties as a college supplying boys with a complete education for the priesthood.

While Aquhorties was the only college to serve the Lowland District, the question of its position in regard to foreign colleges did not arise, and, as one Aquhorties student put it, the boys had to resign themselves to being "heather priests" all their lives.[3] After the defeat of Napoleon in 1815, however, there was a prospect of recovering some, if not all, of the Scots Colleges abroad, and the Aquhorties professors began to view with suspicion colleges which they jealously regarded as rivals of Aquhorties. Mr John Gordon, for instance, in 1816 complained that the foreign colleges insisted on admitting only boys who had already undergone a trial period at Aquhorties. In that way they were spared the expense of trying out a boy who might prove unsuitable after a year or so, while at the same time, if a boy failed while abroad, they could blame Aquhorties for bad selection in the first place. In this way Aquhorties bore all the risks, and the foreign colleges took all the credit, in the selection and training of boys for the priesthood.[4]

Bishop Cameron made it quite clear that he put Aquhorties before the Scots Colleges abroad. In 1818, when instructing Mr Kyle to select some boys to be sent to Paris and to Rome, he added:

> . . . but I cheerfully allow you to keep for Aquhorties those whom you judge most likely to do it honour.[5]

Four months later, after Mr Kyle had selected the boys to be sent to Paris, Bishop Cameron wrote again:

> I was a little astonished to find that you had no objection to parting with James Gillis; and I even thought that you might like to keep John Wilson, to be a pattern and some sort of Monitor to his companions. At present the whole burden of the House lies on your shoulders, and I should be very sorry to deprive you of any little assistance you can receive from any of your young ones . . . At the same time I should be equally sorry to deprive [you of] any one whom you choose in the meantime as an instrument in your own hands, if the means [exists] of cultivating his own mind as much as he could desire or you could advise. I should either give him a season at one of our own universities, or I should send him for a year to any of our foreign establishments. I trust you will think this no very small encouragement, and you may freely hold it out to anyone who you think deserves it.[6]

Bishop Cameron's attitude towards Aquhorties is reflected in the comments made by various priests. In 1820, for instance, Mr James MacDonald, newly appointed assistant rector at Rome, complained that the boys recently sent to Rome from Aquhorties must have been the refuse of that place because

> . . . they neither can spell nor read in any one language, and what is worse appear incapable of learning anything . . . We shall be affronted by them when they go to the public schools.[7]

The rectors of foreign colleges were naturally anxious that their boys should do well when sent to the public universities, so that they should bring honour to their college and their country. They therefore wanted the best students to be sent to them.

Bishop Paterson, Bishop Cameron's coadjutor and successor, although he had worked harder than anyone to obtain bursaries in Paris for Scots boys, made the following comment in 1826:

> . . . I hope to see the day when our college at home will make us independent of all the little etiquette and ceremony and chicanery of these most troublesome colleges abroad.[8]

By the time Bishop Paterson wrote this he was beginning to have hopes that a new college might be opened at Blairs to serve all Scotland. It was therefore probably not on Aquhorties that he was pinning his hopes. In the event his hopes were never entirely realised. Although today the vast majority of Scottish priests are educated in Scotland, a number still go to study at the Scots Colleges of Rome and of Valladolid, or, as bursars, in the French colleges in Paris.

The foreign colleges, whatever their disadvantages, made two important contributions to the Scottish priesthood. Firstly, in the days when Catholicism was proscribed in Scotland, they enabled future priests to see the practice of their religion in a Catholic country. As one priest, who had never been abroad, rather wistfully remarked:

> The want of a foreign education I consider as a loss in different respects, but chiefly because I

have not seen religion in its splendour with regard to its exterior part.[9]

Secondly, at a time when Scottish priests were being recruited from small, rather isolated rural communities, a foreign education must have played an important role in preventing the Scottish Catholic clergy from becoming introspective and parochial in outlook.

When Bishop Hay took over the lease of Aquhorties, it was in the hope that the British Government would give him some financial help. The Government did pay £600 towards the building of the college, and for a few years it made an annual grant of £50. This was a small grant indeed compared with Maynooth's £8,000 per annum, but it was a help. However, it was not paid regularly, nor was it continued after 1805. The college was therefore thrown back on other resources.

It was Bishop Hay's intention to improve the farm attached to Aquhorties so that, in time, it would be able to support the college. In 1797, he sent the following description of the farm to Abbé MacPherson:

> There are upwards of 200 acres of arable ground upon the farm, and double that number of muir and hill; part of which is very capable of improvement and the rest for planting [i.e. with trees].[10]

The land which the Bishop had leased was not vacant land. It was inhabited by a number of subtenants,[11] each of whom grazed a few cows and grew crops on the better patches of land under the old runrig system. The task that faced Bishop Hay and later Bishop Cameron was, therefore, in every respect, a daunting one. They had to organise the draining of marshy land, the clearing away of heather, the removal of boulders from the land, the building of miles of enclosing dykes, and finally the draining, manuring, liming, ploughing and sowing of the newly formed parks. At the same time the old joint tenancies had to be either done away with or the tenants moved to where their smallholdings would not stand in the way of improvements.[12] A steading had to be built for the college farm, stock bought, and men hired as labourers. All this implied a very large capital investment which would see no profits for a good many years. One letter, written in 1808, gives some idea of the expense involved:

> We will have it seems throughout the summer half year six fee'd servants viz three horsemen, the same as last summer, two for the oxen plough, and a cowherd the same as last year. Besides this herd another must undoubtedly be employed occasionally when the cattle are put to graze on pasture grounds not inclosed, but a constant herd need not be fee'd for the purpose, as a day labourer can be employed when there is occasion or even a young boy. Mr Davidson has also employed occasionally of late four persons at slump jobs viz two making drains and two at the cornyard. There have also been 7 persons employed as day-labourers more or less . . . Their work was in the bog, winning stones for the masons, taking up the old foundations of dykes in the turnip grounds, and just now they are making the road behind the byres to the cornyard.[13]

Even though the farm was able to provide fodder for the cattle and horses, and meat, meal, milk, butter, eggs and honey for the college, this could in no way balance out the cost of wages, lime and so on during the years when the land was being enclosed.

Savings were made wherever possible: stones dug out of the fields were used to build dykes and fill field drains, as well as to furnish materials for the farm buildings. Bishop Cameron became obsessive about manure in his anxiety to have the newly laid-out fields fertilised economically. The Bishop was negligent in answering queries from his priests concerning cases of discipline,[14] but he never failed to send Mr Sharp a weekly reminder of the importance of conserving manure. Two letters are sufficient illustration:

> I find we might have had much more dung, not only by Lord Meadowbank's method of mixing three cartloads of moss with every one load of dung, but also by putting a great deal of moss all along below the dung in the court, before the byres, to soak in the urine of the cattle. After lying, in that way, for six weeks, it seems, it is an excellent manure for turnips, without any other mixture . . . It is only from dung that we can expect summer and winter provisions for man or beast.[15]

Even the privies were to be utilised:

> If a good, thick stratum of moss were put below the privy, and fresh moss thrown in once a month, if the pigs always had moss, covered with straw . . . [16]

Manure was of course, in the days before artificial fertilisers, the only way of enriching farmland, and of replacing the good the crops took out of it.

In spite of every possible economy the farm at Aquhorties continued to swallow capital. In 1813 Bishop Cameron pointed out that four times the original value of the land had already been spent on the farm.[17] It has been estimated that about £10,000 was spent on Aquhorties, mainly on the farm, before the lease was finally given up in 1844.[18] Most of this money was spent between 1797 and 1826, and most of it came from the pockets of Bishops Hay and Cameron.

During Bishop Hay's lifetime the main concern was to get the land immediately surrounding the college improved and enclosed so that crops could be grown to feed the students, professors and servants, and also the cattle and horses. In addition a farm steading was built, a farmhouse provided to accommodate the grieve and other servants,[19] and a dam constructed to provide a head of water to power the wheel which drove the threshing mill.[20]

Under Bishop Cameron the improvements which were continuing on the farm became a matter of pride for all concerned. The Bishop's sentiments are well summarised in one of his letters to Mr Sharp:

> We certainly should not be the last to attempt anything which may tend to promote the interest of the farmer. Our honour is in some degree at stake, and the public opinion merits attention. If we are found to be mean, slovenly, negligent or ignorant in any point of which the public at large can form an opinion, the same character will soon be attached to our merit in the execution of every other part of our professional or personal duty.[21]

In an endeavour to keep Aquhorties at the forefront of agricultural improvements Bishop Cameron sent to Mr Sharp a stream of advice, some of it gleaned from farming magazines, and some from talking to the improving landowners whom he met in Edinburgh. Some of his Bishop's advice, such as to use blubber to make compost,[22] or to investigate new types of turnip-sowing machines,[23] Mr Sharp was willing to try; others, such as the burning of subsoil to make fertiliser, he refused to have anything to do with unless and until farmers elsewhere proved them to be practical.[24]

Bishop Cameron's concern with improvements had the desired result. In 1819 Mr Sharp was able to write to him that

> Mr Young, the first improver in Murrayshire . . . recommends Aquhorties as the best school for a practical Farmer,[25]

while in the same year Mr Kyle wrote to him to tell him that Colonel MacKenzie Fraser of Castle Fraser and his father-in-law, Sir John Hay of Edinburgh, had ridden over to Aquhorties especially to see the improvements, and had expressed themselves most gratified at what they seen.[26] So pleased was Mr Sharp with the improvements to the farm, nearly all of which had been carried out under his personal supervision, that he applied to the Board of Agriculture in London for a gold medal in respect of them.[27]

Inevitably Bishop Cameron's enthusiasm for farming proved to be very expensive and, in 1821, in answer to Mr Sharp's request for money to build new byres, he at last refused to spend any more in that way:

> As to my contributing any sum whatever to that or to any other object about the farm, I must tell you plainly that I absolutely cannot advance a farthing. The income of Aquhorties is £204 per annum with which and the produce of the farm you must do the best you can.[28]

Mr Sharp was understandably upset that Bishop Cameron should, after so many years, withdraw his support. In 1822, having installed a two-horsepower steam engine to replace the old, inefficient water-wheel, he felt that the improvements were well on the way to being completed. As he wrote to Bishop Cameron:

> Our operations are now in such a state of forwardness that I would fain see them brought to a conclusion. At all events . . . I have no doubt but that the Farm will ultimately repay us for all our outlays.[29]

One way and another Mr Sharp managed to scrape together enough money to continue, and in February 1826 he was able to report:

> Our great outlays are nearly over, and the Farm will, in the course of two or three years be all brought into a state of cultivation, and will, I trust be yielding us a fair return for our labours and expenses.[30]

By 1826, however, unknown to Mr Sharp, negotiations were proceeding for the acquisition of Blairs as the successor to the college at Aquhorties. Although the Scottish Mission was to retain the lease of the farm at Aquhorties until 1844, improvements were completed too late for the farm to realise its original purpose of maintaining completely the college in its grounds.

The engrossment of so much capital by Aquhorties led naturally to resentment on the part of many of the Scottish priests. In 1801, for example, there was some prospect of reopening the Scots College at Rome if, as Abbé MacPherson wrote to Bishop Hay, the Scottish Mission could send over some money. Much to Abbé MacPherson's disappointment, Bishop Hay said that Aquhorties needed all his available capital and that none could be spared for Rome.[31] Mr Farquharson, too, thought that Bishop Hay was being very shortsighted in his attitude towards Rome:

> Company never will or can contribute thereto even partially, imagining their home foundations will soon suffice, yet, in this they'll find themselves mistaken; outlays even for boys run extravagantly high, but with a poor prospect at long run of success; and in succeeding, but with shallow confreres.[32]

Mr Farquharson believed that Aquhorties could never turn out priests of the same calibre as the Scots College at Rome, and that the latter should be helped at whatever cost to Aquhorties.

Mr Farquharson had his own personal reasons for feeling bitter about

Aquhorties. Between 1795 and 1805 he was stationed in Glasgow. He incurred a large debt there in the building of a very necessary chapel and priest's house. He had understood that Bishop Hay would help him, both personally and by using his influence with his friends, to clear this debt, but this the Bishop had refused to do:

... being himself immediately after a busy and more successful beggar for his new Seminary: of course after having gotten me fairly engaged he thought proper to leave me in the lurch.[33]

Within the college of Aquhorties itself there were many complaints about the meanness of successive procurators: about their refusing to allow sufficient funds to provide an adequate diet, and about their refusing to allow extra fires to be lit so that the older boys could study in a room by themselves. The procurators realised themselves that they were unpopular. Theirs was a difficult task. Each procurator in turn was expected to expedite the agricultural improvements on the farm at the minimum possible expense. At the same time he was expected to finance the necessary expenditure on food and clothes for the boys. Mr Sharp in particular was accused of spending money on the farm to the detriment of the college. The office of procurator, moreover, was regarded with jealousy by the professors in the college, who imagined that it had many perquisites attached to it, such as the use of a horse at any time for transport. Mr Sharp was also suspected of being in league with Mrs Gaul, the housekeeper, to get the best of the food for himself. Mr John Gordon voiced the opinion of all the professors in the following letter:

I never have made a secret of my opinion that the *office of Procurator* of this house must ever be viewed with jealousy and dislike by every mere professor of it, whom I scruple not to say, it reduces to a state of comparative insignificance. I mean that office when possessed of all those privileges, rights and appendages which are supposed to belong to it, (no matter how justly or necessarily) which it has hitherto enjoyed, and actually enjoys; more especially when the person who fills it imagines (as I know to be the case just now) that he has a right to interfere in domestic discipline.[34]

Mr Sharp was quick to defend himself against this last charge:

The least boy of the house is ... told that I have no business with him — a caution by the by extremely unnecessary as I never pretend to exert the least influence over Boy or Master.[35]

Far from encroaching on domestic discipline, Mr Sharp found himself denied any authority over the boys. As he himself realised, however:

... I have the misfortune to occupy a Post, which, it would seem, is an object of ambition in the eyes of some weak Brethren.[36]

Although it was the procurator who was blamed for all economies practised in the college, he was often only obeying instructions from a higher authority. In 1801 Bishop Hay wrote to Mr John Gordon (senior), the first procurator at the college, demanding greater economy. His letter provoked the following reply:

The expenditure of this house principally consists of the following articles viz Provisions, Coals and Candles, Clothing for the boys, the necessary furniture for the masters and boys, and Servants' fees. I shall now give you such observations as occur to me on each of the above heads ... [37]

Mr Gordon's observations ran to some four pages, the contents of which leave the reader in no doubt as to the economy with which the college was run. Incidentally Bishop Hay and Mr Gordon were living under the same roof when this letter was written!

One of the most frequent complaints made at Aquhorties, as indeed at any school then or now, was that the food was inadequate and unappetising, and that there was no adequate supervision of what was produced from the kitchens. Bishop Hay's answer to one such complaint contained the following words:

> ... the managers of the temporals of Aquhorties are obliged in conscience to use the strictest economy least by running the place into debt, they bring it to destruction.[38]

He added that, as the boys looked very well and healthy, and as he had never known anyone to have left the table without having eaten something, he considered the complaints groundless.

The complaints continued and, probably in answer to one such letter from Mr John Gordon (junior), Bishop Cameron made the following notes on the diet:

> (1) The community breakfast is pottage and milk; the portions for each to be given in separate bowls. At such seasons of the year when sufficient quantity of milk cannot be had beer must be substituted instead of milk.
>
> (2) To dinner, on flesh days, about ½lb of meat shall be prepared for each person in the community.
>
> (3) On the other day for soup, rice barley and milk, barley and pease, pease soup, turnips and carrots, potatoes soup, white cabbage soup, greens.
>
> (4) After soup, on meagre days, fish with potatoes and butter, eggs, milk curdled or plain, white cabbage with butter, rice and potatoe pudding, or pudding of any other sort etc.
>
> (5) For supper, pottage, sowens, potatoes differently prepared, rice soup, haddocks when cheap.[39]

The diet at Aquhorties, if not particularly exciting, was at least both plentiful and nourishing — the meat ration in particular is generous by today's standards. It also obviously depended to quite an extent on the produce of the farm. Fish and rice are the only items listed which could not have been produced on the farm of Aquhorties. Throughout the thirty years of its existence, the college of Aquhorties, and the farm there, were economically interdependent. The farm provided food for the boys; and the boys' fees paid the wages of farm servants.

NOTES

1 Bishop Hay, "Remarks on the Regulations of the College of Aquhorties and what is to be Considered in making any Changes in them", 1802, B.L.

2 Bishop Hay to Bishop Cameron, 13th March 1803, B.L.

3 John Cameron to James Gordon, 5th April 1815, B.L.

4 John Gordon to James Kyle, 1st March 1816, B.L.

5 Bishop Cameron to James Kyle, 9th June 1818, Preshome Letters, S.C.A.

6 Bishop Cameron to James Kyle, 28th October 1818, Preshome Letters, S.C.A.

7 James MacDonald to Bishop Cameron, 3rd October 1820, B.L.

8 Bishop Paterson to James Kyle, 30th November 1826, Preshome Letters, S.C.A.

9 James MacLachlan to Bishop Cameron, 10th February 1806, B.L.

10 Bishop Hay to Abbé MacPherson, 1st April 1797, B.L.

11 E.g. John Gordon to Bishop Cameron, 22nd May 1808, B.L.

12 Bishop Cameron to James Sharp, 19th April 1809, B.L.

13 John Gordon to Bishop Cameron, 29th May 1808, B.L.

14 E.g. William Rattray to Bishop Cameron, 21st February 1814, B.L.

15 Bishop Cameron to James Sharp, 8th May 1812, B.L.

16 Bishop Cameron to James Sharp, 8th August 1813, B.L.

17 Bishop Cameron to James Sharp, 5th September 1813, B.L.

18 Alexander MacWilliam, "Aquhorties" typescript, p. 302, S.C.A.

19 John Gordon to Bishop Cameron, September 1808, B.L.

20 John Davidson to Bishop Cameron, 23rd October 1807, Preshome Letters, S.C.A.

21 Bishop Cameron to James Sharp, 30th May 1815, B.L.

22 Bishop Cameron to James Sharp, 9th September 1815, B.L.

23 Bishop Cameron to James Sharp, 27th April 1813, Preshome Letters, S.C.A.

24 James Sharp to Bishop Cameron, 29th May 1817, B.L.

25 James Sharp to Bishop Cameron, 25th May 1819, B.L.

26 James Kyle to Bishop Cameron, 8th July 1819, Kyle Letters, B.L.

27 Bishop Paterson to James Sharp, 5th February 1820, B.L.

28 Bishop Cameron to James Sharp, 28th March 1821, B.L.

29 James Sharp to Bishop Cameron, 12th November 1822, Preshome Letters, S.C.A.

30 James Sharp to Bishop Paterson, 12th February 1826, B.L.

31 Bishop Hay to Charles Maxwell, 13th May 1801, B.L.

32 John Farquharson to Abbé MacPherson, 2nd October 1804, B.L.

33 John Farquharson to Abbé MacPherson, 7th May 1800, B.L.

34 John Gordon (junior) to Bishop Cameron, 11th December 1808, B.L.

35 James Sharp to Bishop Cameron, 11th February 1809, B.L.

36 James Sharp to Bishop Cameron, 15th January 1809, B.L.

37 John Gordon (senior) to Bishop Hay, 24th March 1801, B.L.

38 Bishop Hay, "Remarks on the Regulations of the College of Aquhorties and what is to be Considered in making any Changes in them", 1802, B.L.

39 Written on the back of one of Bishop Cameron's scroll letters, 1805, B.L.

24

The Lowland College of Aquhorties:
The Students and their Life

BOYS who were admitted as students to Aquhorties fell into two categories: boys intended for the priesthood, and boarders who came merely to receive a secular education. Generally speaking the church students were fed and clothed by the College, while the boarders were expected to pay for their keep at an economic rate. It was the church students with whom Aquhorties was principally concerned.

In 1787 Bishop Hay set down on paper some observations on the type of boy who should be accepted as a church student at Scalan.[1] As he pointed out, in the past priests had generally come from among the ranks of the gentry or of the well-to-do tenant farmers who often intermarried with the gentry. By the 1780s, however, most priests were the sons of

> ... the lowest class of farmers, including those who laboured with their own hands on their farms.

Few priests came from the ranks of the generally poor Catholic tradesmen of the towns.

Bishop Hay, though himself of a noble family, felt that neither inferior birth nor previous employment as a servant should bar a boy from entering Scalan as a church student. Bishop Geddes, who was the son of a small tenant farmer, argued that people born in "low circumstances" had to overcome difficulties such as

> ... a littleness of mind, a timidity of temper, a vulgarity of sentiment, and too often the grossness of vice,

difficulties which were not easily overcome. He also believed that a priest who came of a respected family would find it easier to win the regard of his congregation.[2]

The Scalan rules laid down that church students should come of "honest and creditable parents".[3] Bishop Hay believed that an otherwise suitable boy should not be refused admission solely on the grounds that his parents had caused scandal. Mr Kyle, in 1820, when he was professor at Aquhorties, protested against the proposed admission of the sons of a Major Gordon as boarders, let alone church students, because their legitimacy was doubtful. They were the Major's sons by a Mrs Cumming, and although Mrs Cumming had, in the previous year, been declared the Major's lawful wife, Mr Kyle still considered that the stigma attached to the boys' births would be a bad reflection on Aquhorties if they were admitted.[4]

The church students who entered Aquhorties came, with one exception, from respectable backgrounds. The exception was William Ireland, who arrived at Aquhorties in June 1814, bringing with him a letter of introduction from Bishop Cameron to Mr Kyle:

> This will be delivered to you by William Ireland. I do not wish him to be with the farm servants, in any way; for he is nowise connected with them. Let him study *English* and *French* grammatically and *write*, under your care. He may serve at table, *if you judge it proper*, and breakfast, dine and sup after the Community either in the Refectory or kitchen as you please.[5]

Mr Kyle, faced with a boy who seemed to be neither servant nor student, decided to treat him like any other student. In 1816 William was sent as a church student to the Scots College, Valladolid. In 1822 he was dismissed from that college.

Whatever his background, a boy who entered Aquhorties as a church student would be cut off from his family. He would not, unless his health became precarious, return to his home from the time he entered the college at the age of about twelve, until he was ordained when he was twenty-three or so. His formative years would be spent among men of letters, whether the Aquhorties professors in Scotland, or the professors and students he would study with in France or in Rome. By the time he grew to manhood his childhood background would have been overlaid by an academic training which might tend to alienate him from his family. He might well have been educated alongside the sons of landowners. By the time he became a priest he might well feel he had more in common with the landowning classes than with the poorer Catholics of his congregation. A letter from Mr James MacLachlan, priest at Deecastle illustrates this:

> I meet with particular kindness from the family of Balnacraig and I see few other families in my neighbourhood with whom I could wish to cultivate any particular acquaintance.[6]

The landowners, for their part, were probably glad to have the company of men who had been well-educated, perhaps in Paris or in Rome, and who could therefore provide interesting conversation. The Duke of Gordon, for one, frequently invited the incumbent at Fochabers to dine with him. Perhaps, therefore, Bishop Hay was more realistic than Bishop Geddes when he insisted that a boy's home background was relatively unimportant.

Boys were generally accepted for Scalan at about the age of twelve. Bishop Hay saw no objection to admitting young men in their twenties, believing that at that age a man would have the perserverance and dedication which would make him likelier to succeed than a young boy who had greater natural ability. Bishop Geddes disagreed, arguing that a man in his twenties would not find the strict discipline of a seminary easy to accept, or the mode of life there easy to conform to, while a young boy would be more adaptable and more amenable to discipline.[7]

As far as Aquhorties was concerned, twelve was generally considered to be the best age for a boy to enter as a church student. By that time he should be able to read and write proficiently in English — knowledge of Latin was not expected.[8] A few boys were accepted at the age of nine or ten, and a large number between the ages of fourteen and eighteen. Of the six men who began their studies at Aquhorties in their early twenties, four were eventually ordained priests, one died in college, and one gave up his vocation, so the success rate for mature students was high.

Bishop Hay, in 1799, made it quite clear that only suitable boys were wanted for Aquhorties.[9] In both Scalan and Aquhorties church students were given a year's trial before finally being accepted to be trained by the Mission for the priesthood. Bishop Cameron went further than that. He pointed out to Mr Kyle that, even after their first year was over, church students remained on trial in so much as they had no right or title to remain in the college should they fail in any respect to meet the Bishop's wishes and expectations.[10] Bishop Cameron meant what he said. In 1814 he had John Forbes sent down from Aquhorties on the grounds that he had been criticising the economy of Mr Sharp and the house keeper, Mrs Gaul.[11] John Forbes was accepted into the Highland College at Lismore where he was ordained a year later, thereafter serving the Lowland Vicariate as priest until his death in 1855. Bishop Cameron's severity, which was criticised by many, had almost lost the Scottish Mission a valuable priest.

All church students were supposed to be accepted for Aquhorties only on the recommendation of the priests who had instructed them in their religion. This rule, however, was not always strictly adhered to. Mr Kyle voiced a complaint against parents who forced their children upon the college:

> Mr William Reid of Keith sends a strong recommendation of a young boy by the name of Dundas as an ecclesiastical student. . . . And of course I think we should take him. For what other criterion can we have for judging him by? It is a quite different case when we have the pastors singling out and recommending a subject for us, from seeing people, as at Edinburgh and Glasgow, forcing in themselves or their children upon us in the priest's despight.[12]

Sometimes a boy would be sent to Aquhorties as a boarder, and then decide he had a vocation for the priesthood. One such boy was James Kyle, who was to become Vicar Apostolic of the Northern Vicariate, and who had considerable trouble in convincing his relatives that he should be allowed to study for the priesthood.[13] Other parents sent their sons as boarders on the understanding that, should one of them discover a vocation for the priesthood, he be allowed to continue at Aquhorties as a church student. Occasionally a parent would write to Aquhorties to say that he wanted one of his sons to become a priest, without the boy having expressed any such ambition himself.[14] Generally, however, it was the boy himself who decided that he had a vocation and then came to Aquhorties with the consent of his parents, on the recommendation of his priest, and with the agreement of the Aquhorties professors and, usually, the Bishop's permission.

In 1818 Bishop Cameron, waiving the custom that he be consulted about prospective church students, wrote to Mr Kyle:

> I . . . authorise you to choose and receive the requisite number of recruits wherever you find them, except in Towns, this exception not to include Fochabers or Tomintoul.[15]

This preference for boys from the country rather than boys from the town was almost universal. As a result, of the one hundred and twelve church students to be enrolled at Aquhorties during the thirty years of its existence, sixty-nine came from the North-East. In 1822 there were six Glenlivet boys at Aquhorties, one at Valladolid, one in Paris and two in Rome,[16] and Bishop Cameron was moved to protest that no more boys from Glenlivet should be admitted to Aquhorties for twenty years to come.[17]

The only boys from the towns of Scotland to be admitted as church students were, with few exceptions, from families with whom Bishop Hay and, later, Bishop Cameron, were very friendly. Horatio Corri, for instance, was the son of the Edinburgh chapel's singing master. Generally speaking, boys from the towns were considered to have been more exposed to corruption and vice than those who had been brought up in the country, and therefore less likely to fit into the atmosphere of an ecclesiastical college. This meant that the large urban Catholic populations of Irish immigrants were virtually denied the chance of having one of their number ordained priest, not only because of their nationality, but also because of the places in which they settled.

Taking boys from areas like Glenlivet also had its problems, as Mr Kyle was quick to point out:

> ... those who have been so much in the habit of abusing and underveiling Aquhorties should have a tasting of that vexatious, thankless and unostentatious drudgery which we here have to undergo for several years in regard to every student that comes to us uncultivated from the mountains, even those that afterwards turn out the best.[18]

Another problem was attached to choosing boys mainly from the North-East: the accent. One of the Galloway priests, commenting on Aquhorties, wrote the following:

> I rather regret that your establishment is placed so far North, and that it is always peopled by a large majority of Northerners, as by that means an accent is irrevocably fixed on the Tongue of the Pupils, which, to all more Southern persons is far from being pleasant. In any situation this is of far more importance than is generally allowed.[19]

It is not hard to imagine bemused Irish Catholics in Glasgow being harangued from the pulpit by Mr Scott with his broad Banffshire tongue.

There was one practical consideration which had to be taken into account when boys were being selected for entry as church students to Aquhorties: the question of entry money. In 1770 regulations were laid down regarding the admission of boys to Scalan as church students.[20] Boys who were initially admitted on a year's trial had to provide their own clothes and pay for their board at a rate of £6 per annum. In addition each boy had to bring with him two pairs of blankets for his own use, the blankets to remain the property of the seminary when he left. After the year's trial the boy, if accepted as a church student, would have to pay nothing further while he was at Scalan. If the year's trial period was waived, the boy was required to bring only the two pairs of blankets and "Tollerable good cloths, with three shirts at least, three pairs of stockings and new shoes". Board was required only if the boy failed in his vocation. By about 1780 the amount charged for a year's board had been increased to £8.[21]

In 1803 Bishop Hay laid down the entrance requirements for church students coming to Aquhorties. Each boy was to bring sufficient clothes, linen, shoes and stockings to last him for the year's trial period:

> ... if they are then found fit for our business, they will cost the parents no more while they remain here. They must also bring with them two pairs of blankets ... As I require no money for their year of trial I hope the parents will not grudge the above.[22]

Bishop Cameron, unlike Bishop Hay, expected all church students to pay board at the same rate as boarders during their first year's trial. In 1814 he stipulated that the parents of a church student must keep him in clothes and shoes for the first year and pay, if possible, £25 for the first year's board. By 1819 board had risen to £28 if clothes were provided by the parents, and £30 if the College was to provide them. Two pairs of blankets continued to be asked of all boys on entry. In 1822 Bishop Cameron wrote to Bishop Kyle:

> As to your Boys you should receive none who does not pay full board immediately.[23]

From this date the Bishop turned down quite a number of promising boys whose parents were unable to pay the first year's board. Many priests on the Mission felt that such a rigid insistence on board, which prevented boys who came from poor families from becoming priests, was shortsighted in that it meant that boys who could pay board were accepted rather than far more promising boys who could not, to the ultimate detriment of the Mission as a whole.[24] Jealousy was also occasioned on the rare occasions when payment of board was either reduced or waived altogether. Mr James Gordon, priest at Glenlivet, for instance, in 1822, complained that Glenlivet boys had to pay full board while some from the Enzie were admitted free.[25]

The situation was alleviated somewhat in 1817 when Mr Farquharson died, leaving sufficient money in his will to support one student at Aquhorties. The Farquharson scholarship ensured that at least a few boys of poorer families would be given a chance to pursue their vocation for the priesthood.[26]

One other rather curious bequest was made to Aquhorties, on paper at least. In 1822, Gregor MacGregor, self-styled Cazique or ruler of Poyais, wrote to Bishop Cameron as follows:

> I now beg to transmit to your Lordship a grant of Land in the territory of Poyais, consisting of 1280 acres, in favour of your Lordship and the other gentlemen your Lordship mentioned as Trustees for and on behalf of the Catholic Seminary of Aquhorties in Aberdeenshire, and for the education of young men, agreeably to the rules of said Seminary.[27]

At the same time MacGregor made the following proposal:

> It is my wish that your Lordship would select three young men of good character and respectability to be placed at the Catholic College of Aquhorties for three years, during which time I will pay the sum of £30 per annum for each; at the expiration of that period they will of course be ordained, when they are immediately to proceed to Poyais for the purpose of taking charge of the curacy, to which each will be appointed.[28]

It is uncertain whether Aquhorties ever derived any benefit from its acres in Poyais; it is certain, however, that no Aquhorties boy ever went there as a priest.

Aquhorties, like Scalan before it, admitted a few boys as boarders. Of Scalan Bishop Geddes had written:

> The instruction and teaching of a young Gentleman designed for a secular life has always been considered as accidental . . . It was looked upon as a hindrance to the attainment of the primary intention.[29]

The Aquhorties professors held similar views about the inconvenience of having boarders, who were generally admitted to oblige a friend of the bishop. Bishop Hay, in 1801 for instance, wrote to Mrs Kyle regretting that he could not accept her son Alexander free of charge as a boarder as his finances would not permit it. He expressed a hope, however, that when times were better, he would be able to help his friends.[30] During Bishop Hay's time boarders were admitted to Aquhorties because their parents were either Edinburgh friends of his, or because they were of families, generally in the North-East, which were long-standing friends to the Scottish Mission.

At first glance the Aquhorties registers[31] suggest that, in Bishop Cameron's time, boarders were accepted from much more varied backgrounds — from Portugal, America and England as well as from Scotland. A closer examination of individual cases reveals that in nearly every instance the boy had some close connection with the Scottish Mission. In some cases the boy's relatives were Catholics well known to the Mission and living in Scotland. In other cases, including those of boys from England, the link with the Mission was through Mr Menzies of Pitfoddels, perhaps the wealthiest and most influential Catholic in Scotland at that time. One boarder whom Mr Menzies sent to Aquhorties was his young cousin, George Gordon. George was a mischievous nine-year-old who, in spite of being shown every indulgence, ran away twice before being expelled for telling the other boys scandalous stories.[32] Another of Mr Menzies' protégés was Alexander Wood. Alexander's father had been converted to Catholicism while working as Mr Menzies' gardener, and when he had left to go to England, he had kept in touch with Mr Menzies, who retained a personal interest in his convert and requested that the boy be allowed to go to Aquhorties. Alexander proved to be a problem, as Mr Sharp informed Bishop Cameron:

> Mr Kyle and the Doctor [i.e. the two professors] insist upon our sending away the English boy Wood as a hopeless subject of whom they can make nothing — besides there is scarcely any possibility of keeping him clean — he dirties his bed, and his clothes in an unaccountable manner, after all the pains we have taken to correct him.[33]

Although Alexander was patently unsuitable for the college, he was permitted to remain there for six years, and was sent home only after he had run away. In 1826 Bishop Paterson replied to criticisms of some new arrivals at Aquhorties, excusing himself by saying that the boys were Mr Menzies' protégés and — "whatever he asks cannot be refused".[34]

Another example of a bishop obliging an influential friend is that of Captain Dick. In 1813 a Mr Dick of Edinburgh was of great assistance to Bishop Cameron regarding the building of St Mary's Chapel.[35] In the same year Mr Dick's brother, Captain Dick, was released from a lunatic asylum, and Bishop Cameron agreed that he should go to stay at Aquhorties. It was hoped that the Captain would be sane enough to help in teaching the youngest boys. Captain Dick, however, far from being useful, proved to be a considerable embarrassment. He wrote letters to numerous ladies proposing marriage, and he sang bawdy songs to the boys.[36] After six months he was removed to the Aberdeen lunatic asylum. One cannot help questioning Bishop Cameron's judgment in allowing him to go to Aquhorties at all.

The foregoing examples illustrate how much Bishop Cameron in particular was at pains to keep the goodwill of influential Scottish Catholics, who tended to think that they were within their rights when they sent boarders to Aquhorties. As Mr Menzies put it:

> The education of clergymen is, no doubt, the first and essential object of the establishment, but as there is scarcely any other place where other Catholic boys, especially those who cannot have a domestic education accompanied with strict discipline, can be educated with tolerable safety to their principles and morals, it is also of great importance that such should be received there, unless that were inconsistent with the main object . . . [37]

Mr Kyle, one of the professors at Aquhorties, and so one of the people directly involved with the day-to-day management of boarders, had strong opinions on the subject:

> It is not a pleasing tho' it may be a very useful lesson of humility and mortification too that we who in our time have had dealing with Hebrew and Homer and the more sublime and recondite branches of Mathematics and Philosophy should now be condemned to hammer the letters into dolts and infants. And it is for people from whom no success can be expected, and even if success were obtained who would be of no service to the purpose of this establishment, and even derive little advantage from their education here as their senseless parents will not allow them time to have their religious principles firmly formed when they know there is anything promising in their children; it is for such that we are wasting our time, our labour and our strength . . . If you wish the house to thrive and to be really serviceable for the purpose it is designed for . . . remove every secular as soon as possible and let us never see the face of one again. [38]

One wonders if Mr Kyle remembered that he himself had first come to Aquhorties as a boarder.

Boys who came as boarders to Aquhorties were generally destined for careers as merchants or as shopkeepers. Their parents therefore expected them to be taught English, book-keeping and perhaps French.[39] Mr Kyle was understandably annoyed at the extra demands such subjects made on his time:

> Fools! Can I divide myself or multiply the hours of the day, or am I to neglect the essential objects for which I am here, to teach their children to manage a farm or keep a merchant's books.[40]

In the same letter he complained that only stupid boys were sent as boarders to Aquhorties; the clever ones who might do the college credit were sent to other schools, while

> . . . we have got this ignoramus [James Saunders], merely as it may be a cheap way of keeping him out of harm's way, and probably there is not a master in Aberdeen who could not feel affronted at seeing him in his school.

Bishop Cameron was sympathetic to Mr Kyle's problems, but was unhelpful:

> In regard to secular boys I see and feel all the inconveniences, trouble and mortifications to which we are exposed on their account. But I fear the number of clerical students would be too small to gain or keep up any degree of respectability.[41]

A more practical reason for accepting boarders was the money they paid yearly for board and lodging.[42] The farm might provide the basic foodstuffs for the college, but servants' wages and so forth required ready cash, and that was not always readily available from sources other than boarders' fees.

Although boarders' fees provided a welcome cash flow at Aquhorties, they were not crucial to the financing of the college. The English Colleges in France, and Stonyhurst in England, relied on boarders' fees to provide the funds to educate church students. At Scalan and at Aquhorties all that was expected was that a boarder should pay enough to cover his expenses. That Bishop Hay did not set out to make a profit from his boarders is obvious. In 1800 he calculated that it cost him £27 a year to keep a boy at Aquhorties,[43] but in 1806 he set the fees for boarders at

£25 per annum, or £20 in cases of hardship.[44] From 1812 onwards Bishop Cameron insisted that boarders pay £28 per annum if they provided their own clothes, or £30 if the college was expected to provide clothes and shoes.[45]

Mr Menzies wrote to Bishop Cameron in 1812 on the subject of fees:

> Profit from Pensioners I should not apprehend to be a leading object with you, in allowing their admission here, but the good of Religion, in affording to Catholic Boys that education which they can scarcely obtain, with tolerable safety, anywhere else.[46]

Mr Sharp, as procurator at Aquhorties, looked at things rather differently:

> Mr Farquharson and I perfectly coincide in opinion with respect to what ought to be charged for Boarders. Nothing is to be gained by affecting generosity. Parents deem themselves quit of every obligation the moment they pay what is exacted — even though our claims were considerably below what we expended.[47]

Tudhoe and Crookhall in England were, like Aquhorties, colleges founded primarily for the education of church students. In 1801 Tudhoe was charging £40 per annum for boarders' fees — almost double those of Aquhorties.[48] Stonyhurst, which relied on boarders' fees for its income, charged in 1802 at the following rates: thirty-seven guineas per annum for boys under twelve years of age, forty guineas per annum for older boys, and forty-five guineas per annum for students of Rhetoric and Philosophy. Over and above these basic fees, boarders had to pay two guineas' entrance money to cover linen, dishes and books. They were charged extra for lessons in dancing, drawing and music, and for expenses such as doctors' fees, medicines and postage.[49] The average boarder at Stonyhurst in 1802 would have been charged in all at least £50 per annum. In 1801 Aquhorties had ten church students and four boarders. In the same year Stonyhurst had twenty-four church students and more than a hundred and fifty boarders.[50] Boarders at Aquhorties were therefore comparatively unimportant, both numerically and financially. They can have been of even less financial importance at Scalan when the annual fee was £2 plus two blankets.[51]

Generally speaking, when boarders were prepared to fit in with the way of life of a college whose primary function was to train boys for the priesthood, they were regarded as welcome additions. These boarders were usually the ones whose names were put forward by their priests. When, however, a boarder was accepted to oblige someone like Mr Menzies, he was much less likely to be the sort of boy who would conform, either to the routine or to the academic standards of Aquhorties, and it was then that problems occurred. While Aquhorties was under the rule of Bishop Hay, the former type of boarder was more usual; under Bishop Cameron's rule too many unsatisfactory boys were admitted to oblige Mr Menzies, while the acceptance of Captain Dick because of his brother's position was a grave error of judgment.

Most boys who came as boarders to Aquhorties restricted their studies to the subjects that would be most useful in their future careers — Arithmetic, English, and perhaps French. A few, however, studied along with the church students up to and including classes in Philosophy.

The church students were placed in classes according to their ability, which meant that one or two professors might have to cope with anything up to five or six classes, and, occasionally, as many as ten. The number of classes could sometimes be reduced by insisting that new boys all come at the same time, but even then boys from different places were often at different stages of advancement. Classes were generally therefore small but numerous, an onerous task for the professors who had to teach them.

Nearly all church students were proficient in English on their arrival, while a few had received some instruction in elementary Latin from their priests to prepare them for entry into the College. Generally the first year at Aquhorties was spent studying English and perhaps French. From there the church student would advance from Latin grammar through "Cornelius Nepos" to the more advanced authors like Cicero. He would probably study some Greek at least before proceeding to Philosophy, a subject which included Logic, Metaphysics and Natural Philosophy. Finally, at the age of about twenty-one, the student would begin his final years in the study of Theology. The foregoing subjects, from Latin onwards, were what might be described as the "core" subjects for a student intended for the priesthood, and would be taken whether the student remained at Aquhorties or was sent abroad. These were, however, by no means the only subjects taught.

Bishop Gordon's rules for Scalan laid down what other subjects should be taught:

> They should be taught from the very beginning by way of recreation or easy study something of sacred and ecclesiastik history, especially the Lives of the Saints. It were fitt also that they should all learn by way of diversion or easy study something of the French and Irish or Highland language, which they may learn a good deal of that way without constraint and with little trouble; and they may be afterwards of very great use to them.
>
> They may learn also according as they advance something of Geography, Chronology, History and Critick, by the by, without much trouble or application. It is fitt that they all learn some little of the Greek and likewise of Rhetorick, when they know the Latin pretty well. And those who are well advanced in philosophy or divinity may learn somewhat of the Hebrew, if they have a genius for the tongues.[52]

In 1810 Bishop Cameron wrote of Aquhorties:

> I see no reason why hebrew should not be taught before — or at the same time with — the Latin. I hope George MacDonald does not mean to forget the erse. I have a gaelic bible for you and shall procure Irish as well as gaelic books for your philologists. Young people should be *allowed* to study hebrew, like geography, history etc on play days or in play hours. The greek is a little harder, but a quantum sufficient is easily acquired. I should willingly indulge young men who had inclination, talents and time, in the more abstruse and higher branches of learning . . . I should look some inches taller, if I saw the attention of men of letters turned to Aquhorties.[53]

Bishop Cameron's was an ambitious programme of study, particularly when one remembers that there were never more than two teachers at Aquhorties. It is true that sometimes some of the older boys were pressed into service to teach the youngest classes, but Mr Kyle for one was never happy about such an arrangement.[54]

While Bishop Cameron was Vicar Apostolic for the Lowland District, French, Hebrew, Greek and Church Music were taught on a regular basis at Aquhorties. It was on Bishop Cameron's instruction, too, that a new emphasis was placed on elocution and on English grammar. It was at this time that Scottish men of letters were attempting to rid their speech of Scotticisms under the tuition of various people including the Irish actor Sheridan. Bishop Cameron sent a Mr Dunn to Aquhorties each summer for a number of years to teach the boys correct English pronunciation.[55] His plan met with some success, judging by Mr Paterson's report on Charles Stuart, a newly ordained priest whose family came from Glenlivet:

> He is a good English scholar, and pronounces words such as pulpit, cushion, butcher, pullet, bullet etc much more accurately than Mr Sharp or Mr MacDonald or such old-fashioned priests.[56]

In addition to sending them an elocution teacher, Bishop Cameron ensured that, during the years when all the foreign colleges were closed, some at least of the oldest students at Aquhorties should have the benefit of a winter's attendance at classes in Edinburgh University. In 1810, for instance, Mr Kyle attended classes in Chemistry, Natural and Moral Philosophy under Dr Hope, Dr Playfair and Dr Brown respectively. He also took lessons in elocution from Mr William Scott, author of the *Dictionary and Lessons*.[57]

Boys were examined on their lessons every second Wednesday. In addition there were three general examinations during the year. John Geddes, one of the oldest students in 1826, described one such examination:

> ... In it I had to sustain a public thesis; the superiors ... being my opponents. The existence of God was the subject, and the disputation was carried on in Latin.[58]

Much emphasis was placed on oral disputations, not only in examinations but also in class, an important training for boys who intended to become priests.

The academic training which priests had received as boys often paved the way for lifelong hobbies. Mr William MacDonald published a volume of poems in 1808.[59] Bishop Andrew Carruthers, while at Dalbeattie, made such a splendid job of laying out the chapel garden with flowers and shrubs that he was often consulted on matters of landscape gardening. He also conducted chemistry experiments, keeping up with all the latest discoveries.[60] Mr James Carruthers wrote a Catholic *History of Scotland* up to the time of Mary Queen of Scots. Mr George Gordon compiled an account of the history and traditions of Banffshire, and Mr Griffin became an expert on ecclesiastical antiquities.[61] In their diverse interests and hobbies the Scottish priests were very like their Presbyterian counterparts, whose accounts, published in the *Old* and *New Statistical Accounts*, betray their personal enthusiasms and hobby-horses.

The *Regulations of Aquhorties*,[62] drawn up by Bishop Hay, emphasised the importance of keeping church students away from the secular world until they were mature enough and well enough grounded in their faith to resist all temptation. This policy of isolation determined the type of recreational activities which Aquhorties students were allowed to pursue.

One of the main differences between Scalan and Aquhorties lay in the amount of work which the boys were expected to contribute towards the running of house and farm. At Scalan, in the summer months, the boys had been expected to help with the hay and the harvest to save the expense of hiring extra men.[63] At Aquhorties, however, the Rule insisted that:

> None of the Students, even in days of vacation, or in the hours of recreation, must be employed to do any work about the farm.[64]

The ruling as regards Aquhorties was to prevent boys from mixing with the farm servants who were more numerous there than they had been at the little farm attached to Scalan. At Scalan generally only a grieve was needed; at Aquhorties upwards of ten farm servants were employed. Perhaps the fact that Aquhorties students were forbidden to help on the farm goes some way towards explaining why priests who had been educated at Aquhorties and at foreign colleges were far less enthusiastic farmers than the older priests who had received at least a part of their education at Scalan.

The rules for Scalan had stipulated that the boys "do any . . . little things they shall be ordered to keep the house neat and tidy".[65] What these little things were can be gathered from a letter written by one of the boys shortly after he had transferred from Scalan to Aquhorties:

> We have here no ex-lectors, no serving at table, no sweeping of the house etc., nay even our beds are made for us . . . [66]

Life at Aquhorties was rather less spartan than it had been at Scalan.

Although the Aquhorties students were not allowed to work on the farm, they were encouraged to spend their hours of recreation outside wherever possible. Walking was encouraged so long as the boys all stayed together, kept away from other houses, and spoke to nobody from outside the college. Outdoor games included handball and football. Each boy was allowed a small garden of his own, and Mr Charles Gordon, priest at Aberdeen, was kept busy sending seeds, plants and gardening tools to encourage the keen gardeners.[67] One or two of the boarders kept pet rabbits.[68]

Once the farm improvements had got well under way, Bishop Cameron was able to turn his attention to improving the amenities round the college building. In 1811 the ground in front of the college was laid out in grass to provide a permanent play area for ball games.[69] In 1818 a pond was constructed which provided the boys with some place to skate in winter.[70] In 1824 the pond was enlarged and, in 1826, an island was constructed as nesting place for two swans which had been gifted by Drummond Castle.[71] In the same year a large boat, capable of taking fourteen boys at a time, was ordered from Aberdeen, and boating became a popular summer activity.[72]

If bad weather made outdoor activities impossible, games were played indoors in the playroom. Bishop Hay used to join the boys there, telling them stories and organising games like "Hunt-the-Thimble" for which he provided almonds as prizes.[73] The boys were forbidden to read plays and novels for amusement, or to play games involving cards and dice which might lead to gambling.[74] In 1824 a workshop was fitted out, and among the first projects to be carried out there was the building of an organ by Mr Kyle, and the making of a boat for the pond by one of the students, James MacKay.[75]

Music played a large part in the recreational activities of Aquhorties boys. Bishop Hay himself was an accomplished fiddle player. James Kyle played the flute and exchanged fiddle tunes — marches, strathspeys and reels — with his brother,

Alexander.[76] Other students possessed their own flutes and violins, while, for those less fortunate, there were one or two violins belonging to the college which anyone might play provided he contributed to the cost of new strings.[77]

Although there were plenty of opportunties for boys to pursue their own hobbies, life at Aquhorties was not all pleasure. The students were expected to work very hard at their lessons. Inevitably, too, there were complaints about the way the college was run. Boys complained about the food, and about the problems of studying their lessons all together in a noisy classroom.[78] Professors complained about the number of classes they had to teach, about having to supervise study periods and about having little time to prepare their lessons or pursue their own studies.[79] Matters were not improved by the fact that, before 1826, there was no rector in overall charge of the college. The absence of one person with authority over procurator, professors and students led to distressing situations, as when Mr Sharp, the procurator, and Mr Gordon, a professor, almost came to blows over the funeral arrangements for a boy who had died in the college.[80] Another defect in the running of the college arose from the practice of promoting students like James Kyle and John Gordon to professorships in the college, without first giving them a glimpse of the outside world, or of the daily problems met by a Mission priest. James Kyle, for instance, arrived at Aquhorties in 1799, aged eleven, received all his education there for the priesthood and was ordained in 1812. He continued there as professor for twenty-four years before being sent to the Glasgow Mission.

Medical care for the boys was provided by Bishop Hay until he became too ill, and later by Mr Sinnott. Both those men had studied medicine at Edinburgh University. Between Bishop Hay's becoming ill and Mr Sinnott's arrival at Aquhorties, medical advice was sought only reluctantly because of the expense involved.[81] Medical advice, when given, was generally sound, involving fresh air, moderate exercise where possible, and a light but nourishing diet. For more severe cases recourse was had to mercury, to blistering, and, occasionally, to cupping.

Deaths among the students were not uncommon, generally from consumption. At that time it was not realised that consumption was very infectious, and boys were left in the crowded dormitory until their illness reached the terminal stage. Eleven boys in all died during the thirty years that the college at Aquhorties was in existence, four of them, including two brothers, over the winter of 1823-1824. All the deaths occurred after 1817, by which time the number of students at the college had risen from eight to over twenty.

Consumption was the main serious medical problem with which the staff of Aquhorties had to deal. A minor but persistent problem was scabies. New boys frequently arrived at the college badly infested with the "scab" as it was called, and priests were asked to try to ensure that their protégés were free of the condition before sending them to Aquhorties. It was appreciated that scabies was a contagious condition.[82]

Cleanliness was insisted on as a means of preserving the health of the boys.[83] At Scalan daily washing in the Crombie Burn, which flowed past the front door, had kept the boys reasonably clean, even in the winter. At Aquhorties their washing water was provided in the dormitories by the maidservants. Even so, it is hard to visualise how a high standard of hygiene could have been maintained. Proper privies, for instance, were not built at Aquhorties until 1815, sixteen years after the college had been opened.[84] One boy who arrived at Aquhorties in 1814 commented:

> I am not quite reconciled to this place yet; everything around me appears to be very dirty . . . [85]

Although the accounts for the college are full of such items as "To paid for mending 20 pairs of shoes" and "To paid for knitting stockings",[86] the Aquhorties boys seem generally to have been shabbily dressed. Mr Charles Gordon, who witnessed the transfer from Aquhorties to Blairs in 1829, had this to say about them:

> For a considerable time before their leaving the Seminary of Aquhorties, the students had been much neglected as to their persons, so that on their arrival at Blairs I found them in a very tattered state indeed. It may be said that they had not coats for their back, shoes for their feet, nor linens for their bodies.[87]

There was one problem at least which Aquhorties church students did not have to face — service with the Militia. As soon as a boy had been ordained sub-deacon, and the Bishop had written out a certificate to that effect, the boy was exempted from service in the Militia on the grounds that he was an ecclesiastic.[88]

All in all, for the boy who possessed a vocation for the priesthood, life at Aquhorties must have been, generally speaking, a happy one. He would be given the chance to pursue many interests, as well as to receive an academic education which embraced the sciences as well as the arts. Had he not been accepted as a church student at the age of twelve or fourteen, he would have been forced, in most instances, to take an apprenticeship, or to work on the land. Aquhorties provided opportunities that would have otherwise have been denied him. Most important, he would form, at the college, friendships which would sustain him throughout his otherwise arduous and often lonely life as a Mission priest.

NOTES

1 *Scotichronicon*, pp. 266-267.
2 *Scotichronicon*, p. 268.
3 "Regulations for Scalan", *Innes Review* 1963, p. 111.
4 James Kyle to Bishop Cameron, 22nd November 1819, Kyle Letters, B.L.
5 Bishop Cameron to James Kyle, 15th June 1814, B.L.
6 James MacLachlan to Bishop Cameron, 10th February 1806, B.L.
7 *Scotichronicon*, pp. 266-268.
8 Bishop Hay to Bishop Cameron, 29th September 1803, B.L.
9 Bishop Hay to James Sharp, 31st March 1799, B.L.
10 Bishop Cameron to James Kyle, 1813, B.L.
11 Donald Carmichael to Alexander Paterson, 5th November 1814, B.L.
12 James Kyle to Bishop Cameron, 11th November 1821, Kyle Letters, B.L.
13 Bishop Hay to Mrs Kyle, 21st April 1803, Preshome Letters, S.C.A.
14 Peter Mellis to Bishop Cameron, 28th October 1823, B.L.
15 Bishop Cameron to James Kyle, 9th June 1818, Preshome Letters, S.C.A.
16 James Kyle to James Gordon, 28th February 1822, Kyle Letters, B.L.
17 William Reid to James Kyle, 11th November 1821, Preshome Letters, S.C.A.

18 James Kyle to Bishop Cameron, 1st October 1820, Kyle Letters, B.L.
19 Andrew Carruthers, Dalbeattie, to James Kyle, 26th February 1822, B.L.
20 "Regulations for Scalan", *Innes Review* 1963, pp. 111-112.
21 "Regulations for Scalan", *Innes Review* 1963, p. 112.
22 Bishop Hay to Bishop Cameron, 13th September 1803, B.L.
23 Bishop Cameron to James Kyle, 6th May 1822, B.L.
24 William Reid, Kempcairn, to James Kyle, March 1822, B.L.
25 James Gordon to James Kyle, 8th April 1822, B.L.
26 E.g. James Kyle to Bishop Cameron, 30th November 1818, Kyle Letters, B.L.
27 Gregor MacGregor to Bishop Cameron, 20th November 1822, Preshome Letters, S.C.A.
28 Gregor MacGregor to Bishop Cameron, 20th November 1822, Preshome Letters, S.C.A. (Two letters, though of the same date, were sent.)
29 Bishop Geddes, "A Brief Historical Account of the Seminary of Scalan", *Innes Review* 1963, p. 94.
30 Bishop Hay to Mrs Kyle, 29th April 1801, Preshome Letters, S.C.A.
31 There are several Registers extant, all in different hands, in the Scottish Catholic Archives.
32 E.g. John Gordon (junior) to Bishop Cameron, 12th October 1813, B.L.
33 James Sharp to Bishop Cameron, 14th December 1820, B.L.
34 Bishop Paterson to James Sharp, 27th January 1826, B.L.
35 Bishop Cameron to James Kyle, 24th June 1813, B.L.
36 John Gordon to Bishop Cameron, 8th April 1814, B.L.
37 Menzies of Pitfoddels to Bishop Cameron, 6th February 1812, B.L.
38 James Kyle to Bishop Cameron, 24th October 1818, Kyle Letters, B.L.
39 E.g. Forbes Stuart, London, to James Sharp, 26th November 1822, B.L.
40 James Kyle to Bishop Cameron, 24th October 1818, Kyle Letters, B.L.
41 Bishop Cameron to James Kyle, 28th October 1818, Preshome Letters, S.C.A.
42 James Kyle to Bishop Cameron, 27th April 1822, Kyle Letters, B.L.
43 Bishop Hay to Abbé MacPherson, 26th October 1800, B.L.
44 Bishop Hay to Bishop Cameron, 1st February 1806, B.L.
45 Bishop Cameron to James Sharp, 25th April 1812, B.L.
46 Mr Menzies to Bishop Cameron, 9th February 1812, B.L.
47 James Sharp to Bishop Cameron, 21st December 1812, B.L.
48 John Farquharson to Abbé MacPherson, 7th September 1801, B.L.
49 Stonyhurst Prospectus for 1802, B.L.
50 Charles Plowden, Stonyhurst, to Abbé MacPherson, 21st November 1801, B.L.
51 "Regulations for Scalan", *Innes Review* 1963, p. 111.
52 Bishop Gordon's "Rules for Scalan", *Innes Review* 1963, p. 107.
53 Bishop Cameron to James Kyle, 22nd June 1810, B.L.
54 James Kyle to Bishop Cameron, 1st November 1818, Kyle Letters, B.L.
55 Bishop Cameron to James Kyle, 16th June 1815, B.L.
56 Alexander Paterson to Bishop Cameron, 30th November 1816, B.L.
57 James Kyle to James Sharp, 27th November 1810, Kyle Letters, B.L.
58 John Geddes to James Sharp, 14th November 1826, Preshome Letters, S.C.A.
59 William MacDonald to Charles Maxwell, 18th October 1808, B.L.
60 *Scotichronicon*, pp. 475-476.
61 James Carruthers, *The History of Scotland . . . to the accession of the Stewart Family*, 2 Vols. (Edinburgh, 1826) and *The History of Scotland During the Life of Queen Mary . . .* (Edinburgh, 1831); *Scotichronicon*, pp. 533, 555, 562 respectively.
62 *Regulations for the Administration of the College of Aquhorties*, printed by J. Moir, Edinburgh (1799).
63 *Scotichronicon*, p. 351.
64 *Regulations for the Administration of the College of Aquhorties*, p. 41.
65 Bishop Gordon's "Rules for Scalan", *Innes Review* 1963, p. 108.
66 John Gordon to Abbé MacPherson, 5th August 1799, B.L.

67 E.g. Charles Gordon to James Kyle, 16th March 1825, B.L.

68 Charles Gordon to James Sharp, 29th March 1813, Preshome Letters, S.C.A.

69 Bishop Cameron to James Kyle, scroll letter, 1811, B.L.

70 John Geddes to James Sharp, 14th November 1826, Preshome Letters, S.C.A.

71 Alexander MacDonald to Bishop Paterson, 12th June 1826, Preshome Letters, S.C.A.

72 John Geddes to James Sharp, 14th November 1826, Preshome Letters, S.C.A.

73 *Scotichronicon*, pp. 419-420.

74 *Regulations for the Administration of the College of Aquhorties*, p. 53.

75 Peter Forbes to John Forbes, 30th March 1824, Preshome Letters, S.C.A.

76 James Kyle to Alexander Kyle, 19th December 1807, Preshome Letters, S.C.A.

77 John Cameron, Notice about subscriptions for violin strings, 3rd September 1816, CS 2/21/4, S.C.A.

78 "The Dutiful Remonstrance and Humble Petition of John Gordon and James MacLachlan, students of Divinity in the College of Aquhorties", to Bishop Hay, 1800, B.L.

79 "William MacDonald's Proposal for altering some of the Rules of Aquhorties", 1803, B.L.

80 James Sharp to Bishop Cameron, 18th June 1813, B.L.

81 John Gordon (junior) to Bishop Cameron, 11th September 1813, B.L.

82 James Sharp to Bishop Cameron, 27th July 1817, B.L.

83 *Regulations for the Administration of the College of Aquhorties*, p. 45.

84 Bishop Cameron to James Sharp, 12th June 1815, B.L.

85 George Smyth to his mother, 19th October 1824, B.L.

86 Aquhorties Account Books, S.C.A.

87 Charles Gordon, "Memorial Concerning Blairs", 15th July 1835, CS 4/2, S.C.A.

88 William Reid to James Sharp, 20th September 1823, B.L.

25

Catholic Education, 1793-1829

BEFORE the outbreak of the French Revolution in 1793 the wealthier Scottish Catholics had been able to send their children abroad to be educated. The Scots College at Paris, whose charter made specific provision for the education of boys not intended for the priesthood, attracted many such students. While Douay was under Jesuit control it, too, educated laymen: generations of Maxwells from Terregles, Kirkconnell and Munshes, and of Glendonwyns from Parton, were educated there, some of them eventually entering the Jesuit Order, others returning to the family estates in Galloway.[1] Girls, too, were educated abroad, in convent schools in France and in Belgium.

All the Scots Colleges abroad educated some boys who, although intended for the priesthood, ultimately abandoned their vocations. Some, like James Torry, returned to Scotland to become teachers. Many in the eighteenth century became soldiers. Others, particularly after about 1800, became merchants.[2] Some of these men were able to repay the Scottish Mission for the free education they had received by doing it some sort of service. Mr Alexander Sloane, for instance, did much to preserve his old *alma mater*, the Scots College at Rome, during the Napoleonic Wars.

After 1793 those parents who had formerly sent their children abroad were forced to turn instead to educational establishments in Britain. The Aquhorties and Lismore Colleges were not generally contemplated. Although Aquhorties did number, among its boarders, two sons of Sir James Gordon of Letterfourie, and one son of Mr Fletcher of Dunans, most of the Scottish Catholic gentry preferred to send their sons to English schools rather than to the spartan Scottish Colleges. In 1794 the English Catholic school at Tudhoe numbered among its students two sons of Lady Livingstone and one son of MacDonald of Glenaladale.[3] In 1808 Mr Charles MacDonald and Bishop Cameron advised MacDonald of Borrodale to send his son to Crookhall College.[4] In 1814 Lady Gordon's son was sent to school at Ushaw.[5]

When the ex-Jesuit priests who had fled from Liège founded Stonyhurst College in Lancashire, in 1794, they received the support of Scottish families like the Maxwells of Kirkconnell who had had a long-standing connection with the Society of Jesus. The Stonyhurst Register, between 1794 and 1830, includes four sons of Constable Maxwell of Terregles. Another important Stonyhurst pupil was Thomas Fraser, 12th Lord Lovat, who, in later years, did much to help the Catholic religion in Scotland. Other boys who attended Stonyhurst during these years, who were probably Scottish, include three Frasers and two Gordons. Undoubtedly there were others; the Register, unfortunately, does not usually state the family or place of birth of its students.[6]

Scots girls who were educated at the convent school in York include daughters of Maxwell of Munshes, of Glendonwyn of Parton, and of Maxwell Witham of Kirkconnell, as well as of Frasers, MacDonalds, Gordons and others.[7]

The trend of Scottish Catholic landowners towards sending their sons to school in England was duplicated by their Protestant counterparts. Stonyhurst, in particular, came to be the Catholic equivalent of Eton or Harrow. The Scottish nobility no longer went to school in Scotland.

After the Continent became once again a safe place, Sir James Gordon of Letterfourie sent his daughters to school in Paris.[8] This is the only reference, in the letters in the Scottish Catholic Archives, to Scottish children being sent abroad to school between 1815 and 1830. It might therefore be safe to hazard a guess that, English schools, which were easier of access, and where language was no problem, now engrossed most of the support that would, in former years, have gone abroad. The failure to reopen the Scots College in Paris after 1815 may have gone a long way towards ensuring that the sons of Scottish Catholic landowners would, in future, be educated in England.

Most families, however, could not afford even the modest sums charged by Aquhorties for boarders. Aquhorties, in any case, could not accommodate more than eight or ten boarders at a time. The vast majority of Catholic boys, therefore, received their education in a Catholic school, run either by priests or by private individuals, if one existed in their area; or else at a Protestant parish or charity school.

Considering first the Catholic schools which were run by priests, and which might therefore be classed as 'official' Catholic schools, there were, broadly speaking, three phases in their development. The first stage occurred in the last decades of the eighteenth century.

In 1788 Mr Robert Menzies, priest of the Highland Chapel of St Andrew in Edinburgh, opened, in his chapel, a school for poor Catholic children.[9] For some time this school was taught by an Irishman, but he was dismissed in 1790.[10] Mr James Torry, a former student of the Scots College, Valladolid, who was teaching at Aberdeen, was considered for the post, but as he insisted on a salary of £25 per annum over and above his house and school, he was not given the job.[11] Mr Torry continued to teach in Aberdeen until 1825; another teacher was found for Edinburgh. Some time before 1790 a Catholic school was opened in Glenlivet. Its Irish schoolmaster had also been dismissed by 1790. In 1791 Bishop Hay appointed a new schoolmaster at a salary of £5 per annum. In 1791 Bishop Hay also appointed a schoolmaster for Aberdeen. The schoolmaster, Mr Barclay, received an initial salary from the Bishop of £5 a year.[12] The schoolmasters at these three schools, like the masters in Protestant schools, would have supplemented their salaries by charging a small fee of each pupil. The schoolmaster in Glenlivet may have been provided with a small patch of land on which to graze a cow or two. The schools at Edinburgh and Glenlivet had a somewhat faltering existence in their early years; the school at Aberdeen was taught continuously by Mr Barclay until his death in 1831.

These schools had all come into existence before the passing of the Relief Act in 1793, at a time when Catholics were forbidden to teach at all. The 1793 Act contained the following clause relative to education:

> . . . it is hereby enacted and declared . . . that nothing in this Act contained shall extend or be construed or deemed to extend, to enable any Person professing the Roman Catholic Religion, in that Part of the Kingdom of Great Britain called Scotland, to be Governer, Chaplain, Pedagogue, Teacher, Tutor or Curator, Chamberlain or Factor, to any Child or Children of Protestant Parents, or to be otherwise employed in their Education, or the Trust or Management of their Affairs; or to be Schoolmaster, Professor, or Public Teacher of any Science, to any Person or Persons whomsoever within that Part of the Kingdom of Great Britain called Scotland.[13]

This clause expressly prohibited Catholics from teaching Protestant children, and was perhaps to be expected. What worried Bishop Hay was that the concluding part of the clause suggested that Catholics were not allowed to teach even in a Catholic school or seminary.[14] In practice the right of Catholics to teach in Catholic schools, or indeed in any schools, was never challenged. The official Catholic schools which had been opened before 1793 continued unmolested, and other new schools were founded after the Relief Bill had been passed.

In Edinburgh the official school closed for some time for want of a teacher.[15] By 1799 it was open again and was doing well, Bishop Hay helping it financially out of his own pocket.[16] In 1802 Bishop Cameron testified that one James Stewart had been 'parochial schoolmaster of the Catholic Congregation' of Edinburgh for a number of years.[17] Before 1820 the school had again closed.

In 1820 Mr Angus MacDonald wrote to Bishop Cameron:

> I was struck when I heard it announced officially from the pulpit by Mr Reid a few Sundays ago that, from the great want which was felt from the want of a Catholic school in this town, that one of the old Chapels in Blackfriars Wynd was granted gratis by you for the aforesaid purpose — and that the present necessary expenses were to be defrayed by subscription, and that a Teacher had already been appointed.[18]

By 1822 there were two Catholic schools in Edinburgh teaching the rudiments.[19] In 1830 there were two official Catholic boys' schools in Blackfriars Wynd, and in 1831 an official girls' school was opened in Old Stamp Office Close. Between them the three schools were teaching about two hundred and forty boys and about two hundred girls. The schools were supported partly by subscriptions from the Catholic congregation of Edinburgh, and partly by the weekly fee charged for each child.[20]

The school in Aberdeen continued unchanged until Mr Barclay died in 1831. When he died Mr Charles Gordon, the Aberdeen priest, took over and built two new Catholic schools, one for boys and one for girls, in Constitution Street.[21] The schools in Edinburgh and in Aberdeen succeeded, broadly speaking, from the dates of their founding. The school in Glenlivet, by contrast, seems to have closed within a very short space of time, and was not revived until 1828.

The only other attempt to found a school in the North-East before 1800 also failed — in this instance the attempt did not get off the ground at all. In October

1797 Mr Mathison, the priest for Fochabers, wrote to Mr Barclay, the Aberdeen teacher, saying that he hoped to open a school, and offering Mr Barclay the post of schoolmaster. He would have enough ground to keep a cow, and a fixed salary over and above the fees that the children might pay.[22] Mr Barclay, however, preferred to remain in Aberdeen, and the school in Fochabers never materialised.

The second phase in the development of official Catholic schools occurred in the South-West of Scotland. Elsewhere the parish schools and charity schools, between them, gave most children the chance of an elementary education. In Glasgow and the other industrial towns of the South-West the huge influx of Irish immigrants, both Catholic and Protestant, strained the existing educational set-up to breaking point. Some idea of the scale of the problem can be gathered from the statistics compiled by James Cleland for Glasgow:[23]

year	total population	total no. of Irish	total no. of Irish R.C.s
1819	140,000	15,208	8,245
1831	202,426	35,554	19,333

In an attempt to alleviate the situation among their congregations, the Catholic priests began to set up schools with the co-operation of the Protestant middle classes.

In 1817 some Glasgow manufacturers formed the Catholic Schools Society in order to found a Catholic school in their city. The president of the Society was Kirkman Finlay, a Glasgow merchant and M.P. A board consisting of fifteen Catholics and fifteen Protestants laid down a scheme for the teaching of reading, writing and arithmetic. The teachers were to be Catholic, chosen with the approval of the priest. No specifically Catholic doctrine was to be taught, and the Protestant version of the Bible was to be used.[24] Various means were used to collect money for this school, and for the others which soon followed under the auspices of the Society. Many Protestants subscribed to them. Charity sermons were preached on their behalf by popular Presbyterian ministers like Thomas Chalmers.[25] In 1818 a concert of sacred music was given in the Catholic church, the only one in Glasgow to possess an organ, and the money made from the sale of the tickets provided a welcome addition to the funds for the schools.[26]

It is interesting to note the difference in attitude between Mr Scott, the priest in Glasgow at this time, and the English Bishop Poynter. Mr Scott was only too pleased to accept the condition that Protestant Bibles be used in the Catholic schools. Acceptance of that condition meant support from Protestants, without which the schools would be unable to continue. Bishop Poynter, on the other hand, would under no circumstances allow English Catholic children to use the Protestant Bible. He went further: although there were insufficient Catholic schools in England to educate all the Catholic children, he would not give his approval to any suggestion that Catholic children be educated by Protestants, even though no Protestant doctrine were taught.[27] This separatist attitude was to creep into Scotland in the early twentieth century. Fortunately, in Mr Scott's day, Scottish bishops were more enlightened and Catholic children were not denied the right to an education simply because there were insufficient Catholic schools.

In 1831 the following account of Catholic schools in Glasgow appeared in the *Catholic Directory:*

> [The Gorbals Chapel] was purchased in 1825 for a school, it having been previously furnished and used for that purpose. It still continues to serve as a school throughout the week, and on Sunday evening. Besides it, there are in Glasgow and its suburbs five other Catholic schools. The number of children on the roll of attendance, in the six schools, generally amounts to 1400. The five principal schools, have hitherto been supported by subscriptions given chiefly by benevolent Protestant gentlemen of the city . . . and the small fee of one penny per week, paid by each scholar, unless owing to the great poverty of his parents, he be furnished with a line of gratuitous admission from one of the Pastors.[28]

In addition, eleven Sunday schools instructed about three thousand children in their faith.

The same method of organising Catholic schools was followed at Paisley as in Glasgow. In reply to the appeal of M. Despreaux, a French émigré priest living in Paisley, for their help in founding a school for the education of the children of Irish and Highland Catholic immigrants, some of the wealthier inhabitants of Paisley stated:

> . . . While some of the poor persons . . . not having had the benefit of education themselves, are indifferent whether their children receive education or not; others, it is well known, from early prejudices, would rather have their children altogether uneducated, than that they should be instructed by one who was not of their own persuasion. Education by a Roman Catholic teacher, or no education at all seems the alternative. The consequence of a number of young persons growing up amongst us in a state of gross ignorance, cannot be thought of but with alarm and deep regret; and may one day be severely felt. It shall gradually change the very character of the place, and take as much from the comfort as the respectability of the inhabitants. Of persons of the Roman Catholic persuasion, the proportion to the general population of this town is perhaps greater than in any other town in Scotland.[29]

Due to all these considerations they agreed to help to support a Catholic teacher, on the following conditions: that only Catholic children should be taught in the school, that no religious books should be used in it but Bibles and New Testaments of the authorised King James version; and that a Committee of Managers have the right to inspect the school at any time. The Eastern Renfrewshire and Paisley Bible Society agreed to furnish Bibles and New Testaments at a reduced rate, or even free, to those who could not afford to pay the full price. Later in the same year — 1816 — Mr Paterson, at Paisley, reported:

> Our Catholic school was opened upon Monday last. More than a hundred scholars attend already. We have got a good steady lad from Glasgow for schoolmaster. We have a vacant day, every week, for Christian Doctrine and Religious Instruction; in a word all the Gentlemen of the Committee seem willing to give us every possible encouragement.[30]

By 1830 there were three Catholic schools in Paisley, only one of which was an 'official' one.

In 1817 Mr John Gordon, the priest at Greenock, started a fund intended to provide both a school and a chapel organ.[31] In the following year he opened a school in rented premises with about ninety children.[32] He had a meeting with some Protestants, but they refused to give any assistance to the school unless Mr

Gordon promised to give up any idea of teaching the Catholic catechism or giving Catholic instruction in the school, even for as little as two hours a week.[33] By 1819 Mr Gordon had decided that it would be more economical in the long run to build a school and schoolhouse than to continue to pay rent for inadequate premises. In October, 1820 his new school was opened with a hundred children attending during the day, and about twenty coming to the night school.[34] All this he had achieved without Protestant support, as he explained to Bishop Cameron:

> [The magistrates] wish no more new Irishmen and they incline to adopt such measures as may gradually but effectively diminish the number of those here at present. On this account, and least any encouragement should seem to be held forth to them, they in general, with the Chief Magistrate and Sheriff at their head . . . have set their face against a School here for *Catholics* on any plan whatsoever. They may go to the Free School, and *perhaps* they may be dispensed from getting the Protestant Catechism on condition of getting portions of the Protestant Bible in lieu of it.[35]

Only one other official Catholic school was opened in the South-West before 1830. It was opened in Ayr, in March 1823, by the priest, Mr Thomson, and had about sixty children attending it. An evening school was also started which, it was hoped, would attract many adults. Mr Thomson also appointed a few women to instruct Catholic girls on Sunday evenings.[36] Before 1830 the school had been forced to close through lack of funds to pay a schoolmaster.[37]

The third phase in the founding of official Catholic schools concerns those founded in the more rural areas of Scotland where the problem of education was less acute.

In September 1815, as the result of a promise of money by a Mrs MacDonald, Mr Grant, the priest at Braemar, opened a school. Charges made on individual children were minimal because it was expected that Mrs MacDonald's money would provide sufficient funds. As a result over seventy children were attending the school by 1817, when it became obvious that Mrs MacDonald had changed her mind. The congregation was too poor to support the school unaided, and so it was forced to close.[38]

More successful were Mr Badenoch's various ventures at Preshome. His first scheme for raising the necessary money arose from his desire to get an organ for his chapel. He proposed to start a subscription for an organ and a gallery at the rate of a penny a week. The interest from the money collected he intended to use to pay the salary of someone who could double as organist and schoolmaster.[39] A year later, in 1819, he decided to start a Catholic library; as he explained to Mr Sharp:

> This institution is intended not only for the diffusion of useful knowledge, but also for the support of a Catholic Schoolmaster and organist for the parish, and therefore in the Constitution which I have made for it, one of the fundamental laws is that whenever we can procure a schoolmaster and organist he is to be librarian with a suitable salary.[40]

Unfortunately no letters which survive tell us whether either of these ideas was as fruitful as Mr Badenoch had hoped. In 1821, however, he applied for the lease of the croft of Stackhead:

> . . . to be a settlement for my organist — and, if I can bring it about, a Catholic school. As a preparatory step said organist has already opened a school in Port Gordon and has about 70 scholars.[41]

In 1822 he wrote to Bishop Paterson of further developments:

> ... there is a prospect ... of our having two Catholic schools, one to be kept by the organist and the other by one to be established in Buckie by Sir James Gordon.[42]

At Whitsunday in 1822 Mr Badenoch obtained the lease of Stackhead and in 1824 wrote to Mr Charles Gordon:

> John Gordon, your cousin, ... has a school in Buckie of more than 100, and John England, whom I have lately installed at Stackhead, has a school of near 40 and is every week getting more scholars.[43]

In 1825 Mr Donald Carmichael, the priest at Tomintoul, tried to obtain a piece of land, next to his farm at Cults, on which to build a school.[44] He failed in this, and was then faced with the expense, first of adding a gallery to the existing chapel, and then of replacing the latter with a new chapel. The project of building a Catholic school was shelved until 1860.[45]

Apart from Mr Badenoch's schools, the only schools to have opened in the North-East by 1830 were those built by Abbé MacPherson in the Braes of Glenlivet. The Abbé, during a visit to Scotland in 1828, built a chapel at his own expense near the old seminary of Scalan. He also opened a school there, settling £5 per annum on the schoolmaster.[46] In 1832 he financed the building of a boy's school and a girl's school, together with a schoolhouse, next to his chapel.[47]

There were no official Catholic schools at all in the Highlands until well after 1830.[48]

The official Catholic schools which had been opened in Scotland by 1830 can be divided into two categories. There were a few schools in Banffshire serving the Catholics of Glenlivet and the Enzie. Then there were the schools which had been opened in the large towns of Aberdeen, Edinburgh, Glasgow, Paisley and Greenock. All the town schools fulfilled the same function — to educate Catholic children whose parents were too poor to send them to schools like the Royal High in Edinburgh. At a time when the existing Protestant schools were unable to cope with the growing urban population, these Catholic schools provided an invaluable service.

It is relatively easy to trace the development of official Catholic schools; it is not so easy to discover Catholic schools which were in no way connected to the Mission. There were, of course, Catholic teachers teaching in Protestant schools such as Inverness Academy. What we are concerned with here, however, is schools opened by Catholic teachers with specifically Catholic children in mind. There was, from about 1813, at least one such school in Edinburgh.

When the official Catholic school was opened in Blackfriars Wynd in 1820, Bishop Cameron received an indignant letter from Mr Julius MacDonald. Mr MacDonald, for the previous seven years, had been teaching Catholic children in his school in the Lawnmarket, and instructing them in their religion, with no help from the Edinburgh priests. Now these same priests were opening a school which, because it was to charge less than he could afford to, threatened to take away all his pupils and leave him penniless.[49]

Mr MacDonald need not have worried. The *Catholic Directory* for 1832 lists, over and above the official Catholic schools in Edinburgh:

> ... two other schools, the one in the Cowgate, under the direction of Mr Francis Stuart, the other in Gosford's Close, Lawnmarket, under the superintendance of Mr Julius MacDonald. These schools are maintained by the fees paid by the children. Into the latter of these, Protestant Children are also received; but although the teacher be Catholic, the religion of the Protestant children is not interfered with.[50]

The only other unofficial Catholic schools in the south to be mentioned in the *Catholic Directory* are two in Paisley, which were kept by Catholic teachers and supported wholly by the fees of the scholars.[51]

In 1828 an attempt was made to set up a Catholic school at Innerleithen. The project, however, failed miserably, even though it was backed by the Earl of Traquair.[52]

In the North-East there were one or two unofficial Catholic schools. James Torry ran one such school in Aberdeen from 1790 till 1825.[53] In Glenlivet James Michie opened a school at Eskmullich. He then applied to Bishop Cameron, in 1817, for the lease of the farm of Scalan.[54] By 1823, having acquired Scalan, he had given up bothering to teach.[55] No Catholic schools, apart from those of Abbé MacPherson, are mentioned in the *New Statistical Account* for Banffshire, an area with a large Catholic population, so it is safe to assume that there were few if any unofficial Catholic schools in existence, other than the ones mentioned above, in Banffshire at least, and probably in Scotland as a whole.

Obviously very few Catholic children were able to attend Catholic schools. Evidence from Catholic sources, however, suggests, not only that the vast majority of Catholic children were educated in parish, or charity, schools run by Protestants, but that these schools had the active support of the Catholic clergy.

In January, 1790, a charity school opened at Badevochla, in Glenlivet, under the charge of a Mr Fleming. Mr Fleming insisted that Catholic children spend each Saturday morning learning the Protestant catechism. Because this confused the children, who had also to learn the Catholic catechism, the priest in Glenlivet, Mr Carruthers, brought an Irishman from Galloway as Catholic schoolmaster. Mr Fleming threatened to send a memorial to the Society for Promoting Christian Knowledge in Edinburgh to the effect that a Catholic was illegally teaching in Glenlivet. Bishop Hay therefore wrote to Bishop Geddes, asking him to use his influence to prevent any trouble occurring.[56]

In November Bishop Geddes chanced to meet Mr Kemp, who was a prominent member of the S.P.C.K., at a supper party. Bishop Geddes was supported by the other guests when he proposed that Catholic children in charity schools should not be required to learn the Protestant catechism.[57] At subsequent meetings early in 1791 he and Mr Kemp came to an agreement that Catholic children in charity schools should be taught reading, writing and arithmetic. Their religious instruction should be limited to lessons on the morality and history of the Bible, particularly of the Gospels. They would not be taught the Protestant catechism.[58] Meanwhile Mr Fleming, who had been the cause of all the discussions, had been moved from Glenlivet to Deskie. In June 1791 Bishop Hay wrote to Bishop Geddes:

> I am happy at the good dispositions of Mr Kemp; and if you think proper, you may tell him that

as the Braes of Glenlivet stand in great need of a proper hand, . . . if he will send a discreet person to settle class in the Braes, and who will fulfil what he has promised you, I will not only encourage all the people to send their children to the school, but will also most willingly give the Incumbent at least twenty shillings in the year out of my own pocket to be some small help to him . . . [59]

A month later Bishop Hay wrote to say that if the charity schoolmaster proved satisfactory, he would dismiss the Catholic schoolmaster in Glenlivet at the term.[60]

There is other evidence of Catholic boys attending Protestant schools with the concurrence of their priests. James Kyle, the future bishop, had received a good education at the Royal High School, Edinburgh before coming to Aquhorties. So too had another future bishop, John Strain. In 1791 two Catholic boys were lodging with Mr Alexander MacDonell, priest in Badenoch, attending the parish school, and studying with Mr MacDonell in the evenings.[61] In 1796 one of Abbé MacPherson's nephews wanted to enter Scalan as a church student. As the college was full, it was decided that he should stay meantime with Mr MacGillivray, priest at Mortlach. He would be able to either study under the priest himself or to attend the local school. Mr Maxwell, priest at Edinburgh, advised him to attend the Mortlach school where there was a very good schoolmaster. Indeed many priests recommending boys for Aquhorties stressed the good reports they had had of these boys from their schoolmasters in what must obviously have been Protestant schools.

A final example might be taken from the *Catholic Directory* for 1834. Mr James MacKay, the priest in Perth, had just finished building a new house. In order to recoup some of his expense he decided to take in boarders:

. . . he can well accommodate a few young men. Of these he will take the charge himself, or send them to Perth Academy, as may be most agreeable to the parents.[62]

Clearly, Scottish Catholic priests were happy that Catholic children should be educated in Protestant schools, so long as they could receive instruction in their faith in Sunday schools or in classes held by the priests themselves. As far as the Protestant schoolmasters were concerned, in an area where there was a significant proportion of Catholics, it was in their interest to co-operate with the priests concerning religious instruction, such as not teaching Catholics the Protestant Catechism, because their incomes depended to quite an extent on the number of children they could attract to their schools.

In 1827 the question of Catholic children's attending a newly opened charity school at Tomatin in Glenlivet prompted the parents to hold a meeting. There they adopted the following resolutions. They, as British subjects, claimed liberty of conscience. They would send their children to the school, and contribute to its upkeep, so long as their liberty of conscience was respected. Should the schoolmaster interfere with the religious beliefs of the Catholic children, their parents would immediately withdraw their support from the school.[63] This attitude suggests that the Catholics of Glenlivet were well aware that the charity school needed their support, and that they could dictate terms regarding its teachings.

Bishop Hay had been pleased to co-operate with Mr Kemp, and many Catholic priests shared his attitude. Bishop Cameron, however, was less forthcoming. In

1823 he was approached by Principal Baird of Edinburgh University. The Presbytery of Edinburgh had decided to propose to the General Assembly that a fund be set up to help provide more schools, particularly in the Highlands. Principal Baird wanted to know whether Bishop Cameron and the Catholic priests would give these schools their support. He assured the Bishop that Catholic children would not be indoctrinated with Protestant beliefs, but would simply be taught to read the Bible.[64] Bishop Cameron, although he admitted that many Protestant schools in Scotland were very accommodating where Catholic children were concerned, went on to say:

> ... I fear that experience will not tend to encourage either Catholic Parents, or Catholic Pastors, to patronise these schools ... In that part of the country, however, with which I am concerned, few if any additional schools are, I believe needed ... [65]

It is hard to guess why Bishop Cameron was so discouraging in the face of so much evidence that Protestant schools could and did co-operate with the Catholic Church. One explanation might be that the Bishop hoped, in the near future, to have Catholic schools throughout his Vicariate.

The drawbacks of the parish system of education cannot have been too severe where Catholics were concerned. Nearly all the boys who came to Aquhorties had learned reading, writing and arithmetic in the parish or charity schools. Some had learned the rudiments of Latin as well, either at school or from their priests. Mr Kyle might complain that Alexander Grant, when he had been taken from the hills of Glenlivet to go to Aquhorties, had hardly had a book in his hand,[66] but two years later Alexander was doing well in the Roman College of Propaganda, where classes were taught either in Latin or in Italian. He must have had a good grounding in the basic skills of reading and writing, before he came to Aquhorties, to have progressed so quickly. Since nearly all the Aquhorties boys had previously been taught in Protestant schools, it seems clear that their schoolmasters must have respected their religious beliefs, otherwise they would not have discovered vocations for the priesthood.

In the eighteenth century intending university students in Scotland did not matriculate as they do today. They enrolled for specific classes and paid their fees directly to their professors. Since his income depended on the number of students he could attract, no professor refused to admit a student to his class on religious grounds. Bishop Hay, as a young non-juring Episcopalian, before his conversion to Catholicism, attended the Edinburgh medical school in the 1740s. His religion debarred him from graduating and from joining the Royal College of Surgeons but it did not prevent him from attending all the classes.[67]

In 1790 a group of charity students from Portugal came to Edinburgh to attend the medical school. They established what amounted to a Portuguese Catholic College in the city, and Bishop Geddes was appointed its superior. The experiment was a failure, not because of religious intolerance, but because of the unruly behaviour of the students.[68]

English Catholic students, whose religion debarred them from attending Oxford or Cambridge, also came to Edinburgh University. Bishop Cameron was quick to take advantage of this. He bought a house in High School Yards which he filled with English Catholic student boarders. In 1818 when, after Alexander Paterson had been consecrated bishop, it seemed likely that he would settle in Edinburgh, Bishop Cameron offered him the following advice:

> If you should think it proper to receive under your roof a few Catholic young gentlemen who wished to attend our University classes for a season, you and five or six of them might be commodiously accommodated at High School Yards. In so far as I can judge from my own experience, you will not be safe to take less than £200 for each ... Old Hall, Oscot and Stonyhurst are the principal places from which application may be expected.[69]

In 1814 Mr Glover one of the Stonyhurst professors, brought four of his students to Edinburgh to attend the University.[70]

Generally speaking, the period 1793-1829 saw a remarkable degree of tolerance and co-operation between Protestant and Catholic in the field of education.

NOTES

1 *Douay Diary*, entries no. 581, 606, 607, 665, 740 etc., New Spalding Club, 1906.

2 *Records of the Scots Colleges of Rome and Valladolid*, New Spalding Club, 1906.

3 Bishop Hay to Bishop Geddes, 30th May 1794, B.L.

4 John MacDonald, Borrodale to Charles Maxwell, 9th August 1808, B.L.

5 James MacDonald to Bishop Cameron, 29th September 1814, B.L.

6 Information kindly supplied by Father Turner, S. J., librarian at Stonyhurst College.

7 W. J. Anderson, 'Some Notes on Catholic Education for Scottish Children in Pre-Emancipation Days', *Innes Review* 1963, pp. 39-41.

8 Mr Stonor to Bishop Paterson, 2nd August 1826, B.L.

9 *Scotichronicon*, p. 273.

10 Bishop Geddes to Bishop Hay, 24th March 1791, B.L.

11 James Torry to Bishop Geddes, 7th December 1790, B.L.

12 Bishop Hay to Bishop Geddes, 21st April 1791, B.L.

13 *Statutes at Large*, Vol 16, 33 George III c 44 p. 337.

14 Bishop Hay to Alexander Brodie, MP, 19th January 1796, B.L.

15 William Rattray, scroll letter, 3rd August 1797, B.L.

16 Bishop Hay to Charles Maxwell, 6th August 1799, B.L.

17 Bishop Cameron: Certificate, 7th October 1802, B.L.

18 Angus MacDonald to Bishop Cameron, 31st May 1820, B.L.

19 James Kyle's report to Propaganda, reproduced in Robertson's 'Life of Kyle', S.C.A.

20 *The Catholic Directory for Scotland*, 1831, p. 63; 1832, pp. 51-52.

21 Alexander MacWilliam, *St Peter's Church, Aberdeen* (Aberdeen, 1979), p. 12.

22 George Mathison to James Barclay, 30th October 1797, B.L.

23 James Cleland, quoted in James Handley, *The Irish in Scotland, 1798-1845* (Cork, 1943), p. 100.

24 James Handley, *The Irish in Scotland*, 1798-1845, p. 260.

25 Andrew Scott to Bishop Cameron, 21st April 1818, Preshome Letters, S.C.A.

26 Andrew Scott to Bishop Cameron, 21st April 1818, B.L.

27 Bernard Ward, *The Eve of Catholic Emancipation*, Vol II, pp. 164-165.

28 *Catholic Directory for Scotland*, 1831, p. 67.

29 Despreaux, 'To the Humane and Affluent Inhabitants of Paisley'; answered by Alexander Campbell, William Jamieson, Robert Boag and John Findlay in a letter dated 'Paisley, 8 May 1816'. Both letters are contained on a printed sheet, filed under 'Despreaux', 1816, B.L.

30 Bishop Paterson to Bishop Cameron, 9th October 1816, B.L.
31 John Gordon to Bishop Cameron, 12th August 1817, B.L.
32 John Gordon to Bishop Cameron, 4th February 1818, B.L.
33 John Gordon to Bishop Cameron, 6th December 1819, B.L.
34 John Gordon to Bishop Cameron, 1st October 1820, B.L.
35 John Gordon to Bishop Cameron, 1st November 1817, B.L.
36 William Thomson to Bishop Cameron, 4th March 1823, B.L.
37 *Catholic Directory for Scotland*, 1831, p.69.
38 John and William Morgan to Bishop Cameron, 25th March 1817, Preshome Letters, S.C.A.
39 Alexander Badenoch to Bishop Cameron, 21st January 1818, B.L.
40 Alexander Badenoch to John Forbes, 18th January 1819, Preshome Letters, S.C.A.
41 Alexander Badenoch to James Sharp, 27th November 1821, Preshome Letters, S.C.A.
42 Alexander Badenoch to Bishop Paterson, 26th August 1822, B.L.
43 Alexander Badenoch to Charles Gordon, 27th March 1824, Preshome Letters, S.C.A.
44 Donald Carmichael to John Anderson, 24th May 1825, B.L.
45 Odo Blundell, *The Catholic Highlands of Scotland*, Vol I (1909), p. 67.
46 Abbé MacPherson to Donald Carmichael, 24th December 1829, Preshome Letters, S.C.A.
47 *Scotichronicon*, p.600.
48 E.g. Terence MacGuire to Bishop Kyle, 6th December 1828, Preshome Letters, S.C.A.
49 Julius MacDonald to Bishop Cameron, 28th April 1820, B.L.
50 *Catholic Directory for Scotland*, 1832, p. 52.
51 *Catholic Directory for Scotland*, 1831, p. 68.
52 W. Lawrie to Bishop Paterson, 1828, Preshome Letters, S.C.A.
53 Valladolid Register, entry no. 23, 'Records of the Scots Colleges', New Spalding Club, 1906.
54 James Michie to Bishop Cameron, 3rd May 1817, B.L.
55 James Gordon to James Kyle, 27th May 1823, B.L.
56 Bishop Hay to Bishop Geddes, 3rd January 1790, B.L.
57 Bishop Geddes to Bishop Hay, 11th November 1790, B.L.
58 Bishop Geddes to Bishop Hay, 17th March 1791, B.L.
59 Bishop Hay to Bishop Geddes, 12th June 1791, B.L.
60 Bishop Hay to Bishop Geddes, 13th July 1791, B.L.
61 Alexander MacDonell to Bishop Geddes, 7th January 1791, B.L.
62 *Catholic Directory for Scotland*, 1834, p. 54.
63 'Turner et allia' to James Gordon, 15th November 1827, B.L.
64 George Baird to Bishop Cameron, 12th April 1823, B.L.
65 Bishop Cameron to George Baird, scroll letter, 1823, B.L.
66 James Kyle to Bishop Cameron 20th March 1820, Kyle Letters, S.C.A.
67 *Scotichronicon*, p. 19.
68 *Ibid.*, p. 306.
69 Bishop Cameron to Bishop Paterson, 28th August 1818, Preshome Letters, S.C.A.
70 Mr Stone to Bishop Cameron, 12th October 1814, B.L.

26

The Highland College of Lismore

IN 1799 the Lowland college of Aquhorties was opened. The Highland bishop, Bishop John Chisholm, having tried unsuccessfully to have Aquhorties made into a college which would serve the two Vicariates, determined that the Highlands should have their own college. Samalaman having been deemed unsuitable for expansion, the farm of Kilcheran on Lismore was purchased in January 1801 for £4950. One or two of the Highland priests voiced some concern that the Bishop should have chosen a location so far from the heart of the Catholic Highlands. To one such complaint Bishop Chisholm sent the following reply:

> Your moral observation seems to imply my being just now at a greater distance than I really am. Am more accessible here to the world than where I have formerly been in Moydart, nor am I at such a distance from you but you can see me when the spiritual concerns of your flock will allow the Pastor take a little range during which time a Pastor in the vicinity may have the charge . . . Lismore, in answer to your query, agrees with us very well . . . we never had more or so much liberty to applying to learning and spiritual matters in any other place.[1]

The move to Lismore had taken place in June 1803.

The farm at Aquhorties was intended to finance the college there. The farm at Kilcheran was too small to do more than provide its college with milk and meal. To finance the new Highland college, Bishop Chisholm pinned his faith on the manufacture and sale of lime. In 1804 Mr Charles Maxwell, procurator of the Lowland Mission, temporarily left his post in Edinburgh and came to Lismore to superintend the operation of building, not only lime kilns, but also a quay from which the lime could be shipped to what were hoped would be the profitable markets of the Clyde's industrial towns. The building of the quay caused the biggest problems:

> I have been unfortunate in my first attempt but not as yet in any degree discouraged. One dreadful stormy night with a very high spring tide overturned my crane, the frame and all the timber work I had in the sea and I would have undoubtedly lost the whole if we had not taken the precaution to fix the cable of my wherry to the whole timberwork which kept it afloat till we got it ashore next morning. I must now wait till the storms are away and till the great spring ebbs come on before I can lay the foundation of my key. I have got pinches, pickaxes, wedges and blasting materials made by a most excellent tho' drunken english smith at Oban.[2]

By 1805 the kilns had been built and were in operation. Mr Maxwell described their progress to Bishop Cameron:

> We extracted all the limestones put into the two kilns for seasoning them — one of them has been filled to the top last week, and in the space of two days and a half the fire was at the top — we propose drawing this kiln tomorrow — if the stones are well enough burnt, the quantity of coal for each kiln will be ascertained . . . We are just now finishing a reservoir for water from which the water for slaking the lime will be introduced into the lime shade . . .[3]

Bishop Chisholm and Mr Maxwell had high hopes for the lime kilns, and for one year at least these hopes seemed justified. In 1810 Mr Fraser, professor at Lismore, reported that they had already sold that spring 6,000 bolls of lime, and that the kilns could barely keep up with the demand.[4] By the following year, however, Bishop Chisholm was becoming very disheartened. He had sunk all his capital in the enterprise; Bishop Cameron had refused to help him; now he was in financial difficulties and was faced with the difficult choice of trying to struggle on, or else dropping the undertaking and losing his capital. He had made no profit as yet in spite of the good sales of the previous year.[5] In 1814 Bishop John Chisholm died and his Vicariate, with all its problems, fell to his brother, Bishop Angus, who appears to have struggled on with the lime kilns, though with little success.

In 1820 his successor, Bishop Ranald MacDonald, inherited the lime kilns and he, in turn, tried to put the enterprise on a better footing. He rebuilt the pier at a cost of £150 and tried to put the kilns themselves on a 'more beneficial footing'.[6] He met with no more success than Bishops John and Angus Chisholm before him. Lismore was at a disadvantage in that it had no coal of its own, unlike some estates where limekilns were being built. The bishops therefore had to buy in all the necessary coal, which meant that their running costs were higher than those of their competitors.[7]

Financial problems made it necessary for the Lismore students, unlike their Aquhorties counterparts, to work for their keep. Bishop John Chisholm, in 1806, wrote to tell Mr Maxwell that the men who should have been working on the kilns had all disappeared home to see to their peats and potatoes. In consequence:

> The demand for lime being pretty brisk, the Professors and the Scholars wrought, and, among these, Mr William Fraser distinguished himself for the large splinters of rock he drove down. No vessel, at the same time, was allowed to go away without her cargo.[8]

In 1816 Bishop Paterson had this to say about Lismore:

> [Mr Angus MacDonald] says they took along with them £700 from the Farm of Samalaman, and his Lordship [Bishop John Chisholm] had saved £100 more in Strathglass. His Lordship paid to the seminary of Lismore £30 a year for Bed, Board etc. As it was impossible for him to do two things at once — to attend to the direction of the students and to improve the finances of the seminary, it was agreed upon that . . . the later object should be effected — a saving operation was adopted; the boys were employed in digging and trenching especially at Samalaman. Money was borrowed from all quarters and without interest and Angus, being a good seaman, he caught plenty of fish and maintained them all for almost nothing. Partial sums were gradually paid up from the interest of the whole stock they borrowed, and he is sure that his Lordship must have been worth a deal of money at his death.[9]

Bishop John Chisholm may have been worth a large sum of money when he died in 1814, but little had been spent on the college. In 1807 he had admitted that his college building was much too small, but the high cost of timber had inhibited him from carrying out the necessary extension.[10] In 1814 Bishop John died and immediately Bishop Angus began to try to improve the college:

> I am busy repairing and preparing one of the small wings of this house that did not answer great purpose before except for lumber for a domestic chapel.[11]

In 1818 Bishop Angus died and the new Highland bishop, Bishop Ranald MacDonald, formed ambitious plans for expanding Lismore to place it on a par with Aquhorties. By 1824 he had to admit defeat. He had discovered that the establishment had accumulated a load of debt, and so he was forced to reduce, rather than increase, the number of boys in the college.[12]

Burdened from the start by financial problems, the college at Lismore limped from crisis to crisis until, in 1828, the boys were finally moved to Aquhorties, preparatory to the transfer of the boys of both colleges to Blairs. Bishop MacDonald remained at Lismore, alone except for one student, old, ill, and going blind. The farm of Kilcheran, with its college and limekilns, was finally given up when Bishop MacDonald died in 1832.

When, in 1814, Sir Walter Scott was touring round the lighthouses of Scotland in the Lighthouse Commissioners' yacht he wrote the following:

> We coasted the long, low and fertile island of Lismore where a Catholic bishop, Chisholm, has established a seminary of young men intended for priests, and, what is a better thing, a valuable lime work. Reports speak well of the lime but indifferently of the students.[13]

He was demonstrably misinformed about the lime; was he equally misinformed as to the students?

When the college at Lismore opened in 1803, Bishop Angus Chisholm hoped that his brother, Bishop John, would model it along the lines of English colleges like Stonyhurst. As he explained:

> We have not a proper Catholic school in all Scotland. The few gentry we have, and the Gentlemen farmers who can afford it, are obliged to send their children to the great towns where they first ruin their morals and then their Religion in which perhaps they were never properly founded, and then turn out the scandal of that very profession which once they carried on their foreheads. The place of Kilheiron in Lismore is now ours — my brother as I trust is in the eve of going to reside there — I have been preaching to him for more than a year back to begin immediately to enlarge his buildings there, to have a lookout for proper professors in various branches, and to be ready to receive all who might offer themselves for a moderate compensation — and to feed . . . and school them — by which plan, if properly digested and steadily followed, Religion would gain ground and the seminary would turn richer.[14]

The college at Lismore never matched up to Bishop Chisholm's dream. There was rarely more than one professor there besides the bishop, and the latter did not normally teach the boys. The maximum number of boys ever to be in the college at any one time was eleven, but often there were only eight or nine. The college took in one or two boarders,[15] but it never became anything approaching a Highland Stonyhurst. Academically Lismore seems to have been poor. It is true that in 1820 Mr James MacDonald, vice-rector of the Scots College at Rome, favourably compared the Highland boys who had just arrived with their Lowland companions,[16] but this does not seem to have been the general reaction. Two years later some Highland boys who had been sent to Paris were described as having no French and little Latin, which placed them at a considerable disadvantage in the French seminary of St. Nicolas.[17]

It is not surprising that Lismore compared unfavourably with Aquhorties. In the first place it seems never to have been properly equipped. In 1808 one of its professors wrote:

> What makes us so scarce of books here is that we are far from the market, and this house being almost till now a nursery for the colleges abroad.[18]

It was in 1808 that the last Scots College abroad was forced to close its doors, and

Lismore was faced with the necessity of purchasing enough books to see its scholars through Philosphy and Theology as well as Latin. It does not seem to have done this very adequately. In 1814 Charles Stuart, an Aquhorties boy who was in his last year of Theology, was sent for a year to Lismore where he was expected to teach as well as complete his own studies. He complained bitterly that not only did he have very little time to study but also that Lismore lacked the books he needed. He continued:

> I have had all along, and continue to have, a set of scholars as troublesome, I believe, as anyone ever had to teach . . . the quantity of labour and time, requisite to be employed upon them, is absolutely incredible . . . To all this I ought to add another disadvantageous circumstance of my situation, that I am deprived of the infinitely superior opportunities for other useful subjects, which I would have at Aquhorties.[19]

In 1827 Mr Scott was even more scathing about the Lismore students:

> You know that, though advised by the Superior, Mr Frere, to take away the three boys who had been so many years in quatricine without making any progress, that he [Bishop MacDonald] refused to do so. You know that you yourself pressed him to send them to Spain in hopes that they would make some progress under English teachers, but you know he refused to listen to any advice, and there they are still and home they will come without any education. You also know, I presume, that Rector Cameron at Valladolid pressed him repeatedly to recall 'Ruvus' from Spain as an unfit subject for the clerical order, and wrote to him plainly that he would never present him for ordination in Spain. But he obstinately refused to recall him, and now he is on his way home, and will be ordained at Lismore without any examination to add to the number of improper subjects in that District.[20]

In the summer of 1827 Mr Scott paid a visit to Lismore. His report on the college there to Bishop Paterson has unfortunately been lost, but the Bishop's reply leaves little doubt as to its content:

> Your account of Lismore astonishes me. I think the sooner the poor fellows are removed the better . . .[21]

It was not until the college at Blairs opened in 1829 that the Highland students were given an equal education with those of the Lowlands. The old Highland District had never had the resources to found a really satisfactory college. Indeed, given their educational opportunities in Scotland, it is a tribute to the Highland priests that so many of them did satisfactorily in the colleges abroad and came home to be useful priests in the Highlands. Three Highland priests who had been educated at Buorblach, and at Samalaman, went on to become famous bishops in Canada.

NOTES

1 Bishop John Chisholm to Reginald MacDonell, 10th March 1804, Oban Letters, S.C.A.
2 Bishop John Chisholm to Charles Maxwell, 6th February 1804, B.L.
3 Charles Maxwell to Bishop Cameron, 10th June 1805, B.L.
4 Mr Fraser to Charles Maxwell, 30th May 1810, Preshome Letters, S.C.A.
5 Bishop John Chisholm to Bishop Cameron, 23rd September 1811, B.L.
6 Bishop Ranald MacDonald to Bishop Cameron, 15th May 1820, B.L.
7 Bishop John Chisholm to Charles Maxwell, 23rd April 1810, Preshome Letters, S.C.A.
8 Bishop Cameron to Charles Maxwell, 7th July 1806, B.L.

9   Bishop Paterson to Bishop Cameron, scroll letter, 1816, B.L.
10 Bishop John Chisholm to Bishop Cameron, 2nd April 1807, B.L.
11 Bishop Angus Chisholm to Bishop Cameron, 9th August 1814, B.L.
12 Bishop Ranald MacDonald to Bishop Paterson, 5th July 1824, B.L.
13 Quoted in Alexander MacWilliam, "The Highland Seminary at Lismore, 1803-1828", *Innes Review* 1957, p.31.
14 Bishop Angus Chisholm to Bishop Cameron, 26th February 1803, B.L.
15 E.g. Charles Gordon to James Kyle, 9th August 1819, B.L.
16 James MacDonald to Bishop Cameron, 30th October 1820, B.L.
17 John MacPherson to James Gordon, 17th April 1822, B.L.
18 Evan MacEachan to Charles Maxwell, 8th August 1808, B.L.
19 Charles Stuart to Bishop Cameron, 18th May 1814, B.L.
20 Andrew Scott to Bishop Paterson, 24th May 1827, Preshome Letters, S.C.A.
21 Bishop Paterson to Andrew Scott, 24th December 1827, B.L.

R

27

Blairs and the Formation of the Three Vicariates

THE Highland college on Lismore was never very satisfactory. By 1818 even the much larger and better equipped college at Aquhorties in the Lowland Vicariate was being criticised. Its building, which must have seemed so spacious after the small house at Scalan, was no longer large enough to house comfortably the growing number of students. In 1818 Bishop Cameron wrote to Mr Sharp:

> You also want — *and must have* — a Chapel, Library and Refectory.[1]

Although Bishop Cameron kept returning to the subject, no building work was carried out. In 1826 Mr Scott visited Aquhorties on Bishop Paterson's behalf, and reported that the college lacked the proper accommodation to put it on a good footing.[2] In 1827 Mr Badenoch, rector at Aquhorties, wrote to Bishop Paterson:

> ... our vile Chapel affords no accommodation — the Schoolroom floor is mostly worn — holes in some places and so dirty it cannot be cleaned, and the long forms being fastened to the floor cannot be moved.[3]

By this time, however, there was every hope that the college might soon be moved from Aquhorties.

In 1826 Mr Menzies of Pitfoddels, who was by then an old man and in poor health, decided to gift his house and estate of Blairs to the Lowland Vicariate to be used as a college instead of Aquhorties, which he considered to be cold, damp, unhealthy, overcrowded and uncomfortable.[4] He subsequently altered his decision and gifted Blairs to become a college for the Lowland and Highland Vicariate together. Bishop Paterson explained the reason for this decision to Mr Kyle:

> The case runs thus: no matter why, or from what cause, the Highland Mission was almost reduced to a state of starvation for want of education on the part of the students, and want of subsistence on the part of the Missionaries. Mr Menzies, influenced, I believe, to a great degree by the lamentable account given by Eishop MacDonell of Canada, was resolved, tho' a Lowlander, to take them in for their full share of the revenues of Blairs, and of this he informed me when we lived together in France. It struck me at once that a Highland and a Lowland Bishop could vix ac ne vix quidem be expected to agree in respect to all concerns on one common seminary. It struck me that we would have a far better chance of agreeing, if there were three instead of two Apostolic Vicars. It struck me too that our union and harmony would be much more closely cemented if we could break up and abolish the Highland District altogether and give a part of it to the Western and another part to the Northern District. Mr Menzies approved highly of that idea.[5]

In other words, Mr Menzies, seeing the great need of the Highland District, wished it to share equally with the Lowland District in the estate of Blairs. This led to Bishop Paterson's idea of dividing the Mission into three new Vicariates, Western,

Map 3. The Scottish Mission in 1830

Northern and Eastern, in place of the old Highland-Lowland division. In this he had logic on his side. Ever since the Mission had been divided into two Vicariates in 1731, the Highland and Lowland bishops had argued with each other, particularly about finance.

The Scottish Mission had always been short of funds, and it was inevitable that the division of the Mission into two Vicariates should have resulted in competition for available money. In 1734 the Highland priests asked that their Vicariate be allowed to control its own funds, instead of depending on a Lowland-based procurator.[6] Their request was refused on the grounds that such a split would be harmful to the Mission. Abbé MacPherson, in his 'History', made the following comment on this episode:

> Any impartial man must disapprove of the conduct of the Highland clergy through the whole of this business. It was insulting to their great benefactor, Bishop Gordon, who had formerly taken upon himself for the public good, the superintendancy of their money; a charge highly distracting and troublesome, especially to him overloaded with the numerous duties of his character. It was extremely unfair to the Lowlanders. They then and even till of late [i.e. 1794] had no means of procuring the necessaries of life, but the miserable pittance they received from the Mission funds, and that pittance was already greatly inferior to their necessaries and even conveniences of life. The Highland Mission was principally formed at first by Irish Friars; as Irish, and more so as Friars, it can be well supposed they did not fail to exact contributions from their flock. The same custom was religiously observed by the Scots secular Clergy, their successors, nor did it meet with any opposition on the part of the laity, as they saw the justice of it, and felt little or no inconvenience from it. The contributions demanded were in kind, of which there was no scarcity in the Highlands, and for which there was no market because of the little trade or communications with other countries. Hence the Missioners were provided liberally by their people in every article of consumption, and had their 28 crowns to dispose of at pleasure.[7]

Abbé MacPherson was, of course, a Lowland priest. By 1799, as even he had to admit, things had changed:

> Of late years the scene is changed. A very great proportion of the Highland Catholics have emigrated to America, or changed the barren hills of the Highlands for the fruitful plains of the Lowlands; the few still remaining in their native soils find now ready market, and ready money, for any article they can spare. They find also greedy Chieftains and Lairds ready to catch at their miserable superfluities, and nothing is left for the poor clergy. In the Lowlands till of late nothing was demanded and little expected by the Missionary from his people. But now that everything is so increased in value that the Clergy's small allowances cannot possibly procure them the mere necessities of life, their hearers, more in number and better in circumstance than formerly, consider their situation and generously do not refuse assistance.[8]

Abbé MacPherson painted a rosy picture of life in the Highlands in the earlier years of the eighteenth century. Such a picture is not borne out by the facts. Each Highland seminary in turn faltered, if it did not close altogether, for want of cash. After the '45 rebellion many districts of the Highlands were devoid of any priest, sometimes for thirty years, because of the dangers attached to serving them. The Highland priests may have received food from their congregations; they still had to pay for many other necessities such as clothes, vestments, books and, often, lodgings. Their life must have been at least as harsh as that of their Lowland counterparts.

The Abbé's assessment of the lot of a Highland priest at the end of the eighteenth century is more accurate. Bishop Angus Chisholm, writing in 1808, described the financial situation of the Highland Vicariate:

> . . . in the Highlands [the clergy] are certainly at this precious moment in a forlorn situation, for eleven pounds cannot do, and support from their hearers is almost in vain to ask it. The principal laiding Catholic families who used to be their support are now by the rapacity of the great landholders scattered in the four quarters of the globe, and the great Lairds themselves, who used, tho' not of the persuasion, to be of some service, seem now, suadente diabolo no doubt, to take a certain pleasure in seeing the distress of the Catholic body . . . The bulk of the commonalty, who have as yet stuck to their country, seem to be staunch in their creed, but they were never accustomed to touch their purses. Indeed the penurious situation, the pressure of their heavy rents, and the uncertainty of their small-holdings, it puts out of their power to do much . . .[9]

Emigration to America had removed many Catholics from Scotland. Those who remained in the Highlands often did so only because they could not afford to go. These people were in no condition to support their priests.

During the first thirty years or so of the nineteenth century the priests of the Lowland Vicariate built large, handsome churches, installed organs and even, in some areas, built schools and schoolhouses. The priests in the Highlands built only a few modest chapels. They could afford neither organs nor schools. In 1828 Mr MacSween, priest in Strathglass, described his situation:

> I am most disagreeably situated here with regard to a house. The house I occupy is small, uncomfortable, and every way inconvenient; it is fully two miles distant from the chapel . . . and with all that I have to pay the unchristian rent of £8 yearly for this miserable hut and a horse's grass.[10]

In spite of the disadvantages under which the Highland priests laboured, the Lowland District would not allow them to join its Friendly Society.[11] Although one reason for this exclusion was undoubtedly Bishop Cameron's fear that Bishop John Chisholm, a devotee of the Society of Jesus, might filter off Mission funds into that Society, which seemed, in 1807, to be on the brink of restoration, another more obvious reason was that the Lowland priests did not want to see their hard-earned savings being used to help the poorer Highland priests. Highland priests, on the other hand, were most offended at being excluded, seeing their exclusion as a rupture between the Highland and Lowland Vicariates. It was natural that the Highland priests should be offended, especially as the formation of the Friendly Society was accompanied by a change in the regulations governing the election of administrators from each district who met each year to review the Mission's finances. Bishop Angus Chisholm expressed the views of the whole Highland Vicariate when he wrote to Bishop Cameron:

> My own conceptions of affairs are that the Scotch Mission was constituted by the head of the Church as one body and that you both [i.e. Bishops Cameron and John Chisholm] act under him as his vicars with particular spots allocated for you to discharge the duties incumbent on faithful stewards, but that neither of you has or had canonical authority to bring about a separation or disunion without consulting superior authority. The election of ten new administrators without consulting your sister district, since as yet the funds are considered as common, was and is by some called a deviation from the very fundamental rules and regulations of the Scotch Mission. Be that as it will I would not wish you to infer . . . that I am the person that would oppose a division of funds, when brought forward on liberal terms, and when sanctioned by superior canonical authority.[12]

In many ways the Lowland District treated the Highland District as its inferior rather than its equal. Superiors for the Scots Colleges abroad, for instance, were almost invariably chosen from among the Lowland priests, and when, in 1825, Mr Angus MacDonald, a Highland priest, was appointed superior of the Scots College at Rome, many of the Lowland priests protested at the appointment of a Highlander to such an important position.[13]

Administrators' meetings, too, were a bone of contention. They were always held in the North-East, at Huntly, Preshome or Aquhorties. Highland priests, particularly those from the Hebrides, found it both difficult and expensive to attend them, so the Lowland priests, many of whom lived in the North-East, dominated the meetings.[14]

Against such a background of Lowland mistrust of Highlander, and Highland resentment of Lowlander, it is not surprising that Bishop Paterson's plan for the division of the Mission into three Vicariates should have been greeted with horror by all the priests of the Lowland Vicariate. Bishop Paterson saw the proposed new divisions as the only way to eliminate the old Highland-Lowland animosity, by splitting up, and so doing away with, the Highland Vicariate altogether. As he saw it, the Eastern District would be composed of the east coast of Scotland from Dundee to Berwick and west to include Stirlingshire and Kirkcudbrightshire. The Northern District would be composed of Aberdeenshire, Banffshire, Kincardine-shire, Moray and Nairn — all parts of the old Lowland Vicariate — to which would be added Strathglass, Kintail and Inverness-shire as far west as Fort Augustus, from the old Highland Vicariate. The Western District would be composed of Galloway and the West of Scotland north to the Clyde, to which would be added the remainder of the Highland Vicariate: Argyllshire, western Inverness-shire and the Hebrides.[15]

This was not how the proposed divisions were seen by the Lowland priests. They all saw the divisions as giving to the old, impoverished Highland District their newest, most promising and potentially rich Mission stations, those of Glasgow, Paisley, Greenock and the other industrial towns of the South-West. In effect they saw the divisions as a Highland takeover which would rob them of their best stations, a takeover which would be the ruin of those stations because of the incompetence and greed of the Highland priests, and in particular of the Highland Vicar Apostolic, Bishop Ranald MacDonald.

For months the Lowland Vicariate seethed with discontent; almost every single priest of that District penned indignant letters to Bishop Paterson.[16] The latter, however, had obtained approval of his plans from Rome, and the priests of the North-East, although they were unhappy about the plan, agreed at length to bow to Bishop Paterson's episcopal authority. The situation in the South was quite different.

In 1818 Bishop Cameron had written to Bishop Paterson, who was his coadjutor, informing him that he was going to retire and hand over all the Mission's affairs to him, as soon as he had completed his business in Paris.[17] In 1826 Mr William Reid, Mission procurator, who was living in Edinburgh in the same house as Bishop Cameron, admitted that the latter had placed all the

Mission's affairs in Bishop Paterson's hands.[18] By this time, in any case, Bishop Cameron had had a bad stroke, his mind was going, and he was demonstrably incapable of making rational decisions. Bishop Paterson, however, had antagonised Bishop Cameron when he had applied to Rome and been granted full powers without Bishop Cameron's prior knowledge; and once the news of the proposed three Vicariates became public, Bishop Cameron, making use of the fact that few priests knew he had retired, organised a strong resistance to Bishop Paterson and his plan. He was actively supported in this by the two Edinburgh priests, Mr Reid and Mr Bremner, and by the Greenock priest, Mr John Gordon. As a result the Lowland Vicariate was split in two, those in the North supporting Bishop Paterson, and those in the South, with the exception of Mr Andrew Scott, supporting Bishop Cameron.

The contention of the southern faction was that, if there must be three districts, then the Lowland District should be divided into north and south, leaving the Highland District *in statu quo*. There was some logic to this suggestion. The Highlands were still Gaelic-speaking, while the Lowlands — and the Lowland priests — were not. Also there was already a tendency for the priests of the North-East to split off from those of the South-West. This is not surprising; there was little in common between the farmer-priests of the North-East, ministering to their scattered rural congregations, and the priests of the South-West, battling against dirt and disease among the Irish Catholics in the slums of the industrial towns. The North-East priests considered themselves to be an élite in that their congregations had a long, continuous Catholic history. Those in the South-West felt that to them fell the most onerous tasks, while their North-East counterparts received all the glory.

As a result of priests' taking sides behind one or other of the two Bishops, ridiculous disagreements occurred. Bishop Paterson ordered Mr Lee to Banff; Bishop Cameron ordered him to stay in Dundee; Mr Lee resolved to ask Rome which Bishop he should obey.[19] Bishop Paterson ordered Mr Bremner to Huntly and Mr Reid to Dumfries, and both priests refused to move from Edinburgh until specifically ordered to do so from Rome itself.[20] Mr John Gordon went in person to Rome, where he spent several months trying to persuade the Pope and Propaganda that the proposed divisions would spell the ruin of Catholicism in Scotland.[21] Even congregations joined in the fight. A self-styled committee of Edinburgh Catholics lampooned Bishop Paterson for his attempt to remove Mr Reid and Mr Bremner, and even appealed to Rome against their removal.[22]

Ultimately the new divisions of the Mission into Eastern, Western and Northern went ahead as Bishop Paterson had planned. Bishop Paterson became Vicar Apostolic of the Eastern District, and Bishop MacDonald Vicar Apostolic of the Western. Mr James Kyle was consecrated Vicar Apostolic of the Northern District in 1828 and, at the same time, Mr Andrew Scott was consecrated as Bishop MacDonald's coadjutor in the Western District. Bishop Cameron had died six months before these two consecrations took place. It was several years, however, before the ill-feeling generated by this innovation began to fade away, and Bishop Paterson, when he took up residence in Edinburgh, was not accepted by the

Catholics there for quite some time.

While the entire Lowland Vicariate was in a turmoil over the proposed three Vicariates, work was going ahead steadily at Blairs under the supervision of the Aberdeen priest, Mr Charles Gordon. The house at Blairs was altered and enlarged to provide accommodation for about sixty boys. The thousand-odd acres attached to the house were improved by enclosing, draining and fertilising fields. New farm buildings were put up to house the black cattle and also the additional harvest that was expected from the improved land. A playground was laid out, with a 'superb granite wall, for the convenience of ball-playing', two workshops were built, and a 'piece of excellent ground [was] laid out as pleasure gardens for the students'.[23]

In August, 1828 six boys arrived at Aquhorties from the Highland College of Lismore, and on 2nd June, 1829 the move was made to Blairs:

> On the morning of that day the whole Family, superiors and students (the students were, I think, twenty-six in number) came down to Inverury, where they took the Fly-Boat on the Canal to Aberdeen, where, after dining at George Hay's, Queen Street, they arrived about Five o'Clock p.m. in Five Carriages at Blairs.
>
> Most of the Books of the Library of Aquhorties had been sent down beforehand . . . and, along with the Superiors and Students, or at least on the same day that they arrived, Five or Six Carts or Carriages arrived with such Furniture as the house of Aquhorties had to produce. This furniture was, in fact of little value: it was mostly of the common kind, old, and a good deal of it was in a broken state.[24]

Aquhorties became the residence of Mrs Violet Leslie, widow of Leslie of Balquhain who had leased the property to Bishop Hay thirty-two years before. The Mission, however, retained the lease on the farm, which was supervised by one of the priests until the lease was finally given up in 1844.

The move to Blairs symbolised the end of the old order. After a hundred years the old linguistic division of the Scottish Mission had finally given way to a three-way division which took account of the new urban Irish Catholic congregations of the South-West.

Another event of wider import than the opening of Blairs also took place in 1829. At last, after years of negotiation and argument, the Catholic Emancipation Act was passed. Politically speaking Emancipation had been, for the previous twenty years or so, an Irish question. English Catholics had become deeply involved in the negotiations, but the Scottish Mission had played very little part. The Irish Catholics of the South-West, as might be imagined, had been enthusiastic supporters of O'Connell, and had formed Catholic Associations aimed at furthering his cause. Bishop Cameron had occasionally been consulted by the English Catholic Association, and Mr Menzies of Pitfoddels had been deeply involved with the same Association, but judging by their letters, the Scottish priests were little concerned. As Mr James Carruthers put it in a letter he wrote to Mr Sharp in 1828 about his Irish Catholic congregation in Dumfries:

> We have great hopes of Catholic Emancipation even under the premiership of the Duke of Wellington. It is a desirable event even tho' it will make little difference to you and me.[25]

In 1829 one of the oldest students at Aquhorties wrote to his parents:

> The Emancipation or Catholic relief bill which you mention and of which you wish to know my

opinion is one of the most useful, just and beneficial measures which could possibly be devised. Without passing this bill, England was incapable of engaging in war because all her forces were required to keep discontented, justly discontented Ireland in allegiance; but now that the measure is passed, in the event of a war, England can not only employ all her own troops but will find many a gallant Irish soldier who will voluntarily offer himself to fight her battles . . . It would be necessary to picture to you the state and condition of Ireland to show you all the beneficial effects which the bill will produce, but let it suffice to say that no measure except the present could ever have been acceptable or beneficial to Ireland, or could have paved the way to redeem that unhappy country from misery, beggary and starvation.[26]

As far as the Scottish priests were concerned, Catholic emancipation was a just and long-overdue measure, but they felt detached from the issues. When emancipation was being discussed in Parliament, they were far more concerned about the question of dividing the Scottish Mission into three Vicariates.

The Bill, when it was passed, allowed Catholics who took the prescribed oath to vote and to sit in Parliament on the same terms as Protestants; to hold, with certain exceptions, civil and military appointments under the Crown; and to become members of lay corporations. Scottish Jesuits were allowed to return to Scotland. Other religious orders were still prohibited — but this clause was quietly ignored. The Act did not change the status quo regarding universities.[27]

As far as the Scottish priests themselves were concerned, they were forbidden to sit in the House of Commons, so only two sections of the Act were immediately relevant to them. The clause concerning lay corporations was of particular importance as it allowed the Scottish Mission to own property in its own name as a corporation, rather than in the names of individuals. The clause concerning universities has often been wrongly interpreted. It did not, as Sister Dealy has stated,[28] prohibit Catholics from attending English and Scottish universities, although it did prohibit Catholics from becoming professors in them. As far as students were concerned, the Act allowed universities to carry on as before or to amend their regulations as they saw fit. Oxford and Cambridge had previously excluded Catholics by their insistence on all students taking an anti-Catholic oath. The Act did nothing to alter this situation. In Scotland Catholics had always attended the universities although they had not been permitted to graduate. They were as free to attend these universities after 1829 as before. In 1828 a practising Jew was allowed to graduate from Edinburgh University without taking the customary oaths.[29] It is likely that Catholics were extended the same courtesy.

Only a small number of Scottish Catholics were affected by the political clauses of the Emancipation Act, because of the very limited franchise then obtaining. It was not until the Reform Act of 1832 broadened the franchise that more than a tiny percentage of Scottish Catholics were given the right to vote. Perhaps this is one reason why only the Irish Catholics in Scotland had been deeply committed to the fight for emancipation.

NOTES

1 Bishop Cameron to James Sharp, 2nd April 1818, Preshome Letters, S.C.A.
2 Andrew Scott to Bishop Paterson, 10th April 1826, Preshome Letters, S.C.A.
3 Alexander Badenoch to Bishop Paterson, 15th May 1827, Preshome Letters, S.C.A.

4 Mr Menzies to Bishop Kyle, 3rd December 1828, Preshome Letters, S.C.A.

5 Bishop Paterson to James Kyle, 8th May 1827, Preshome Letters, S.C.A.

6 Abbé MacPherson's continuation of Thomson's 'History', Vol II, under 1734.

7 *Ibid.*, pp. 56-60.

8 *Ibid.*, p. 60.

9 Bishop Angus Chisholm to Bishop Cameron, 22nd March 1808, B.L.

10 Alexander MacSween to Bishop Kyle, 29th October 1828, Preshome Letters, S.C.A.

11 E.g. Bishop John Chisholm to Bishop Cameron, 18th July 1810, B.L.

12 Bishop Angus Chisholm to Bishop Cameron, 14th December 1809, Preshome Letters, S.C.A.

13 Bishop Cameron to James Kyle (under 'Reid'), 17th March 1826, B.L.

14 Norman MacDonald to Charles Maxwell, 21st October 1809, Preshome Letters, S.C.A.

15 Bishop Ranald MacDonald to Bishop Paterson, 18th June 1827, Preshome Letters, S.C.A.

16 E.g. James Kyle to Bishop Paterson, scroll letter, May 1827, Kyle Letters, B.L.

17 Bishop Cameron to Bishop Paterson, 28th August 1818, Preshome Letters, S.C.A.

18 Mr Reid to Bishop Paterson, 21st April 1826, Preshome Letters, S.C.A.

19 Constantine Lee [to?], 5th November 1827, B.L.

20 Bishop Paterson to Bishop Kyle, 12th December 1828, Preshome Letters, S.C.A.

21 Angus MacDonald to Andrew Scott, 10th November 1827, B.L.

22 Bishop Paterson to James Gordon, 20th October 1828, Preshome Letters, S.C.A.

23 Charles Gordon, 'Memorial Concerning Blairs', 15th July 1835, pp. 9-10, S.C.A.

24 Charles Gordon, 'Memorial Concerning Blairs', 15th July 1835, pp. 10-11.

25 James Carruthers to James Sharp, 17th March 1828, Preshome Letters, S.C.A.

26 John Geddes to his parents, 28th April 1829, Preshome Letters, S.C.A.

27 *Statutes at Large*, Vol. II, George IV, 10 George IV, especially p. 695.

28 Sister Mary Bonaventure Dealy, *Catholic Schools in Scotland* (Washington D.C., 1945), p. 123.

29 D.B. Horn, *A Short History of the University of Edinburgh, 1556-1889*, (Edinburgh, 1967), p. 151.

Conclusion

FOLLOWING the Reformation of 1560 the Roman Catholic faith was proscribed in Scotland. Acts of Parliament condemning "popery" culminated in the Penal Acts of 1700 which spelt out in detail the penalties for adhering to Catholicism. Not only were Catholics banned from practising their faith, but they were prohibited from teaching even Catholic children, and they risked losing their property to their nearest Protestant relatives. But in spite of their harshness the Penal Laws failed to stamp out Catholicism in Scotland. They failed politically because a number of powerful families, notably the Dukes of Gordon, remained Catholic and protected their Catholic tenants against persecution. They failed ecclesiastically because of internal dissensions between Protestants. Throughout most of the seventeenth century Episcopalianism vied with Presbyterianism for the government of the Established Church of Scotland. Because of this struggle neither form of protestantism was capable of mustering sufficient strength to take over all of the Gaelic-speaking West Highlands, and part of that area remained resolutely Catholic for almost two hundred years after the Reformation had taken place. In 1764, for example, Bishop MacDonald reported to Propaganda that Moidart and South Morar were still entirely Catholic and Arisaig almost entirely so.[1]

Catholicism in the Highlands did, however, suffer after 1689 for political reasons. In 1689 Catholic James VII fled to France. For the next sixty years in Scotland Catholicism, like Episcopalianism, was equated with Jacobitism. Nor is this inexplicable. Scottish Catholics from 1700 onwards had virtually no legal rights and saw, in the restoration of the Stewarts, their only hope of obtaining a repeal of the Penal Laws against them. In the years after the defeat of the '45 Rebellion it became obvious that the Stewart cause was a hopeless one, and with the death of Prince Charles in 1788 Jacobitism receded rapidly into the realm of historical romance. After 1788 the only surviving royal Stewart was Prince Henry, Cardinal Duke of York, and by 1794 even he was on friendly terms with the House of Hanover. In 1799 the British Government granted the Cardinal Duke a life pension of £4,000 per annum. The dynastic claims of the senior stem of the royal Stewarts were thus finally abandoned.

Even before the death of Prince Charles, Scottish Catholics were demonstrating their loyalty to the House of Hanover by enlisting in the army for foreign service, in spite of the fact that, in order to do so, they had to take an anti-Catholic oath. By 1764 an estimated 6,000 Scottish Catholics were serving mainly in the East and

West Indies. It was because of the fighting potential of the Highland Catholics that the question of repealing the Penal Laws was first raised in the House of Commons, in 1770, by General Burgoyne. Although nothing came of this attempt, the subject was again raised in 1778 when Sir John Dalrymple questioned Bishop Hay as to the loyalty of Scottish Catholics, and their willingness to serve in America, should the Penal Laws be repealed. The ultimate outcome of Dalrymple's enquiries was, ironically, the passing in 1778 of the first English Catholic Relief Act. A second English Relief Act followed in 1791. Irish Relief Acts were passed in 1778, 1782 and 1792. Finally in 1793 Scotland received its first Relief Act, by which Catholics were secured in their property and were permitted to worship freely so long as they took an oath of loyalty to the Hanoverian government. In practice Scottish Catholics, generally speaking, had been able to worship freely for many years before 1793, so in this respect the Act was an acknowledgement of an existing situation. The clause concerning property was of immediate relevance, application for a Scottish Relief Bill having been precipitated by a threat to the property of Maxwell of Munshes by his nearest Protestant heir.

The tardiness in passing the Scottish Relief Act was due partly to the anti-Catholic riots which had broken out in 1779 in various towns throughout Scotland. It was also probably due in part to the relative unimportance of Scottish Catholics. In Ireland the situation was quite different: there most of the population were Catholic and so the Penal Laws applied not, as in Scotland, to a small minority, but to almost everyone. At the same time Irish Catholics were forced to pay tithes to an established Anglican Church. In short, religion in Ireland was inseparable from politics, a fact which was crucial when the question of Catholic emancipation came to be raised in the early nineteenth century. In England too, although Catholics made up only a small minority of the population, they included in their number powerful and wealthy men whose political influence could not be ignored. In Scotland, however, in the eighteenth century, the vast majority of Catholics were impoverished tenant farmers and farm labourers living in fairly remote areas. By 1789, of the landed families, only the Earl of Traquair, and a few lairds in Galloway and the North-East, remained Catholic. Of these lairds, only Menzies of Pitfoddels backed the Scottish Mission financially to any significant extent. For these reasons Scottish Catholics, with a few exceptions, were, in the early nineteenth century, to play little part in the struggle for emancipation. It was left to the Irish Catholic immigrants to the industrial West to embrace the cause of their compatriot, O'Connell. It was in Ireland that the political implications of emancipation were a burning issue.

The death of Prince Charles Edward Stewart in 1788 purged Scottish Catholics of the last taint of Jacobitism; the French Revolution which broke out in the following year cemented their allegiance to the House of Hanover and brought about a political alliance between the British Government and the Vatican.

The French Revolution began in 1789. In 1790 the Revolutionary Government ended Papal jurisdiction over the Catholic Church in France, converting it into a state Church controlled by government departments. In August 1792 all priests who refused to conform to the new regime were ordered to leave France within eight days. Many found their way to Britain. Many more French Catholics, laymen as well as priests, followed after the Paris massacres of September 1792. In 1793 Britain declared war on France. In the same year the Pope appealed to the British government for protection in the face of the French threat to Rome. The British fleet was despatched to Italy and cordial relations were established between the Vatican and the Court of St James. Sir John Cox Hippisley was sent to Rome as agent of the British government and the Pope sent Cardinal Erskine to London as his unofficial ambassador.

This new amity between the British Government and the Vatican was reflected on a domestic level within Britain itself in government grants to the French émigré refugees, priests as well as laymen; in grants to the Irish Catholic college at Maynooth; and, finally, in a grant to the impoverished Scottish Mission.

After the Reformation the Roman Catholic Church lost all its property in Scotland, except in remote areas where the reformed faith failed to penetrate. More important, the whole structure of the Church disintegrated, with no bishop remaining in Scotland to co-ordinate the efforts of the priests who stayed on, or to consecrate new chapels or bestow the sacrament of confirmation on Catholic children. Throughout the seventeenth century the survival of Catholicism in Lowland Scotland depended on the protection of powerful individuals like the Dukes of Gordon who maintained priests as chaplains in their households and protected their tenants from the severest effects of the Penal Laws. In the West Highlands, where there was little pressure from the Protestant churches, Irish Franciscan priests did much to keep Catholicism alive, and even in areas which did not have the benefit of these priests many people remained Catholic in spirit even when they received no instruction in their faith. But by 1700 there were only two main regions where Catholicism continued in strength: Banffshire in the North-East and a large area of Inverness-shire in the West. Outwith these areas there remained small pockets of Catholics in Edinburgh and Aberdeen, and on the estates of Traquair, Stobhall, Munshes, Terregles and Kirkconnell.

In 1694 Catholicism in Scotland was reinforced with the appointment by Propaganda of Bishop Nicolson as the first Vicar Apostolic of the Scottish Mission. Bishop Nicolson had powers to control the regular clergy operating in Scotland and to consecrate more secular priests to augment the few already on the Mission. He was also able to revive the faith in many areas by providing them with priests and by reintroducing the sacrament of confirmation after a gap of over a hundred years.

Although Bishop Nicolson's consecration represented a significant break-through, there still remained the problem of language: over half of the Catholics in Scotland spoke only Gaelic, while most of the priests were not native Gaelic speakers. This problem was solved in 1731 when the Scottish Mission was divided into two Vicariates, Highland and Lowland, and Hugh MacDonald was consecrated as the first Highland Vicar Apostolic. The success of this appointment was apparent by 1747 when the first Highland boys selected by Bishop MacDonald to train for the priesthood arrived home ordained from the colleges abroad.

Throughout the first half of the eighteenth century ministers of the Church of Scotland made strenuous attempts to have the Penal Laws against Catholics rigidly enforced. In this, however, they were largely unsuccessful. Only when Jacobite rebellions occurred, converting Catholicism from a religious to a political threat, did the Scottish Mission suffer materially from government action. It was in the aftermath of Culloden that the Mission received its severest setback when many of its chapels were looted and burned and a number of priests, Highland for the most part, were forced into exile in France. So severe was this setback to the Highland Vicariate that several of its mission stations remained without a priest for the next thirty years. The Lowland Vicariate was quicker to recover. As Jacobitism ceased to be a political threat, government pressure on Catholics relaxed and the Vicariate began to regain its lost ground. By 1790 all the chapels which had been destroyed in 1746 had either been rebuilt or replaced by other premises nearby. In 1789 several priests, among them, significantly, the priest stationed in Edinburgh, were petitioning to be allowed to introduce singing in their chapels. Such confidence was the result of a growing spirit of toleration among the Moderates within the Church of Scotland, a spirit which was acknowledged in the passage of the Scottish Relief Act in 1793.

By the end of the eighteenth century some of the Highland priests were tenants of small farms where they were able to supplement their salaries by growing a few crops and keeping a cow or two. Others were still forced to board with members of their congregations, an unsatisfactory state of affairs as it left these priests with little privacy. By 1830 all the Highland priests had their own houses, leased from local landowners, but often these houses were little more than hovels, uncomfortable and inconvenient. Poverty prevented the Vicariate from obtaining better houses because, between 1770 and 1830, almost all of the better-off Catholics had emigrated to North America, while many of the poorer had migrated to the industrial towns further south. At a time when the overall Highland population was rising, the Catholic population fell dramatically.

Throughout the eighteenth century most of the Lowland priests were concentrated in the North-East. The number of chaplaincies, which had been crucial to the continuance of Catholicism in the seventeenth century, gradually dwindled throughout the eighteenth and early nineteenth centuries until by 1830 only Traquair remained. The place of these chaplaincies was generally taken by small farms where the priests lived, saying mass for their congregations in converted barns. The few priests who served towns rather than country areas lived in houses of which one floor was converted to provide a chapel. By the beginning of the nineteenth century chaplaincies, small farms and town houses alike were gradually being replaced by purpose-built churches with adjoining priests' houses. Several reasons lay behind the move towards purpose-built churches. In the North-East an increase in the Catholic population was occasionally a contributory factor, but far more prevalent was the desire of Catholics to present a respectable face by worshipping in chapels which were as imposing architecturally as neighbouring Protestant churches.

In the cities and industrial towns of Scotland new chapels were not so much a matter of prestige as of necessity. In Glasgow, for instance, between 1786 and 1822 the number of Catholics rose from about seventy to over fifteen thousand. In 1822, by comparison, there were only about twelve hundred Catholics in Glenlivet. This phenomenal increase in the number of Catholics in Glasgow was repeated throughout industrial Renfrewshire and Ayrshire, and was brought about by a growing tide of immigrants arriving from Ireland in search of employment. It was the tide of Irish Catholic immigrants, more than anything else, which altered the pattern of Catholicism in Scotland, not only because of the sheer weight of numbers, but because the immigrants formed an urban slum population quite different in outlook, temperament and religious tradition from the indigenous Catholics of the Highlands and the North-East. These differences led ultimately to a clash of interests within the Mission itself. The general public, on the other hand, came gradually to equate Catholicism with Irish nationality. Such an equation was erroneous on two counts: firstly because as many of the immigrants were Protestant as were Catholic, and secondly because a strong tradition of Catholicism continued unbroken in areas of Scotland like the North-East. It was a persuasive equation, however, and its legacy is exemplified today in the rival support given to the Rangers and Celtic football teams.

The growing Irish Catholic population in Scotland meant heavy demands on the Scottish Mission for chapels and for priests. The Mission was therefore forced to rethink its financial policies. Traditionally Scottish priests had received their salaries from the Quota Fund, which consisted partly of an annual allowance from Propaganda and partly of interest from bequests of money which the Mission had invested, some in the Bank of Scotland and some in the Paris funds. Congregations were not asked to pay anything towards the support of their priests. From the Quota Fund country priests were paid about £10 a year and town priests about £15.

By 1793, due to the French Revolution, the Mission had lost all the money it had invested in the Paris funds, and town priests' salaries had been reduced to £10. In 1798 the progress of the French Revolution ended the Mission's allowance from Propaganda. All that remained were funds invested in the Bank of Scotland. A temporary relief was obtained when the British Government agreed to provide an annual grant which would give each priest £20. The first instalment of the grant was paid in 1799; the grant finally petered out with the 1803 instalment which was not paid until 1805.

In any case, by 1805 most of the priests and many of the congregations of the West and South-West considered £50 to be a minimum salary. In the North-East a priest could augment his income by farming and by teaching foreign languages; in the industrial South-West neither of these alternatives was feasible and a priest had to depend completely on his salary. There was no way the Quota Fund could meet such high demands, and so other methods of raising the necessary money had to be found.

Nor was it only for salaries that the money had to be found but also for the new, very large chapels that were needed in places like Glasgow and Paisley. It had long been the custom for better-off Catholics to pay seat-rent for their chapel pews.

Now in the industrial West the renting of seats became, if not obligatory, at least strongly urged. It was seat-rents and Sunday collections which largely paid for St Andrew's Chapel — later Cathedral — in Glasgow.

The French Revolution had caused the Scottish Mission to lose much of its traditional income; it was the demands made by Irish immigration which forced the Mission to turn to its congregations and place on them the responsibility of paying for their priests and chapels.

Much the same pattern of influence can be seen in educational development within the Scottish Mission. From the Reformation until 1714 Scottish priests received all but the most elementary schooling on the Continent, at the Scots Colleges of Paris, Douay, Rome and Madrid, or in the Benedictine monasteries at Ratisbon and Wurzburg. In 1714 these colleges were supplemented for the first time by a seminary in Scotland, a tiny establishment founded by Bishop Gordon on an island in Loch Morar. A year later the Loch Morar seminary was forced to close when soldiers were stationed throughout the Highlands after the failure of the 1715 Rebellion. It reopened almost immediately at Scalan in the Braes of Glenlivet, and remained there from 1716 until 1799, preparing boys for the colleges abroad and even training a few completely itself. One priest who received all his training at Scalan was Hugh MacDonald who, in 1731, was consecrated as the first Highland Vicar Apostolic.

After 1732 Scalan became the seminary for the Lowland Vicariate, Bishop MacDonald having founded a Highland seminary on the site of the very first little establishment on Loch Morar. Scalan had an almost continuous history for over eighty years; the Highland seminary was less fortunate. Dogged by financial problems, it had a chequered existence at Loch Morar (1732–c1738), Guidal (c1738-1746), Glenfinnan (1768-1770), Buorblach (1770-1774, 1776-1779) and finally at Samalaman (1783-1803).

By 1793 the Scots Colleges at Paris and at Douay had been forced to close, and the Scottish Mission was faced with the necessity of providing alternative colleges in Scotland. The situation became even more urgent with the closure of the Rome college in 1798. Initially both the Scots and the English bishops had hoped that they might be able to claim compensation, through the British Government, for the losses they had sustained in France. The Napoleonic Wars, however, shelved all thought of compensation until 1815. In 1825 the Privy Council finally rejected the English claim for compensation and, as a result, the Scottish bishops abandoned all hope of reimbursement from that quarter.

Even without having received any compensation Bishop Hay had, in 1794, considered purchasing the farm of Oxhill as a site for his proposed new college. After mature consideration, however, he discarded the idea of Oxhill, settling two years later, in 1796, for a ninety-nine year lease of the estate of Aquhorties, near Inverurie. For thirty years Aquhorties served as a college for the Lowland Vicariate. Indeed, for eight years, it was the Vicariate's only college, the Napoleonic Wars having at length closed even the Scots College at Valladolid. Bishop Cameron refused almost without exception to allow any Irish priest to serve in his Vicariate, and so Aquhorties trained only one boy of Irish descent for the priesthood. It was, however, the presence of so many Irish Catholics in Scotland which ensured that, even though most of the Continental colleges had reopened by 1829, more and more Scottish priests in the future would complete all their training in colleges within Scotland, as the colleges abroad could no longer provide nearly enough places to serve the growing demands of the Mission.

It had been the hope of John Chisholm, the then Vicar Apostolic of the Highland District, that Aquhorties could be made into a large enough college to serve the Highlands as well as the Lowlands. This, however, Bishop Hay refused to consider, and Bishop Chisholm was thrown back on his own resources. In 1803 he opened a Highland College at Kilcheran on the Island of Lismore. The Lismore College lacked the resources of its counterpart of Aquhorties and, although it produced many excellent priests, it was never really adequate for the needs of the Highland district. Not until 1829 were Highland and Lowland put on a par. In that year, thanks to the generosity of Menzies of Pitfoddels, a new college opened at Blairs in Aberdeenshire, a college which was to replace both Lismore and Aquhorties, providing excellent facilities for an increased number of students. At the same time the old Highland and Lowland Vicariates, with all their long-standing frictions and jealousies, were swept away, to be replaced by three new Vicariates, Northern, Eastern and Western, which acknowledged the changes that had taken place over the previous forty years in the distribution of Catholics throughout Scotland.

Although much attention was always paid by the Scottish Mission to the education of Catholic boys intended for the priesthood, surprisingly little was paid to the education of lay Catholics until well into the nineteenth century — surprising, that is, when one considers the emphasis placed today on educating Catholic children in Catholic schools. True, there were, before 1745, a few small Catholic schools tucked away in remote glens, but these schools catered for only a handful of children. Generally speaking, priests and parents alike were happy to see Catholic children educated at Protestant schools so long as they were not forced to learn Protestant doctrine; and the Protestant schools, perhaps moved in part by financial considerations, were happy to co-operate. Between 1770 and 1829 one or two country priests attempted to set up Catholic schools in their areas, but, of these, only the two opened in 1824 by Mr Badenoch, priest at Preshome, survived for any length of time. It was in the cities that Catholic schools were first established, and not in the country areas. The reason for this is clear: in the cities the old system, under which each parish was obliged to provide a school and schoolmaster, broke down when the population grew too large. This was particularly true of the industrial towns in the West. Catholic schools had been founded by priests in Aberdeen and Edinburgh before 1800, and in Glasgow, Paisley and Greenock by 1829. These schools were set up to cater specifically for the urban poor and not for Catholics well enough off to be able to send their sons to schools like Edinburgh's Royal High School. In other words, they were founded to meet an educational rather than a religious demand. Indeed, particularly in the West, the success of the Catholic schools owed much to the financial assistance of well-to-do Protestants. In return for Protestant help the priests were happy to

S

agree to the condition that they use the Protestant King James translation of the Bible in their schools.

In conclusion, it may be said that the French Revolution had an immediate impact on the Scottish Mission, but that many of its effects were only temporary. True it promoted toleration for Catholics in Britain; it forced the Scottish Mission to open colleges in Scotland, and to look to its congregations to support their priests, and it finally healed the breach between Scottish Catholics and the British Government. On the other hand, the closure of the colleges abroad was only temporary, as was the loss of an income from Propaganda.

Irish immigration, however, permanently changed the whole pattern of Catholicism in Scotland. By 1829 Irish Catholics were numerically greater than indigenous Scottish Catholics. The industrial South-West replaced the rural Highlands and North-East as the main concentration of Catholics, and Catholicism began to develop racial connotations. It was the flood of Irish Catholic immigrants that promoted the founding by priests of large schools, the financing of priests from seat-rents and collections instead of from the old Quota Fund, and the building of very large purpose-built chapels. Today Catholicism in Scotland is an urban rather than a rural phenomenon, and Catholics of Irish descent dominate the Roman Catholic Church of Scotland.

NOTE

1 R. MacDonald, "The Highland District in 1764", *Innes Review* 1964, p. 148.

Bibliography

Sources

THIS book is largely based on the study of the extensive collections of letters and documents which are housed in the Scottish Catholic Archives in Columba House, Edinburgh. For the period 1789 to 1829, approximately 20,000 such letters survive. These collections are particularly valuable in that they contain many virtually complete series of letters, such as the correspondence between Bishop Hay and Bishop Geddes, and the correspondence between Bishop Cameron in Edinburgh and Mr James Sharp at Aquhorties. Almost all the letters which were written to the bishops of the Lowland Vicariate have survived. These include letters from France, Rome and Valladolid, letters from Government Ministers and queries, complaints and comments from individual priests on the Mission. Even the most unpleasant anonymous letters to the bishops have been carefully preserved. Only those letters which referred to private matters such as queries concerning the confessional were deliberately destroyed by the bishops.

Other important letters which survive include those written by Scottish priests to the successive Scots agents at Rome. These letters are full of news and gossip about the Scottish Mission. Of equal importance as source material are the copy letters of correspondence between the bishops and men such as Henry Dundas, Viscount Melville. Such copy letters were always preserved for future reference, and are of great value in tracing negotiations between the Scottish Mission and the British Government.

Finally there are the letters exchanged by individual priests. A sufficient number of priests preserved the letters they received to make this source particularly interesting. A priest was removed from his family at about the age of twelve. His education and his vocation from that time onwards ensured that it would be among his fellow priests that he would find his closest friends. Many such close friendships can be discovered, as, for instance, between Mr John Farquharson and Abbé MacPherson. As such friends were often stationed at considerable distances one from another, they relied on letters to keep in contact, and these letters are full of personal details about their lives as Mission priests.

Letters are a valuable source in that they describe events as they occur. They also reflect the enthusiasms, opinions and prejudices of individuals. They do, however, leave tantalising gaps. For instance, very few letters written by Highland priests have survived. It is sometimes difficult to fill such gaps. The Scottish Catholic Archives contain a number of contemporary memoirs which are helpful. Some of this material derives from the Scots Colleges abroad. Of particular national interest are the 'Memoirs' of James VII, although unfortunately the original manuscript from which these memoirs were compiled, and which was kept in the archives of the Scots College in Paris, was destroyed during the French Revolution. Of less national interest, but of importance in the study of the history of the Scottish Mission, is material that has been compiled in the archives of the different Scots Colleges by priests stationed there. Of particular note are the works of two of the Scottish Agents in Rome. The 'History of the Scottish Mission' was begun by Mr Thomson in 1789 and was continued by his successor, Abbé MacPherson. It makes extensive use of archive material and, so long as the anti-Jesuit prejudice is discounted, it is an extremely valuable source. Abbé MacPherson has also provided us with a 'History of the Scots College, Rome', as well as accounts and comments concerning contemporary events. Other priests, although less prolific writers than the Abbé, have copied material from foreign archives which they felt might interest friends at home.

For the period from 1750 onwards a useful secondary work is Stothert's 'Life of Bishop Hay', printed in J.F.S. Gordon's *Journal and Appendix to Scotichronicon and Monasticon*. This work is based on the Blairs collection of letters in the Scottish Catholic Archives, and contains much valuable material. It is, however, limited in that it provides only a chronological digest of those letters which immediately concern Bishop Hay's life.

The resources of the Scottish Catholic Archives, which were for many years inaccessible to the general public, contain a vast amount of largely untapped source material. It is on this material that my book is based.

I. Manuscript Sources and Unpublished Material

1. The Blairs Letters (B.L.); Scottish Catholic Archives (S.C.A.). The Blairs Letters include the "Kyle Letters".
2. The Preshome Letters, S.C.A.
3. The Oban Letters, S.C.A.
4. "Folder of manuscript including Aquhorties material", S.C.A.
5. Folder: "Some Letters Relating to Scotch Colleges" — includes various Rules for Scalan, S.C.A.
6. Aquhorties Account Books, some of which include registers of students, S.C.A.
7. Charles Gordon, "Memorial Concerning Blairs", 15th July 1835, S.C.A.
8. Abbé Paul MacPherson, "Account of the Mission of Scotland: Memoirs for the end of 1792 and the whole of 1793", S.C.A.
9. John Thomson, "A History of the Scottish Mission", continued by Abbé MacPherson — the whole bound into two manuscript volumes (Thomson, and MacPherson's continuation of Thomson).
10. "Register of the Actings and Proceedings of the Committee of the General Assembly of the Church of Scotland for Reformation of the Highlands and Islands of Scotland and for the management of the King's Bounty for that end," Register House CH/5/51.
11. James Kennedy Robertson, "The Life and Times of James Kyle, D.D., Vicar Apostolic of the Northern District", typescript, S.C.A.
12. Alexander MacWilliam, "Aquhorties", typescript, S.C.A.
13. *Regulations for the Administration of the College of Aquhorties*, printed by Moir, Edinburgh, 1799, S.C.A. (printed book but very rare).

II. Printed Source Material

1. *Acts of the Parliaments of Scotland*, edited by T. Thomson and C. Innes, Vols. 10 and 12 (Edinburgh, 1823 and 1875).

2. *Statutes at Large*, Vol. 16 (London, 1794).

3. *State Trials*, editied by T.B. and T.S. Howell, Vol. XXIV (London, 1809-1828).

4. *Scotland's Opposition to the Popish Bill: A Collection of all the Declarations and Resolutions . . . Against the Proposed Repeal of the Statutes . . . for Preventing the Growth of Popery* (Edinburgh, 1780).

5. *List of Popish Parents and Their Children in Various Districts of Scotland as given to the Lords of the Privy Council and to the Commission of the General Assembly 1701-5*, Maitland Club *Miscellany*, Vol. III, Part II (Edinburgh, 1843).

6. William Forbes Leith, *Memoirs of Scottish Catholics during the XVIIth and XVIIIth Centuries* (London, 1909).

7. *Report on the Laing Manuscripts, University of Edinburgh*, Historical Manuscripts Commission, HMSO (London, 1925).

8. *The New Statistical Account of Scotland* (Edinburgh, 1845).

9. *The Catholic Directory for Scotland* (Edinburgh and Dundee, 1831-1835).

10. *Scottish Population Statistics, including Webster's Analysis of Population 1755*, edited by J.G. Kyd (Edinburgh, 1975).

11. W.J. Anderson, ed., "The College for the Lowland District of Scotland at Scalan and Aquhorties: Registers and Documents," *Innes Review*, 1963.

12. "The Autobiographical Notes of Bishop John Geddes", edited by W.J. Anderson, *Innes Review*, 1967.

13. "Ambula Coram Deo: The Journal of Bishop Geddes for the year 1790", edited by W.J. Anderson, David MacRoberts (two parts), *Innes Review*, 1955.

14. Abbé Paul MacPherson, "History of the Scots College, Rome", edited by W.J. Anderson, *Innes Review*, 1961.

15. "Records of the Scots Colleges at Douay, Rome, Madrid, Valladolid and Ratisbon, Vol. I, Registers of Students", New Spalding Club (Aberdeen, 1906).

16. "The 'Encrease of Popery' in the Highlands, 1714-1747", Presbyterian documents edited by Noel MacDonald Wilby, *Innes Review*, 1966.

III. Secondary Works: Books

1. *The Catholic Encyclopaedia* (London, 1911).

2. Peter Anson, *Underground Catholicism in Scotland* (Montrose, 1970).

3. Alphons Bellesheim, *History of the Catholic Church in Scotland*, translated by David Hunter Blair (Edinburgh, 1840).

4. Dom Odo Blundell, *The Catholic Highlands of Scotland*, two Vols. (Edinburgh and London, 1909, 1917).

5. Henry Cockburn, *Memorials of his Time* (Edinburgh and London, 1910).

6. John Davidson, *Inverurie and the Earldom of Garioch*, Edinburgh, 1878.

7. Sister Mary Bonaventure Dealy, *Catholic Schools in Scotland* (Washington DC, 1945).

8. Mark Dilworth, *The Scots in Franconia* (Edinburgh, 1974).

9. Gordon Donaldson, *The Scottish Reformation* (Cambridge, 1960).

10. Gordon Donaldson, *Scotland: James V-James VII* (Edinburgh, 1971).

11. William Ferguson, *Scotland: 1689 to the Present* (Edinburgh, 1968).

12. Franklin L. Ford, *Europe 1780-1830* (London, 1976).

13. W.M. Gloag and R. Candlish Henderson, *Introduction to the Law of Scotland*, 6th edition (Edinburgh, 1956).

14. J.F.S. Gordon, *The Book of the Chronicles of Keith* (Glasgow, 1880).

15. J.F.S. Gordon, *Journal and Appendix to Scotichronicon and Monasticon* (Glasgow, 1867) — includes Stothert's "Life of Bishop Hay" — (*Scotichronicon*).

16. James Handley, *The Irish in Scotland, 1798-1845* (Cork, 1943).
17. James Handley, *Scottish Farming in the 18th Century* (London, 1953).
18. Sir Paul Harvey, *The Oxford Companion to English Literature*, 4th edition (Oxford, 1967).
19. M.V. Hay, *The Blairs Papers, 1603-1660* (Edinburgh and London, 1929).
20. D.B. Horn, *A Short History of the University of Edinburgh* (Edinburgh, 1967).
21. Kathleen Hughes, *The Church in Early Irish Society* (London, 1966).
22. Dr Samuel Johnson, *Journey to the Western Islands of Scotland* (Oxford, 1970).
23. Edith Mary Johnston, *Ireland in the Eighteenth Century* (Dublin, 1974).
24. Tom Johnston, *A History of the Working Classes in Scotland*, 4th edition (Glasgow, 1946).
25. Calum MacLean, *The Highlands* (Inverness, 1975).
26. David Milburn, *A History of Ushaw College* (Durham, 1964).
27. H.W. Meikle, *Scotland and the French Revolution* (London, 1969).
28. *Munroe's Western Isles of Scotland and Genealogies of the Clans*, ed. R.W. Munro (Edinburgh, 1961).
29. Gearoid o' Tuathaigh, *Ireland before the Famine* (Dublin, 1972).
30. John Ritchie, *Reflections on Scottish Church History* (Edinburgh and London, 1927).
31. James Robertson, *Narrative of a Secret Mission to the Danish Islands in 1808*, ed. Alex. C. Fraser (London, 1863).
32. Bernard Ward, *The Dawn of the Catholic Revival in England, 1781-1803* (London, 1909).
33. Bernard Ward, *The Eve of Catholic Emancipation* (London, 1911).

IV. Secondary Works: Articles and Pamphlets
1. Margaret Adam, "The Highland Emigration of 1770", *Scottish Historical Review (SHR)* xvi, (Aberdeen, 1919).
2. Margaret Adam, "The Causes of the Highland Emigrations of 1783-1803", *SHR* xvii, 1920.
3. W.J. Anderson, "The Edinburgh Highland Chapel and the Reverend Robert Menzies", *Innes Review (IR)*, (Glasgow, 1966).
4. W.J. Anderson, "Some Notes on Catholic Education for Scottish Children in Pre-Emancipation Days", *IR*, 1963.
5. W.J. Anderson, "David Downie and the 'Friends of the People'", *IR*, 1965.
6. P.F. Anson, "Catholic Church Building in Scotland from the Reformation until the Outbreak of the First World War", *IR*, 1954.
7. James Darragh, "Bishop Andrew Scott", Catholic Truth Society of Scotland, (Glasgow, 1946).
8. James Darragh, "The Catholic Population of Scotland since the year 1680", *IR*, 1853.
9. F. Forbes and W.J. Anderson, "Clergy Lists of the Highland District, 1732-1828", *IR*, 1966.
10. Roderick MacDonald, "The Highland District in 1764", *IR*, 1964.
11. Roderick MacDonald, "Bishop Scott and the West Highlands", *IR*, 1966.
12. James MacGloin, "The Abbé Nicolas", *IR*, 1963.
13. James MacGloin, "Some Refugee French Clerics and Laymen in Scotland, 1789-1814", *IR*, 1965.
14. William MacGoldrick, "The Scots College, Madrid", *IR*, 1953.
15. David MacRoberts, "Abbé Paul MacPherson, 1756-1846", Catholic Truth Society of Scotland, 1946.
16. David MacRoberts, "Romana Robertson", Clan Donnachaidh *Annual* (n.p., 1971).
17. David MacRoberts, "The Scottish Catholic Archives 1560-1978", *IR*, 1977.
18. Alexander MacWilliam, "The Glasgow Mission 1792-1799", *IR*, 1953.
19. Alexander MacWilliam, "The Highland Seminary at Lismore 1803-1828", *IR*, 1957.
20. "Glenlivatensis" (i.e. Alexander MacWilliam), "The Highland Seminaries I, Loch Morar and Arisaig", *St Peter's College Magazine*, Vol. 19, no.75, December 1950.
21. "Glenlivatensis", "The Highland Seminaries II, Glenfinnan and Buorblach", *St Peter's College Magazine*, Vol. 20, no.76, June 1951.

22. "Glenlivatensis", "The Highland Seminaries III, Samalaman", *St Peter's College Magazine*, Vol. 20, no.77, December 1951.

23. "Glenlivatensis", "Scalan, 1719-1799", *St Peter's College Magazine*, Vol. 17, no.67, December 1946; and no.68, June 1947.

24. Alexander MacWilliam, *St Peter's Church, Aberdeen*, Aberdeen, 1979.

25. J.K. Robertson, "What our Great-Grandfathers Remembered", *Aberdeen University Review*, Vol. XXXV, no.4 (Aberdeen, 1954).

26. J.K. Robertson, "The Young Bishop Kyle", *IR*, 1950.

Index